# Popular Culture and the Civic Imagination

# Popular Culture and the Civic Imagination

Case Studies of Creative Social Change

**Edited by**
**Henry Jenkins,**
**Gabriel Peters-Lazaro,**
**and Sangita Shresthova**

NEW YORK UNIVERSITY PRESS
New York

NEW YORK UNIVERSITY PRESS
New York
www.nyupress.org

References to Internet websites (URLs) were accurate
at the time of writing. Neither the author nor New York
University Press is responsible for URLs that may have
expired or changed since the manuscript was prepared.

Cataloging-in-Publication data is available from the
publisher.

New York University Press books are printed on acid-
free paper, and their binding materials are chosen for
strength and durability. We strive to use environmen-
tally responsible suppliers and materials to the greatest
extent possible in publishing our books.

Manufactured in the United States of America

10 9 8 7 6 5 4 3 2 1

Also available as an e-book

*To Maxine Hope,*

*who shines a light into our future.*

# Contents

# Popular Culture and the Civic Imagination

Foundations

## Henry Jenkins, Gabriel Peters-Lazaro, and Sangita Shresthova

We all—adults and children—have an obligation to daydream.
We have an obligation to imagine. It is easy to pretend that nobody can change anything, that we are in a world in which society is huge and the individual is nothing: an atom in a wall, a
grain of rice in a rice field. But the truth is individuals can change
the world over and over. Individuals make the future, and they
do it by imagining that things can be different. . . . Political movements, personal movements, all begin with people imagining another way of existing.
—Neil Gaiman (2013, 8, 14–15)

In 2016–17, Broadway performer and composer Lin-Manuel Miranda
emerged as a key spokesman for a more inclusive civic imagination. The
success of his historical stage musical *Hamilton* increased his personal
celebrity, and he used this visibility to call attention to various social
justice struggles: he supported LGBTQ rights during his Tony Awards
acceptance speech; he protested the Trump administration's inadequate
response to the devastating effects of Hurricane Maria on Puerto Rico,
where Miranda's family is from; he performed at the March for Our
Lives; and he defended immigrants and their contributions to American society against President Donald Trump, who insists that "a nation
without borders is not a nation." *Hamilton*'s line "Immigrants, we get the
job done" was often a showstopping moment, as audiences applauded
and shouted comments to express their frustration with Trump's policies rolling back the protections offered to Dreamers (undocumented

1

youths who arrived in the United States as children), blocking Muslims from entering the country, and proposing a wall to be built along the US-Mexico border.

For the 2016 *Hamilton Mixtape* album, Miranda collaborated with recording stars ranging from the Roots and John Legend to Kelly Clarkson to reimagine his songs from the musical. One cut, a remix of "Yorktown (The World Turned Upside Down)" was produced as a music video, with the proceeds supporting the Hispanic Federation and Miranda's own Immigrants: We Get the Job Done Coalition. Here, Miranda joins forces with musicians K'naan (Somali-born), Residente (Puerto Rican), Riz MC (British-Pakistani), and Snow Tha Product (Mexican American). With roots in New York City's black and Latino communities, global hip hop speaks for oppressed and marginalized groups, and thus the song can forge solidarities between immigrants with different national origins, each struggling with a hostile political climate. Each verse of the song, which is partially in English and partially in Spanish, describes immigrants' struggles to overcome prejudice, to work underpaid and undervalued jobs, to escape violent situations, and to forge new identities. The song ends with the following refrain:

> Look how far I come
> Look how far I come
> Look how far I come
> Immigrants, we get the job done
> Not yet

In the music video's opening, a newscaster defines a core paradox: "It's really astonishing that in a country founded by immigrants, 'immigrant' has somehow become a bad word." The camera moves through a train full of the dispossessed, evoking the postapocalyptic 2013 film *Snowpiercer*. *Snowpiercer*—a Czech–South Korean coproduction based on a French graphic novel, performed in English with a multinational cast and directed by South Korean filmmaker Bong Joon-ho—itself used a coalition of diverse artists to call attention to class inequality and environmental degradation. *Snowpiercer*'s postapocalyptic story is set on board an endlessly traveling train that is a stratified microcosm of earth's class structure. If each train car in the original film was occupied by a particular class, each car in the music video represents refugees from different countries. Immigrants are shown performing low-wage jobs, such as stitching American flags, picking fruit, packing meat, washing dishes, sweeping floors, and constructing buildings. A final zoom out reveals an entire planet crisscrossed by railroads, each car containing huddled masses seeking a better life someplace else.

These trains constitute something like Michel Foucault's (1967) "crisis heterotopia"—a space where different people are thrown together out-*Free* side of their everyday space and time and, in Foucault's account, freed from fixed roles. Such profound disruptions allow us to imagine alternative social arrangements—not utopias (which are about order and hierarchy, at least according to Foucault) but heterotopias as defined by diversity and inclusion. Foucault's prime example is the boat, "a place that exists by itself, that is closed in on itself," a resonant metaphor for many immigrants. He concludes, "In civilizations without boats, dreams dry up, espionage takes the place of adventure, and the police take the place of pirates" (1967, 27).

What you do when "dreams dry up" is a question being raised by many of those confronting seemingly endless crises and catastrophes, disruptions, and displacements. There can be no politics without hope, *Hope* and it is through imagination that our hopes are rekindled. Somewhere between hope and disappointment is ambivalence and precarity—words that describe what many feel at the current moment. This book assembles case studies of popular culture shaping the civic imagination of people involved in political struggles and social movements around the *2 times* world. Stories have always been vehicles for people to pass along shared wisdom, question current actions, and direct attention to shared desires. Neil Gaiman reminds us that we have a civic obligation to daydream not only on behalf of ourselves but for others with whom we share this planet.

Miranda fits within a long tradition of progressive or radical artists doing what used to be called "culture work" (Denning 2011; Iton 2008; Mickenberg 2005)—using vernacular forms to express alternative perspectives to a broader public. In today's struggles for immigrant rights, other change-making organizations are demonstrating how popular culture might be appropriated, remixed, and redeployed at the grassroots level.

When Jolt Texas, a Latinx advocacy group, organized their "Quinceañera at the Capitol" protest on July 19, 2017, they tapped the fifteenth-birthday rite of passage to create a "celebration . . . and call to action against SB4 [Senate Bill 4]" (Martinez 2017), a measure that empowered Texas law enforcement to demand immigration status information when investigating minor infractions. Jolt also encouraged supporters to upload their quinceañera photos through social media in solidarity with the protest. The quinceañera theme increased the protest's visibility, as young women stood in front of the state capitol in their formal and often opulent dresses; it also imbued protesters and bystanders with hopes of a bright, youthful future. These protesters tapped a popular and well-known cultural tradition in ways that resonate with the participatory practices Arely Zimmerman and Liana Thompson (2016) identify in their discussion of Dreamer activists. Mock college graduation ceremonies—like those staged on "Dream for America: National DREAM Act Graduation Day" on June 23, 2009—similarly combined onsite and online protests, shaping public perceptions of the Dreamer movement via images broadly associated with youth, aspiration, and ultimately, success.

By contrast, Trump's campaign to build a wall along the southern border depends on a divisive "us versus them" rhetoric, pitting immigrants' dreams against "American" values. When the Trump administration announced plans in 2017 to terminate the Deferred Action for Childhood Arrivals Act (DACA), which sought to protect the Dreamers from deportation, activist Eric Huerta (2017) blogged,

> All these years later and now the day has come in which DACA "must be defended" because the program is going to be shut down by the current administration. Can't say that I didn't see this day coming, oh wait, yes I did. I watched the '90s X-Men animated cartoon on Saturday mornings. I saw how the mutant registration program and Sentinels targeted mutants unjustly because they signed up for a program. I have analogies for days when it comes to making sense of what's going on, it's the reactions I've been seeing from those impacted, those in solidarity, and those who are new to this that has me doing double takes. Some of the rhetoric and narratives being used are by the books. Highlight that individuals with DACA are the best of the best, they contribute economically, are highly

educated, they are Americans without papers. They deserve to keep their
temporary work permits because the country would lose X amount of
money. Oh and let's not forget that they're all innocent kids who were
brought here as children and they themselves are still children. We have
to think of the children.

Huerta worries that such rhetoric differentiates "deserving" youths
from "other" immigrants. He nods to the X-Men universe as informing his own more dystopian, and contested, civic imagination. Similarly,
Miranda's "We Get the Job Done" music video offers alternative visions
of immigration—ones that do not rely on the us/them and desirable/
unwanted immigrant frames. These examples scarcely encompass the
available images. The focus on walls as a defense against zombie inva-
sion in *Game of Thrones* led activists to create a mash-up between the
HBO fantasy series and Trump's campaign speeches (Jenkins, Billard et
al. 2018). And Pixar's film *Coco* depicts the dead having to show papers
or risk an illegal crossing to reunite with loved ones.

## Defining the Civic Imagination

Through the diverse cases represented in this collection, we model the
different functions that the civic imagination performs. We define *civic
imagination* as the capacity to imagine alternatives to current cultural,
social, political, or economic conditions; one cannot change the world
without imagining what a better world might look like. Beyond that, the
civic imagination requires and is realized through the ability to imagine
the process of change, to see oneself as a civic agent capable of making
change, to feel solidarity with others whose perspectives and experiences are different than one's own, to join a larger collective with shared
interests, and to bring imaginative dimensions to real-world spaces and
places. Research on the civic imagination explores the political consequences of cultural representations and the cultural roots of political
participation. This definition consolidates ideas from various accounts
of the public imagination, the political imagination, the radical imagination, the pragmatic imagination, creative insurgency, or public fantasy.
In some cases, the civic imagination is grounded in beliefs about how
the system actually works, but we have a more expansive understanding,

stressing the capacity to imagine alternatives even if those alternatives tap the fantastic. Too often, focusing on contemporary problems makes it impossible to see beyond immediate constraints. This tunnel vision perpetuates the status quo, and innovative voices—especially those from the margins—are shot down before they can be heard.

When the University of Southern California's Media, Activism, and Participatory Politics (MAPP) research group interviewed more than two hundred young activists for our 2016 book *By Any Media Necessary: The New Youth Activism*, many felt that the language of American politics was broken: it was, on the one hand, exclusive in that policy-wonk rhetoric was opaque to first-time voters and, on the other hand, repulsive in that partisan bickering displaced problem solving and consensus building (Jenkins, Shresthova et al. 2016). The young leaders we interviewed wanted to address their generation on its own terms, and activists around the world were appropriating and remixing popular culture to fuel their social movements. This discovery informed our own thinking about the civic imagination. This collection's three editors lead the Civic Imagination Project, funded by the MacArthur Foundation. Many contributors are members of our University of Southern California–based Civic Paths research group or our expanded research network. Our project conducts workshops across the United States and around the world designed to harness the power of the civic imagination as a tool for bridge building and problem solving. Our conceptual work here is coupled with efforts to test, strengthen, and expand these ideas through practice.

We need a robust civic imagination now more than ever. A 2015 CNN/ORC poll found that only three in ten Americans believe that their views are well represented in Washington, and many feel that the nation is as divided politically as it has been at any point since the Civil War and Reconstruction. The current plight of American politics has global counterparts, as witnessed, for example, by the Brexit vote outcome, the rise of right-wing populism across Europe, political unrest in Brazil, and the destabilizing violence and suffering perpetrated by the so-called Islamic State.

Like Peter Dahlgren (2009), we feel that the term *civic* carries "the implication of engagement in public life—a cornerstone of democracy." The civic for Dahlgren always has an affective and imaginative dimension: "The looseness, openendedness of everyday talk, its crea- *Empathy* tivity, its potential for empathy and affective elements, are indispens- able resources and preconditions for the vitality of democratic politics" (90). As Dahlgren further specifies, the term *civic* is also connected to the pursuit of a "public good" as a "precondition" for other forms of political engagement. Eric Gordon and Paul Mihailidis (2016) expand on Dahlgren's notion, observing that "while the concept of 'common good' is deeply subjective" (2), the term "invoke[s] the good of the com- mons, or action taken that benefit a public outside the actor's intimate sphere." The civic supports community connections toward shared goals. Dahlgren's (2003, 139) civic culture circuit model is composed of six di- *six* mensions: shared values, affinity, knowledge and competencies, prac- tices, identities, and discussion. Neta Kligler-Vilenchik's account of the Harry Potter Alliance illustrates how each of Dahlgren's dimensions are built into this oft-cited example of fan activism (Jenkins, Shresthova et al. 2016), exploring how the group mobilizes youths around a shared fan interest (affinity); taps fan skills to mobilize politically (knowledge and competencies); creates a shared identity around being imagina- tive, socially caring beings; builds in supports for engaged discussion of social issues; and translates this new civic knowledge into a shared set of practices. We are building here on what was perhaps her study's most controversial aspect—the idea that fantasies about wizards and magic might inspire real-world social action, seeing popular culture as a provocation for civic engagement rather than as escapism. Let's be clear that there is always a political dimension to culture, and our defini- tion of the civic contains a heavy cultural component, but we are inter- ested in the ways cultural practices and materials are deployed toward overtly political ends, whether by established institutions or grassroots movements.

Civic engagements with popular culture involve complex negotia- tions between oppositional world views with fraught relationships with commercial institutions. Consider, for example, how technological tools and platforms inform the civic imagination. We reject both the idea of technological determinism and the myth of total autonomy, seeing the individual as constantly negotiating with the culture around them, which includes the technologies that increasingly shape our contempo- rary environment. Read in that way, Twitter hashtags and rudimentary virtual reality headsets, as discussed here, are potential vectors along which personal identity can be tested and political agency reimagined.

Many changemakers maintain a passionate relationship with popular culture, using that cultural vocabulary to broker relations across different political groups. Indigenous peoples are tapping *Avatar* to dramatize their struggles (Brough and Shresthova 2012). *The Hunger Games'* three-finger salute is being deployed by resistance movements in Thailand and Hong Kong. Media makers in the Muslim world and Russia are developing their own superheroes to reflect their own social mission (Jenkins, forthcoming). In her report *Spoiler Alert: How Progressives Will Break through with Popular Culture*, Tracy Van Slyke (2014) sums up the logic: "Pop culture has power. We can either ignore it, letting dominant narratives as well as millions of people who interact and are influenced by popular culture slide by, or we can figure out how to double down and invest in the people, strategies, products, and experiences that will transport our stories and values into mainstream narratives" (15). Michael Saler (2012) has coined the phrase "public sphere of the imagination" to describe the communities that form around popular narratives, spaces where discussions about hopes and fears are staged, often outside of partisan frameworks, one step removed from real-world constraints. Not simply escapism, such discussions work through real-world issues that participants might not be able to confront through other means.

## The Politics of Popular Culture

Our approach is informed by the cultural studies tradition. Cultural studies began with Raymond Williams's ([1958] 1989) simple and poignant observation that "culture is ordinary," which allowed him to reclaim rural working-class British culture as worthy of study and reflection. Stuart Hall (1981) further broke down the concept of popular culture. On the one hand, popular culture is often understood in terms of its commercial success, "the things that are said to be 'popular' because masses of people listen to them, buy them, read them, consume them, and seem to enjoy them to the full" (512). Sometimes a distinction is made between mass culture (culture mass produced, distributed, and consumed) and popular culture (which may also refer to niche, subcultural, and folk forms that may never achieve mass appeal). Some of this book's cases deal with the political impact of Hollywood blockbusters (*Star Wars*), best-selling young adult novels (*Harry Potter*), highly rated sitcoms (*All in the Family*), Oscar acceptance speeches, and brand icons (Smokey Bear). But others deal with grassroots projects (such as Chicano street murals or virtual reality and urban games initiatives) whose impact is felt mostly on the local level. Here, Hall's second definition of the popular, as having to do with "the people," comes into play. Forms of cultural expression—memes or hashtags, for example—that rely on vernacular forms are "popular" even if the works themselves do not reach mass attention. Social movements tap into imagery from commercial texts (Miranda's music videos, *Coco*) but also into the vernacular modes of expression (graduations or quinceañeras). Hall does not believe we can simply inventory popular culture because of the dynamic nature of its relationships with high culture, prevailing ideologies, the marketplace, and other forces determining what culture "counts." Rather, popular culture might be better understood in terms of how everyday symbols are assigned meanings within particular contexts.

Some activists dismiss mass culture as speaking only for corporate interests, serving dominant ideology, and thus manipulating the masses. Hall (1981), conversely, saw popular culture as "a battlefield where no once-for-all victories are obtained but where there are always strategic positions to be won and lost" (513). Hall is not alone in seeing popular culture as a space for fomenting social change. Here's bell hooks (1990): "It's exciting to think, write, talk about, and create art that reflects passionate engagement with popular culture, because this may well be 'the' central future location of resistance struggle, a meeting place where new and radical happenings can occur" (394). hooks celebrates a critical "engagement with popular culture" even if she sees mass media as saturated with white supremacist ideologies. In hooks's account, black people in particular, but also all marginalized groups, "yearn" for alternative forms of popular culture that more fully express their fantasies of social change.

Writing about the "creative insurgency" of the Arab Spring movements, Marwan M. Kraidy (2016) demonstrates that popular culture—here understood as grassroots forms of expression—may be deployed toward revolutionary ends: "Creative insurgency celebrates heroes, commemorates martyrs, and sustains revolutionaries. . . . It triggers debate and contributes to a vast, crowd-sourced archive of revolutionary words, images, and sounds" (17). "Creative insurgency" arises when people find their voice through practices that first take shape around popular media but are now deployed for more explicitly political purposes. Linda Herrara (2012) documents how Arab youths were drawn together through their recreational use of digital media—downloading popular music, trading Hollywood films, gaming, or engaging in social media practices—where they encountered unfamiliar ideas and forged solidarity with others. Many Arab youths, as Yomna Elsayed and Sulafa Zidani remind us in their contribution, have returned to social media as tools for creative insurgency after new repressive regimes gained power.

Thinking of popular culture as offering resources for social change leads to several important observations. First, just as it matters whether you are making your purse from silk or a sow's ear, the quality of the raw materials also matters: not every popular culture text speaks for all groups. Most acts of appropriation are not acts of resistance as traditionally understood. In many cases, these fan-activists feel ownership over these works and see congruence between the original texts and the causes to which they are being deployed. The Harry Potter Alliance can use J. K. Rowling's fantasy world for human rights advocacy because of the author's history of involvement with Amnesty International, and the Dreamers can use Superman's story to tell of their own struggles to be accepted as Americans in part because the character was created by immigrants from another generation and ethnic background (Jenkins, Shresthova et al., 2017). This is not to say that such texts can speak only these truths—the construction of revolutionary politics in the Hunger Games series is deeply contradictory, as is the concept of a radical text marketed by a major media corporation. As Hall (1981) writes, "The danger arises because we tend to think of cultural forms as whole and coherent: either wholly corrupt or wholly authentic. Whereas they are deeply contradictory; they play on contradictions, especially when they function in the domain of the 'popular'" (513).

Over the past few decades, popular culture—from the multicultural, multiracial, and multiplanetary communities of *Star Trek* to the depiction of an American Muslim superhero in *Ms. Marvel*—has increasingly offered resources people have drawn upon to spark the civic imagination. Many narratives address particular subcultural, niche, or generational cohorts, but these narratives are often hotly contested by others from different political, spiritual, or ethnic backgrounds. Many minor groups struggle for inclusion and representation within popular media after decades of negative stereotyping or exclusion. In other parts of the world, American popular culture remains a dominant but not unquestioned influence alongside local alternatives (Bollywood, K-Pop, telenovelas). In part because of its pervasiveness, references to American popular culture are traded across different political movements, with superheroes or zombies widely used in debates and protests. Stuart Hall (1992) writes, "Popular culture, commodified and stereotyped as it often is, is not at all, as we sometimes think of it, an arena where we find who we really are, the truth of our experience. It is an arena that is profoundly mythic. It is a theatre of popular desires, a theatre of popular fantasies. It is where we discover and play with the identifications of ourselves, where we are imagined, where we are represented, not only to the audiences out there who do not get the message, but to ourselves for the first time" (382). So cultural scholars work to identify which resources from which narratives speak to which communities with which meanings. We do not live in a semiotic democracy. Cultural resources are not evenly distributed. And some communities must work harder to bend those symbols to their will, face greater opposition to their proposed interpretations, and have a difficult time getting others to understand what they are trying to say.

## The Utopian Imagination

Harry Potter series author J. K. Rowling evoked the power of fantasy as a tool for social change during a 2008 Harvard commencement speech: "Imagination is not only the uniquely human capacity to envision that which is not, and therefore the fount of all invention and innovation. In its arguably most transformative and revelatory capacity, it is the power that enables us to empathise with humans whose experiences we have never shared. . . . We do not need magic to change the world, we carry all the power we need inside ourselves already: we have the power to imagine better" (n.p.) By "imagine better," Rowling advocates two closely related goals: that activist do a better job imagining alternatives to current social conditions and that they imagine better worlds that they then work to achieve. Rowling also expresses a third goal—that an empathetic imagination may better understand and respond to others' suffering.

Supporting and exercising the imagination is crucial to the community work the Civic Imagination Project performs; workshop participants repeatedly tell us that they rarely are invited to engage their imaginations, which are often perceived as separate from reason and rational thought, unless it directly relates to their professional or artistic practices. This separation leaves their civic lives mired in the what Stephen Duncombe (2012b) has called the "tyranny of the possible"—that is, the inner voice that says that change is not possible, that opposing forces are too strong, that we can never afford what would be ideal, that we are stuck with the status quo. Duncombe is one of several contemporary writers seeking to reclaim a utopian tradition: "For the revolutionary, utopia offers a goal to reach and a vision to be realized. For the reformer, it provides a compass point to determine what direction to move toward and a measuring stick to determine how far one has come. . . . Without a vision of an alternative future, we can only look backwards nostalgically to the past, or unthinkingly maintain what we have" (n.p.). Duncombe (2017) acknowledges why utopianism has gotten a bad name, given the number of utopian projects that became rigid and doctrinaire. Rather than seeing utopias as blueprints, he sees utopias as provocations: "By asking 'What if?' we can simultaneously criticize *and* imagine, imagine *and* criticize, and thereby begin to escape the binary politics of impotent critique on the one hand and closed imagination on the other" (12). In some cases, the utopian imagination envisions absurd, unworkable, unthinkable things precisely so that in shooting them down, we articulate shared values and visions: "The paramount question, I believe, is whether or not Utopia can be opened up—to criticism, to participation, to modification, and to re-creation" (Duncombe 2012b, n.p.). This is what he calls an "open utopia."

Duncombe's concept of the "open utopia" resonates with a broader literature on the role of imagination. Philosopher Mary Warnock sees the imagination as that "which enables us to see the world, whether present or absent as significant, and also to present this vision to others, for them to share or reject. . . . Its impetus comes from the emotions as much as from reason, from the heart as much as from the head" (196). According to Warnock, the imagination allows us to "detach" ourselves from the

*Detach ourselves*

reality to "think of certain objects in the world in a new way, as signifying something else" (197). In *Pragmatic Imagination,* Ann Pendleton-Jullian and John Seely Brown similarly reject the perceived dichotomy between reason and imagination to chart a related set of cognitive processes: perception (the ways imagination reconciles between a subject position and the world beyond us), forms of reasoning (deductive, inductive, and abductive), speculation (the ability to conceive of possible futures and related actions), experimentation (the willingness to tap existing skills toward something never tried), and free play (characterized through intentional disruption and boundary crossing; pp. 43–56). This collection's cases explore how creative engagements with popular culture can support a journey along this continuum as people turn to the imaginary and even fantastical to reenergize their civic lives. The imagination gains civic power when it is no longer personal or private but rather can *share* be translated into a form that can be shared intersubjectively. As participants at a 2013 ReConstitutional Convention hosted by the Institute for the Future concluded, "Any democracy requires a thriving public imagination, in order to make visible, sharable and understandable to *democracy* all the people new ideas, new models, new potential policies. We cannot make any kind of collective decisions unless the collective can understand what is at stake, and envision where it may lead. . . . We must strive to understand the private imaginations of others, whose reality is defined by different lived experiences and assumptions" (n.p.).

Exploring links between social movements and superhero comics, Ramzi Fawaz (2016) argues that the civic imagination need not be grounded in realism in order to help us see the world from a new perspective: "Popular fantasy describes the variety of ways that the tropes and figures of literary fantasy (magic, superhuman ability, time travel, alternative universes, among others) come to organize real-world social and political relations. . . . [Such popular fantasies] embody and legitimate nascent cultural desires and modes of social belonging that appear impossible or simply out of reach within the terms of dominant political imagination" (27–28). Fawaz describes how The X-Men's mutant narratives expand conceptions of the human, offering new recognition to "gender and sexual outlaws, racial minorities, and the disabled" (13). Eric Huerta's use of the X-Men to talk about DACA is in this same spirit. Superheroes are culturally pervasive and thus handy for political deployment. They offer a shared vocabulary for talking about personal and cultural identity. Different superheroes embody different conceptions of justice and the social good. The genre deals directly with issues of power and its responsible use. Superheroes never doubt their capacity to change the world. The superhero comic articulates who the good guys are, their mission, and also what they are fighting against. Across several essays, Civic Paths researchers have explored superheroes as an extended example of the civic imagination at work (Jenkins, Shresthova et al., 2017; Jenkins, forthcoming).

Fawaz references sociologist Deborah Gould (2009), who sees such "structures of feeling" as triggering and sustaining social movements that express the "desire for different forms of social relations, different ways of being, a different world. . . . In articulating and enacting what previously might have been unimaginable, a movement offers a scene and future possibilities that surprise, entice, exhilarate, and electrify" (as quoted in Fawaz 2016, 29).

Such popular narratives were neither designed to last nor intended to convince. Duncombe (2012a) discusses how *Star Trek* fans became activists: "Our political imagination was inspired by the presentation of Roddenberry and company's SF [science fiction] scenarios. . . . Yet the sheer campiness of the series kept us from accepting the future it presented as a real possibility, or, rather, a valid fantasy" (n.p.). Fans may not want to board the *Enterprise*, but they may want to collaborate with a diverse community to achieve shared missions; they may not want to live in the Federation, but they may want to inhabit a world where making money is secondary to other goals; they may not want to travel into deep space, but they desire the discovery of difference and a sense of wonder. People yearn for the value these stories place on rationality and the pursuit of knowledge all the more in a culture that sometimes has declared war on science. Richard Dyer (1985) tells us that entertainment embodies "what utopia would feel like rather than how it would be organised." Entertainment captures a utopian sensibility; it offers a taste of a better world but leaves us unsatisfied. In Duncombe's account, this dissatisfaction propels activism.

By now, we've identified multiple reasons why popular culture matters for social movements: because it is ordinary, because it can be appropriated and transformed so freely, because it constitutes the realm where we might imagine alternatives, because it fosters shared desires that may fuel struggles for social justice, because it addresses feelings that might not be expressed in any other way, and because it may bridge cultural divides. Certainly, other stories—religious narratives, folk tales, historical epics—also perform some of these functions. But for many young people, popular narratives are particularly valued as resources for the civic imagination.

## Counternarratives

We do not offer a civics grounded in popular culture as a panacea for all the challenges confronting contemporary democracy. Critics remind us that popular culture does not speak for everyone, that not everyone feels comfortable within its imaginary worlds or has access to the means of production and circulation, and that certain toxic elements in popular culture repel many whom social movements might seek to attract. Because popular culture is not the language most commonly spoken in the corridors of power, messages framed within its terms may be trivialized and dismissed by those who have the ability to act on the articulated concerns. Expressing real-world issues in fantastical language runs the risk of simplifying messages so that they may be circulated more easily, and some causes may be impossible to articulate within the limited range of fantasies currently on offer. And still others see such a mechanism as too gradual to address urgent problems.

Sarah Banet-Weiser (2018) considers what is gained and lost as feminism becomes popularized, fearing that its vision of social change is being smoothed over to ensure that its ideas travel faster across a networked society. Popular feminism may have inspired a new generation, but it has also brought out the trolls as patriarchy defends its privilege: "Misogyny is popular in the contemporary moment for the same reasons feminism has become popular: it is expressed and practiced on multiple media platforms, it attracts other like-minded groups, and it manifests in a terrain of struggle, with competing demands for power. . . . The relationship between popular feminism and popular misogyny is deeply entwined: popular feminism and popular misogyny battle it out on the contemporary cultural landscape, living side-by-side as warring, constantly moving contexts in an economy of visibility" (n.p.). Banet-Weiser asks what voices get silenced, what ideas get sidelined, as a political movement enters a new "economy of visibility." If popular culture is a terrain of hegemonic struggles, as Hall suggests, then such resources may also form the basis for conflicting narratives or counternarratives. Such conflicts surface across this book—the different conceptions of the American Revolution that spawned *Hamilton* and the Tea Party, divergent definitions of the Indian American experience channeled through Bollywood, or alternative responses to Star Wars's gender and racial diversity.

Naomi Klein (2017) compares her "shock" and "horror" over Donald Trump's election to watching "dystopian fiction come to life." She describes Trump as a "mirror" that reflects our worst aspects back at us. Klein encourages her readers to identify "the stories and systems that ineluctably produced him" and to ensure wider circulation of counternarratives: "The forces Trump represents have always had to suppress those other, older, and self-evidently true stories, so that theirs could dominate against so much intuition and evidence. . . . Which is why part of our work now—a key part—is not just resistance, not just saying no. . . . We also need to fiercely protect some space to dream and plan for a better world" (n.p.). Klein sees the creation, circulation, and promotion of alternative stories as the key means by which progressive groups may defeat "Trumpism."

We share Klein's desire to shatter entrenched narratives and renew the resources from which we may collectively construct our own futures. Too often, academic work overvalues critique at the expense of advocacy. Critical writers offer a clear sense of what they are fighting against but rarely commit to what they are fighting for. Critique is valuable as part of a larger political cycle, which includes an analysis and description of a current problem, a critique of the powerful forces that created these circumstances, and advocacy for ways power might be distributed differently. There is a tendency to shoot down alternatives before they have been fully explored and to assume that future struggles will necessarily follow the same logics as those that have come before. The result is academic fatalism, a posture that blunts the power of critique, because in the end (shrug), What are you gonna do?

The temptation is to see utopian fictions as pure advocacy and dystopian fictions as pure critique, but as Duncombe's emphasis on provocations may suggest, the reality is more complex. Most utopian writing contains at least an implicit critique of the current realities that its alternative hopes to displace. By the same token, most dystopian writing contains a utopian alternative—often, in the form of a resistance group struggling to transform the society. We can only wish that critical studies were equally committed to this contestation between rival visions.

## Nostalgia

Just as science fiction debates alternative visions of the future, nostalgic conceptions of the past also offer a yardstick against which to identify flaws in the current system. Such nostalgia is no less utopian simply because it references the past. Svetlana Boym (2002) writes, "Nostalgia . . . is a longing for a home that no longer exists or has never existed. Nostalgia is a sentiment of loss and displacement, but it is also a romance with one's own fantasy" (xiii). Boym argues that nostalgia is only partially about looking backward and can also speak to the future, as the Trumpian mantra "Make America Great Again" suggests. Boym distinguishes between two forms of nostalgic imagining: "Restorative nostalgia does not think of itself as nostalgia, but rather as truth and tradition. Reflective nostalgia dwells in the ambivalence of human longing and belonging and does not shy away from the contradictions of modernity. Restorative nostalgia protects the absolute truth, while reflexive nostalgia calls it into doubt" (xviii). Restorative nostalgia has a fixed agenda, whereas reflexive nostalgia incorporates the dialogic process, the movement between critique and imagining that Duncombe locates within the "open utopia." Both look to the past to better understand what might be desirable in the future, but only reflexive nostalgia sees the past as open to critique. Civil War epics, such as *Gone with the Wind* or *Birth of a Nation* represent restorative nostalgia at its most forceful, reproducing what people have described as the "Lost Cause" ideology. Such mythologies have fueled recent backlashes against the removal of Confederate monuments from public places. Yet there are also revisionist or reflexive narratives that revisit this same era—Octavia Butler's *Kindred*, for example—to imagine what alternative social orders might look like (McPherson 2003).

Dark side

Boym's restorative nostalgia is susceptible to decidedly uncivic, even violent applications. Propaganda for the Third Reich—a nostalgic yet transformative vision of the "perfect" racialized society—embodies this dark side of the civic imagination. According to Alon Confino (2014), the imagination that animated the Nazis included both a careful construction of a shared nostalgic past (a story of national origin that placed the Jews as villains at its center) and a radically aspirational future ("the dream of an empire," "a world without Jews"; 12). The Nazis combined restorative nostalgia (a sense of restoring dignity to the "Heimat," or motherland) with a utopian imagination of a more perfect Aryan culture, drawing on the vivid theatrics and iconography some have called "fascinating fascism."

Significantly, the Nazi imagination was only one of several competing models for the past and future of Europe to emerge during this era. For example, a much more anarchistic and pluralistic vision of German society inspired the Edelweiss Piraten, a loose network of youth communities linked through a shared affinity for jazz, nature hikes, and free time, all things the Nazi regime despised. Others had visions of a more pluralistic German society that tapped a more reflective nostalgia. The student-led White Rose movement distributed flyers that drew on biblical and literary texts as they urged Germans to resist the Nazis. The White Rose's first flyer included this quote from Johann Wolfgang Goethe's *The Awakening of Epimenides* (act 2, scene 4):

> Though he who has boldly risen from the abyss
> Through an iron will and cunning
> May conquer half the world,
> Yet to the abyss he must return.
> Already a terrible fear has seized him;
> In vain he will resist!
> And all who still stand with him
> Must perish in his fall.
> HOPE:
> Now I find my good men
> Are gathered in the night,
> To wait in silence, not to sleep.
> And the glorious word of liberty

They whisper and murmur,
Till in unaccustomed strangeness,
On the steps of our temple
Once again in delight they cry:
Freedom! Freedom!

In quoting Goethe, the White Rose not only evoked nostalgia for Germany's past but also directly contested the Nazis' claim on his works as exemplifying their ideal Aryan nation. The White Rose further supported their alternative vision through the white rose, a flower associated with purity and truth. The image of the rose subtly suggested an alternative, nonviolent, and extremely fragile German society. Tragically, the White Rose was crushed when its two key members, siblings Sophie and Hans Scholl, were arrested, tortured, tried, and executed after distributing flyers at the university in Munich in 1943.

Nazis used brutal violence to maintain their hold on Germans' civic imagination. As Hannah Arendt (1966) reminds us, "In the totalitarian government, . . . terror becomes total when it becomes independent of all opposition; it rules supreme when nobody any longer stands in its way" (464). Terror represents an efficient mechanism for silencing dissent and isolating individuals. The resulting culture operates, in Arendt's words, as "One Man of gigantic dimensions" (466). In this scenario, there is no room for contested or competing visions that might threaten the totalitarian state.

Czech playwright, dissident, and later president Václav Havel (1991) offers a useful continuation of Arendt's formulations on power and totalitarianism. In the context of posttotalitarian (or late totalitarian Soviet-era) regimes, as Havel explains, Nazi terror is largely replaced with "manipulatory devices so refined, complex, and powerful that it no longer needs murderers and victims" (332). The real challenge to posttotalitarianism then comes from "fiery Utopia builders spreading discontent with dreams of a better future," for they open the possibility of change and invite people to continue to dream rather than slide into apathy. People's ability to sustain alternative visions empowers them to resist "creeping totalitarianism" (332).

In Cold War Czechoslovakia, Havel identifies a loose network that operated outside the political realm as a productive space of engagement when real political change remains unrealistic. In January 1977, Charta 77, the protest document initiated after the arrest of Plastic People of the Universe band members, exemplifies such "antipolitical politics" (with real political repercussions for those who signed it). Havel explains, "Everyone understood that an attack on the Czech musical underground was an attack on the most elementary and important thing, something that in fact bound everyone together: it was an attack on the very notion of living in truth, on the real aims of life. The freedom to play rock music was understood as a human freedom and thus as essentially the same freedom to engage in philosophical and political reflection, the freedom to write, the freedom to express and defend various social and political interests in society" (119). Havel's commitment to cultural dissidence is confirmed in this excerpt from the original document, viewable through the Freedom Collection at the George W. Bush Institute (translated by the authors): "Charta 77 is not an organization; it has no constitution, no permanent institutions, no formal membership. Charta 77 is not a fundamental oppositional movement." Stressing its connection to popular culture (in this case, rock music), Charta 77 affirmed that fostering alternative civic imaginations is crucial to popular dissent in posttotalitarian regimes.

We take seriously the power of the civic imagination, for better and for worse, as scholars and as citizens (recognizing that we are among those with the privilege to take citizenship as given). As we write this, the Nazi- and Soviet-era efforts to shape and police the imagination weigh heavily on our minds. We need to diligently interrogate how the Nazis managed to construct, deploy, and maintain their vision and justify to themselves the atrocities committed by the so-called Third Reich. We need to remember the dangers of apathy and dearth of imagination that Havel articulated. Making a case for the value of the "public imagination" in the wake of Donald Trump's rise to power, Drucilla Cornell and Stephen D. Seeley (2017) also identify the dangers of constraining the public's ability to explore alternative futures:

> [Democracy] allows us to be affected by as many people as possible, in all of their diversity, and this in turn promotes the maximal clarification of inadequate ideas. The more open we are to being affected by others who are different from what we currently imagine ourselves to be, the more

our imagination is enriched and the more we are empowered in both body and mind. In this light, what we are seeing now is the dearth of collective imagination. Trump and his supporters want us literally to be walled off from México, blocked off from the tragedy in Syria. He wants to keep us from interacting and creating new, enriched images of people in different religions through his grotesque Muslim ban. He wants to turn women into things whose impact on public life is as limited as possible, imagined instead as nothing other than their reproductive organs to be "grabbed" and controlled. These walls and barriers clearly block democracy . . . as the widest engagement with each other.

They cite the influence of Baruch Spinoza, but we see congruence also with the vision outlined and enacted by Havel—the desire to expand and diversify the contents of the imagination as a means of resisting and ultimately overturning any systems of power that curtail or criminalize the rights of all people to imagine and work toward a world that allows them to thrive in happiness, security, and humanity. We recognize grave threats within the rhetorics and actions of contemporary politics. We recognize that this moment is but one in a larger cycle of struggle; we see the need to continually bolster, refine, and adapt our tools for collective progress. In the end, it is imagination, more than information, that wants to be free.

## ❧ Our Guiding Questions

This book assembles a diverse set of cases exploring the civic imagination at work in contemporary social movements. Each essay offers critical insights at a time when once again there are threats of authoritarianism and a need for resistance movements. These cases come from many parts of the world; they reflect contemporary struggles by people of diverse ethnic, cultural, and economic backgrounds; they deploy many cultural materials and political tactics; and they address a range of issues (environmentalism, wealth inequality, gender and sexual politics, and systemic racism, to cite a few). Often, they represent conflicting or clashing imaginations as people struggle over what constitutes a better world. We have organized the essays around the functions of the civic imagination, adding new layers to our understanding of this core concept with references to a broader range of theoretical perspectives (as will be discussed in the introductions to the sections).

We will break down the key questions here using the example of *Black Panther,* a Marvel-Disney film that many have described as movement building. If we want to take these claims seriously and on their own terms, we can use the functions of the civic imagination to identify what imaginative resources *Black Panther* offers the diverse publics who have gathered around it. The idea that such a franchise movie might become a tool for social change is not farfetched: Define American and Fandom Forward developed a study guide around the film that organizations could use to foster discussions about refugees, immigrants, and borders; the Electoral Justice Project organized voter registration drives around film screenings, urging supporters to "Wakanda the vote." Let's consider how *Black Panther* maps onto the functions of the civic imagination that organize this book.

### How Do We Imagine a Better World?

*Black Panther*'s fictional Wakanda provides a vivid contrast to the poverty and hopelessness depicted in Oakland in the film's opening and closing scenes. Oakland was the setting of director Ryan Coogler's first film, *Fruitvale Station,* and the birthplace for the Black Panther Party (no direct relation). Interestingly, the conclusion's agenda for social reform through community schools and health clinics owes much to the Black Panther Party's original platform. *Black Panther* envisions an imaginary African nation where black peoples exercise self-determination, having no history of colonization; where Africans develop advanced technologies while controlling their natural resources; where traditions persist despite modernization; and where warring tribes have developed practices for resolving conflicts.

### How Do We Imagine the Process of Change?

Killmonger—the American-born terrorist who seeks to take over Wakanda—is not a villain in a traditional sense: the film has sympathy for his goals but differs over means. Killmonger's advocacy for the export of arms to help rebels overturn oppressors inspires T'Challa's move from isolationism toward diplomacy and social services. Some of the most intense debates around the film have centered on these competing visions of the process of social change.

## How Do We Imagine Ourselves as Civic Agents?

T'Challa—the Black Panther—undertakes the classic hero's journey, moving from the young prince to the ruler of his country following the death of his father, taking on new responsibilities, embracing an expanded mission, and learning to make a difference on both a local and a global scale. It is this acceptance of social responsibility that makes the character such a great model for young activists. When, at the end of the film, T'Challa steps up at the United Nations in the face of sniggers and skepticism from other world leaders, he models what it means to demand respect that has not been granted before, a key theme in the black radical imagination literature. As Gabonese filmmaker Manouchka Labouba explained during an interview for Henry Jenkins and Colin Maclay's *How Do You Like It So Far?* podcast: "I remember . . . being a kid and female in Africa [that] the superhero that I imagined was a white male . . . because all of the superheroes that I watched back then were white. Superman, Batman, Spiderman, all of them were white. . . . It is important to have a character [like Black Panther] because it gives an opportunity for kids nowadays to imagine their superhero in a different way." And even though the film's producer, Walt Disney Studios, may be seen as a corporate "colonizer" by many critics, the story can nevertheless be appropriated and reconfigured on the ground as a resource that speaks to young people across Africa and around the world.

## How Do We Imagine Our Social Connections with a Larger Community?

A striking aspect of *Black Panther* is the range of different conceptions of power, courage, responsibility, wisdom, and knowledge within the Wakandan community. Unlike most superhero sagas, success rests on collective rather than individual action. Consider, for example, the film's different representations of black women: Nakia, who is on a mission to rescue captive women in Nigeria; Okoye, who experiences conflicting loyalties but remains true to her principles as leader of the royal guard, the Dora Milaje; Shuri, who embodies her society's technological and scientific advancement; and Ramonda, who carries regal dignity and deep-rooted traditions. These women clash but rally as their country turns outward and becomes a superpower dedicated to a more just distribution of resources.

### How Do We Forge Solidarity with Others with Different Experiences Than Our Own?

Having developed a stronger Wakandan community, Black Panther joins the Avengers, directing his newly claimed leadership against the villain Thanos and his allies in *Infinity War*. Here, he fights alongside a Norse god (Thor), a Russian assassin (Black Widow), two World War II veterans (Captain America and Winter Soldier), and a scrawny kid from Queens (Spider-Man), to cite just a few. Each defends a different community, but they join forces against threats so big that they put everything they love at risk.

### How Do We Bring an Imaginative Dimension to Our Real-World Places and Spaces?

Many *Black Panther* fans have expressed a desire to visit or even live in Wakanda because the film's Afrofuturist fantasy is that powerful. Here, they are seeking not simply the imagined versions of Hogwarts or Pandora being offered by contemporary amusement parks but a reconfiguration of social relations animated by the shared vision of a better life. University of Southern California PhD candidate Karl Bauman partnered with artist/organizer Ben R. Caldwell to run a community-building project that used elements of Afrofuturism to reimagine Los Angeles's Leimert Park as it might take shape over the next few decades (Jenkins 2017). The project, Sankofa City, "worked with community participants to define their preferable futures, often tied to local African-American cultural norms and social practices." Participants deployed practices of world-building and transmedia storytelling to create a vision for their future that could be shared intersubjectively both within and beyond their community.

Ta-Nehisi Coates, the black sociologist whom Marvel hired to reconstruct the Black Panther comic book series in anticipation of the film's release, spoke for many when he said, "I didn't realize how much I needed the film, a hunger for a myth that [addressed] feeling separated and feeling reconnected" to Africa (Beta 2018). This response connects *Black Panther* to a much longer history of what Robin G. Kelly (2002) calls "freedom dreams," which he describes as "many different cognitive maps of the future" that through the years have allowed African Americans to maintain hope in the face of oppressive conditions and continue to struggle for something better: "The most radical art is not protest art, but works that take us to another place, envision a different way of seeing, perhaps a different way of feeling" (25). "Freedom dreams," in Kelly's particular formulation of the black radical imagination, "produce a vision that allows us to see beyond our immediate ordeals" (12), "Mother Africa," Kelly suggests, occupies a central role in those dreams as a place from which African Americans have been separated against their wills and as a place with which they hope to be spiritually and culturally reunited. The desire to reimagine Africa as a source of strength for the black community has only intensified in recent years. *Black Panther* fits within a larger strand of Afrofuturist art, music, and literature: for example, a generation of science fiction and fantasy writers, many of them with cultural ties to Nigeria—Nnedi Okorafor and Tomi Adeyemi, among others—are reclaiming African mythology and culture as the inspiration for groundbreaking works of speculative fiction.

In his piece for the *Atlantic*, "The Provocation and Power of *Black Panther*," Van R. Newkirk II (2018) explores the ways the film might fuel the black radical imagination:

Blackness invites speculation. The very idea of a global African diaspora creates the most fertile of grounds for a field of *what-ifs.* What if European enslavers and colonizers had never ventured into the African continent? More intriguing yet: What if African nations and peoples had successfully rebuffed generations of plunder and theft? What if the Zulu had won the wars against the Voortrekkers and the British, and a confederation of Bantu people had risen up and smashed Belgian rule? What if the Transatlantic children of the mother continent had been allowed to remain, building their empires with the bounties of the cradle of civilization? (22)

Here, Newkirk suggests that young black creators and fans are retracing their roots in order to forge a path forward into the future. In doing so, Newkirk addresses a question Kelly raises early in his book: "What are today's young activists dreaming about? We know what they are fighting against, but what are they fighting for?"

No wonder *Black Panther* captured the imagination of so many people in spring 2018, offering a shared myth desperately needed in the age of Trump: the film inspired many different forms of participatory culture (memes, fan fiction, cosplay) as people fused its iconography with their personal and social identities. As this example suggests, any given case is apt to tap multiple functions of the civic imagination, and thus the placement of essays within this book may sometimes feel arbitrary. But in flagging these questions, we encourage you to think about how these functions work together to constitute a model of social change, one that also shapes our own community-building practices. And it goes without saying that this book does not exhaust the possible range of examples. For every case we included, there are many more we were not able to include. We hope this book will inspire students and faculty researchers alike to develop their own case studies, exploring different aspects of popular culture and the civic imagination that they recognize as playing out within their own communities.

## Our Mission in Practice

The link between theory and practice is an integral part of our process. We believe that democracy works best when we can bring together diverse perspectives, encouraging people to share their memories, dreams, and hopes with each other. Such diverse perspectives provide the social foundation for civic life, especially when coupled with supports for people to find their voice and talk across their differences. Such are the primary goals of our practice-based community work. Our team is based in Los Angeles at the University of Southern California, and we are keenly aware of the role that place plays in our own work; we actively endeavor to build bridges from the university to the outside world. Our collaborations and interventions attempt to harness the active imagination of disparate groups and create opportunities for creativity and network building. The six core concepts introduced above have grown out of and informed the work we have been doing with communities since 2013.

Our community engagements have included the design and implementation of civic imagination workshops in Europe and the Middle East, with teachers in Missouri, economic development professionals in Kentucky, water agencies in California, and faith-based communities in Arkansas. Accounts of this work can be found online and in our book *Practicing Futures: A Civic Imagination Action Handbook* (Peter Lang, forthcoming), which is both an analysis of our activities and a manual for those wanting to run workshops with their own communities. Here we will focus on a single three-week engagement in Salzburg, Austria, in the summer of 2016 as a way of further illustrating these six core concepts of the civic imagination.

In 2016, the three editors taught at the Salzburg Global Seminar's Academy on Media and Global Change. We worked with educators, scholars, and approximately seventy college-aged students from around the world. The Salzburg Global Seminar is a nonprofit organization that organizes events and dialogs on global issues such as health care, justice, economics, and human rights. Since 1947, the seminar has been housed at an eighteenth-century palace, its neighboring farmhouse, and its grounds. That year, the focus of the academy was on immigration and the global refugee crisis. One of our team's goals was to design a series of civic imagination workshops that would help the attending students form a productive community founded on mutual respect, understanding, and empathy. This foundational work provided a strong basis from which the participants then worked toward engaging with the difficult issues of immigration and refugees.

## 1. How Do We Imagine a Better World?

In many of our community engagements, we imagine a better world by starting with a wide-ranging brainstorming session based on the ideas of world building. In Salzburg, this meant bringing all the participants together in a space, setting up whiteboards, and asking them to imagine a future world in the year 2066 where anything is possible. We asked them to set aside what they thought might actually occur in the future and open themselves to the full potentials of their imaginations. Our approach here is informed by the work of production designer and University of Southern California professor Alex McDowell and his Worldbuilding Institute. The idea is to identify key characteristics of the future world within categories such as education, transportation, economics, and so on. As the process gains steam, participants riff off and inspire each other to explore alternative possibilities. The Salzburg participants imagined a world where battles are relegated to outer space, women lead the world, teleportation is a telepathic action, and the people are united by an apocalyptic depletion of natural resources. We asked participants to craft specific narratives to explain how the world came to be this way, and then in a surprise twist, we asked them to perform their stories for the whole group of almost seventy. This exercise kindled a great deal of energy, laughter, embodied creativity, and wide-open imagination.

## 2. How Do We Imagine the Process of Change?

In the second part of our work, we asked the students to surface and share inspiring stories from their lives. These narratives could come from any source and fit within any genre—family stories, folk tales, popular culture, and so on. We were looking for something that had resonated with people over time. We asked participants to explore what within a story inspired them and consider how that narrative kernel could be leveraged to inspire collective action. The goal was to make a link between personal inspiration and change making. Movements arise from the connections and bonds of individuals who find engagement and purpose by identifying common ground. We asked participants to consider specific communities and circumstances in which they thought their stories could inspire change and to identify how a successful social movement campaign might build on those foundations.

## 3. How Do We Imagine Ourselves as Civic Agents?

Participants composed brief write-ups of their inspiring stories and uploaded them to a central location online along with geographical information about where their stories came from. We then assembled the stories in a navigable Atlas of the Civic Imagination using the Scalar platform, which rendered each participant's work viewable, shareable, searchable, and navigable. Participants then worked in small groups to get to know each other's stories. They shared with us that they experienced a deep sense of connection within a small timeframe by sharing stories that mattered in their own lives. They also enjoyed a sense of satisfaction when they were able to share new perspectives with their collaborators, introducing them to new ideas, histories, or communities. Creating a context in which personal voices and values can be heard and acted upon is a valuable step in helping young people recognize their civic agency. As students began to see themselves as storytellers, they saw how similar creative processes could be channeled into civic action and global change.

## 4. How Do We Imagine Our Social Connections with a Larger Community?

Next, we brought participants together in groups of three to create new stories by combining elements from each of the sources. We suggested that they employ several strategies for these story migrations, including but not limited to moving a character from one story into another; creating a new character by combining aspects of several characters; adapting a key moment, event, or theme from one story to another; or moving a story from one location to another. Participants spoke of the initial challenges of finding common ground among their seemingly very different stories. Through negotiating the imaginative terms of a new narrative, they each gained a deeper understanding of the potentials for bridging between the national cultures from which these stories originated. Storytelling again provided a vehicle and framework through which to connect individual experience with a collective and emergent identity. The act of unearthing, exploring, and playing with the values and ideas that excite and sustain us is a powerful mechanism for strengthening our connections with larger communities.

## 5. How Do We Forge Solidarity with Others with Different Experiences Than Our Own?

Empathy, recognition, and a sense of community all arise through the process of shared narrative creation and the migration of stories. Solidarity comes when that sense of connection translates into real action. When participants become invested in the stories of their peers and when they create new work together, they are building foundations for future solidarity. They recognize the humanity in other stories, asking how they might join forces with the people behind those stories. We saw this in the Media Academy when participants met with refugee families living in Austria. Stories became people; journalism became real life. And students learned how to be more effective advocates for their own interests and the needs of others.

## 6. How Do We Bring an Imaginative Dimension to Our Real-World Places and Spaces?

The Schloss Leopoldskron, where the Media Academy takes place, was a filming location for the immensely popular American musical film *The Sound of Music*. This connection to such a touchstone of pop-cultural history was somewhat neglected within the course of the academy. Upon reflection, our team has seen that perhaps there was a missed opportunity to be explored, considering how history is always re-created and reimagined. *The Sound of Music* is, after all, about a family who must navigate uncertain times and identify the right moment and means by which to flee their home amid encroaching violence. Places have stories. We should be on the lookout for ways to engage with, learn from, and contribute to those local narratives.

Imagining is a process, not a panacea. Imagining can be powerful and enriching, challenging and surprising, light and dark, sublime or overwhelming depending on where it takes us. Across the examples in this casebook, readers are encouraged to search for opportunities to enhance civic imagination in their own lives, work, and communities. Imagining, of course, is never enough if it does not inspire action. We all need to imagine better and imagine bigger.

# PART I

## How Do We Imagine a Better World?

**B**efore you can change the world, you need a vision of what a better world might look like—this is the primary function of the civic imagination. Essays in this section consider different narratives through which publics identify what they are fighting for and what they are fighting against.

Science fiction writers have long thought about their works as "thought experiments," as encouraging readers to discuss potential futures, speculating beyond what was currently known. Recently, designers have begun to consider science fiction world-building as a means to prototype alternative directions for their work. Writers and practitioners such as Brian David Johnson (2011), Julian Bleecker (2009), Paul Dourish and Genevieve Bell (2011), and Anthony Dunne and Fiona Raby (2013) have advocated for the use of critical design, speculative design, and "design fictions"—scenarios or prototypes that allow users to imagine future technologies and the contexts within which they might be used. They argue that such "design fictions" anticipate how technological change shapes—and is shaped by—social, cultural, and political change and how desired technologies depend on implicit assumptions about the people who might use them.

Drawing on his experiences on large-scale Hollywood film productions such as *Minority Report*, production designer Alex McDowell (2015) envisions a methodology of critical speculative design that imagines future worlds and the peoples and systems that inhabit and sustain them. Through his World Building Lab based at the University of Southern California, multidisciplinary and geographically dispersed teams collaborate to explore the potential repercussions of developments such as climate change while making room for fantastical elements such as giant flying whales. They collectively generate social action narratives that often go beyond familiar story arcs, recognizing the multiple points of entry for imagining change. Engaging in critical speculative design helps center concerns about agency, privacy, and inclusion that might otherwise be overlooked.

Following a similar logic, science fiction has become a battleground as different groups demand a voice in how the future is represented. William Lempert (2015), for example, has documented how Native American, First Nation, and Aboriginal peoples use science fiction as a means of contesting the frontier and settler mythologies that run through so many space operas: "By assuming that Native peoples are not just relics of the past, but have as many complex cultural and political futures as Western societies, Native sci-fi has the potential to help reimagine the assumptions that inform the social and policy treatment of contemporary Indigenous peoples." Curtis Marez (2016) similarly considers what he calls "farm worker futurism," alternative conceptions for the economic and social arrangements sustaining agribusiness that emerged from those seeking to organize farm workers for collective action. One recent anthology, *Octavia's Brood* (Brown and Imarisha 2015), created as a tribute to the legacy of Octavia Butler, assembled science fiction stories by, for, and about social movements: "Whenever we try to envision a world without war, without violence, without prisons, without capitalism, we are engaging in speculative fiction. All organizing is science fiction. Organizers and activists dedicate their lives to creating and envisioning another world, or many other words—so what better venue for organizers to explore their work than science fiction stories" (3). The visions that emerge in these debates are often contradictory and polyvalent. Michael Saler describes them as "contingent"; they cannot be reduced to classic utopias and dystopias. Minority writers in particular struggle to think through how their communities might fit within the genre vocabulary of speculative fiction as it has evolved since the pulp magazine era in the early twentieth century: their narratives reflect their ambivalence about whether they will be allowed a meaningful future, whether they can redefine the society in which they currently live or escape and build a new world for themselves elsewhere.

Science fiction imagery surfaced often at feminist protest marches against Trump in 2017. On the one hand, the image of Princess Leia from Star Wars was newly revitalized by the character's digital reconstruction in *Rogue One* and had gained greater cultural resonance following actress Carrie Fisher's death. Her heroic posture of holding a blaster evokes a utopian possibility for women: "A woman's place is in the resistance." On the other hand, a number of women adopted the restrictive dress of the Handmaids from Margaret Atwood's *The Handmaid's Tale*, recently adapted into a television series for Hulu. This dystopian narrative reminds participants of the stakes in their struggles against greater restrictions on women's reproductive rights.

Several of the essays in this section explore the politics of speculative fiction. In chapter 1, William Proctor focuses on the alt-right backlash against Star Wars and other media properties for what some perceived as "politically correct" messages. Here the push to imagine more inclusive futures was seen as having gone too far, too fast—at least by some white men who felt displaced from and threatened by these new narratives.

In chapter 2, Lauren Levitt considers the growing popularity of dystopian young adult fiction, "mass-market narratives about revolution." Levitt traces the growing popularity of the Hunger Games series—with its narrative about wealth inequality, government surveillance, and media manipulation—at the same moment that Occupy Wall Street and the Bernie Sanders campaign directed attention to similar real-world problems. She explores what happens as activist groups mobilize around such narratives and how market demands smooth away their more radical potentials.

A world can be "better" without being perfect or ideal. We may never reach a consensus about what a better world looks like, and one group's utopia may be another's dystopia. But this is what Duncombe means when he describes utopian rhetoric as a provocation rather than a blueprint. In chapter 3, Michael Saler depicts the communities around speculative fiction as examples of what he calls "public spheres of the imagination"—places where ideas are debated, positions are questioned, and people evolve. He shares two stories about the horror and fantasy writer H. P. Lovecraft: The first is about how Lovecraft himself evolved away from a reactionary worldview through conversations with readers and writers who saw things differently. The second deals with how contemporary genre-fiction writers, especially those of color, wrestle with his legacy, trying to write their way past the racism, misogyny, and xenophobia they identify in works that have proven foundational to the fantasy tradition.

Of course, speculative fictions are not the only popular genres inspiring debates about what a "better world" looks like. In chapter 4, Taylor

Cole Miller and Jonathan Gray narrate the political history of the television sitcom, a genre often accused of offering a nostalgic and sanitized conception of the American family. Yet their account shows how the sitcom has been a contested space, where different ideas about gender, sexuality, race, and class are staged and debated. In the final chapter of this section, Raffi Sarkissian considers award shows as a space where we celebrate what is best in our culture or, more recently, where minority winners counter prevailing narratives within popular media. Tracing the 2016 award show cycle, he demonstrates how acceptance speeches called attention to struggles over representation, moving beyond personal success stories to consider systemic constraints on whose stories are told.

# 1

## Rebel Yell

The Metapolitics of Equality and Diversity in
Disney's Star Wars

### William Proctor

Since Disney's acquisition of Lucasfilm in 2012, the Star Wars saga has
been a lightning rod for political quarrels and conflicts. On the one
hand, the three Star Wars films that Disney has produced so far—*The
Force Awakens* (2015), *Rogue One: A Star Wars Story* (2016), and *The Last
Jedi* (2017)—have each been critically championed for enacting positive
shifts in representation, opening up the imaginary world as an ideological space for inclusion and equality through new characters played
by a culturally diverse cast as well as an increase in female actors. On
the other hand, a small band of rebels asked audiences to boycott Disney's Star Wars in order to resist such shifts by attacking (what they saw
as) a significant uptick in politically correct entertainment. Indeed, the
reemergence of the Star Wars film franchise has been paralleled by
the ascendancy of the so-called alt-right, "an amorphous, ideologically diffuse, and largely online movement," which has grown into "an
umbrella term for white supremacists, MRAs [men's rights activists],
neo-Nazis, white tribalists, and other ideological groups" (Heikkilä
2017, 2). Whether for progressive or reactionary ends, a battalion of
digital commentators tapped into the Star Wars civic imagination by
voluntarily enlisting as soldiers in the new culture wars being fought
across the battlefields of the internet, with social media platforms functioning as "public spheres of the imagination" (Saler 2012).

This is not the first time that Star Wars has been a hotbed of political
antagonism. In 2005, *Revenge of the Sith* was criticized by members of
Patriotic Americans Boycotting Anti-American Hollywood (PABAAH)
for promoting anti-Bush rhetoric, the most offensive element being a

line spoken by Anakin Skywalker, at this point descending rapidly to the dark side, to Obi-Wan Kenobi: "You're either with me or you're my enemy." For dissenters, this was clearly a pop at Bush's War on Terror, when the POTUS stated unequivocally, "Either you're with us, or you're with the terrorists." In fact, George Lucas made no secret of the film's political analogies and promoted the film as a commentary on the War on Terror and US involvement in Iraq and Afghanistan. In response, PABAAH attempted to mobilize a boycott of the film via available online channels prior to the ascendancy of Twitter and other social networking services. But if box office receipts are an indicator of a film's success, it failed to spark anything much beyond mainstream ridicule. Writing for the *Guardian*, John Sutherland (2005) mocked the boycotters of the right as "hilarious," drawing on other campaigns, such as one by the American Family Association that protested Disney's *The Lion King* "on the grounds that Timon the Meerkat and Pumba the Warthog were inter-species homosexual lovers."

On Twitter, the first hashtag campaign directed at Disney's Star Wars allegedly occurred in December 2014 following the release of the teaser trailer for *The Force Awakens*. The inclusion of black actor John Boyega in Stormtrooper uniform reportedly led to the hashtags #boycottStarWarsVII and #BlackStormtrooper becoming trending topics on Twitter. As I have written about elsewhere (Proctor 2018), many news outlets claimed that the hashtags were used to promote virulent racism, and the media drew from Twitter as source material for a bevy of news reports. The hashtag #BlackStormtrooper, it was argued, had been created specifically to protest Boyega's involvement in the film. However, the hashtag had been created in 2010 to publicize Donald Faison's LEGO parody *Black Stormtrooper*. Across social media, there were fannish arguments about the genetic makeup of Imperial Stormtroopers and, in particular, the way in which Boyega's racial identity raised significant questions regarding Star Wars canon. In *Attack of the Clones* (2001), Jango Fett (played by Polynesian actor Temuera Morrison) provides the genetic material for the creation of an army of clones. The main canonical issues pivoted on comments and queries relating to Jango Fett's race, perhaps best exemplified by one commentator who tweeted, "Pretty sure the galaxy is patrolled by bad ass Polynesians" (quoted in Proctor 2018). Other commentators marshaled textual evidence from a variety of sources that demonstrated that Clonetroopers and Stormtroopers are, in fact, different kinds of soldiers: the former grown from the genetic soup of Jango Fett and the latter recruited from civilian populations.

Similarly, the hashtag #boycottStarWarsVII rapidly became a trending topic on Twitter. However, it was the welter of news media reporting that catapulted the hashtag into prominence, not the social media platform itself. The website Mashable employed social media analytics firm Fizziology to scrape the hashtag and provide quantitative data centered on racism within the thread as well as robust challenges from the twitterati. According to the data, 94 percent of comments were critical of the hashtag, with 6 percent being "racist trolls trying to get people mad" (Dickey 2015). As with #BlackStormtrooper, the discussion around the hashtag mostly attracted antiracist comments, many of which were hostile themselves, perhaps signaling that Twitter is, in the main, a left-leaning platform. What is impossible to determine is whether progressive tweets were acts of "virtue signaling" to draw attention to liberal politics as a bid for cultural capital or if the cacophony of invective directed at an imaginary and imagined community of fan racists was also the work of trolls. That said, there has certainly been an escalation of right-wing pushback within and across a variety of other digital spaces, especially those Adrienne Massanari (2015) describes as "toxic technocultures," such as Reddit, 4Chan, and the men's rights activist website Return of Kings (ROK).

Following the theatrical release of *The Force Awakens* in December 2015, ROK published opinion pieces on how the film was nothing more than "social justice propaganda" within which women are granted power that they could never obtain in the real world (Brown 2015a). Although new character Rey, played by Daisy Ridley, was largely celebrated across news media as "a game-changer," "a feminist-punch-in-the-air moment we've all been waiting for" (Carvelas 2016), and "a female Jedi that kicks ass" (S. Cox 2015), ROK writer David G. Brown singled out Rey but also criticized other female characters, such as Captain Phasma, who "is given command of the First Order's elite Stormtroopers but has the same biology as in our world where no woman has ever passed the Marine Corps' Infantry Officer Course" (2015a).

Contextually, ROK is an online hive of scum and villainy composed of what can only be described as misogynist, reactionary, antifeminist, and antifemale content. Articles include non-ironic titles such as "Seven

*conservative* (margin note)

*Rey / women* (margin note)

*Phasma* (margin note)

Ways Women Are Just like Abandoned Dogs" (Sharpe 2017), "How Toxic Femininity Turned Men into Tranny Chasers" (Jones 2017), and "Why Are So Many Women Sluts?" (Sebastian 2016). Created by misogynist Daryush Valizadeh—who goes by the pseudonym Roosh V—ROK is a container for right-wing propaganda, often marshaling falsehoods such as Brown's astonishing claim that the boycott of *The Force Awakens* was triumphant, costing Disney $4 million in box office receipts only four days after its theatrical release. If true, then that would account for just 0.21 percent of $2 billion, the global box office tally, which is hardly indicative of a meaningful impact. But of course, it isn't remotely true, and even a cursory glance at Brown's methodology and his claim that ROK contains "balanced critical reporting" should cause scholars to twitch and squirm (Brown 2015b).

The first Disney spin-off movie, *Rogue One*, also attracted the ire of right-wing commenters in the months leading up to its theatrical release, with a spate of racist articles and another hashtag campaign (#dumpstarwars). In the aftermath of Donald Trump's election victory, *Rogue One* screenwriter Chris Weitz tweeted the progressive message "Star Wars against hate. Spread it" above an image of the rebellion insignia with a safety pin attached—a signifier of solidarity with immigrants, refugees, and other exploited parties that was first used in the wake of the Brexit referendum in the United Kingdom and adopted in the United States following the election. Others responded by calling out Weitz for dressing the franchise in political robes: "Just let Star Wars be Star Wars," said one early commenter. In response to another follower who said, "I'm with the empire," Weitz tweeted, "Please note that the Empire is a white supremacist (human) organization." To this, writer Gary Whitta added that the Empire is "opposed by a multi-cultural group led by brave women."

These comments served to inflame members of the so-called alt-right, with both sides playing a game of social media volleyball between interpretative and ideological communities, striking abusive comments back and forth across digital platforms. Recognizing that Weitz's and Whitta's tweets had provoked an angry backlash from Trump supporters, Disney CEO Bob Iger attempted to calm the fracas, claiming that *Rogue One* "is not a film that is, in any way, a political film. There are no political statements in it, at all. [*Rogue One*] has one of the greatest and most diverse

*[handwritten margin notes: "Star Wars against Hate" and "everything Political"]*

casts of any film we have ever made and we are very proud of that, and that is not a political statement, at all" (Galuppo 2016). Iger's insistence that *Rogue One* is not political "at all" had more to do with appealing to multiple audiences by attempting to paratextually neuter the movie's politics in order to promote it as nonpartisan and ideologically agnostic, "a film that the world should enjoy." As the *Hollywood Reporter's* Tatiana Siegel (2016) argued, "What Disney and Lucasfilm might not be thrilled about is that a Trump 'Empire' versus [Hillary] Clinton 'resistance' narrative might alienate the 61-million-plus voters who backed the real estate mogul, a group too large to ignore when a company is in the tent-pole business. . . . In the Trump age, if the right-leaning media can help tip a presidential election, it's reasonable to assume it can impact grosses."

Moreover, right-wing voices protested Disney-Lucasfilm for allegedly ordering expensive reshoots so as to add anti-Trump messages to the film. This rumor—set in motion by right-wing troll Jack Posobiec, who tweeted that "Star wars [*sic*] writers rewrote and reshot Rogue One to add in Anti Trump scenes calling him a racist"—gained traction across various news media platforms. As absurd as ROK's claims about box office damage, the notion that Disney would spend an extravagant amount of money to insert progressive ideologies into a film Iger rendered politically neutral in an interview is clearly nonsense. But then equally ridiculous was the volte-face that Disney ordered reshoots not to embed anti-Trump sentiments within *Rogue One* but instead *to remove them altogether*. In response, ROK's Brown (2015b) wrote, "Rogue One shows that Hollywood is listening to our complaints about feminism in films"—talk about delusions of grandeur—and that "the film industry is quickly becoming aware of viewers' anger at SJW [social justice warrior] madness being forced down their throats." Despite such claims, research conducted by the Creative Artists Agency (CAA), which found that "the average opening weekend for a film that attracts a diverse audience, often the result of having a diverse cast, is nearly three times [greater] on average [compared to] a film with non-diverse audiences. . . . Across every budget level a film with a diverse cast outperforms a release not so diversified" (T. Anderson 2017). That said, it would be wrong to dismiss these various boycott campaigns as the exploits of nefarious, ironic trolls who are only in it for "the lulz" (Whitney 2017). As Niko Heikkilä (2017) puts it, to see these digital instantiations as "mere trolling, on the basis of which one might dismiss the behavior, distorts the actual message and downplays the ideology behind it" (8). Indeed, sowing dissension and discord is part and parcel of the alt-right's "metapolitical strategy," a discursive culture war "that would gradually transform the political and intellectual culture as a precursor to transforming institutions and systems" (10). In other words, alt-right criticism is centered on the production and circulation of *ideas* transmitted via digital means and methods, such as by flooding online territories with weaponized memes that tap into the civic imagination. The alt-right's attacks have resulted in mainstream news exposure, offering prime space to these marginal voices and giving valuable oxygen and decibels to the movement, a phantom menace no longer.

According to Whitney Phillips and Ryan M. Milner (2017), the alt-right moved from the margins and into the mainstream during the 2016 US presidential election, in which Trump proved to be "a particularly unifying force for the Ku Klux Klan, splinter white nationalist groups, and the cacophony of reactionists, antagonists, and neo-supremacists that have come to be known as the alt-right, all of whom have declared, publically and enthusiastically, their support for a candidate who 'gets it'" (180). However, the alt-right have also set their sights on critiquing objects of popular culture with the goal of grinding the March of Diversity to a halt. As Brown has recognized, ROK is "not the only positive source of non-mainstream news, self-improvement advice and cultural commentary. What happens when we add together the reach of Breitbart, the Daily Caller, Gotnews.com and a host of other sources with our own?" (2016b).

Other films have also become a site of protest for alt-right ideologues and anarchic trolls. It appears that they will attack anything that does not fit their scurrilous views on multiculturalism and egalitarianism. ROK's Aaron Carey deemed *Mad Max: Fury Road* (2015) a wolf in sheep's clothing, a "feminist piece of propaganda posing as a guy's flick. . . . A piece of American culture ruined and rewritten before their very eyes" (2015). Forgetting that Mad Max is of Australian heritage, not American—hardly an example of fan cultural capital there—his central thrust is that the film is nothing but a kind of ideological black magic that will undoubtedly spellbind vulnerable men with explosions and action sequences while simultaneously conditioning the male populace to feminist ends. "Not all of them [men] have the same keen eye as we do here at ROK," argues Carey.

Perhaps stranger still are the rightist voices that bemoan the latest incarnation of Star Trek for containing progressive politics (emblemized by the hashtag #politicalcorrectness) when the franchise has included a multicultural cast from its inception. Alt-right commentators have adopted fannish rhetoric in many instances, but when it comes to the accumulation of fan cultural capital, they often fall short. As the right's protests and boycotts against franchises, stars, and brands supposedly sympathetic to multiculturalism have diversified, it becomes harder to tell whether the critics are actually fans of what they are railing against: Boycott Kellogg's (Woolf 2016). Boycott Jennifer Lawrence. Boycott Google. Boycott Star Trek and *Mad Max: Fury Road*. Boycott Stephen King's *IT*. Boycott Pepsi, Oreos, Doritos, and Netflix. And of course, boycott Disney's Star Wars.

Web 2.0 has become a figurative bullhorn for both the spread of right-wing ideologies and critiques from progressive quarters. Even though various news media have reported on "the dark side of geek culture" (Rosza 2014) as the province of "angry white nerds" (Lachenal 2015), we simply do not know the identities of these people or their fannish or ideological affiliations. Obviously, if "we are all fans now" (Gray et al. 2017, 2), then it stands to reason that those on the far right of the political spectrum are fans too (fans of what, however, is another question). But there is also evidence that the alt-right's appeal to fandom, perhaps as a recruitment strategy, contains little fan cultural capital, which might be one way that scholars can investigate the truth claims of alt-right commenters. The idea is not to protect fandom as a utopian community—fans can no doubt be toxic too (Proctor and Kies 2018)—but to drill deeper down into hashtags and other user-generated mechanisms to tease out an accurate representation of discursive publics rather than reproducing journalists' appropriations of tweets without much in the way of methodological rigor or even basic fact-checking.

We should not forget that in each of the hashtag campaigns discussed here, the majority of voices are those attacking reactionary comments, despite news media highlighting the latter as the loudest. News media certainly prefer controversy over fact, spectacle instead of authenticity.

The way in which journalists cherry-pick from an armada of social media expressions is perhaps what should concern scholars most of all. Conversely, we should also remember that the metapolitical strategy of right-wing voices and activists is arguably more about facilitating the spread of insidious ideologies than it is about legitimate fans expressing their antagonism (although I am equally certain that there are conservative Star Wars fans criticizing shifts in the politics of representation). Both progressive and reactionary audiences see themselves as rebels fighting an ignominious Empire, and perhaps it is time we acknowledge that right-wing audiences are also tapping into the civic imagination, whether we like it or not.

For many fans, however, Star Wars signals freedom from tyranny and oppression, perhaps best illustrated by the way in which female protestors appropriated and politicized the image of Princess Leia during the 2017 Women's March in Washington, DC. It is quite remarkable how often Star Wars has been evoked in political debates over the past four decades or so, demonstrating that popular culture is often a valuable resource for hope. And "rebellions are built on hope," as Jyn Erso states in the trailer for *Rogue One*.

Star Wars against hate. Spread it.

## 2

# The Hunger Games and the Dystopian Imagination

## Lauren Levitt

If you walk into a major bookstore in the United States, you might find a shelf labeled "dystopian young adult fiction." Although dystopian science fiction and the young adult (YA) novel have long been established genres in their own right, the proliferation of dystopian stories for young adults is a relatively recent phenomenon. The current popularity of the genre originated with Suzanne Collins's best-selling Hunger Games trilogy: *The Hunger Games* (2008), *Catching Fire* (2009), and *Mockingjay* (2010). All three of these novels have subsequently been adapted for the screen and have been massively successful. *The Hunger Games* was released in 2012, grossing about as much at the box office as the most popular of the YA fantasy films from the Twilight series (Booker 2013, xxvi). Then in 2013, *Catching Fire* was released to further box office success. Finally, *Mockingjay* was split into two parts that were released in 2014 and 2015, and both were well received critically and by the public.

YA dystopian narratives take up sociopolitical issues such as wealth inequality and governmentality that are particularly timely considering the growing inequities in our own world and the use of surveillance and manipulation by the media and governments in order to maintain social control. Following the subprime mortgage crisis in the United States in 2007 and the global financial crisis in 2008, in September 2011, Occupy Wall Street activists took over Zuccotti Park in the financial district of New York City to protest wealth inequality, sparking similar protests nationally and worldwide. Then in 2015, Vermont senator Bernie Sanders announced that he would run for the Democratic Party's nomination in the 2016 presidential election on a platform of addressing wealth inequality. Sanders had previously served in the US House of Representatives and Senate as an Independent, and he was not taken seriously as a candidate at first. Raising most of the money for his campaign from individual donors, Sanders mobilized younger voters and narrowly lost the nomination to party favorite Secretary of State Hillary Clinton, winning 43 percent to Clinton's 55 percent.

YA dystopian texts may be particularly suited to offer radical critique, as they are essentially stories about revolution, but there is a certain irony to this, since these are *mass market* narratives about revolution. YA novels and films are big business, and they have grown exponentially over the past twenty years. By 2012, when the first Hunger Games film was released, YA fiction was the world's fastest-growing literary genre. The number of YA novels published each year had increased from three thousand in 1997 to twelve thousand in 2009 (Martin 2012). In 2012, the Hunger Games trilogy replaced the Harry Potter series as Amazon's top seller, and as of 2014, the trilogy had sold more than sixty-five million copies in the United States alone (Bosman 2012; G. Hall 2014).

This chapter will first examine the themes of wealth inequality and governmentality in the Hunger Games multimedia franchise to show how the series both promotes and forecloses radical politics. Here I define *radical* as that which is outside the bounds of what is considered possible or practical in a given political context. Thus radical politics is highly contingent on historical and geographic contexts: mainstream politics in one time and place may be considered radical in another. For example, while democratic socialism is well established in Nordic countries such a Sweden or Finland, it remains radical within a contemporary US political context. Next, following from Duncombe's (2012a) suggestion that the utopian imagination leads to social change in a dialectical fashion, this chapter proposes that the dystopian imagination, as a subset of the utopian imagination, may function in a similar way. Finally, this chapter turns to the ways in which real-world activists have taken up symbols from the Hunger Games in order to combat world hunger and wealth inequality in the United States; push for minimum-wage reform in several US states; protest police brutality and social injustice in Ferguson, Missouri; and fight for democracy in Thailand and Hong Kong.

## Wealth Inequality

The Hunger Games series takes place in a postapocalyptic North America following a global environmental disaster. The nation of Panem comprises twelve districts controlled by the Capitol. After an unsuccessful uprising of the districts against the Capitol in which a thirteenth district was allegedly wiped out, the Capitol established the Hunger Games as a punishment for the districts and a source of entertainment. Each year two youths, one male and one female, are selected as "tributes" from each district to fight each other to the death on a nationally broadcast reality television program.

As Fischer (2012) points out, the socially, economically, and politically inferior position of the districts links them to the "periphery" of the Global South as posited by postcolonial theory. The districts extract resources and produce goods for the use of elites in the Capitol, with those districts located closest to the Capitol involved in the production of luxury items such as gemstones and occupying a privileged position vis-à-vis the other districts. As in the Global South, both socioeconomic and physical mobility are extremely difficult, but there is some stratification within the districts. Moreover, the series provides a critique of neoliberal capitalism within the United States. The citizens of Panem receive no social welfare services and have no organized labor. People in the districts appear to have little access to medical facilities, and during the rebellion, President Snow, Panem's totalitarian leader, raises the work quotas for the districts with impunity.

## Governmentality

As Hector Amaya (2013) suggests, the media are key players in systems of oppression, and the criticism of contemporary media is perhaps the clearest message of *The Hunger Games*. Both media manipulation and surveillance constitute what Foucault refers to as "governmentality," the nondisciplinary strategies through which populations are controlled. The clearest way in which the citizens of Panem are controlled through the media is by the games themselves. The Capitol believes that if it keeps the masses satisfied with mindless entertainment, then they will not rise up against the government.

Propaganda

When Katniss unintentionally starts a rebellion with the poison berries at the end of the first games, President Snow punishes her with another media spectacle, a Quarter Quell, in which the tributes will be chosen from the remaining victors. However, the games themselves are by far not the only instance of media manipulation in the story; both the Capitol and District 13 extensively use propaganda toward their ends. Both *Mockingjay* films are heavily concerned with President Coin, the stern leader of District 13, and head gamemaker Plutarch's plan to use Katniss as a symbol of their revolution against the Capitol and their production and broadcast of "propos" featuring her. The Capitol counters these broadcasts with propaganda of its own: televised interviews between Caesar Flickerman (the host of the Hunger Games) and Peeta (Katniss's fellow tribute from District 12, who is captured by the Capitol at the end of *Catching Fire*), in which Peeta urges the rebels to lay down their arms. Apart from this, both Snow and Coin make use of the media to directly address the citizens of Panem.

Surveillance

Aside from media manipulation, power is asserted over the districts through surveillance. During the games, every action of the tributes is watched and recorded, but surveillance occurs outside of the games as well. The riot-suited Peacekeepers are a ubiquitous presence in both the Capitol and the districts. Surveillance is also conducted during the rebellion with the use of surveillance cameras in both the Capitol and the districts. The constant surveillance of the districts and the Capitol by both Peacekeepers and security cameras corresponds to what contemporary theorists have called "the surveillance society" and to their worries about the dystopian consequences of surveillance technologies (Gates 2011, 4).

## The Dystopian Imagination

Although typically utopian narratives are thought to lead to social change by modeling more perfect worlds, in "Imagining No-Place," Duncombe (2012a) suggests that utopian narratives invite us to imagine radical alternatives through a dialectical process, since utopia is not only ideal but also impossible, and in his introduction to *Open Utopia* (2012b), an online, interactive version of Thomas More's *Utopia*, he elaborates on how this process occurs. The dystopia, Duncombe (2012b) writes, serves a critical function; it shows us what could happen in the future if things continue as they are. However, criticism "has become ineffectual at best and self-delusional at worst" because it does not offer an alternative vision of society (2012b).

Klein (2017), by contrast, offers an opposing view of dystopian narratives. These stories "take current trends and follow them to their logical conclusion"; they "hold a mirror up" to the world. In other words, the dystopian imagination serves a hortatory function: it exhorts us to make changes in the present to avoid disastrous future consequences. By this token, the dystopian imagination may also operate in a dialectical fashion, and dystopian narratives may be doubly effective, since they present us with *undesirable*, as well as impossible, worlds. Like utopian narratives, of which they are a type, dystopian narratives may also encourage us to make changes in the present in order to create a better future. This ability to imagine different possibilities may inspire political action, as suggested by Imagine Better's Hunger Games–related campaigns and the adoption of the symbol of the series by global political activists (Kligler-Vilenchik 2016).

## Imagine Better

Although it is now a separate organization run by Harry Potter Alliance (HPA) founder Andrew Slack, Imagine Better started off as a branch of the HPA (a fan activist organization) dedicated to fandoms other than the Harry Potter series. In 2012, to coincide with the release of the first Hunger Games film, Imagine Better partnered with Oxfam's GROW campaign to launch their Hunger Is Not a Game campaign combating global hunger. Hunger Games fans were encouraged to sign Oxfam's GROW pledge, which called for governments to create policies to encourage the growth of crops for food rather than fuel, food aid reform, and support for small farmers (Martin 2012). Canned food drives were held at local movie theaters, and on March 23, activists attended midnight release parties, asking people to sign the pledge and tweet with the hashtag #notagame to create a sense of global community (Bird, personal communication, June 1, 2017; Martin 2012). However, the day before the movie was released, Lionsgate, the film's production company, issued a cease-and-desist letter to the campaign through Oxfam, claiming that the campaign was damaging to Lionsgate and their marketing efforts. In response, twenty-six-year-old fan Holly McCready created a Change.org petition asking Lionsgate to retract the letter. Eighteen thousand people signed it, and the studio capitulated within hours, resulting in the fastest-resolved petition in Change.org history (Bird, personal communication, June 1, 2017).

In conjunction with the release of *Hunger Games: Catching Fire* in 2013, Imagine Better shifted its focus from global food justice to economic inequality, launching the Odds in Our Favor campaign. That year, CoverGirl announced their Capitol Collection as a marketing tie-in with the film, and Slack (2013) wrote an op-ed in the *Los Angeles Times* arguing that through its collaboration with CoverGirl, Lionsgate had positioned itself as the Capitol. Imagine Better encouraged fans to rise up as the people of the districts in response, posting real-world facts about economic inequality and pictures of themselves doing the three-finger salute, a symbol of the districts' rebellion against the Capitol, on Lionsgate's social media pages. Moreover, Imagine Better started the We Are the Districts campaign, inspired by Occupy's slogan "We are the 99 percent," which came up with real-world causes of systemic inequality to correspond with each of the districts, and the Tumblr for this campaign garnered more than three thousand followers in the first year (Bird, personal communication, June 1, 2017).

The following year, in conjunction with *Mockingjay, Part 1*, Imagine Better urged fans to share their personal stories of inequality with the hashtag #myhungergames, which received widespread press coverage and was even retweeted by Anonymous, a global, collaborative hacktivist group that has taken action against religious groups, governments, and corporations. In 2012, *Time Magazine* called Anonymous one of the one hundred most influential "people" in the world.

Although the hashtag spread well beyond Imagine Better's following, it also highlighted how many within the HPA had experienced economic marginalization themselves. Whereas previously the organization had thought of its members as primarily white, middle-class youths fighting for the rights of others, this showed that the membership of the HPA was more diverse than anyone had expected, which marked a shift within the organization toward listening more to its members (Bird, personal communication, June 1, 2017). At this time, the We Are the Districts Tumblr became a space for the discussion of economic inequality, three-finger salute selfies, and #myhungergames posts.

In 2014, Imagine Better also worked with some workers' rights organizations, including Fight for $15, an organization devoted to increasing the minimum wage. Fight for $15 held national protests for fast-food workers to increase the minimum wage to $15 per hour, and some members attended the protests and demonstrations (Bird, personal communication, June 1, 2017). Imagine Better also asked members to support the protests by posting, with the hashtag #myhungergames, a three-finger-salute selfie in front of their local fast-food restaurants and by giving the organization's letter about fair wages for employees to restaurant managers. Some members expressed anxiety about handing letters to managers, showing that it could be difficult to translate online activism to real-world activism, but the workers' marches embraced the Hunger Games imagery (Wiedeman 2014). The organizers of one protest made a board with life-size photos of some of the characters from the film with their faces cut out where protestors could take photos, and Slack convinced organizers to get the protestors to use the three-finger salute at protests in Brooklyn, Atlanta, Chicago, and Manhattan (Bird, personal communication, June 1, 2017; Wiedeman 2014). Finally, a worker from the South rewrote the song "The Hanging Tree" from the movie to be about the movement and sang it at a demonstration there (Bird, personal communication, June 1, 2017). Imagine Better continued working with Fight for $15 through the release of *Mockingjay, Part 2*.

## Other Protest Movements

Activists also employed Hunger Games symbolism in other protest movements worldwide. For instance, on August 9, 2014, protests and riots broke out in Ferguson, Missouri, a suburb of St. Louis, following the fatal shooting of Michael Brown, an unarmed black teenager, by Darren Wilson, a white police officer. Following the release of *Mockingjay, Part 1* in November, protestors awaiting the grand jury decision about whether Wilson would be tried for murder graffitied a line from the movie—"If we burn, you burn with us"—on an arch in the Shaw neighborhood of St. Louis (Bates 2014). Then in May, following a military coup in Thailand, prodemocracy activists began to use the three-finger salute from the films as a sign of resistance against the military regime in the first instance of the international adoption of the symbol (Mydans 2014). The three-finger salute reemerged as a prodemocracy symbol in September during the Umbrella Movement in Hong Kong. Following a decision by the Standing Committee of the National People's Congress on reforms to Hong Kong's electoral process, which requires candidates for Hong Kong's chief executive to be selected by a nominating committee, tens of thousands of protesters led by student activist groups took to the streets to demand free and fair elections. As in Thailand, the protestors adopted the three-finger salute as a sign of defiance against the Central People's Government in Beijing (Sim 2014).

## Implications

As these examples suggest, engagement with popular culture can lead to civic engagement through the civic imagination (Jenkins, Shresthova, Gamber-Thompson, and Kligler-Vilenchik 2016; Jenkins et al. 2016). Duncombe's (2012a) concept of the utopian imagination helps us think about the ways in which utopian fiction can allow us to imagine a better future through a dialectical reaction to utopia's "no place," and the dystopian imagination may work in a similar way by warning us about what could happen if we do not make changes in the present. Though we must always be aware of its commodity status and its ambiguous stance on issues related to racial inequality, the Hunger Games series offers negative examples of what might happen if contemporary wealth inequality and governmentality are left unchecked.

**3**

## Spinning H. P. Lovecraft

A Villain or Hero of Our Times?

**Michael Saler**

The legacy of horror writer H. P. Lovecraft (1890–1937) has been sharply contested in recent years, providing insights into how stories—both fictional and nonfictional—inform the civic imagination. During his lifetime, his stories had a limited following, appearing primarily in pulp magazines; they became more widely known in succeeding decades through hardcover and paperback reprints, as well as adaptations in film, comics, and games. By the turn of the new century, Lovecraft had been tacitly inducted into the canon of North American literature through the publication of his stories by the prestigious Library of America (Lovecraft 2005).

The attendant publicity brought greater attention to his racism and xenophobia, which had been noted by earlier biographers and critics. In 2011, Nnedi Okorafor wrote a widely circulated blog post about her conflicted feelings about receiving a 2010 World Fantasy Award (WFA), which since 1975 had been known informally as "the Howard" and cast in Lovecraft's visage. As the first person of color to win this award, Okorafor was shocked when she learned the extent of his bigotry, and she was determined to incite a debate "about what it means to honor a talented racist" (Okorafor 2011). Another writer, Daniel José Older, started a petition in 2014 to have Lovecraft's image replaced, which garnered more than 2,500 signatures. This controversy received wide media coverage and spurred extensive online discussion. Some objected to changing the award on the grounds that Lovecraft was one of the most influential fantasy writers, his objectionable views more a reflection of his times and psyche than a central feature of his fiction. Whatever this argument's merits, he clearly had become an inflammatory figure within the fantasy field, which had increasingly diversified since at least the 1990s. In 2015, the organization bestowing the award agreed to replace it, commissioning an abstract design for the statuette.

The controversy had several salutary consequences. Lovecraft's fears of ethnic, sexual, and social differences—and the ways that he expressed these in his fiction—were fruitfully discussed in terms of how horror's rhetorical strategies have historically been deployed politically and socially to exclude difference and vilify outsiders. The online debate also suggested that such narratives can be combatted by the promotion of more inclusive counternarratives. Following the WFA controversy, numerous writers from groups whom Lovecraft ignored or denigrated, such as women and minorities, began to reclaim his imaginary worlds, writing stories celebrating cosmopolitanism and gender equality.

These results demonstrate how fantasy can inform the civic imagination through vigorous discussions about fictional representations. These "public spheres of the imagination" first appeared in the early twentieth century, when readers began to discuss stories in new public venues such as the letters pages of fiction magazines, clubs (such as those dedicated to science fiction and Sherlock Holmes, both arising in the 1930s), fanzines, and conventions. Discussions about fantasy worlds often segue into related issues concerning the real world, a process now ubiquitous online (Saler 2012).

However, the controversy also highlights an ever-present danger within the civic imagination itself: replacing one set of simplistic narratives with another. Just as Lovecraft could resort to stereotypical labels, several critics have branded him as an extreme racist and misogynist who must be understood primarily in these terms. Rarely mentioned is the striking fact that Lovecraft repudiated many of his most disturbing prejudices in his final years, largely as a result of discussions with others who maintained different views. Lovecraft even might have abandoned his virulent adherence to a "color line" had he continued to reconsider long-held beliefs.

One of Lovecraft's most important legacies for our consideration is his own understanding of the civic imagination as a collocation of stories that are constantly being revised to capture new understandings based on new circumstances. He differentiated between reality and fantasy, but for him, both depend to some degree on pragmatic interpretations:

provisional, contingent narratives underlie fiction and nonfiction alike and are largely the product of intersubjective negotiations. He wrote to a friend in 1928, "Value is wholly relative. . . . No one thing, cosmically speaking, can be good or evil, beautiful or unbeautiful" (Joshi 1990, 90). Lovecraft emphasized both the psychological necessity and the social utility of contingent narratives, humanity's conduit to scientific, moral, and aesthetic truths. He believed that writers had an ethical responsibility to capture such truths in all their complexity. For this reason, he insisted, informed debate among citizens was indispensable "because it enables us to test our own opinions and amend them if we find them in any way erroneous or unjustified. One who never debates lacks a valuable chart or compass in the voyage for truth—for he is likely to cherish many false opinions along with sound ones for want of an opportunity to see each opinion viewed from every possible angle. I have modified many opinions of mine in the course of debate, and have been intensely grateful for the chance of doing so" (Lovecraft 2010, 459). While contemporary writers advocate that similar discussions take place in public spheres of the imagination in order to enlighten the public about racism and sexism, they usually don't give Lovecraft sufficient credit for the strides he made in reconsidering his own biases and recrafting his narratives accordingly. He too embraced the important civic functions of respectful, rational dialogue among individuals with different views and a willingness to reconsider one's most cherished opinions in the light of evidence and argument. His critics might respond that he only applied these ideals in a concerted way at the end of his life, an instance of "too little, too late." Yet when compared to the prejudices expressed without remorse by many others of Lovecraft's generation, such as T. S. Eliot and Martin Heidegger, his radical reconsiderations are remarkable. If the "arc of the moral universe is long, but it bends towards justice," as Martin Luther King averred, then "better late than never" has a virtue of its own.

## The Colors Out of Space

Prior to the WFA controversy, Lovecraft's fiction was usually discussed in terms of its philosophic implications and aesthetic strategies (or lack thereof) rather than in terms of its political and social implications.

Many of his stories have been categorized under two informal labels—lushly narrated tales about "dreamlands" and more realist-style "mythos" tales concerning humanity's encounters with extraterrestrial entities. The latter were popular partly because they reconciled transcendental concerns with modern secularism and rationalism. The Lovecraft mythos recast supernatural tropes into scientific and existentialist terms, providing readers with the sublime qualities of fear and awe generated by a vast and inexplicable cosmos.

Lovecraft encouraged other writers to borrow from and contribute to his imaginary universe. Mythos stories continued to be generated, primarily by white men, through the early twenty-first century. Discussions about the mythos in these decades tended to focus on the metaphysical dimensions of Lovecraft's legacy, such as his philosophy of "cosmic indifference" and whether his extraterrestrials might be analogous to—or distinct from—the pantheons of traditional religions. While the racism, xenophobia, and near-absence of women in his fiction as well as his life were explored in biographical works by L. Sprague de Camp (1975) and S. T. Joshi (1996), among others, these issues were rarely highlighted by writers contributing to the evolving mythos. Perhaps the first Lovecraft pastiche to deliberately redress his exclusionary outlooks was Joanna Russ's "My Boat" (Russ 1976)—and even here, her canny deployment of a black girl as protagonist probably eluded those unfamiliar with his original stories.

Since the WFA controversy's advent, however, discussions of Lovecraft's fiction have focused on their social and political dimensions. The controversy also stimulated an efflorescence of new mythos fictions reflecting these debates. Ruthanna Emrys observes, "[This] does feel like one of those moments of sudden condensation, a feedback loop where interest leads to discussion leads to art leads to interest. . . . That discussion is key" (quoted in Cunningham 2016). Emrys is among a host of recent writers who have reimagined Lovecraft's universe to include those whom he shunned or ignored. (Others engaged in this reclamation project include Caitlín Kiernan, Matt Ruff, Kij Johnson, Alan Moore, Victor LaValle, Cassandra Khaw, and Paul Lafarge; in 2015, Silvia Moreno-Garcia edited a World Fantasy Award–winning anthology of mythos tales by women, *She Walks in Shadows*.) Many such narratives redescribed difference as a source of strength rather than degeneration (as in Lovecraft).

Three accomplished works can stand for many others. Victor LaValle's *The Ballad of Black Tom* (2016) reenvisions Lovecraft's "The Horror at Red Hook" (1927) from the perspective of a working-class African American living in Harlem. Readers needn't know the latter story, with its overtly racist depictions, to be alerted to LaValle's political intentions. He makes it clear through his dedication: "For H. P. Lovecraft, with all my conflicted feelings." (For good measure, the tale features a bigoted detective named "Mr. Howard.") LaValle's protagonist, Charles Thomas Tester, finds that the meaningless nature of the cosmos is not nearly as horrific as the casual cruelties inflicted within Jim Crow America. After discovering that his father has been killed by a white police officer, Tester reflects, "A fear of cosmic indifference suddenly seemed comical, or downright naïve. . . . What was indifference compared to malice?" (LaValle 2016, 66). When faced with a choice between evils, Tester avows to the police, "I'll take Cthulhu over you devils any day" (LaValle 2016, 144.) Kij Johnson's *The Dream-Quest of Vellitt Boe* (2016) revisits Lovecraft's *The Dream-Quest of Unknown Kadath* (1926) from the perspective of a female protagonist, underscoring the complete absence of women from Lovecraft's dreamworld (and from much of his fiction). Johnson's dedication—"For everyone who had to find her way in"—would not inform the uninitiated about the gender imbalance in the mythos, but her acknowledgments page is unambiguous. She recalls reading Lovecraft's story as a child, "uncomfortable with the racism but not yet aware that the total absence of women was also problematic" (K. Johnson 2016, 168). Emrys's *Winter Tide* (2017) is a revisiting of Lovecraft's "The Shadow over Innsmouth" (1934) from the perspective of a female "Deep One," the hybrid species Lovecraft represented as monstrosities worthy of extermination. Emrys aligns their denigration in his story with the internment of Japanese Americans during World War II and the blood libel against the Jews. Like Johnson, she makes her purpose explicit in her acknowledgments: "This book owes its greatest debt to Howard Phillips Lovecraft, who invited everyone to play in his sandbox—even his monsters" (Emrys 2017, 364).

Emrys's tale is also explicit about how the civic imagination comprises contingent stories that too often are reified as normative truths and about the necessity of revising them based on evidence and experience. Lovecraft expressed similar views to those of one of her characters: "If there's one thing I've learned . . . it's to be suspicious of the stories every-one knows" (Emrys 2017, 183). Despite Lovecraft's insistence on the con-tingent and provisional nature of culture, he retained—for most of his life—stereotypical representations that were too gratifying to his fragile sense of self to be easily questioned, let alone abandoned. His gradual process of challenging his own prejudices is as instructive—and as heartening—as the contemporary turn to rewriting the mythos in terms of inclusivity and alterity.

## "Fandom's Favorite Racist"

Many who participated in the WFA debate admitted their conflicted feelings about Lovecraft. While they acknowledged his important influ-ence and creative imagination, Lovecraft tended to be smeared after 2011 as an unrepentant, hateful racist. As a consequence of the recent contro-versy, this has become the predominant image of him in the media. His late-life reconsideration of many of his attitudes is not widely known, or it is mentioned only to be dismissed as immaterial. In an interview, the Lovecraftian writer Cassandra Khaw stated, "I've heard people remark on the fact that Lovecraft became more tolerant as he grew older, but I don't think that's relevant. You can be a bigot and then you can stop being a bigot, but that doesn't change the fact that you were a bigot, if you get me?" (quoted in Cunningham 2016).

The heated language used by some veered perilously close to Love-craft's inflammatory invective against ethnic groups. China Miéville la-beled him a "bilious anti-Semite," stating that he had turned his own WFA toward the wall, "punishing the little fucker like the malevolent clown he was" (Okorafor). Older's petition acknowledged that while Lovecraft "did leave a lasting mark on speculative fiction, he was also an avowed racist and a terrible wordsmith." In other remarks, Older called him "fandom's favorite racist," who "used literature as a weapon against entire races" and "enthusiastically advocated for genocide" (Flood 2014).

When reading some of Lovecraft's remarks, one can understand such views. For example, in a letter to his friend James F. Morton on June 12, 1933, Lovecraft opines that Hitler's racist conceptions are mistaken—for the most part: "A real colour-line needs to be drawn only against certain definitely alien physical types—chiefly the biologically underdeveloped black races." For the Caucasian races, he insists that the important differences are cultural, not racial. Lovecraft, an impoverished writer, clung desperately to his WASP heritage as one of his few marks of distinction, resenting its apparent dilution by the influx of immigrants: "A hideous example of what Hitler is honestly—if crudely—trying to prevent is the stinking Manhattan Pest Zone. Faugh! Everything gone Yiddish— radical, effeminate psychology dominant . . . publishing houses . . . gobbled by squint-eyed, verminous kikes. . . . There's an Augean stable for the future Nazis of America! . . . I'd like to see Hitler wipe Greater New York clean with poison gas—giving masks to the few remaining people of Aryan culture (even if of Semitic ancestry). The place needs fumigation & a fresh start. (If Harlem didn't get any masks, I'd shed no tears . . . & the same goes for the dago slums!)" (Lovecraft 2011, 324). It is revealing, however, that he wrote this to Morton, a political radical who had long campaigned for black civil rights, the rights of women, and other progressive causes. The two became friends after they met as members of an amateur press association in 1915, one of the many new public spheres of the imagination of the period. Morton recognized that his conservative opponent was not only gifted but open to persuasion; he noted in his first response to Lovecraft's views in 1915, "The one thing in his favor is his evident sincerity. Let him once come to realize the value of appreciating the many points of view shared by persons as sincere as he and better informed in certain particulars, and he will become less narrow and intolerant" (Lovecraft 2011, 410). The two continued to argue, as friends, throughout Lovecraft's life.

Morton was not in the habit of wasting time with closed-minded bigots, and by late 1936, it appeared he was right about Lovecraft's capacity for change. The Depression had opened Lovecraft's eyes to social and political issues that he had never seriously considered. Between 1931 and 1936, he shifted from conservative Republicanism to Fabian Socialism, supporting Roosevelt's New Deal and eagerly reading works by progressive writers he would have scorned earlier. "Virtually *all* the reputable authors & critics in the United States are political radicals," he wrote to C. L. Moore in 1937, confessing that he could "understand the inert blindness & defiant ignorance of the reactionaries from having been one of them" (Lovecraft 2016, 217).

Lovecraft himself was somewhat bemused by the great distance he had traversed in such a short time. Writing to Clark Ashton Smith in 1934, he said that if he were a Californian, he'd vote for the socialist candidate for governor, Upton Sinclair: "A decade ago I thought he ought to be chloroformed. . . . Such are the mutations and ironies of time & growth!" (Lovecraft 2017, 570). He was also rethinking his attitudes toward Jews—many of whom he now perceived as fellow travelers within a "Popular Front"—as well as Nazis, whom he now linked with WASP plutocrats. He told Moore how he had attended a New Deal rally in late 1936 "with the eminent Rabbi Wise of New York as principal speaker. He sized up the changes in the national mind with phenomenal penetration & wit—so that I can well imagine the polite Nazis of Wall St. cursing him as a blasphemous non-Aryan intellectual!" (Lovecraft 2016, 218). Women, too, received more consideration. "I do not regard the rise of woman as a bad sign," he wrote Smith in 1934. "Rather do I fancy that her traditional subordination was itself an artificial & undesirable condition. . . . To expect [the feminine mind] to remain perpetually in the background in a realistic state of society is futile—despite the most feverish efforts of the Nazis and Fascisti" (Lovecraft 2017, 583). Even his depictions of extraterrestrials became more accepting in the 1930s, reflecting his increasing acceptance of difference (Saler 2012, 151–55).

Lovecraft died just as he was, in effect, being reborn. As Morton had predicted two decades earlier, he had become more tolerant as a consequence of widening his circle of friends and considering alternate points of view across spirited debates. He recognized that many of his prejudices were a consequence of his sequestered life. As he ruefully told Moore, "That earlier illness had kept me in seclusion, limited my knowledge of the world, & given me something of the fatuous effusiveness of a belated adolescent . . . is hardly much of an excuse" (Lovecraft 2016, 218). He confessed to having been too "one sided" in his education, favoring the arts, the natural sciences, and abstract philosophy over more immediate social and historical issues: "God! the things that were *left out*— the inside facts of history, the rational interpretation of periodic social crises, the foundations of economics and sociology, the actual state of the world today . . . & above all, the *habit* of applying disinterested reason to problems hitherto approached only with traditional genuflections, flag-waving, & callous shoulder-shrugs!" (Lovecraft 2016, 217). Had

Lovecraft survived beyond 1937, there is every reason to believe that this trend toward inclusivity and progressivism would have continued, perhaps challenging his lifelong scorn for blacks—especially should he have witnessed the logic of racism culminating in the Holocaust, an event he had presaged in his "callous" jokes about gassing minorities in 1933.

In her blog post that stimulated the WFA controversy, Okorafor imagines that Lovecraft must be "spinning in his grave" because she won the award. She then proposes another possibility, which comes across as incredible: "Or maybe, having become spirit, his mind has cleared of the poisons and now understands the error of his ways. Maybe he is pleased that a book set in and about Africa in the future has won an award crafted in his honor. Yeah, I'll go with that image" (Okorafor). It's meant as a hopeful—if perhaps snarky—picture.

But if more people knew about Lovecraft's late-life conversions, they might be slower to dismiss him with simple labels, just as he was finally learning to do in terms of others. In the world of the civic imagination, which he and his critics agree is constructed from contingent narratives, Lovecraft had the integrity to begin revising himself long before others did. Today, he is usually maligned for the racism that marred his life, whereas he should be celebrated as a hopeful example of how the civic imagination can change hearts and minds.

# 4

## Family Sitcoms' Political Front

### Taylor Cole Miller and Jonathan Gray

American politics is a televisual phenomenon: elected through ratings, characters serve as our representatives; elections build dramatic, serialized tension over the course of a season; and politicians and pundits alike appeal to our understanding of history as seen on TV. When borne out, for example, Donald J. Trump's presidential campaign slogan "Make America great again" oozes with sentimentality and nostalgia for the days gone by of "conservative" morals and "wholesome" family values, a mythical civic imagination most familiar to modern audiences through reruns of classic television shows like *Leave It to Beaver*, *Father Knows Best*, and *The Adventures of Ozzie and Harriet*. Trump's commonplace racist and sexist remarks, meanwhile, have led people to refer to him as a modern-day Archie Bunker, a fitting characterization considering how his signature refrain echoes *All in the Family*'s own nostalgic theme song, "Those Were the Days" (see Rolsky 2019 for examples).

Politics and television have long shared a mutually constitutive relationship that has even led to public feuds between television's fictional and first families. While campaigning for reelection in 1992, for instance, President George H. W. Bush and First Lady Barbara Bush took on *The Simpsons*, a show the first lady referred to as "the dumbest thing [she] had ever seen" and a failed family the president promised he could lead the country away from and toward the more wholesome family future of *The Waltons* (O'Neill 2015, A-2). Meanwhile, in a speech about LA's Rodney King riots, Bush's vice president, Dan Quayle (1992), bemoaned the cultural rot of our cities, extemporaneously citing *Murphy Brown*'s titular character as representative of TV's "poverty of values" for her choice to raise a child as a single working woman. What such examples demonstrate is how powerful a role not only television writ large but specifically its *families* can play in crafting our political and civic imaginations such that even those sitting in our nation's highest office react to the simplest tele-transgressions as if they were real or could become representative given their symbolic power to construct ideas of everyday normality for the nation.

Family sitcoms show their political hand in myriad ways. Overt politicization was not a common programming strategy for the 1950s and 1960s, for instance, and rarely did sitcoms give attention to the civil unrest happening out on the streets. But their collective inattention to such unrest and gleeful if paranoid retreat to suburbs and small towns that, as David Marc (1989) has noted, were "located not merely miles from the modern city but the better part of a century as well" (53) made them conservative tools. Renowned historian of the American family Stephanie Coontz (1992) has written of the powerful nostalgia for the 1950s that lives within contemporary conservative politics yet singles out *Leave It to Beaver*, *The Adventures of Ozzie and Harriet*, and their peers as playing a particularly important role in the construction of conservative myths and delusions of what American families could and should be. The 1960s also saw a small handful of sitcoms that addressed contemporary politics, but only metaphorically, as *I Dream of Jeannie* and *Bewitched* literalized the threat of the women's movement in women with magical powers whose male partners struggled to contain and manage them (see Marc 1989; Spigel 1991) and *The Munsters* transposed fears of minorities "ruining" the neighborhood onto a tale of the monsters next door. The television landscape of the 1970s is, of course, famed for the head-on approach of Norman Lear, whose slate of family sitcoms tackled all manner of political issues, from integration to abortion and impotence to cultural ambivalence surrounding the Vietnam War, staging heated arguments about the issues rather than hiding them delicately behind metaphor. In making their case for television's power to inspire and encourage dialogue about the political world around us, Horace Newcomb and Paul Hirsch (1983) therefore invoke numerous sitcoms as examples.

As we will discuss, this political legacy of, and the symbolic resource represented by, the family sitcom continues. For example, television's most thoughtful serialized depiction of a transgender character has come from Amazon's *Transparent*, and *black-ish* has regularly engaged racial politics. Via *Leave It to Beaver, Ozzie and Harriet, Father Knows*

*Best*, and its peers and via their many later throwbacks—whether *Happy Days* or *Full House*, *Growing Pains* or *Fuller House*—the family sitcom is known for first imagining and second policing a conservative image of family and nation. But in what follows, we explore several nodes across a broad history of the family sitcom's more progressive engagements in and contribution to the civic imagination.

* * *

Federal Communications Commission (FCC) regulations in the 1970s led to the rise of independent TV studios that used subversive politics and taboo topics as programming strategies the networks had shied away from in their own productions, thereby giving America some of its first openly progressive sitcoms. In addition to some of his more well-known shows that focused on culture clashes within fairly normative nuclear families, such as *All in the Family*, *Good Times*, and *The Jeffersons*, Norman Lear in particular also produced series that challenged the structure of families as TV understood them, often by hiring writers and producers with lived experience to create them. *One Day at a Time*, for instance, focused on the family of a divorced mother of two teenage daughters, based in part on cocreator Whitney Blake's personal life (Oliver 2002). Lear's *Hot l Baltimore* and *Apple Pie*, meanwhile, centered on the lives of nonbiological families. And taking network rejects *Mary Hartman, Mary Hartman* and *All That Glitters* to first-run syndication gave Lear and his writers more creative control over content, furthering transgressive possibilities for sitcom families and challenging the limits of the tele-visible by representing leads in extramarital relationships, often with queer characters not elsewhere represented (Miller 2017).

Lear's notoriety as the "face" of the shows he produced—especially as he continuously explained his intention behind Archie Bunker—also created a few lasting political advantages by transforming television comedy into a hotly debated political sphere and megaphoning the political voices of sitcom stars. On the one hand, reverend and TV star Jerry Falwell used Lear's celebrity as a lightning rod to help organize the Moral Majority movement by bemoaning Lear's shows' liberal agenda and corruption of gender norms, going so far as to label him the "number one enemy of the American family." On the other hand, it legitimized the possibilities of TV as a cultural space for negotiating politically relevant topics and making room for more overt, activist messages by TV personalities such as Lear and others who followed, especially in the 1980s and early '90s under the Reagan and Bush administrations. Years before she herself became a caricature of Archie Bunker, Roseanne Barr, for example, insisted Lear's work taught her social relevance because "wherever he saw a barrier, he ran over there and kicked it in" (Itzkoff 2014). Indeed, in response to criticism of his political leanings—and with his ratings slipping alongside a cultural rightward shift—Lear created People for the American Way in 1981 to funnel money directly into liberal causes. The now-common refrain that President Trump is like the modern-day Archie Bunker, a nostalgic, supposedly "lovable misogynist," has refocused both the sitcom's and Lear's place in the political spotlight (Wiener 2017).

Advancements in TV technologies in the 1980s and '90s spawned more channels of distribution, along with new possibilities in cable and satellite, creating television fragmentation and more competition, which led to the networks picking up ever-edgier content. Barr argued that Reagan's use of television in the presidential campaign had been "swallowed like a big fat turd that smells like chocolate" and that she agreed to do Roseanne in 1988, a show about a working-class family in the Midwest suffering the "trickle-down" economics of the era, to help swing the political pendulum back by imprinting "a generation of women through television itself . . . to use it for the betterment of the world, and not the way it is always used, as a method to tranquilize the minds of women" (Miller 2011). Chuck Lorre (2012) recalls that he was nearly fired for his first script for Roseanne, since Barr "had a pretty good instinct for glibness; she wanted to write an honest comedy, about what real families say and do. . . . The glibness got burned out of you really quickly or you were gone, and it was quite an education." Like Lear, Barr became a symbol of her show and women in the '90s as an unruly, outspoken critic of male dominance, and as such, she was transformed into a political chess piece. In 1990, President Bush took the time to publicly remark on her performance of the national anthem at Working Women's Night of a baseball game as a "disgrace" to the nation, boosting traction and support with viewers who despised her show and what it represented (Letofsky 1990).

Inspired by his time at *Roseanne*, Lorre went on to write *Grace under Fire*, about a divorced, single mother and survivor of domestic abuse raising children without a financial safety net. Contemporary with both shows, *Murphy Brown* highlighted the life of a divorced woman and recovering alcoholic as she reentered the workforce as a famous investigative journalist and TV news anchor. In the 1991–92 season, Brown became pregnant and decided to raise the child alone despite "several people [who] do not want me to have the baby. Pat Robertson, Phyllis Schlafly, half of Utah" ("Birth 101"). The jabs at these conservative figures were returned when Vice President Quayle (1992) criticized Brown for "mocking the importance of fathers by bearing a child alone and calling it just another lifestyle choice." Writers and producers incorporated footage of the speech as if it occurred in the story world in "You Say Potatoe, I Say Potato," an episode that honored the multiplicity of what it meant to be an American family in the 1990s.[1]

Meanwhile, the newly formed Fox Network developed a slate of family sitcoms in the late 1980s and '90s that were designed to compete not only economically but also tonally with established network fare. The first of these, *Married . . . with Children*, offered a "dysfunctional" family, but as much as critics often applied that moniker to the subsequent *Simpsons* and *Malcolm in the Middle*, both are remarkable less for moments of actual dysfunctionality and more for their parodic attack on past domestic sitcoms. *Married* invites the audience to laugh derisively at its characters, but the clear object of humor in *The Simpsons* and *Malcolm* is the set of norms that many prior sitcoms had established for how families should behave. When President Bush raged against the show, he surely knew the stakes: if many prior sitcoms had tried to build conservatism into the very form of the family sitcom, *The Simpsons* particularly set about disassembling that structure parodically while showing enough love and "functionality" in the family to suggest that families— much less the family as societal institution—didn't need conservatism to work.

Granted, sitcom families today rarely make it into the speeches of politicians, though prior to running for office, Donald Trump tweeted out disapproval of ABC's *black-ish*, asking, "Can you imagine the furor of a show, 'Whiteish'! Racism at highest level?" Certainly, while Bush and Quayle could rely on *The Simpsons* and *Murphy Brown* being well-known enough for political shorthand, the postnetwork era limits any one show's reach. Nevertheless, this era has also seen a flourishing of different types of families. As Trump's tweet suggests, ABC is particularly deserving of recognition here, as they have adapted their (and parent company Disney's) brand identity as a family channel to focus on a range of American families. *Modern Family* contains a biracial family and a white gay couple with an adopted Asian American daughter, *black-ish* joins it with a black family, *Fresh Off the Boat* with a family of Taiwanese American immigrants, *The Middle* with a working-class family, and *Speechless* with a family that includes a son (and corresponding actor) with cerebral palsy. All of these adopt a similar approach and style inasmuch as they regularly move back and forth between centering episodes on "issues" associated with the identities of their families—*black-ish*'s much-lauded episode "Hope," in which the family discuss police killings of black Americans, stands out here—and allowing the humor in other episodes to stem from more banal sources.

In interviews, *black-ish* showrunner Kenya Barris often frames his show as a conversational resource for American families and has expressed particular pride at moments when viewers tell him the show facilitated otherwise tough discussions. American popular culture, he said on *The Daily Show with Trevor Noah* in October 2017, could make "us think like, 'Everything's all good' and then all of a sudden we look up and I feel it's almost like the cicadas, like they were buried and we think it's all good, and next thing you know it's like [makes cicada noise] because everyone was repressing." By contrast, Barris says, he wants his show to "have those conversations," and he has framed his and his writer's room's dedication to this cause as redoubled following Trump's election, telling NPR (2016) just days later that after this election, "We were like, 'You know what? . . . We have to dig in deeper and stay later and have more real conversations and argue amongst ourselves more and really bring our emotions to the surface and really say things that people want to hear, have said.' We have to do that more. We have a responsibility."

Meanwhile, FX's *Louie* and *Better Things* offer families helmed by, respectively, a single father and a single mother. Showtime's *United States of Tara* starred Toni Collette as a mother with dissociative identity disorder. NBC's short-lived *The New Normal* focused on a gay couple who welcome their selected surrogate mother and her daughter into their home. Netflix's *Atypical* follows a family with a teenage boy on the autism spectrum. And Amazon's *Transparent* follows the Pfefferman family coming to terms with a parent's transition and their own fluid sexualities. To this, we might add special episodes of other prominent sitcoms, such as *Master of None*'s "Thanksgiving," which focuses on Denise and her relationship with her mother as both come to terms with Denise's sexuality as a lesbian over several years. Upon winning an Emmy for writing the episode, Lena Waithe (who plays Denise) noted how keen she was for the episode to offer a broader image of family to a wide range of viewers: "Straight, white people have come up to me and say how much they like it," she explained. "And that, to me, is progress. When a straight white guy is, like, "'Thanksgiving" was my favorite episode,' that's when art is doing its job when he can look at my character and go, 'I can see myself in her'" (Villarreal 2017). And *Transparent* creator Jill Soloway echoes Waithe here, noting pride at moments "when I meet people who tell me they were able to come out because of the show. People say, 'My parent is trans. My family stopped talking to them ten years ago. I called them up and said have you seen this show?' [*Transparent*] becomes like a bridge for people to reconnect and a model for love and family" (Vanity Fair. 2016).

Of course, television reruns and streaming platforms' large catalogs of older shows mean that television has hardly turned into a nonnormative sphere. But few contemporary sitcoms with families feature straight, white middle-class nuclear families, as it has become more common to depict the nation's families more broadly. What's more, reviews and press for these shows regularly focus on their inclusive image of an American family, seeing significant value in stretching the formerly contained limits. Many of them have won Peabody Awards, no less—the preeminent nod for "stories that matter" and that are deemed to have served the American polity.[2]

Fans' discussions on social media regularly frame the shows as refreshing, expansive, and inclusive. And although the shows all clearly direct themselves in part at an out-of-group audience, fans' discussions illustrate the shows' ability to serve as resources for in-group community-building too. *black-ish* and *Fresh Off the Boat* both have successful podcasts that broadcast following each week's show, for instance, and both speak directly to black and Asian audiences, respectively. The latter, *Fresh Off the Show*, is hosted on YouTube by Jenny Yang and Phil Yu, founder of *Angry Asian Man*, a key site for the Asian American on-line community. Yang and Yu have featured guest appearances from *Fresh Off the Boat* stars, offering a sign of the production team's wel-coming of the "unofficial" podcast. Their banter habitually focuses on their excited reactions to seeing elements of Asian American culture on network television. *afterbuzz's black-ish after show's* hosts Stacey New-some and DeAnjilo Platt similarly often contextualize black culture in *black-ish*. In both cases, the shows' cultural work extends beyond the television, as activists and fans have recognized the potential for these shows to serve as springboards to larger discussions and to community construction and development.

Like politics itself, civic reimagination must at some level begin at home. Given that we have likely all seen more families and seen inside more homes through television than we have or will outside of televi-sion, the medium's power to create a sense of national norms, of the politics of the home, is immense, especially in the medium's preeminent domestic genre of the family sitcom. Cultural historians have thus noted the role that 1950s and '60s sitcoms have played in constructing Ameri-can suburbia as an entire mythological system, and it is no surprise that this system is regularly referenced via its sitcom representatives of June Cleaver, Ozzie Nelson, and the quintessential "Father Who Knows Best." As such, the domesticom attempts to reimagine the genre and its fami-lies as key resources for a similar reimagination of American politics, of who belongs, and of its rules and norms for gender, sexuality, class, race, and power.

## Notes

1   For more on this incident, see Fiske (1996).
2   We note that Gray and editor Jenkins were on the board of jurors for some of these victories. However, the board consists of eighteen members, and winners must receive unanimous support.

# 5

## "To Hell with Dreams"

Resisting Controlling Narratives
through Oscar Season

**Raffi Sarkissian**

[*Moonlight* playwright] Tarell Alvin McCraney and I are this kid.
We are Chiron. And you don't think that kid grows up to be nomi-
nated for eight Academy Awards. It's not a dream he's allowed
to have. I still feel that way. I didn't think this was possible. But
now I look at other people looking at me and if I didn't think it
was possible, how are they going to? But now it's happened. So
what I think of possibility, let's take it off the table.
—Barry Jenkins (quoted in Sperling 2017)

Dreams are a rather common trope in the rhetoric of winning awards.
This is encapsulated best by the Academy of Motion Picture Arts and
Sciences's own advertising campaign for the 2016 Oscar telecast, featuring a series of posters with a racially diverse array of past winners that
read, "We all dream in gold." Gold here signals singular achievement—
placing first—but it also implies a color-blind erasure of the Academy's
fraught racial politics made egregiously visible by two years of all-white
acting nominees that spurred #OscarsSoWhite. Barry Jenkins's planned
speech above breaks the illusion of this shared dream. Hollywood's cinematic imaginary does not carry the images projected in *Moonlight*, and
its industry accolades and success narratives rarely ever step outside
familiar, studio-sanctioned tropes, especially when it comes to the work
and stories of queer artists and artists of color. For this reason, the acceptance speech transforms the televised award show into a prime stage for
actors and artists to either keep playing—dreaming—along or disrupt
the script. The 2016–17 Oscar season provides a unique opportunity to

study this dynamic, as three films centering black narratives—*Fences*, *Hidden Figures*, and *Moonlight*—dominated the industry awards. Yet I caution against reading this as either an anomaly or a watershed course correction to Hollywood's institutionalized ideologies and practices. Rather, this chapter tracks the actors and filmmakers of these films across the 2016–17 award shows to demonstrate how they used their acceptance speeches to collectively challenge Hollywood's controlling black narratives, expanding the parameters of our cultural and cinematic imaginations.

Oscar season is understood as the months-long timeframe from late summer and fall film festivals to year-end critics lists and televised awards. Every season tends to develop a first-order narrative, overarching—or competing—themes borne from industry trends and cultural politics. Oscar season is, then, a continuous text, stitched together through all its component award shows and paratexts and shaped by the various films, actors, and studios in play that year. Within the developing themes of a given Oscar season, though, are countless second-order narratives that focus on individual actors, craftspeople, or films. These individual "Oscar narratives"—akin to political campaigns—that drive momentum for nominations and wins are constructed through an unspoken negotiation among special awards publicists, the industry press, and the actors' speeches themselves (Thompson 2014). A smart Oscar campaign, notes Mark Harris (2010), makes someone or a film part of a larger story, "makes voters feel that, by writing a name on a ballot, they're completing a satisfying plotline." These developing narratives, says Harris, are largely built on familiar tropes: the little movie that could, the ingenue, the comeback, and most commonly, "It's time." The latter narrative is often used for actors or directors with remarkable career performances but no Oscars to show for it: "It's their time; they are due."

When it comes to cast, crew, and subject matter from underrepresented and marginalized communities, these narratives tend to be in part or overwhelmingly defined by their identity-born differences or accompanying superlatives: the "gay cowboy movie" (*Brokeback Mountain*), first woman to win Best Director (Katherine Bigelow), or first black woman to win Best Actress (Halle Berry). These may overlap with the gendered, racialized, and queer-specific "Oscar bait" tropes known to land such corresponding screen roles and film subjects nominations and wins, such as the long-suffering wife, the maid, or the queer martyr. While these tend to be implied by industry players and campaign strategists, Fox Searchlight's Oscar marketing behind 2013's *12 Years a Slave* notably ran an ad campaign across billboards, newspapers, and television featuring images from the film accompanied by the simple phrase "It's Time." Oscar journalists like *Hollywood Reporter*'s Pete Hammond (2014) purported this ambiguous tagline was a message about finally rewarding a black-subject film Best Picture, while *Slate*'s Aisha Harris weighed this as a potentially shaming, moral dog whistle geared toward voters' white guilt. Whether callous or coincidental, the sentiment is a clear function of the lack of black-centered—and otherwise nonwhite, -straight, -cis, -male—representation not only on screen but behind the camera as well. Just the next year, #OscarsSoWhite would be a trending directive, using the optics of racial disparities to reveal the structural inequalities at the root of these exclusions.

An important reason black films' and actors' Oscar narratives are consistently racialized is best understood through what Patricia Hill Collins calls controlling images. Collins argues that stereotypes of black women, such as the mammy, matriarch, welfare recipient, and hot momma, work to make "intersecting oppressions of race, class, gender and sexuality . . . and other forms of social injustice appear to be natural, normal, and inevitable parts of everyday life" (2000, 69). Dominant, elite groups with the authority to assign social value exercise their power to objectify subordinate and Othered groups, defining, sanctioning, and thus controlling their images. In an interview, actor David Oyelowo (2015) explicates the tendency to celebrate and recognize black people and their stories more for when they are slaves, subservient, or criminals than when they are leaders, kings, or at the center of their own narratives. He remarks that *Selma*, the first major film to ever feature Martin Luther King Jr., was only greenlit after the commercial success of *12 Years a Slave* and *The Butler*. The phenomenon he describes stems largely from the limits of Hollywood's representational capitalism—a risk-averse unwillingness to trust or invest in nonwhite (or female or LGBTQ) filmmakers and subjects—which perpetuates the stereotyped roles for which black artists receive recognition, including Oscars (see Sexton 2009 and Murch 2003). I propose extending and applying Collins's notion of controlling images to the structural limitations on black roles and film subjects, particularly through the lens of Oscar discourse, as *controlling narratives*.

Controlling narratives may not be part of the conscious discourse around a film's or actor's awards campaign but nonetheless contributes to the systems of inequality that perpetuate reductive, racially rooted ideologies throughout the entertainment industries, including colloquial sentiments about diversity quotas—such as a specified "slot" in a spread of nominees—or that the Academy won't award black-subject films two years in a row. Controlling narratives not only encompass the limited range of available roles for black actors and filmmakers but also affect who benefits most from campaigns for black narratives. For instance, *Straight Outta Compton* and *Creed* both received Oscar nominations in 2016, but for their white writers and actor, respectively. In a different vein, when it comes to queer-subject films—which already feature straight actors in prestige LGBTQ roles—studios and their hired marketers actively de-queer the trailers and "For Your Consideration" ads to consistently spin a "universal love story" rhetoric on the awards and press circuit (Cabosky 2015; Richards 2016). These practices reinforce the values, capital, and ideologies of those in power.

This is not to say that controlling narratives are not malleable. Acceptance speeches and the active role nominees and award recipients play in shaping the meaning of their participation in this economy can make an impact. For instance, after winning Best Actress at the Screen Actors Guild (SAG) awards in 2012, Viola Davis was considered the front runner at the Oscars for playing the role of a 1960s maid in Disney's *The Help*, a film with a white lead, based on source material written, adapted, and directed by white filmmakers. Stepping onto the Oscar red carpet wearing her natural hair for the first time in public, I have argued elsewhere, allowed Davis to flip the typical controlling narrative of playing such subservient characters (Sarkissian 2015). While Davis did not get the opportunity to make it on stage, this is an example of why acceptance speeches and other paratexts (the red carpet, interviews, the box office) along the campaign trail are important. With proliferating precursor award shows, there are numerous opportunities for actors to undermine controlling narratives and shape their Oscar narratives.

The 2016–17 Oscar season provided an unusually fruitful year for challenging black controlling narratives. *Fences, Hidden Figures,* and

*Moonlight* represented not only black-led casts but projects authored almost completely by black writers and directors. *Fences*, based on a fictional play about a 1950s black patriarch and the emotional havoc his social upbringing wreaks on his family, was written by late playwright August Wilson. Denzel Washington stars as Troy Maxson and directs Wilson's play for the screen opposite Viola Davis, who plays his wife, Rose Maxson. Davis swept the Best Supporting Actress awards throughout the season, culminating to the Oscar stage. Accepting her Oscar, Davis starts with a bold metaphor: "You know there's one place where all the people with the greatest potential are gathered. One place. And that's the graveyard. People ask me all the time, 'What kind of stories do you want to tell, Viola?' And I say exhume those bodies. Exhume those stories. The stories of the people who dreamed big and never saw those dreams to fruition. . . . So here's to August Wilson, who exhumed and exalted the ordinary people" (Davis 2017b). This was the last of Davis's three major televised acceptance speeches, and while making each one distinct, she built a consistent thematic narrative across them all, expounding on the importance of telling stories about ordinary people in all their specificity.

In the first of the three speeches, at the Golden Globes, she concludes by likening her own father's story as a stable boy with a fifth-grade education to that of Troy in *Fences*: "But you know what? He had a story and it deserved to be told, and August Wilson told it" (2017c). Davis expands on this in her second act at the SAG awards: "What August did so beautifully is he honored the average man, who happened to be a man of color. And sometimes we don't have to shake the world and move the world and create anything that is going to be in the history books. . . . We deserve to be in the canon of any narrative that's written out there. And that's what August did. He elevated my father, my mother, my uncles, who had eighth- and fifth-grade educations, and he encapsulated them into history" (2017a). The repeated refrain on Wilson should not be overlooked here. While many award speeches focus on a dedication, what Davis—who herself runs JuVee Productions and greenlights media projects—implies and emphasizes here, more than her role in making the film or the impact of her particular trophy, is the importance of creating, and thus putting into our imagination, the common stories that don't have a voice. Despite any imposed narrative on superlative statistics or her "due" award, Davis's speeches, including her Emmy acceptance a couple years prior about the lack of opportunity for black women, all cohere not around personal or historic achievement but instead on acknowledging and challenging the systems that structure and limit those narratives.

*Hidden Figures* weaves the stories of three African American female mathematicians who worked at NASA and spearheaded crucial innovations during the 1960s space race. Adapted by Allison Shroeder and Theodore Melfi—both white—and directed by Melfi, the film is based on black author Margot Lee Shatterly's nonfiction book and is among the very few studio films to ever feature a predominantly black female ensemble. The film caught fire at the box office, eventually grossing $169 million, the highest of any of the nine Oscar Best Picture nominees. *Figures* debuted late in the awards season but managed to upset other films to claim SAG's top award: Best Ensemble Performance. Speaking on behalf of the cast, Taraji P. Henson exclaims,

> Listen, this film is about unity. We stand here as proud actors, . . . but the shoulders of the women we stand on are three American heroes: Katherine Johnson, Dorothy Vaughan, Mary Jackson. Without them, we would not know how to reach the stars. These women did not complain about the problems, their circumstances, the issues—we know what was goin' on in that era. They didn't complain, they focused on solutions. Therefore, these brave women helped put men into space. . . . Thank you so much for appreciating the work we've done. Thank you so much for appreciating these women. They are hidden figures no more.

Like Davis, Henson takes this opportunity not simply to make a statement but to link the work of the cast—and SAG voters—to the unrecognized work the subjects they portrayed accomplished fifty years earlier. She is mapping a trajectory of the undervalued labor of black women across both science and the arts not just to imply that a wrong has been righted with an award but, like Viola Davis, to call out systems of oppression that have left us without black women heroes in history books and as stars on movie screens.

Earlier at the same SAG ceremony, Mahershala Ali won his first major award as supporting actor for *Moonlight*. At what was an overwhelmingly and explicitly political event—taking place the weekend after Trump's inauguration—Ali revealed that what he learned most from working on *Moonlight* was "what happens when you persecute people: they fold into themselves." *Moonlight*, made on an independent $1.5 million budget, featuring an exclusively black cast, tells the story of Chiron, a queer black kid in the south Florida projects, through three vignettes—portrayed by three different-aged actors—as he deals with bullying, queer intimacy, and a drug-addicted mother. Continuing his speech, Ali expresses gratitude for playing the father figure to Chiron, "a gentleman who saw a young man folding into himself as a result of the persecution of his community and taking the opportunity to uplift him, to accept him." He concludes by disclosing that his mother is an ordained minister and he is a Muslim, and their ability to see and love each other through these differences, or minutiae, is a choice as opposed to going to war over those differences. I argue that his speech dramatically transforms his own and *Moonlight*'s narrative at this juncture in the season from the indie underdog—or, more reductively in the press, the "black" David to *La La Land*'s whitewashed Goliath—into one about the specific and intersectional impact of oppression. An acceptance speech like Ali's at the SAG awards drowns out the campaign's competitive milieu and performs a crucial move, enshrining the importance of his accolade and, by synecdoche, *Moonlight* within a narrative of solidarity and resistance.

Where *Moonlight* and its actors, in both the professional and civic sense, most subtly upend controlling narratives, though, is through the affection and fraternity expressed among its all-black, intergenerational cast across many texts, from the nine-member cast coming on stage to accept the Gotham Jury Award for Best Ensemble in November 2016 to the MTV Movie Awards the following May, where Ashton Sanders and Jharrel Jerome accepted the award for Best Kiss—as well as numerous paratexts, including festival and trade interviews with the cast, crew, and director.

Along these lines, it is of no small significance that black queer playwright Tarell Alvin McCraney, who wrote the unpublished semiautobiographical play the film is based on, and director Barry Jenkins—who is straight but also grew up in south Florida's Liberty Square—stand side-by-side accepting the award for Best Adapted Screenplay at both the Independent Spirit Awards and the Oscars. There is a palpable intimacy they share in bringing this story—their story, Chiron's story—to the screen and broadcast stage. Speaking at the Indie Spirits, McCraney states, "I come from a little neighborhood that little people know, but we fell into diverse temptations Barry Jenkins and I. And I just want to thank him, first and foremost, for looking at those temptations, that life, and thinking it was a story worth telling and sharing because there are a lot of people who pushed that script away." The following night, on the Oscar stage, McCraney proclaims, "Two boys from Liberty City up here on this stage representing 305. This goes out to all those Black and brown boys and girls and non-gender conforming who don't see themselves. We're trying to show you you and us." As McCraney's speeches make clear, *Moonlight* is representative of the very untold stories Viola Davis speaks about in her speeches, and McCraney's and Jenkins's appearance on stage is a testament. Together, they provide a powerful intertextual reading of this moment as dreaming not in gold but in full color.

Throughout a given Oscar season, narratives rise and fall; some prevail, while others fade from memory. Their remnants are enshrined mostly in acceptance speeches, living on in YouTube clips and cultural lore. The winners chronicled in this chapter all shirk any narrative based on personal achievement or Oscar history. Their speeches refrain from framing these accolades within the rhetoric of Hollywood's diversity panic. While it is difficult to top the spectacle of *Moonlight*'s upset as the dominant story of that year, I argue that these actors use their broadcast performances on the award-show stage to offer up an alternative narrative for the 2016–17 season, one that defies the limits placed on our cultural and cinematic imaginations. As *Moonlight* receives the Best Picture award, Jenkins exclaims, "Even in my wildest dreams, this could not be true. But to hell with dreams. I'm done with it, 'cause this is true." These "wildest dreams" could not be true because they never included Katherine Johnson, Rose Maxson, or Chiron. Through their speeches, these actors challenge the controlling narratives of Hollywood and Oscar season by valorizing the specificity of these stories and the value of black—and brown, queer, and Muslim—artists to be authors of their own narratives, and in doing so, they carry out the work of reconstructing our imaginations.

## PART II

# How Do We Imagine the Process of Change?

The essays in this section explore how social movement tactics and strategies emerge from shared theories of change and how communities acquire the skills and resources necessary to act upon such visions.

Writing about her own experiences growing up in Oakland as an African American woman, Christina Evans (2015) recounts, "I had neither the experiences nor the resources to imagine a world where police protected and served me and the people in my community" (n.p.). These constraints on the civic imagination reflect the harsh realities her community confronted but also a lack of any available models within mainstream media that addressed such concerns. Much writing on the radical imagination have emerged from such conditions, as marginalized communities sought ways to imagine freedom, equality, dignity, respect, and safety before they had actually experienced them. Today, Evans is helping Bay Area high school students to develop more diverse models for how they might advocate for their community's betterment: "Unlike when I was a teenager and grappling with issues of systemic injustice, new technologies and virtual spaces are now potential spaces where young people can map/articulate their civic imaginations in ways that serve as a bridge to empowered civic and political engagement" (n.p.). Inspired by such examples as Black Lives Matter and the Dreamer movement, she sees fostering digital literacies as requiring the development of alternative models for civic and political action.

Evans's emphasis on promoting media literacy and other civic skills is mirrored by several contributors to this book. In chapter 7, Elisabeth Soep, Clifford Lee, Sarah Van Wart, and Tapan Parikh discuss the work of YR Media and its community partners as they help Bay area youths acquire computational thinking and design skills. Inspired by Maxine Greene and bell hooks, YR Media helps young people identify and address local problems, providing the adult supports required to help these youths translate their civic imaginations into sustainable projects. *Tracking Ida*, developed by game designer Lishan AZ and a team of graduate students of color from the University of Southern California, introduced investigative journalist Ida B. Wells's historic struggles against lynching to a Watts public high school. In chapter 8, Emilia Yang recounts how this project taught young participants about the roots of contemporary struggles with police. Media literacy and research skills, coupled with activities intended to enhance their political voices, were seen as increasing civic agency for marginalized youths.

While we have so far adopted a more expansive notion of the civic imagination, valuing popular fantasies as motivating struggles for social change, Evans writes about the digital civic imagination as offering models of social change that can be operationalized in a particular life-world. This more grounded model emerged as social scientists sought to understand the choices civic agents make. For example, Gianpaolo Baiocchi and his colleagues (2014) write, "Civic Imaginations are people's theories of civic life. They are cognitive roadmaps, moral compasses and guides that shape participation and motivate action" (55). For them, the civic imagination takes shape as communities work together, "identifying problems and solutions, envisioning better societies and environments, and developing a plan to make those visions of a better future into a reality" (55). In their case studies of local government meetings, they identify several different ways people set priorities for how civic life could be conducted depending on whether they placed the greatest value on "distributing power and privilege," "building community solidarity," or "solving problems." Each of these forms of the civic imagination, though, are much more grounded and practical than the forms we are generally discussing here, and a key question may be, How do we go from thinking about world building or transformative fantasies to these more pragmatic approaches?

This version of the civic imagination builds on what Ethan Zuckerman (2016) has described as "theories of change." Social movement tactics, he suggests, are ideally calibrated to what participants and leaders see as the best mechanisms for social change. Drawing on a framework developed by Lawrence Lessig to describe different forms of regulation, alternative tactics might rely on law, code, markets, and norms: "Asking if an act has a well-defined theory of change is asking whether it is instrumental or symbolic, whether the action is designed to influence people through passing laws, influencing norms, leveraging markets, or coding new possibilities, or whether an act's importance is through the raising of voice" (71). Different participants may deploy different tactics based on their skills and resources, and there may be more than one path to victory, but these forms of operationalized civic imagination are vital in defining goals, tactics, and measures of success.

In chapter 6, Sarah Banet-Weiser explores the discourse of "empowerment" in popular feminism, comparing the Girl Scouts and the Radical Monarchs as two projects that seek to prepare young women to take action in the world: one adopts an entrepreneurial model, and the other adopts a social justice frame. And in chapter 9, Andrea Alarcón considers the mechanisms by which the political leaders of Colombia sought to overcome the longest-running insurgency in the Western Hemisphere, coming to understand "peacebuilding" as an ongoing process rather than looking toward "peace" as a steady state. She outlines multiple "peacebuilding" approaches, including mass marketing and local art initiatives.

# 6

## Imagining Intersectionality

### Girl Empowerment and the Radical Monarchs

**Sarah Banet-Weiser**

In the past fifteen years, there has been an exponential rise in "girl empowerment" organizations in the United States, which are variously corporate, nonprofit, and state funded (Banet-Weiser 2015, 2018). During this time, girls have been generally seen to be "in crisis"—whether because of the media, education, or public policy—and thus are in need of support (found in empowerment organizations). Of course, the kind of "crisis" often depends on the kind of girl: a given reaction to crisis or its resolution is contingent on both race and class. Girls are also widely recognized as one of the largest and most significant consumer groups within neoliberal capitalism (Banet-Weiser 2007, 2015). Importantly, these two positionings of girls—as in crisis and as powerful consumers—are mutually sustaining. In both subject positions, girls are seen as in need of empowerment, and in both, the definition of empowerment focuses on the individual girl as an entrepreneurial subject.

The Girl Scouts, which was founded in 1912 and now boasts 2.6 million members in 92 countries, has more or less created the standard for organizations that empower girls in the United States (www.girlscouts .org). While the Girl Scouts has long focused on building confidence in young girls, its current emphasis on building feminine leadership skills and entrepreneurship seems unique to the current context—that is, while the Girl Scouts has always been committed to building girl-centered communities, like all organizations, the shape and logic of these goals shift given the parameters of cultural, social, and economic priorities. In the twenty-first century, those priorities have been deeply connected to neoliberal capitalism, entrepreneurship, and economic success, with the self-branded entrepreneur as the key subjectivity. The imagination that fuels the Girl Scouts and its goal of empowering girls, in other words, is limited by a set of dominant ideologies that privilege the girl as an economic subject.

As of 2018, the Girl Scouts' mission states that the organization will help each girl "unleash her inner G.I.R.L. (Go-getter, Innovator, Risk-taker, Leader)." While the Girl Scouts has always focused on individual girls' confidence, historically the group has also emphasized a *community* of girls, or what founder Juliette Gordon Low called a "circle of friendships, united by ideals" (www.girlscouts.org). Indeed, a kind of sisterhood was central to the Girl Scouts; Low founded the organization in the midst of the Progressive Era and a burgeoning US feminist movement to grant women the right to vote. In the 1960s, the Girl Scouts launched the "ACTION 70" project "to help overcome prejudice and build better relationships between people"; in the 1970s, the group took a stand on environmentalism with their "Eco-Action" project (www.girlscouts.org). Certainly throughout the history of the organization, the Girl Scouts has focused on individual growth and self-sufficiency. Yet, at the risk of waxing nostalgic, self-sufficiency in 1912 or 1965 did not necessarily mean embracing a trademarked slogan that validates capitalist economic subjects such as G.I.R.L. If we examine the context for this acronym, some of the logics of the current manifestation of the Girl Scouts become a bit clearer: the current Girl Scouts' "Leadership Experience" is described as "a collection of engaging, challenging, and fun activities like earning badges, going on awesome trips, selling cookies, exploring science, getting outdoors, and doing community service projects" (www.girlscouts.org). These projects are organized around four areas that form the foundation for the Girl Scouts "Leadership Experience": STEM (science, technology, engineering, and math), outdoors, life skills, and entrepreneurship. There is certainly nothing wrong with these areas of experience, but they also are formulated within a set of parameters that encourages some girls to succeed and others to fail. For example, the effort to include more girls in the STEM fields is a key component of contemporary popular feminism; because the technology industries are increasingly the centers of power (financial, political, cultural) and because the gender and racial disparities in employment in giant technology companies such as Google have moved into the media spotlight, it makes sense that popular feminism would focus its efforts on including women in these industries (Banet-Weiser 2018). However, the attention to the technology industries is also indicative of the limitations of a market-focused popular feminism, where encouraging girls and women toward technology aligns with broader neoliberal principles about expanding markets and an increasing GDP and often works to implicitly and explicitly devalue other career paths whose economic rewards are less certain.

The second area of focus in the Girl Scouts Leadership Experience, "life skills," again seems important—after all, who couldn't use life skills? But whose "life" are we talking about here? Life skills are decidedly different if one must learn to navigate a racist landscape or if one is poor and needs to figure out how to live within very limited means. The Girl Scouts' definition of *life skills* involves community and civic engagement but also financial literacy: "Grounded in real-life situations, Financial Literacy badges give girls a deeper understanding of financial issues, providing them with insight, skills, and practical knowledge in areas such as budgeting, philanthropy, making smart buying decisions, financial planning, and more" (www.girlscouts.org). But what does "making smart buying decisions" mean if one is on food stamps? Or how does a girl think about "financial planning" if there are no finances to plan? Who can afford to be "philanthropic"? Like "life skills," it is not that "financial literacy" isn't important (especially for those who have surplus finances), but it does assume a particular kind of privileged life. Similarly, the mission of the Girl Scouts claims a girl will "get to lead her own adventure (it's her world!)"—but when the context and equipment for living are geared toward those individuals who are privileged by race and class, the idea that it is "her world" becomes a bit more tenuous.

It needs to be said that the goal of the Girl Scouts has historically been, and continues to be, about imagining a better life for girls and a space for them—in a culture based on gender inequality where maleness is a default standard. The Girl Scouts also has a record for being inclusive. My critique of the Girl Scouts is that its definition of "empowerment" usually means empowering girls to be better economic subjects in the world, and this is an avenue of opportunity that is not open to all girls in the same way. That is, the acronym used by the Girl Scouts, G.I.R.L., stands for all the components of a neoliberal entrepreneur: go-getter, innovator, risk-taker, leader. They all gesture toward succeeding in business and becoming a better economic subject.

Indeed, "unleashing your inner G.I.R.L." is perhaps best realized in the fourth area of the Girl Scouts Leadership Experience: "entrepreneurship." Entrepreneurship has a particular meaning within neoliberal capitalism, where to be an "entrepreneur" means to be unfettered from ties to the state or other forms of organized governance and to succeed economically as an individual, as a "free" person in a "free market." Despite the fact that the Girl Scouts is ostensibly about building girls' communities, in the current moment, the areas of leadership that are emphasized are all centrally focused on the individual girl—especially the competitive individual girl. The neoliberal individual entrepreneur, like the liberal subject, succeeds based on a theory of meritocracy, where one's merits are the key to economic success. As many have pointed out, the theory of meritocracy works only if there are those who are found to be without merit—and this is often naturalized into categories of race and class (see especially Littler 2017). The Girl Scouts Leadership Experience assumes that racism and classism are not barriers to success— that one need only acquire apparently universal "life skills" in order to unleash her inner G.I.R.L. It is not a surprise, then, that the Girl Scouts' most visibly recognized activity, and its most lucrative, is selling cookies, where troops are rewarded depending on how much money they make from the sales.

Imagining a different world for girls is a crucial beginning for social change. But the thing about imagination is, of course, that it is never static. It has to be constantly practiced; as author Ursula K. Le Guin has said, "One of the troubles with our culture is we do not respect and train the imagination. It needs exercise. It needs practice" (Streitfeld 2017). If the empowerment goals of girls' organizations fall within the already established parameters of dominant power dynamics and neoliberal capitalism, the ways in which this empowerment can be imagined are limited. The Girl Scouts emerged as a way to address the lack of organizations devoted to girls, which is important. But there are other gaps in organizations, such as addressing the complexities and specificities of the lives of girls of color and those who are disproportionately impacted by structural racism and socioeconomic class inequities. For most girl-empowerment organizations, there is a norm of whiteness and middle-class status, and so the activities engaged in by the girls also validate this norm, such as entrepreneurship or "life" skills. To actually reimagine what empowerment is for girls, organizations need to think of the different skills needed for different lives: in other words, girl-empowerment organizations need to adopt an intersectional framework.

Intersectionality, a theoretical and methodological framework developed by feminist legal scholar Kimberle Crenshaw, insists on examining how different types of discrimination—based on race, gender, class, sexuality, and so on—interact. Importantly, intersectionality refers not merely to personal identities but to institutions: Crenshaw asks us to consider how structural and political formations such as the law and public policy privilege singular identity, thus rendering intersectional identities invisible. The law, for example, addresses gender discrimination or race discrimination, but not the complexities of both gender and race on discriminatory policies (Crenshaw 1991; Lipsitz 2006). Thus the varied ways that women of color are discriminated against in the law, in the workplace, in policy, and in social life cannot be addressed with existing frameworks. Rectifying that, as Crenshaw has said, "has been the project of black feminism since its very inception: drawing attention to the erasures, to the ways that 'women of colour are invisible in plain sight'" (Adewunmi 2014) Part of the project of intersectionality is thus revealing the inadequacies of existing law (such as antidiscrimination law) to address and remedy intersectional discrimination. As Crenshaw states, "You've got to show that the kind of discrimination people have conceptualised is limited because they stop their thinking when the discrimination encounters another kind of discrimination. I wanted to come up with a common everyday metaphor that people could use to say . . . it's well and good for me to understand the kind of discriminations that occur along this avenue, along this axis—but what happens when it flows into another axis, another avenue?" (Adewunmi 2014).

This is precisely the project of the Radical Monarchs, a girls' empowerment organization created and practiced around intersectionality. The group is an alternative girls' organization founded in 2014 in Oakland, California, founded by women of color who felt that traditional girls' organizations, such as the Girl Scouts (and their younger affiliated group, the Brownies), didn't recognize some of the unique experiences their daughters and other young women of color experience in the United

States and across the globe. The foundations of the organization are in the pursuit of social justice, especially for young women of color. More specifically, the goals of the Radical Monarchs are not necessarily about the individual girls involved—the G.I.R.L. experience of the Girl Scouts—but rather about community building and recognizing structural discrimination and unequal dynamics of power. Their mission statement is to "create opportunities for young girls of color to form fierce sisterhood, celebrate their identities and contribute radically to their communities." Their vision is to "empower young girls of color so that they step into their collective power, brilliance, and leadership in order to make the world a more radical place" (http://radicalmonarchs .org). The focus of the Radical Monarchs is community and collectivity, and while some of the same rhetoric as the Girl Scouts is used, such as leadership, the continued use of the word *radical* in both their mission and their vision—and in the badges the girls earn—needs to be acknowledged. The conventional definition of *radical* is "advocating or based on thorough or complete political or social change" (Dictionary .com), and to have this goal as the basis for a girls' empowerment organization in the United States does, in fact, require some imagination. The aims of the Radical Monarchs are not limited to figuring out a way for girls of color to find a place in a world that has already been determined for them; rather, they are expanded to guide girls to think about how to actually practice political and social change in a sexist, racist, heteronormative landscape.

For example, the Radical Monarchs group recognizes that the "playing field" of life is structurally unequal; the Girl Scouts assumes this field can be leveled by empowering girls with individual skills, including (or perhaps especially) that of becoming better economic subjects. The Radical Monarchs thus turns its imagination to this *field* rather than to the individuals who are positioned at its starting line. The cofounder of the Radical Monarchs, Anajuette Martinez, noticed that girls of color are scarce in the Girl Scouts and wondered what a troop that focused on the experience of girls of color would look like. What are some of the issues a girls' organization can tackle that go beyond service learning and volunteering? The explicit intention was to build a kind of sisterhood with girls of color. The different units in the troop ask the girls, "What are the social justice issues that impact your lives as a girl of color?" Rather than earning badges in entrepreneurship or STEM fields, girls in the Radical Monarchs earn badges in Black Lives Matter, Radical Beauty, Environmental Justice/Racism, and Global Trans Rights (http://radicalmonarchs .org).

What does it mean to "earn" these sorts of badges? While the traditional Girl Scouts earn badges that, even if important and helpful, are seen as conduits for girls to become "successes" within neoliberal culture, such as Financial Literacy, the badges of the Radical Monarchs are about the process of addressing the specificities of the lives of girls of color. Earning a badge, for the Radical Monarchs, means learning about social justice "and self-empowerment-focused topics through experiential field trips and workshops." In order to earn the Black Lives Matter badge, for instance, the girls attended a civil rights march in Oakland. In a twist on celebrating Valentine's Day, the group "practiced 'Radical Love' by reading bell hooks and writing kind notes to themselves and their fellow Monarchs" (Lindsay 2015).

The Radical Monarchs march in protest, visit historical sites that were key in social justice movements in Oakland, and have workshops with activists from the Black Panthers. Indeed, the "uniform" of the Monarchs includes a beret, which symbolizes the group's commitment to "movements grown by the community" and is an explicit homage to the Brown Beret and Black Panther movements (http://radicalmonarchs .org).

The earning of badges, however, not only encompasses specific activities but also has an ideological dimension. To earn a badge in Black Lives Matter, for instance, is a direct challenge to the liberal response of "All Lives Matter." Of course all lives matter, but as the Radical Monarchs group insists, they do not all matter in the same way. Only when we begin to imagine, and thus recognize, how lives are intersectional can we address what it truly means to "matter." The refusal to easily shift from "Black Lives Matter" to "All Lives Matter" is crucial; while the focus on leadership and entrepreneurship in the Girl Scouts is a key issue for the contemporary moment, it also assumes that all girls have the same starting place, that structural racism and homophobia do not somehow impact different girls in different ways. Ironically, the move to "all lives" rather than the specific lives of African Americans in the United States is one that refocuses attention on individuals—and particularly white individuals. The founders of the Monarchs, Martinez and Marilyn Hollinquest, "hope to expand the Radical Monarchs to include girls of all races and cultural backgrounds in multiple chapters across the country, while maintaining its primary focus on girls of color and issues of social justice" (Lindsay 2015).

Predictably, there has been a backlash to the Radical Monarchs, a response that precisely refuses a reimagination of girls' lives as intersectional and historically specific. Indeed, the backlash to the group follows the same path as "All Lives Matter," where the idea that young women of color have a specific experience in a nation with a history of slavery, structural racism, segregation, and white nationalism is seen as *too* specific and contrary to the goals of an expansive "girls' culture." Thus, not surprisingly, the focus on the specificities of black girls' culture in a historically racist society garnered a response from the right-wing media. Sean Hannity of FOX news argued that this troop was "radicalizing young girls" and that earning badges in social justice represented their "indoctrination" (http://radicalbrowniesmovie.com). These critiques are interesting in that the first, that "radicalizing" is the natural result of recognizing historical and present racism, is a familiar one, especially in the past decade in the United States. Almost any challenge to the status quo has been seen as radicalizing—except if it is the expression of those who are the "extreme" of dominant society, such as the white working class (as we witness in the contemporary rise of white nationalism in the United States, where this demographic is often portrayed as "authentic" or about the "silent majority"). FOX news continued in this vein, with one reporter criticizing the Radical Monarchs by claiming that it is "better to learn how to sew than to raise little racists" (http://radicalbrowniesmovie.com). The idea that there is a specificity to nonwhite individuals and that specificity is immediately seen as racist reveals the presumption that whiteness is the norm and all other ethnic and racial groups should adapt to it. "Radical" is also positioned ideologically in opposition to "innocent"—much of the backlash was focused on the "innocence" of girls. Yet we know from history that the category of innocence has been one primarily reserved for white girls; it is their bodies that are woven into a national script about innocence and value (Egan 2013). Part of the goal of the Radical Monarchs is to reveal the racial politics of "innocence"; as the founders say, it is important to be honest about the contemporary climate in the United States in terms of race and not cover it up with platitudes about being a "leader" and an "entrepreneur."

The second critique, that of "indoctrination," is also a familiar one; of course, all media, because they are in the business of representation, could be accused of "indoctrinating" the norms of race, gender, and sexuality to their audiences. Obviously, the threat of the Radical Monarchs to conservative media is that the group is practicing the wrong kind of indoctrination: one that refuses the normalization of racism and classism, one that insists upon the specificities of racialized lives, one that demands that we reimagine what empowerment looks like and what we are empowering girls to do.

In many ways, the recent increase in organizations dedicated to empowering girls is something to celebrate. And to be clear, the Girl Scouts has been, and continue to be, an important organization for inclusion. Here, what I intend is not necessarily a general critique of the Girl Scouts but more of a plea for expanding our imagination for what we can empower girls *to do*. The Radical Monarchs' mission to "empower young girls of color so that they step into their collective power, brilliance and leadership in order to make the world a more radical place" is a creative example of this kind of expansion of imagination. Imagination is not truly imaginative when it refuses to go beyond the boundaries of the hegemonic status quo or when badges in "financial literacy" are coveted and rewarded over badges of "radical love."

# 7

## Code for What?

### Elisabeth Soep, Clifford Lee, Sarah Van Wart, and Tapan Parikh

*Fresh produce*

Imagine if there were a way for people who have fruit trees in their back-yards to easily share with neighbors the abundant plums or figs that would otherwise fall to the ground and rot and for families that struggle to afford fresh produce to have access to it as a result.

Imagine a map you could find online that showcased stories from residents of a rapidly gentrifying city. You could add to the map and use it to grapple with what it means for the new resources to be so unevenly distributed across neighborhoods in this city and for so many working- and middle-class families to be pushed out.

*emotion*

Imagine you are fifteen years old and perhaps struggling with feelings of isolation, sadness, or anxiety. What if you had an app that allowed you to track your moods on a moment-to-moment basis using the same symbolic vernacular—emojis—that you feel so comfortable with in your everyday communication with friends? And what if the app uncovered patterns in your emotions over time and encouraged you to reach out to trusted others when you were feeling down or alone?

These are the very sorts of imaginings that guided a series of proj-ects in the San Francisco Bay Area over the last five years, where young people both used and created technology to see their worlds in new ways and to work toward transformation in their own trajectories and communities.[1] The first concept led to a prototype for a web-based food-sharing tool called "Forage City," designed by a group of young people matched with professional developers in a free after-school pro-gram. The second idea became a website called "Oaktown," a map that a team of young people and adult partners at that same organization developed and filled with audio and video stories, hand-drawn illustra-tions, and narratives centered in gentrifying neighborhoods across the

89

city. Another group of young people came up with the third idea and turned it into "Mood Ring." It's a free mobile app that counters conventional wisdom that frames cell phones as sources of distraction, addiction, abuse, and other forms of trouble for teens. Here young people programmed their mobile devices as tools for personal and community agency.

What all these projects have in common is the centrality of imagination as a driving force in shaping both the learning process and digital products. Imagination is what allows us to look "through the windows of the actual, to bring as-ifs into being," in the words of the late philosopher of learning Maxine Greene (1995, 140). "Of all our cognitive capacities," Greene argued, "imagination is the one that permits us to give credence to alternative realities. It allows us to break with the taken for granted, to set aside familiar distinctions and definitions" (3). Educating for the imagination makes it possible for people to conceive of things as if they could be otherwise. To tap into imagination is to create a state of what Greene called "wide-awakeness" and "to become able to break with what is supposedly fixed and finished, objectively and independently real" (19).

We tend to associate imagination with fiction, fantasy, escape. "How I envied Dorothy her journey in *The Wizard of Oz*, that she could travel to her worst fears and nightmares only to find at the end that 'there is no place like home,'" said critical theorist bell hooks (1991, 61), reflecting on her own longing for alternatives to the life she was living and the world as it was. hooks went on to describe how imagination could turn out to be practical, instrumental, grounded in reality, and emancipatory. One especially powerful form of imagination for hooks was theorizing—essentially a way of spinning imagination into an explanatory framework through which to understand complex and often vexing phenomena. hooks said that through theory, she learned to make sense of what was happening around her in a way that unlocked new options: "I found a place where I could imagine possible futures, a place where life could be lived differently. This 'lived' experience of critical thinking, of reflection and analysis, became a place where I worked at explaining the hurt and making it go away" (1991, 2).

The four of us are adults who work in learning environments where young people create media and technology. Part of our job is to foster the kind of critical thinking, reflection, and analysis hooks talks about and to ground the practical work of building such tools, apps, and sites within their imaginations and their sense of a new "possible future": a future where healthy food is more freely available, where communities undergoing change honor the experiences of those who made them, where teens can access positive mental health resources free of stigma, and where young people underrepresented in the technology field can create transformative tools and platforms. How do we promote this kind of critical imagination as a key dimension of computational thinking—a literacy young people need if they are to become makers and not just users of technology?

## Code for What?

To foster civic imagination via computational learning and vice versa, we need to challenge the frequent call to teach "Code for all!" with a provocation we don't ask often enough: "Code for what?" What good will this code do? How do we mitigate possible harm? Whose well-being does it serve? What difference does the technology make, and how do we know? How is it part of a larger context, and how does it evolve with that context? Our work prioritizes equity in terms of who and how we teach and in the products we make. Using a "critical computational literacy" framework (Lee and Soep 2016), we teach teens and young adults to create web- and mobile-based interactive projects that address inequities and give voice to communities that contend with various systems that stifle their growth and freedom. For young people, creating these projects entails both forming a critique of what's gone wrong in the area they aim to address (food, housing, violence, health, etc.) and developing a clear and specific vision of what a better world might look like as a result of the technology they produce.

Without an insistence on "Code for what?" we risk narrowing projects only to those that match the current marketplace. We end up teaching code for code's sake and not also as a way to engage young people meaningfully in civic life. We prepare young people for what is and not what could be. When young people create digital tools and platforms that awaken them and their intended users to conditions they wouldn't otherwise see and solutions they wouldn't otherwise have access to, they are, in hooks's sense, developing a critical lens and set of working theories through hands-on design. They work toward explanations for collective hurts and new concrete realities that make that hurt recede. They nudge us closer to equitable social and civic conditions in which, in the words of Danielle Allen (2012), members of society "take turns accepting losses in the public sphere, and . . . acknowledge and honor the losses that others have accepted" (1).

There's nothing particularly unexpected about arguing that imagination plays a key role in developing technology along the lines of the mobile apps and interactive content we've described. In software development, traditions of user-driven design hinge the entire product-development cycle on what users need and want and how they behave. Rather than design in a vacuum, rely on hunches, or base decisions on a nonrepresentative group (e.g., the people creating the technology, who may not reflect the target audience), user-centered technologists gather a whole lot of data on the actual people they imagine to be their future consumers. The process can be highly empirical and ethnographic, informed by focus groups and surveys, rounds of structured testing, and careful observation of "naturalistic" use cases. That said, while even a traditional user-driven approach often depends on acts of imagination, it does not always frame that work as emancipatory, geared to foster greater empathy and equity. In our work, when a group of youths was tasked with redesigning an underused local park, it took an act of *critical* imagination for them to reenvision that park with a graffiti wall and walking paths and safe places for youths to gather and relax and to document that vision in the form of a physical model and map that they could use to communicate their vision. They took everyday experiences, observations, and desires and channeled them into new visions of how products, places, and technologies can be designed in ways that speak to people's passions and often-misunderstood realities.

The learning environments where we both teach and carry out research incorporate these powerful aspects of user-driven design in the service of building critical computational literacy. Two of us (Lee and Soep) work at YR Media (formerly Youth Radio), a national youth-driven production company headquartered in Oakland, California, that has operated an Innovation Lab for seven years. Young people who are part of the lab partner with professional designers and developers to create mobile apps and web-based interactives, including the ones that open this chapter, that are featured on outlets including the Google Play Store, the Apple App Store, the *Atlantic*, Vox, and NPR. The other two of us (Van Wart and Parikh) have worked with a range of youth-serving organizations in Oakland and Richmond, California, to develop and deploy data collection, analysis, and mapping tools for community-relevant projects. All these projects involve predominantly youths of color and those dealing with poverty and other structural drivers of inequality. In many but not all cases, they *are* the intended users of the tools and platforms they produce, so we have the user "in the room" in ways other technologists who target youth consumers do not. But our approach reaches beyond conventions of user-driven research. We balance a focus on what currently exists for the communities we engage against an understanding of how the tools young people use and make can be drivers of greater equity and full-fledged participation in civic life.

To reveal what that balance looks like in action, we take you behind the scenes in the making of two projects: Know Your Queer Rights and Local Ground.

## Critical Computational Literacy in Action: Making the Know Your Queer Rights App

Know Your Queer Rights, a mobile app conceptualized in YR Media's Innovation Lab by two high school students, Kwan and Myra,[2] provides knowledge and resources to support LGBTQ+ youths and young adults. Over nearly two years with a team of six additional youths and three adults, the aesthetics and functionality of the project have changed, but the focus has remained largely the same. Young people were responsible for every stage of making the app, including ideation, research, design, coding (using MIT's App Inventor, a tool that enables novice programmers to create Android apps), testing, promotion, and launch.

Know Your Queer Rights allows users to learn about various LGBTQ+ leaders and the laws that protect the community, report discriminatory acts through text and photos, and alert preprogrammed contacts through text messaging when they are in trouble (see figure 7.1a–c). Presenting the laws that protect the LGBTQ+ community was

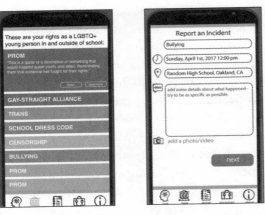

**Figure 7.1a–c.** Features from the Know Your Queer Rights app

a demanding process for youths and adult staff, who sifted through, analyzed, and in some cases translated complex national and state laws for a general audience of youths and young adults. Each function of the app needed to be programmed from scratch, which is why when young people set high standards for the social goals they seek to achieve through their products, they need corresponding supports to develop the necessary computational thinking and coding skills to achieve those ends.

In discussing the importance of including laws that protect LGBTQ+ youths, Myra pointed out, "Instead of kind of letting it [discrimination] happen and just being like, 'There's nothing I can do,' . . . it would empower people to be like, 'Oh, I actually have a legal right to do this.'" Myra, who uses they/them pronouns, recognized the struggles they and other LGBTQ+ youths face and noted that they too often resign themselves to ongoing harassment and abuse via discriminatory words, behaviors, actions, and policies. Often young people do not know the laws that can support their resistance and embolden their fight for equality and freedom. Myra hypothesized that the tool their team was creating had the potential to "lower a lot of rates of suicide and self-harm" (Personal communication, 2:8, 2016). They saw their app as one possible antidote against that suffering by enabling queer youths to reframe abusive behavior as something that in some cases went beyond meanness or bullying—it broke the law.

The team behind Know Your Queer Rights also incorporated evocative black-and-white images and descriptions of leaders from the LGBTQ+ community. Again, this functionality required a compelling design, an efficient code base, and tireless research into official sources and peer networks to generate a list of well-known and less-visible leaders in the community who would resonate with other young people. Kwan and Myra reflected on the value of highlighting "queer icons":

> KWAN: Using these role models [is] really to show [that] this is what other people have done in the past, and it has worked.
> MYRA: And you can do it too!
> KWAN: And you can do it too, because you're just like them!

These two youth creators dreamed and populated the world they wanted to see not only for themselves but also for others by way of their platform. The team felt a special urgency to create that space in light of the timing: the coming-into-power of a new administration that championed the rolling back of LGBTQ+ rights to marriage, military service, and freedom from workplace and school-based discrimination.

## Mapping Civic Imagination: Local Ground

"You cannot make a change if you don't know there's a problem, so therefore you have to recognize it and allow others to acknowledge it so [that] the process of coming up with a solution can be even possible." These reflections come from Lionel, a youth researcher-collaborator who was part of an after-school initiative in the San Francisco Bay Area in which he and his peers used the Local Ground platform to collect, analyze, and map data. We have examined some of the ways the platform can support the development of a civic imagination, knowledge vital to communities, and new resources, including programs, apps, and even local policies (Van Wart, Tsai, and Parikh 2010). With the help of facilitators, peers, and adaptable digital technologies that are intuitive and accessible, youths can be supported in naming and disrupting systems of injustice.

In one such project, one of us worked with a local initiative that brought together youths, facilitators, and city agencies to collectively reimagine a local park, housing complex, and community center. As youths collected and analyzed data, which entailed going outside, walking around, and observing a place together, they talked about their shared observations and experiences, as well as the constraining and enabling factors that produced these local realities. Inviting youths to use their own symbols, language, and local knowledge (e.g., figure 7.2), Local Ground supported candid, often playful conversations. For example, the blue icons you see in figure 7.2 indicate places on a school campus where students can "cupcake" (a.k.a. flirt, in Bay Area parlance). Other maps identified places where young people did and did not feel safe. Taken together, the maps make visible an ecosystem of experience few adults in their lives had previously understood.

Whether young people are mapping the social cliques at their school, documenting healthy places, or identifying blighted buildings, the process of gathering evidence and discussing it enables them to understand their current social worlds and imagine how those worlds could change.

While we aim for young people to drive these explorations, our research suggests that adults play an important role as well. They bring knowledge of history and current events and introduce young people to relevant creative practices, initiatives, ideas, and solutions that have worked elsewhere. For instance, in students' local park and community center proposals, the young people blended a number of different design ideas from other cities that were introduced by adults (dynamic water features, an amphitheater, and winding pathways) with their own ideas (a graffiti wall, a snack bar, and a skate park) in order to instantiate their visions (figure 7.3).

Within these projects, youths spent the majority of their time articulating, debating, resolving, representing, and designing solutions with one another. The process of mapping and the shared data corpus and representations generated as a result served as a means to activate young people's collective imagination. As was the case with Know Your Queer Rights, any resulting artifact (a map, tool, or policy proposal based on collected data) is only one of a wider set of outcomes that enable young people to work in solidarity and, through evidence-based arguments, advocate and set agendas for their communities.

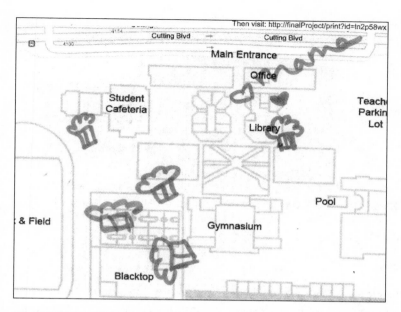

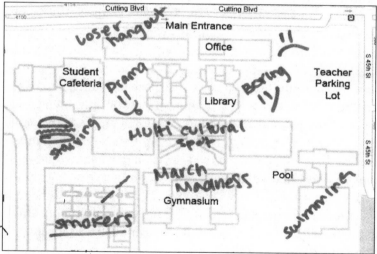

**Figures 7.2a and b.** Local Ground maps

**Figure 7.3.** Local park and community center designs

## Collective Hope

The development of a critical civic imagination through digital projects such as the ones we have described can both require and help generate what Shawn Ginwright (2016) calls "collective hope": "Collective hope is a shared vision of what could be, with a shared commitment and determination to make it a reality. Collective hope can be likened to the soul of the community as it bolsters and protects the existential dimensions of community life, its faith, purpose, meaning, and collective imagination" (21). Ginwright's framework of collective hope helps make sense of the ways in which young people grapple with shared experiences that include stigmatization, criminalization, discrimination, violence, and isolation. To cultivate civic imagination within these conditions requires that young people see the unequally distributed "traumas of everyday life" as both "wrong and subject to redress" (23). Without actionable steps, reliable scaffolds, and enduring support from peers and adult allies, the civic imagination can dissipate, curdle into disappointment, harden into fixed ideologies, and eventually reinforce a sense of powerlessness. Our research and practice suggest that with community, pedagogical, and technological supports in place, young people can both use and produce digital tools to identify what can be done—or, more precisely, what *they* can do—to be a part of civic solutions for the future that are rooted in knowledge of the past and grounded in a clear view of the present.

This research is supported in part by the National Science Foundation under Grant No. DRL-1513282 and Grant No. DRL-1614239. Any opinions, findings, and conclusions or recommendations expressed in this material are those of the author(s) and do not necessarily reflect the views of the National Science Foundation.

## Notes

1 This research was funded in part by the National Science Foundation (WAVES: #1614239 and From Data to Awesome: #1513282).
2 Both Kwan and Myra, as well as Lionel, are pseudonyms.

# 8

## Tracking Ida

Unlocking Black Resistance and Civic Imagination
through Alternate Reality Gameplay

**Emilia Yang**

Historically, radical black and feminist tellings of history are not to be
found in schools. The denial of black people's experience and humanity
inherited from slavery and present in the legislative and justice systems of the United States is also ever-present in its public and private
education systems. Racial bias reveals itself through school discipline
and curricula choices, which perpetuate the false mythology that "black
children are less capable scholastically" (Cullors 2017). For example,
one McGraw-Hill textbook downplayed the horror of slavery by calling
slaves "workers" who "emigrated" to the United States. It is common
knowledge that history lessons focus almost exclusively on white lives,
and black students are expected to stay engaged and interested in
courses that do not recognize the reality of their lives and do not cover
the contributions of black political leaders and artists. For example,
educators in South Carolina say that even though they want to teach students about topics more central to communities of color, the guidelines
for history courses to prepare students for state exams make it difficult
to stray from a focus on the white Founding Fathers and other cultural
milestones. Students and teachers say, "Even when Black historical figures and contemporary political and cultural leaders are discussed, their
lives are whitewashed" (Quinlan 2016). There is an obvious disconnect
between students' and their ancestors' experiences and what they are
learning at school.

The civic imagination is theorized by Henry Jenkins and members of
the Media Activism and Participatory Politics research group, of which
I am an active member, as the capacity to imagine alternatives to current

cultural, social, political, or economic conditions in order to imagine a better world. This capacity is fueled by icons and narratives borrowed from popular media and our cultural image bank. Thinking about the context described above and the civic imagination as our "ability to imagine ourselves as agents of change in order to change the world" (Jenkins et al. 2017), I ask, Whose imagination are we talking about? How can young students of color imagine any change if the history they are taught and the media they consume deny their experience in the first place? How can they imagine their connections with their community and their place in a shared collective identity? What are the tools or experiences needed to talk about the issues that concern them? How can they foster hope to create a collective vision of what could be?

Because black history, transmitted mostly through families and oral history, is rich in its history of struggle, strength, and hope in the face of adversity (Cullors 2017), there is a strong case for students to learn black history at their schools and most importantly encounter examples of black feminist resistance that connect to the issues students face today. This chapter analyzes *Tracking Ida*, an educational alternate reality game (ARG) inspired by the pioneering investigative journalism of Ida B. Wells in the 1890s. *Tracking Ida* was created by game designer Lishan AZ with a team of University of Southern California graduate students of color, including me, with interests in activism and social justice; we wanted to address black and brown youths who have limited access to radical tellings of history by feminists and people of color (*Tracking Ida* n.d.), ARGs use transmedia storytelling that "takes the substance of everyday life and weaves it into narratives that layer additional meaning, depth, and interaction upon the real world" (Watson 2010; Martin et al. 2006) to deliver a story that may be altered by players' ideas or actions. They are participatory in the sense that players construct the story—advancing through the experience requires collective action and problem solving. Discussing *ilovebees*, one of the pioneer examples of ARGs, Jenkins states, "ARGs teach participants how to navigate complex information environments and how to pool their knowledge to solve problems" (2004).

*Tracking Ida* is a hands-on group endeavor in which students manipulate archives and historical artifacts in an immersive set design with the intention of reanimating Ida's history in a way that feels proximate and relevant—something that is not often experienced in history class. In the pilot version of the game, at King Drew High School in Watts, Los Angeles, in 2016, players uncovered Wells's crusade against lynching and used her strategies to investigate police and vigilante killings today. Along the way, they solved puzzles, decoded messages through a phonograph, role-played as investigative journalists, conducted interviews, and harnessed social media to spread awareness. Transferring the struggle of racial violence to the present, students interviewed members of the community of Watts and the larger Los Angeles area who have worked closely with the issue of police and vigilante killings, such as community organizers, mothers and fathers of youths who had recently been killed by the Los Angeles Police Department, and journalists who cover police-community relations.

In the following section, I present, discuss, and analyze how Wells's story is told through the game and how the combination of story and gameplay created experiential and embodied knowledge for students, exposing players to the history of black resistance (personified, in this case, by a black woman) in order to refine shared visions of the past, present, and future. The game fosters civic action by giving players a taste of archival research, investigative journalism, and activism in a compelling, safe, and immersive environment. All the activities teach them media literacy and production skills to cover social and political events with a critical lens; such skills allowed participants to transform their own narratives as black and brown youths in Trump's America by connecting earlier history to present struggles. Throughout this chapter, I link my own critical commentary with testimonies of students who played *Tracking Ida*, as recollected by creator Lishan AZ and Gabriela Gomes in their study "Tracking Ida: Civic Engagement Evaluation" (n.p.). Their evaluation shows that the game allowed students to see themselves as agents capable of making change by providing participants with the opportunity to interview figures dedicated to social justice.

## Ida's Story

The game starts by contextualizing the time of Reconstruction following the American Civil War in which Wells lived with a companion curriculum taught by historical consultant and writer Jasmin A. Young, a

PhD candidate in the Department of History at Rutgers University. In this exercise, students dissected three political cartoons that depict the reality of black people at the time. Students stated they learned about what was going on and how people felt instead of learning just the "facts."

On day two of the companion curriculum, the students dissected excerpts from Wells's first published book, *Southern Horrors*, in order to get into her complex investigations. Wells was a journalist, newspaper editor, suffragist, sociologist, and feminist who, after the murder of her close friend Thomas Moss in Memphis in 1892, started researching the real reasons for the lynchings nationwide. Her pamphlets refuted the justification for lynching as a punishment for black-on-white rape by revealing that only a third of reported lynchings even involved the charge of rape. As Wells (1892) wrote, "Lynching was merely an excuse to get rid of Negroes who were acquiring wealth and property and thus keep the race terrorized and 'keep the nigger down'" (2013). Furthermore, not only men but women and even children were lynched. Her findings became the cornerstone of all subsequent arguments against lynching by a wide range of reformers and critics. Wells's work was "a substantial body of innovative writing, reporting, and analysis in U.S. intellectual history, combining statistical analysis, muckraking journalism, and a kind of 'talking back' to power" that was appropriated and transformed by other social reformers who, in many cases, erased her contribution and marginalized her as an author and leader (Schechter 2015).

## Alternate Reality Gameplay

After the curriculum companion, players are guided through the ARG experience by a video recording of Jordan Moss (a fictional character played by an actress), descendant of Wells's friend Thomas Moss. Jordan is a graduate from King Drew High School and is now away at her first year of college. She's troubled by recent police killings striking closer and closer to home—first eighteen-year-old Richard Risher getting shot by the police near her home in Watts (the same neighborhood where the students live; Mather 2016) and now another black man shot down the street from her college. She looks toward Ida B. Wells's work for guidance because of her family connection. Her

grandmother finds Wells's old trunk in their attic, and Jordan recruits
players to investigate the trunk and find information on Wells's tactics while she's away at school. In the game, Jordan communicates via
email, instant messaging, and social media, asking students for their
help and giving them hints. The trunk contains the salvaged pieces
of Wells's investigation into Memphis lynchings—what she was able
to preserve after her newspaper office was burned down by a lynch
mob in 1892. In order to understand her investigative practices, players must solve puzzles in order to unlock each compartment. The
first puzzle contains a set of headlines from the *Memphis Free Speech*
(Wells's newspaper) and the *Memphis Scimitar* (a popular white newspaper) describing the stories of the lynchings of Thomas Moss, Calvin
McDowell, and William Stewart, which were "the climax of ugly events
in Memphis" (Giddings 1984) and also led to Wells's persecution. The
puzzle recounts the story of how the three black men opened the People's Grocery, a beloved gathering place for Memphis black folks and
the focus of white resentment and target of provocations by white grocery owner William Barrett. After a fight started over a children's game
of marbles that involved the store owners, white people got a warrant
for the three black men, who were arrested and later taken from their
cells and lynched. Wells's editorial embraced Moss's dying words: "Tell
my people to go West, there is no justice for them here." Memphis's
white press stirred the community into a frenzy over the incident. The
black men were painted as "brutes" and "criminals" who victimized
"innocent" whites (Giddings 1984, 13).

Players must match the polarized headlines describing each event
and arrange them into a story in order to unlock the next compartment. Comparing the coverage of white and black papers taught students media literacy skills in decoding biases. The *Tracking Ida* team
re-created archives and artifacts. As AZ mentions, "*Tracking Ida* is in
part about reclaiming history destroyed. Whenever possible, we used
newspaper articles from the time period—articles that were important
to Wells' investigations. What we couldn't find, we reconstructed using
a combination of primary documents and secondary sources." A student claimed that it allowed them to "see different things through different lenses," and another commented about being "shocked" at the
major gaps between stories.

The second puzzle involves a set of letters to the editor and an audio recording of Wells's voice revealing messages with the combination to unlock the next compartment. The audio recording is in the form of a phonograph cylinder, with a note urging the Moss family to find a library that will play the cylinder. (Wells heard that libraries in California were open to negroes.) The recording is played in a library, where they borrow the phonograph to play it (made for the game with Arduinos[1] and planted in the library). Students hear the audio while finding lynching postcards. The audio states, "Letters to the editor were particularly cruel. . . . Lynching postcards carried death threats with happy salutations. . . . Yet what kept my sanity were the letters of support." A second audio states Wells's call to action: "We must continue to fight injustice wherever and however it may present itself. No matter the age, we must push on to victory."

*Fight*

The use of antique artifacts—the phonograph, lynching postcards, a typewriter, a handkerchief embroidered with "T. Moss," and a photograph of Wells with Moss's widow and children—helped give the ARG the feeling of real life rather than a game. Students stated they had not seen any of these artifacts before and described the game as "vivid" and "realistic." The use of group puzzles also enabled collaboration and teamwork. One student mentioned that she liked to work independently but suddenly "being in a group was actually exciting and it made everything easier." bell hooks (2014b) mentions that excitement about ideas is not sufficient to create an exciting learning process—that our capacity to sustain excitement is deeply affected by our interest in one another, in hearing one another's voices, and in recognizing one another's presence.

The following section describes the leap from the classroom to the real world. In order to unlock the final compartment, players must put Wells's investigative tactics into action. Wells's tactics include the following:

1. Discern between fact and fiction. Use data to deepen your reporting.
2. Listen and decipher what's not being said.
3. Develop sources (eyewitnesses, family, friends of the victim, community members, law enforcement, undertakers, lawyers, race men/women).
4. Talk to other reporters or knowledgeable people.
5. Write compelling investigative narratives.

Students conducted interviews with community members who became activists against police violence through their personal experiences, legal means, activism, social services, art, and so on. A field trip was arranged to the Watts Labor Community Action Commission, and a diverse group of interviewees was invited. Students role-played as investigative news teams, with each student taking on a specific role (producer, videographer, public relations specialist, reporter), and camera gear was provided on-site. In the end, students prepared a three-minute highlight video to show in class and post on social media.

In this lesson, students learned media production skills that allowed for capacity building; they also heard activists' stories and, as they said, learned "how they [activists] see things differently and do things differently." Student participants stated that these experiences boosted their confidence to be open with other people. They were able to draw instant connections between the past and the present. One student shared, "Ida, she investigated lynchings. Then we talked to Ms. Helen Jones, and her son was hung; he was found hung in jail, and they tried to call it suicide. It was just one of those things that shed light on the situation of Black Lives Matter [and] deaths in the black community that nobody ever likes to talk about." Students also mentioned the interviews being "no longer part of a class and not part of the game."

## Black Historic Resistance, Memory, Activism, Imagination, and Learning

As described in this chapter, *Tracking Ida* uses the reality of historical violence and resistance as a source of learning, empowering students to take action toward a different future. The combination of narrative and gameplay in *Tracking Ida* taps into students' civic imaginations, enabling, first of all, their self-affirmation of their own history. In *White Rage: The Unspoken Truth of Our Racial Divide*, Carol Anderson discusses how white rage resulted in not only the overt tactics of white supremacists but a range of more covert policies that can be threaded through US history, from post-Reconstruction racial terror and lynching to the enactment of Black Codes and peonage and from the blocking of black people from fleeing repression during the Great Migration to Reagan's policies in response to the gains made during the civil rights movement (C. Anderson 2016). Michelle Alexander also has demonstrated how mass incarceration and the war on drugs are part of a well-disguised system of social control in response to the abolition of slavery and the civil rights movement (Alexander 2012). Students imagined themselves as part of a larger community through the collective identification of the black struggle against white rage. They were able to identify a collective black memory. Students reported that they were "learning about themselves and their community" and "acting in it" while learning about possible mentors and role models: "It makes you feel more connected to the subject in a way. . . . When you're just reading about old white people who made America—it gets boring, but [when] you go out and you listen in your community [to those] who are actually helping others to become better people, it inspires you to become a better person. It might inspire you to follow that same career choice and go help others as well and give back to your community that helped to raise you." In addition, *Tracking Ida*'s game mechanics tap the radical imagination, defined by Max Haiven and Alex Khasnabish as one that sees society's problems and the power that impacts our lives as deeply rooted in systemic and structural inequalities and exploitation (2014). Students learned to identify the persistence of a white supremacist version of history, which will consequently help them understand how the privilege of whiteness works today. As bell hooks (2014) argues, we need a schooling that is a practice of freedom, not one that merely strives to reinforce domination through stereotypes. Finally, by role-playing as journalists who are fighting against police brutality and killings today, the game positioned students as actors who followed Wells's call to "continue to fight injustice wherever and however it may present itself." Jordan's fictional narrative based on real events invited participants to influence reality by talking to real people and crafting their own stories. As one of the students mentioned, "In the history class, we learn from what others did, but in *Tracking Ida*, it's kind of like we are creating our product, with the interviews and with the game—whatever we get out of it. We kind of have an impact, and people get to see what we did." Jenkins states that "a well-designed ARG also changes the ways participants think about themselves" (2004), and *Tracking Ida* did just that. This embodied game fostered a new form of learning through action that activates possibilities for students to be authors of their own narratives and to envision a new world in which they have a place, a history, and a community to guide them.

## Note

1  *Arduinos* are single-board microcontrollers and microcontroller kits for building digital devices and interactive objects that can sense and control objects in the physical and digital worlds.

# 9

## Everyone Wants Peace?

Contending Imaginaries in the Colombian Context
of Peace Creation

**Andrea Alarcón**

Utopia is on the horizon. When I walk two steps, it takes two
steps back. I walk ten steps, and it is ten steps further away.
What is Utopia for? It is for this, for walking.
—Eduardo Galeano

"Everyone without exception wants peace," said Colombian president
Juan Manuel Santos during his 2016 Nobel Peace Prize acceptance
speech. Winning, he said, aided the "impossible dream" of ending his
country's fifty-four-year-old conflict (Associated Press 2016). Ironically,
the Colombian people had recently voted against the peace agreement that he spearheaded. Evidently, not "everyone without exception"
wanted *his* definition of peace. Similar to the Brexit vote that same year,
the "no" vote took the country and the international community by
surprise. Santos achieved exceptional support for the deal at the international level. Nonetheless, winning a peace prize while losing the vote
showed the nation's internal struggle. To the Colombian people, the
prize lacked authenticity.

Before the imaginary of peace, there was an imaginary of war. Colombia's conflict is considered the longest-running one in the Western
Hemisphere; it is multisided and complex but, in terms of numbers,
relatively small. Nonetheless, the guerrilla groups have imposed fear
on the general population from their remote, rural fighting spaces
for more than fifty years. The peace agreement was between the state
and the largest and most relentless of these actors, the Revolutionary
Armed Forces of Colombia, or FARC, which formed during the 1960s

as a Marxist-Leninist peasant movement pushing a political line of agrarianism. Up until the cease-fire, they practiced kidnapping of civilians, extortion, forced recruitment (including that of minors), and drug trafficking.

Several administrations attempted peace negotiations with varying results, including the FARC gaining control of more territory (Baquero 2006). In February 2012, after many preparatory talks, the Santos administration, the FARC, and Norwegian mediators sat down in Havana, Cuba (picked as a neutral zone between parties), to begin negotiations. The process gave political legitimacy to the FARC, since the United Nations and the international community had previously identified it as a narco-terrorist organization. The following four years included many controversies, civic actions to spur forgiveness and peace, and the opposition to what former president Álvaro Uribe called a "peace with impunity."

The contending visions among the Colombian people about the meaning of the agreement, the vote, and the mobilization of media strategies for and against the deal embodied what Baiocchi et al. (2013) call a "variability in civic imaginations." For example, the rural areas that suffered the most from the violence voted "yes" on the referendum, showing an ability to forgive that the urban areas lacked. Critics saw the most visible symbol, the Nobel Prize, as a strategic political win for Santos but not necessarily for Colombia.

According to peace scholar Jean Paul Lederach (2005), the first step in the *process* is understanding that dialogue requires continuous hard work, and conflict "does not end with a ceasefire or the signing of a paper. . . . Authentic engagement recognizes that conflict remains." The contention points highlighted in this chapter include a private-sector-led media and marketing campaign asking citizens to forgive, political and civic actions for and against the treaty, and the signing. Lastly, the government's call for art made of turned-in weapons asks for the creative imagination of what reconciliation and healing may look like. What Benedict Anderson (1991) terms the "imagined communities" of nation-states require symbols such as sporting events, museums, flags, newspapers and so on to maintain unity. Following this logic, most people understand that these are indeed just symbols and steps in the *process* and are not the *endpoint* of peace, the same way a flag is a symbol of a nation and not the nation itself.

Therefore, in this chapter, I propose two uses for the civic imagination. First, since conflict remains, agreements, campaigns, prizes, art, and other symbols are needed to concretize a peacemaking that seems too abstract and utopian: the role of the civic imagination as *process*. The second, the utopian *endpoint* of peace, as Uruguayan writer Eduardo Galeano said, is for walking. The endpoint serves as a beacon illuminating the direction to walk in but also as motivation in order to improve current social, political, or economic conditions.

## The "Soy Capaz" Campaign

One of the hardest issues faced by demobilized combatants in postconflict nations is rejection from the societies they are seeking to reenter. The population's feeling of resentment is justifiable and, as a result, hard to resolve. To tackle the resentment, mainstream media, national soccer teams, major musicians, the Catholic church, schools, and many others united in a communal, national campaign led by the private sector called the #SoyCapaz campaign. The way to depoliticize peace, they agreed, was to unite nonpolitical actors, since "peace does not belong to those who inflict violence, nor to politicians. It belongs to the citizens: it has no color nor party" ("Campaña Soy Capaz: Reporte final" 2014). Millonarios and Independiente Santa Fe, two soccer teams that are traditionally major rivals, put on white "Soy Capaz" shirts before their "clásico" match. The goal was to show that if competing soccer teams, competing brands, and media conglomerates can put aside their differences for peace, so could the rest of Colombia.

The phrase "Soy Capaz" roughly translates to "I am able" or "I am capable," with the connotation of overcoming a challenge. It also utilizes the singular "soy" (I am) because the campaign aimed to spur individual commitments and actions. Many other civic initiatives across the nation sprouted to either support peace creation or oppose the agreement (Lombana Bermudez 2016). Nonetheless, the campaign was unique in its scope and in involving nonpolitical actors who would not work together under other circumstances. Victims of the conflict as well as demobilized combatants called radio stations to tell their stories of war and violence, but especially of forgiveness, following the hashtag #SoyCapazdeEscuchar (I am capable of listening). The hashtag #SoyCapazDeEscuchar was promoted on air for people to share their stories and get theirs told on the radio. Approximately 140 companies (including McDonald's, telecom giant Claro, and Avianca airlines) changed their product packaging to white and printed phrases such as "I am capable of growing" or "I am capable of cheering with my rival" on their products (Campaña Soy Capaz: Reporte final 2014). According to the campaign's founder, Marc De Beaufort, the goal was to "create a conversation at the dinner table: attack apathy. . . . The sugar packet at the restaurant . . . would say it and cause a family to have to talk about it." In the main goal of creating conversation, it succeeded. Yet in its goal of remaining nonpolitical, it failed. Thinking back, De Beaufort expressed, "[We] might as well have used the government's help, given the wave of criticism we received."

Critics complained that releasing white-packaged products, wearing T-shirts, and hosting shows was a much easier feat than what they asked from the public: allowing demobilized FARC members into their communities. The campaign served as one of the first mirrors of the polarization (and politicization of peace) within the country. While the Santos administration espoused it, the opposition, led by former president Álvaro Uribe, denounced it. Some boycotted Soy Capaz products, with the hashtags #nocomprosoycapaz (I don't buy Soy Capaz) and #nosoycapaz (I am not capable) trending on Twitter. The opposition took advantage of its magnitude to attack the campaign in mainstream media. "I am *not* capable of signing peace in exchange of turning the country over to the FARC" was the common complaint. Famed satirist and columnist Daniel Samper Ospina (2014) supported the campaign, using the controversy surrounding it to mock the opposition: "Integrating the guerilla into society is the true way to defeat them. I can imagine them in a couple of years attending the Hay Festival, rubbing shoulders with Vicky Turbay [Colombian socialite] and reading poetry: isn't that a way to pay for their crimes? What impunity is Uribe talking about?"

## The Agreement: Contending Imaginaries for the "Yes" and "No"

On September 26, 2016, after four years of negotiation, infamous FARC leaders, Santos, and other parties dressed in white shook hands and signed the agreement on a national broadcast from the historical city of Cartagena. Against advice, Santos made the deal approval into a plebiscite for the general population to have the final say: yes or no. A slim majority listened to former president Álvaro Uribe's argument that the government could have driven a harder bargain with the FARC. The agreement had the potential outcome of FARC leaders accused of massacres and kidnappings avoiding prison by confessing, but many Colombians wanted to see the perpetrators behind bars. Yet the government argued it was the only way to convince the FARC to lay down weapons. Andrei Gómez-Suárez (2016) wrote about the opposition's affective strategy (and what could be called the mobilization of a civic imagination) to win that "no" vote, including the exploitation of fear, indignation, and resentment: "The acts of Uribe-ism were accompanied by rhetorical devices that interpreted reality and justified their decisions. . . . They consolidated in mainstream media and became trending topics in social media, until they became part of the everyday discourse, through which many Colombians delegitimize the developments of the peace process" (38). These included #nopazconimpunidad (No to peace with impunity) as well as "Castro-Chavismo," a coined term summoning the leftist governments of Cuba and Venezuela as the direction Colombia would be heading in by allowing the FARC into the political process. The intelligibility of the final deal and its ensuing simplification by the opposition created an imaginary of the deal that equated it to impunity. Therefore, the Colombians who voted against the agreement saw it as a "triumph of justice" (Miranda 2016).

The massive abstention rate was the first indication that the country had expected a "yes" vote. According to a study by economists Juan Sebastián Muñoz and Juan David Herreño (2016), the departments with the most victims, particularly in rural areas, overwhelmingly supported the agreement. For example, in the municipality of Bojayá in the West Pacific region of the country's department of Chocó, the FARC once threw a cylinder bomb into a church during an engagement with paramilitaries. Approximately eighty people died, including forty-eight minors. The district voted 95.78 percent in favor of the peace agreement. The vote surfaced the blatant disconnect between the victims in rural areas and the residents of urban areas, who experienced the conflict much more indirectly.

In what was called the "March of the Flowers," thousands of students and Indigenous people poured onto the streets in reaction to the "no" win after much pushing and organizing through Facebook, Whatsapp, and Twitter. They gave white roses to victims of the conflict to tell them that they would not be forgotten. During the march, protestors shouted and held signs that read, "¡Acuerdo, ya!, ¡acuerdo, ya!" (Agreement, now!) and "the people who voted 'no' are those who have not suffered the war. We, in the rural areas, suffered, and now we want to live in peace" (*El Tiempo* 2017). The government listened to the opposition and edited part of the deal, and it was eventually signed and passed. Nonetheless, the signing of the revised agreement lacked the performativity and showmanship of the first one. Even though it incorporated some of the concerns from the "no" side, it continued (and still continues) to have detractors. Writer Héctor Abad Faciolince (2017) complained about the resistance to "good news" in a column in newspaper *El Espectador*:

> This is a country that is allergic to good news, well, half of the country.... When the peace process began, they said that the FARC would never sign an agreement. When they signed it, they said it was a terrible deal. When they changed it following the suggestions of the "No," they said the FARC would not comply. When they began to comply by demobilizing and going to the concentration zones, they would not surrender their weapons. And now that the delivery of arms arrives, they return and begin again with the same string of denial and lies.

He listed the pushback and contending imaginaries at each step of the *process*. The treaty was signed, edited, then signed again. The Nobel was won. But the cynicism endured. When the FARC turned in seven thousand weapons to the United Nations, it did not have the emotional impact the government had envisioned, as some speculated many weapons were not turned in. This could be partly due to the cease-fire implemented a few months before: turning in weapons was only the final point in the *process* of nonviolence and disarmament. Also, this was not a first-time occurrence: the demobilized paramilitaries, as well as other rebel groups, such as the M19, had already gone through this process in the 1980s, 1990s, and 2000s. Many speculated exhaustion:

after fifty-four years of war, the Colombian people had to endure five years of the peace process. Each step demanded the public's attention and emotional energy, but the process was hopefully a much smaller cost than a continuing armed conflict.

## Transforming Weapons into Art

By the time of publication, the government made a call for three pieces of art made from melted, turned-in weapons: one for the United Nations, one for Cuba for serving as the space of dialogue, and one for Colombia. Artist Doris Salcedo is creating the Bogotá sculpture, titled "Fragments," which consists of a simple floor of gray-colored tiles built with melted rifles. Salcedo says her work is an attempt to symbolically narrate the memories of war through a space that is "radically empty and silent." The tiled floor monument will become part of a museum documenting the conflict. The artist explains it as follows: "Standing on this floor, any person stands as equal, balanced and free. From here it is possible to remember and not forget the legacy of war. This space has the task of accepting antagonistic memories in order to generate from here a great polyphony of voices. The main task of art is to accommodate multiple readings of the same fact. Therefore the memory-art relationship becomes an essential tool to build contact zones or meeting areas where, as Colombians, we can cohabit." The art piece serves as a convening point for competing imaginaries, where the unified statehood, or the larger "imagined community," can share one space. The floor is a literal "common ground" in the capital, and as a literal "thing," it takes a symbolic role in both peace creation and nation building.

## Conclusion

By conflating the civic imagination of a full utopian peace with concrete moments in the process, the country contended and wavered. The international flattening of the *process* into what is known as "peacebuilding" also has "become a 'non-space,' part of the supermodern aid industry" (Denskus 2010). As we move into understanding peace as a *process* instead of an *endpoint*, it is important to keep in mind the tendency to make "peacemaking" into a "thing" in itself, reducing it to a checklist.

Floating between the treacherous dualism of peace and war remained deep-rooted social problems that did not disappear with the agreement or with the disarmament of the FARC. First, FARC members are receiving mixed responses as they attempt to reintegrate into towns. Politicians associated with Uribe and the opposition are running (in 2017) on campaigns against the agreement and what they still call "impunity," contesting the agreement. Other violent rebel military groups such as the National Liberation Army (ELN) remain. According to the US Drug Enforcement Agency, what are known as Bandas Criminales (BACRIM) gangs are taking over the country's cocaine production. Other problems that an agreement cannot dissolve include failing state control over many territories, general criminal activity, inequality, and a lack of access to education. Nonetheless, the FARC created their own logo and branding for their political party in summer 2017 (Faiola 2017). Whether it is accepted or not, the shift between a violent approach and a more democratic process is palpable.

# PART III

# How Do We Imagine Ourselves as Civic Agents?

In this section of the book, we see powerful examples of how popular culture and the civic imagination play important roles in building agency. Popular culture provides tools for identifying problems and marshaling the resources at hand (even when they seem less than up to the task) and overcoming the odds. Such stories also provide role models as individuals learn to see and exercise their own potential as agents of change; they also provide metaphors as participants reflect on different aspects of their lives, often by stepping away, momentarily, from their own real-world problems.

Our understanding of this dynamic formation of civic agency is informed by Paulo Freire's *Pedagogy of the Oppressed* (1970, 2005). Freire's Marxist-inflected language can be a hard sell to American audiences, but we resonate with his consideration of how individuals learn to move beyond fixed imaginaries and question inherited terms in order to struggle against unfair conditions. Moreover, we share the sense that uncritical participation in the status quo will allow malignancies to persist. Per Freire, without alternatives, people will accept dominant narratives: "Submerged in reality, the oppressed cannot perceive clearly the 'order' which serves the interests of the oppressors whose image they have internalized" (62). For Freire, educators ideally become partners in this self-emancipation process, contributing to what he sees as a struggle toward perpetual revolution and universal liberation.

In chapter 10, Diana Lee illustrates this process within a pop-culture context. Lee details how one young woman sharpens and articulates her own identity in response to the perceived shortcomings of a fictional character, Cho Chang, in the Harry Potter books. Lee specifically invokes Freire in her description of this process and suggests that "when we don't see diverse, nuanced characters that look and sound and think and love like real people, it can limit not only the possibilities we imagine for ourselves but also what others see as possible for and with us."

Similar themes arise in chapter 11 in Brooklyne Gipson's account of the phenomenon of #BlackGirlMagic, an empowerment movement involving both everyday people and celebrities. Here messages are shaped via social media and circulated within a larger conversation about the intersections between race and gender. In this formulation, magic offers a metaphor for the power women deploy in their everyday lives, encouraging women to resist forces that might constrain their ability to act upon the world. Gipson invokes both Afrofuturism and Afropessimism as powerful currents in this struggle, reading this current movement in its relation to a larger history of the black radical imagination.

In *Freedom Dreams* (2002), Robin G. D. Kelley engages this larger historical arc of black radical imagination and includes autobiographical reflections alongside his accounts of black political and cultural history, recounting the unfolding of his own civic identity. Kelley sees creative vision—especially as defined through the blues and other black musical traditions—as a key tool for emancipation: "Fantasy remains our most pre-emptive critical faculty, for it alone tells us what can be. Here lies the revolutionary nature of the blues: through its fidelity to fantasy and desire, the blues generates an irreducible and, so to speak, habit-forming demand for freedom and what Rimbaud called 'true life'" (163–64). While trying to avoid essentialism, we may embrace imagination as something that is core to our humanity and something that all people should enjoy as their birthright. We all have an origin story. We all work to grow and overcome obstacles in our lives. Ideally, we learn to see ourselves as part of something larger and recognize that our own contributions, however small, can help turn the wheels of progress in the right direction. Freire helps us identify tools and practices through which we may work together to liberate the imagination.

In chapter 12, Jocelyn Kelvin explores how contemporary pop divas enlist differing strategies as they adapt their artistic personas to the tasks of political action. Kelvin compares the personas that artists such as Madonna, Katy Perry, Lady Gaga and Beyoncé Knowles have crafted for themselves in the name of female empowerment. As women spoke out more and more in 2017, these artists adopted different stances, spoke for different communities, or in the case of Taylor Swift, faced backlash because of their refusal to take a political position. Kelvin explores both the ways these identity transformations play out in the public eye and their implications for the millions of fans (especially young women) who look to these performers as role models.

The power of performance and the license to explore identity on stage and for an audience is also a central aspect of chapter 13 by Manisha Pathak-Shelat. In her essay, the stakes are rooted more directly in local and regional histories and the legacies of identity that entrap local youths in the city of Ahmedabad in the Gujarat state of India. Young people of the Chhara tribe struggle to break from the historical associations of criminality that ensnare their community. By creating and staging plays that narrativize the real struggles of their pasts, the youths of the Chhara create a place and way for themselves to shape and claim an identity in which they are active, empowered, and capable of charting new future paths.

Other communities described in this volume find their path to agency through online performances of identity. In chapter 14, Donna Do-own Kim analyzes feminist activism in South Korea, and in chapter 15, Yomna Elsayed and Sulafa Zidani explore creative youth activism through satirical digital cultural production in the Arab world. Both pieces examine how online engagement with and reworking of familiar cultural forms help participants articulate their own evolving sense of agency. In Kim's case, women adopt a mirroring strategy to expose the deeply misogynistic nature of popular online speech and inspire greater awareness of their country's problems with gender inequality. For Elsayed and Zidani, the moves toward activism are more circumspect, taking the form of humorous digital content, familiar memes, photos, and remix videos as Arab youths confront political corruption after the collapse of the Arab Spring movement.

Finally, in chapter 16, Gabriel Peters-Lazaro argues that the material forms of new technological platforms can make space for the civic imagination. He describes how a low-cost virtual reality headset made out of cardboard allows users to see themselves as potentially intervening within the cycles of technological innovation. He uses Google Cardboard as an example to think about how to enable more openness, more opportunities for agency, and more room for grassroots exploration and experimentation.

A key dimension of the civic imagination is this capacity to imagine ourselves as agents of change, to value our own stories, visions, and voices. This focus of agency, in the Freirean tradition, places an emphasis on finding our own voices but also on ethical listening as we work to make sure that other voices are heard within a process of social change. This section's essays consider how popular texts and practices offer resources for critical media pedagogy, whether formal or informal.

# 10

## Learning to Imagine Better

A Letter to J. K. Rowling from Cho Chang

**Diana Lee**

To: J. K. Rowling
From: Cho Chang

When you put me in your books, millions of Asian girls across America
rejoiced!
Finally, a potential Halloween costume that wasn't a geisha or Mulan!
What's not to love about me? I'm everyone's favorite character!
I totally get to fight tons of Death Eaters and have a great sense of humor
and am full of complex emotions!
Oh wait.
That's the version of *Harry Potter* where I'm not fucking worthless.

These fiery lines open "To JK Rowling, from Cho Chang" (Button
Poetry 2013), a poem by Asian American spoken-word artist Rachel
Rostad, who utilized the dynamic oratorical conventions of spoken-
word poetry and the well-known content of the Harry Potter world to
challenge stereotypical and limited representations of Asian women in
Western popular culture. A video of Rostad's rousing performance of
this poem at an annual college poetry slam was posted online in April
2013 and immediately struck a nerve with the Harry Potter generation.
Viewed more than one million times and counting, the video raced
across the internet and sparked heated debates about her critiques of
the beloved fantasy series. While the content and performance of her
poem were undeniably powerful and necessary in drawing attention to
an industry landscape that continues to marginalize Asian characters
in mainstream cultural stories, what she did in response to the sudden

notoriety of her video was even more remarkable. Through her creative engagements with a process of acting, learning, and teaching, we are able to imagine the liberating possibilities of harnessing popular cultural narratives, personal testimony, and mediated communication as tools for transformative education and social change.

## The Poem

Spoken word is meant to move audiences, and Rostad and her poem deliver. Through clever phrasing, shifts of tone and cadence, dramatic pauses, and soaring crescendos, we hear her frustration with how Asian women in the United States are constantly misrepresented in shallow and stereotypical roles in popular books, movies, and television shows. We follow along as she highlights the subtle but pervasive ways these caricatures are presented—with accented "Asian" English and as the butt of racial and ethnic jokes; with anglicized "foreign" names that often make little sense in actual Asian languages; as disposable sidekicks there to set up white leading women who are the "real" love interests; and as hypersexualized, "exotic" conquests used and then discarded so that white male protagonists can advance through their heroic plot lines. We cringe with recognition as she glaringly lists example after example of these gendered tropes in widely celebrated, famous works: the Harry Potter series, *Ms. Saigon*, *Madame Butterfly*, *Memoirs of a Geisha*. She evokes other familiar images that bring even more stereotypes to mind: "Lucy Liu in leather," "Schoolgirl porn," "Subordinate. Submissive. Subplot." "Go ahead," she challenges. "Tell me I'm overreacting." Never mind that these stereotypes are spread through four hundred million Harry Potter books worldwide and are plastered on billboards and movie screens around the globe.

At the end of the poem, she brings it down to a quieter, more personal level and talks about why these representations matter for our everyday lives. When we don't see diverse, nuanced characters that look and sound and think and love like real people, it can limit not only the possibilities we imagine for ourselves but also what others see as possible for and with us. This moment of quiet vulnerability and exposed pain lingers before the poem shifts and ramps up again for the conclusion of the performance. Empowered once again in her defiance of these stereotypes, she spits out the last words, turns, and walks off stage to a roar of cheers and applause from the audience.

Through her carefully chosen words and rousing performance, Rostad asks us to imagine what a more diverse, intersectional, and representative popular culture landscape might look like. She urges us to think critically about the narratives we participate in consuming and perpetuating every day and directly asks influential cultural producers such as J. K. Rowling to please do better. She used her voice—amplified through a compelling art form, networked communication, and a passionate Harry Potter fan base—to spread her message about the impact of perpetuating damaging stereotypes, and she got a lot of people listening. But consciousness-raising was not the only thing she did that we should highlight and celebrate. She also showed us what it looks like to learn from our mistakes and grow.

## The Response

Although many people appreciated and supported Rostad's poignant challenge of Asian stereotyping through the prism of the Harry Potter world, the video of her spoken-word performance also brought on an onslaught of sharp criticism. Remarkably, instead of ignoring or dismissing these responses or getting pulled into destructively defensive and combative flame wars, she used the opportunity to reflect, learn, teach, and engage in a (public) conversation. She did this in a number of ways, but the most visible one was the follow-up video she created and posted two days later.

In her "Response to Critiques of 'To JK Rowling, from Cho Chang,'" Rostad (2013) smiles affably and speaks directly to the camera (beginning with "Hey there, Internet!") and sincerely and calmly addresses the criticism that came flooding in. Referencing a prepared statement to help organize her thoughts, she talks through the five main points of contention she received about her poem, demonstrating through her words and actions that she took seriously the feedback she received and was now using this same socially mediated forum to further engage with the people who engaged with her. In this carefully considered response video, she uses each point to both talk about what she herself learned through this process and also encourage her audience to reflect on their own experiences and actions as well.

She starts with what many people reacted to most strongly, that "Cho Chang" could be a legitimate Chinese name despite what she said in her poem about "Cho" and "Chang" (only) being two Korean last names. Rostad admits ignorance of Chinese naming practices, acknowledges that the line in the poem about Cho's name was problematic, and apologizes for marginalizing and misrepresenting parts of a community she was trying to empower. She also asks viewers to not only focus on this mistake but take into consideration the other points she is trying to make throughout her poem.

Rostad then emphasizes that she does not speak for all Asian women and was not claiming to do so through her work. She apologizes again for unintended mischaracterizations, especially to those who reached out to her saying they felt misrepresented by her poem and performance, and then uses these interactions to encourage further reflection about why diverse cultural portrayals matter. Building on key points about to-kenization and the burdens of limited representation made in her poem, she says, "I'm very sorry I misrepresented you. But I don't think either of us is to blame for this. I would ask you, what conditions are in place that make it so that you are so defensive that I, someone with a completely different experience of oppression, am not representing your voice? It's sad that we live in a society where my voice is so easily mistaken for yours, where our differing identities are viewed as interchangeable" (Rostad 2013). What might it look like, she asks us to consider, when one solitary representation doesn't have to carry the burden of representing us all?

Rostad's third point is about narrative marginalization via shallow character development. She asks us to consider what realistic portrayals of grief might look like for a well-developed central character versus a weepy, one-dimensional character there as plot development for the white leads. Yes, Cho was sad about boyfriend Cedric Diggory's death and confused about her developing feelings for Harry, so she was cry-ing, pensive, and sad for most of the story, but Rowling set up Cho as weak to make Ginny Weasley, Harry's eventual love interest and a white woman, look stronger. Playing into this pervasive stereotypical trope may not have been intentional on Rowling's part, but our ignorance of how we perpetuate structural and systemic discrimination does not re-lieve the effects of our actions. This is a tired and damaging theme that

recurs in mainstream films and stories, and the more we see it repeated *(color*
with no alternative portrayals of complex, nuanced characters of color, *Important*
the more it has the potential to seem "natural" that people of color do
not belong at the center of important stories. We see how strong this
hold on centering whiteness as the representative "norm" is when people
accept each new white male iteration of Batman, Spider-Man, and Sher- *Idris*
lock Holmes but vehemently oppose the idea of a black James Bond *Elb*
played by Idris Elba and fiercely condemn the casting of black actress
Noma Dumezweni as Hermione Granger in the play *Harry Potter and
the Cursed Child* (2016).

Rostad then discusses other ways that problematic representations
take form, explaining why she talked about Dumbledore's sexuality,
which some argued seemed tangential to the main themes of her poem.
She reminds us that thinking about representation and whose stories
are privileged is not only about who is invisible from the story or the *Development*
limited roles people are allowed to play. It is also about considering that
even when in prominent positions within stories, aspects of characters'
identities aren't developed in ways that illustrate the depth and complexity of our lived realities.

Speaking directly to fans at this point, Rostad then emphasizes that
contrary to what many of her critics think, she does not hate Harry Potter or J. K. Rowling but rather is a big fan of the series who grew up on
the books and went to all the midnight movie showings. Her words remind us that it is possible to think critically about and critique a world
that one also enjoys and loves. This idea, after all, is also what the foundation of democracy is based on.

And finally, at the end of her response video, Rostad (2013) closes
with this message:

> It's been humbling and amazing to watch people respond to this video. I
> think that the presence of so much passionate dialogue means that this is
> an issue that needs to be talked about. And yes, I made mistakes . . . but
> what I hope people realize is that dialogue about social justice is . . . about
> calling attention to mistakes, which I'll be the first to admit, is painful,
> and using those mistakes as an opportunity to grow. I personally have
> learned so much from the mistakes I've made in this process, and I want
> to thank the community for calling me out on that. Social justice is about

holding each other accountable, and I hope as a devoted fan base and as an amazing community, we can continue to use my piece as a jumping-off point for further dialogue, growth, and reflection.

Thank you.

We should celebrate this as an exemplary instance of reflexivity, of praxis—of the liberating power of reflection, awareness, and action. Of an intelligent, passionate young person invested in learning from and contributing to her community. Of the engaging, participatory possibilities available through working with popular culture and using technology, media, and newer forms of mediated communication as tools for transformative education. This is also a great opportunity for educators and families to unpack the pedagogical implications of what happens when you find something young people are excited about and engage in this kind of expression and communication with a larger community. And this is also an example of what media scholar Henry Jenkins (2011) calls participatory culture—specifically in relation to new media literacies and civic engagement.

In other words, Rostad's critical engagements illustrate what we hope that people of all ages are doing when they are participating in mediated communication, enjoying popular culture, and otherwise interacting out in the world. We hope that people are actively engaged with their media and popular cultural stories and with each other. We hope that people are thinking about ideas, sharing them, playing with and acting on them, challenging each other and working out responses, incorporating new information, helping each other learn and grow, and then repeating that process again and again.

## Learning Is a Connected Process

This case study reminds us to see learning as a social and interactive ongoing process, not simply something that occurs once, linearly, and within the confines of individual, solitary minds. As critical pedagogy scholar and activist Paulo Freire (2000) teaches, dialoguing and developing the ability to reflect on what is learned through the process of sharing experiences and perspectives with others is "an indispensable component of the process of both learning and knowing" (17). This social, iterative, and transformational practice of critical thinking and acting is what ultimately allows us to see beyond the confines of our present situations in order to make changes in the world toward a better future.

By following the example of Rostad's videos and active online engagement with a larger community, we can literally see and hear this messy, discursive, and interactive transformative learning and teaching process unfold not just for her but for those she was in conversation with. In one instance, for example, a blogger posted on Angry Asian Girls United (2013) calling Rostad out for her glaring misrepresentation of South Asians and for ignoring Pan-Asian solidarity and identity. The blogger also critiqued her for taking up the term *brown* as an East Asian and for conflating the varying meanings of the "Asian" label when considering US versus UK contexts (where the Harry Potter world is set). In the poem, Rostad speaks of "Asians" as if they equate to East Asians and does not count Indian characters Padma and Parvati Patil, which is a common erasure when people have not fully unpacked the inherent privileges and inconsistencies within volatile US (and global) racial and ethnic categories. The identity term *brown* is a similarly slippery and contentious point. In the poem, Rostad includes the Patil twins, as well as herself, as *brown* and *minority.* As an Asian American woman myself, I read her use of the terms inclusively, as an attempt to empower and connect with discourses of identity politics that are specific to the contemporary US cultural context, but whether (East, South, Southeast, Central, Middle Eastern, or Pacific Islander) Asians are included under that umbrella term or whether she should or can claim the term *brown* is a separate conversation. The point here is that multiple people with different backgrounds and experiences were actively engaged with these complex issues, challenging both their own and each other's thinking through these creations. Thanks to digital and networked communication, these processes were also happening in a public square, allowing even more people to witness, learn from, and join in on the discussion.

## Imagining Better

In the end, Rachel Rostad wanted us to use her creations as "a jumping off point for further dialogue, growth, and reflection" about identity and social justice issues. By tapping into the Harry Potter world and amplifying her voice via spoken word and networked media, she tore down stereotypes and asked us to envision a more diverse, intersectional, and inclusive popular cultural landscape. She showed how popular stereotypical stories can impact people's actual lived realities and encouraged us to challenge the limiting narratives we participate in consuming and perpetuating in our own lives. She also modeled what it looks like to seek common ground civilly across difficult divides, to listen to those whose opinions and perspectives differ from one's own, and to learn from the mistakes we make so that we can continue to grow. Rostad's actions inspire us to imagine a world where we each are brave and take it upon ourselves to participate in ongoing processes of critical thinking, action, reflection, and dialogue about our experiences. Imagine what could be possible if we all learned to honor ourselves and our connections with one another so that together we could build a more representative, more inclusive, more just and loving world.

# 11

## Black Girls Are from the Future

### #BlackGirlMagic as an Extension of the Black Radical Imagination

**Brooklyne Gipson**

> Black Girl Magic is a rallying call of recognition. Embedded in the everyday is a magnificence that is so easy to miss because we're so mired in the struggle and what society says we are.
> —Ava Duvernay

In the Western world, typical imaginings of the "future" often include the assumption that it will be somewhat of an improvement on the present and certainly should be far better than the past. In the United States in particular, the ideal of progress is a throughline that has serviced the American mythos of development. Progress has been constructed through fictionalized accounts of the nation's history that obscure the travesties of colonialism and re-present them as "progress"—a notion that is privileged as not only inevitable and unavoidable but also wholly positive, linear, and forward-moving. However, when said "progress" comes at the expense of certain bodies, it can be anything but truly positive. Think of the nineteenth-century ethos of Manifest Destiny, for example; in its pursuit, the United States waged a violent war with Mexico over their land and forcibly removed and/or slaughtered the Native American inhabitants along their path to the Pacific Ocean.

For those oppressed individuals whose political history is mired in intermittent achievements and setbacks that appear to exist solely to cancel one another out, the linear conception of time does not resonate. The notion of an "absolute future," or a future that can be forecasted by empirical evidence or statistical notions of "likelihood," stands on a shaky foundation for those for whom the promise of tomorrow is a constant uncertainty. For those living at the margins, the thought of future is a nerve-racking unpredictability that looms with promises of negativity, making it challenging to imagine a "future" in the traditional sense, often because it is too painful and/or impractical.

#BlackGirlMagic serves as an exemplar for how one oppressed group—black women—has chosen to reimagine its current condition. What started out as a simple thought expressed in a tweet by Cashawn Thompson—"Black girls are magic"—has now become a rallying cry for self-love and self-affirmation for hundreds of thousands of black women who have used the internet to co-construct a narrative of otherworldly strength and beauty. Julee Wilson, a writer for the *Huffington Post*, defines #BlackGirlMagic as "a term used to *illustrate* the universal awesomeness of Black women. It's about celebrating anything we deem particularly dope, inspiring, or mind-blowing about ourselves." The rhetorical shift from the phrase "Black girls are magic" to the digital shorthand #BlackGirlMagic shifted the sentiment from claim to self-evidentiary fact. In colloquial terms, "Black girls are magic" is the charge and #BlackGirlMagic is the receipt.

#BlackGirlMagic is black women doing things they never thought they would be able to do in places they never thought they would be able to do them. Consider Beyoncé parading into the 2016 Super Bowl halftime show (the ultimate prime-time American media event) in Black Power–era garb, stealing the show from headlining act Coldplay to sing "Formation," a song about the beauty of two prominent phenotypic markers of her blackness—her "negro nose and afro." Recall the first images of the Obama White House and the humble brag that Michelle Obama was the first and only First Lady of the United States to attend and graduate from Ivy League universities for both undergraduate and graduate school—Princeton and Harvard Law, respectively.

#BlackGirlMagic is black women being successful at things others are not able to do. The 2016 Summer Olympic Games in Rio served as a primary stage to showcase #BlackGirlMagic: Simone Biles was the first woman to win all-around titles in world gymnastics in three consecutive years; Ibtihaj Muhammad became the first fencer to compete in the Olympics wearing a hijab; Kristi Castlin, Nia Ali, and Brianna Rollins, all representing America, dominated the medal ceremony, winning gold, silver, and bronze; and Allyson Felix, the most decorated Olympic runner, broke a record in winning her sixth gold medal in track and field.

#BlackGirlMagic is black women defying the odds. During the 2016 Miss USA pageant, it was noted that only 13 percent (seven out of fifty-two) contestants were black women. However, two out of three finalists, one of which ultimately became the winner, were black (Hume 2016). In 2015, *Fortune* magazine identified black women as the fastest-growing group of entrepreneurs in America, with a 322 percent increase in business ownership since 1997 (Haimerl 2015). The National Center for Education Statistics (2010) also recently named black women as the most educated group (by race and sex) in America, with a higher percentage of black women (9.7 percent) enrolled in college than any other group: Asian women (8.7 percent), white women (7.1 percent), and white men (6.1 percent). #BlackGirlMagic is also the "one up." It is the moment we realized that tennis star Serena Williams had won her twenty-third grand slam at the Australian Open *while pregnant*.

#BlackGirlMagic is the unexplainable fuel that propels black women to achievement in spite of the double burdens of racism and sexism. Postslavery, popular and visual culture has maintained the marginalization of the black female body. The stereotypical tropes of the sexless workhorse "Mammy" figure, the hypersexed "Jezebel," and the angry, attitudinal "Sapphire"—many of which were popularized by racist minstrel shows—were later adapted for television and radio and still endure today. The contemporary stereotypes of black women as domestic servants, as sexually insatiable, as animalistic, or as enraged are all legacies of these popular images. Now that barriers to media production have been broken down, black women actively work to subvert these images—the Twitter platform and the hashtag #BlackGirlMagic have become major tools for doing this.

As a new discursive site for the black public sphere, the hashtag #BlackGirlMagic allows social media users to categorize and therefore archive digital evidentiary support for the claim that black girls and women are indeed magical in that they possess hair that defies gravity, beauty and mystery that defy mainstream media castigation, unexplainable success, and the power to perform feats of greatness. The open-source nature of Twitter's search/hashtag functions act as collaborative spaces where participants are invited into a genre-defining dialogue that establishes the parameters of what is meant by terms or tags employed. A simple Twitter search of the term #BlackGirlMagic yields a seemingly never-ending queue of cultural artifacts, updated in real time, of all other public tweets containing the same tag. However, #BlackGirlMagic is not a viral phenomenon, as it only increases in momentum and popularity over time.

Communication theorist Catherine Squires (2002) highlights how the marginalization of the black voice has resulted in the creation of multiple public spheres to address the needs of disenfranchised groups. According to her theory, "enclave publics" developed as a subset of the black public sphere in response to the hostility that members of mainstream publics may have had to their ideas or sheer presence. The existence of #BlackGirlMagic points to the necessity of safe spaces for black women where they can define themselves without being subjected to further objectification or silencing but also reimagine their current social standing. Patricia Hill Collins (1990) describes "self-definition" as "the power to name one's own reality." #BlackGirlMagic is an exercise in self-definition because it allows black women to define themselves for themselves.

However, the #BlackGirlMagic movement has not been without its ideological issues. Though popularized by Thompson, black women online can be credited with the co-construction of its meaning and cultural significance. In addition to mutually constructing an easily accessible aggregate of examples, #BlackGirlMagic also constructs a particularly narrow definition of black womanhood that could be understood as reinforcing both the politics of respectability and racist ideology. In fact, in an article written for *Elle* magazine, Dr. Linda Chavers argues that #BlackGirlMagic did not subvert the "strong black woman" archetype at all but actually contributed to it: "Saying we're superhuman is just as bad as saying we're animals, because it implies that we are organically different, that we don't feel just as much as any other human being. Black girls are women and women are humans. That's all we are. And it would be a magical feeling to be treated like human beings—who can't fly, can't bounce off the ground, can't block bullets, who very much can feel pain, who very much can die" (Chavers 2016). In response to

Chavers critique, another scholar, Ashley Ford, acknowledges the strong black woman archetype and its parallels within the #BlackGirlMagic framework: "Black girls and women have been routinely denied their humanity in the face of a world ruled by racism, sexism, colorism, classism, and the enduring belief that our backs were built to carry what others would consider unimaginable burden" (A. Ford 2016). However, she highlights how #BlackGirlMagic worked to reclaim the imagery of the black female body and do some of that "self-definition" work that Collins (1990) spoke of. "It's not for them. It's for us," Ford writes. "It's not about tapping into something supernatural, it's about claiming or reclaiming what others have refused to see." The intermittent invisibility and hypervisibility of the black female body has meant that black women are ignored at the same rate that they are made a spectacle. In her book *Black Looks: Race and Representation*, black feminist scholar bell hooks (1992) analyzes the commodification of blackness as a major contributor to not only racism but internalized black self-hate. She necessitates the decolonization of the minds of black Americans in order to contest media representations that disseminate white supremacist ideology. As one way to do this, hooks suggests that black women work to de-essentialize images of themselves via more radical representations of black female subjectivity. In "Representations of Whiteness in the Black Imagination," hooks (2014a) calls for a redirecting of the "ethnographic gaze"—the "investigating state of white supremacy" that influences black people's self-perception. In interrogating self-hate and self-love as products of both media consumption and production, hooks (writing in a predigital world) touches on an early version of debates surrounding how mediated public discourse can either reinforce or deconstruct the racist ideology disseminated by mainstream media.

Afrofuturism is one ideological framework and cultural aesthetic through which many black people have chosen to envision and reimagine futures outside the confines of their lived reality. As defined by Alondra Nelson, Afrofuturism is a collection of "African-American voices" with "other stories to tell about culture, technology and things to come" (2002). Originally coined by Mark Dery in a 1993 essay, the term *Afrofuturism* is described as "speculative fiction that treats African-American themes and addresses African-American concerns in the context of the 20th century technoculture—and, more generally, African-American signification that appropriates images of technology and a prosthetically enhanced future" (Dery 1993) Kodwo Eshun describes the art classified as Afrofuturism as being focused in "one way or another on the intersecting imageries of pastness and future in Black culture, setting out not so much to rewrite the history of the African diaspora, but to systematically deconstruct it, rendering Africa an 'alien future'" (Akomfrah 1996). However defined, I would argue that #BlackGirlMagic acts as an extension of the Afrofuturistic tradition in that it employs an invocation of the fantastic to combat social realities such as "misogynoir" (M. Bailey 2010), or misogyny against black women that is prevalent throughout the history of American visual and popular culture.

On the converse, Afro-pessimism has been identified as a framework some black scholars have employed to articulate a disenchantment with idealized narratives of "home" or a natural "homeland" for displaced people of the African diaspora. In the Afro-pessimist tradition, "social death" (Patterson 1982), or the complete rejection of the humanity of a person through mechanisms of isolation and alienation, is a guiding logic. In this view, enslavement completely alienated black people from their ancestry, and as a result, they are permanently displaced. In this perspective, "Blackness" is not a cultural identity but a way of living or being. The concept of social death is integral for understanding the narratives #BlackGirlMagic reinforces and those it subverts. At first glance, the construction of the black woman as beautiful, strong, powerful, and worthy of attention, praise, and love could be read as a humanizing act. However, #BlackGirlMagic does not simply humanize the black female body; it constructs a narrative of the black woman as superhuman or supernatural and uses the reality of her alienated and denigrated social position to underscore this reality.

The reimagining of the black female body as "in the world but not of the world" is indicative of a desire to sidestep current social realities. This reimaging also places the popular hashtag #BlackGirlMagic squarely within the Afrofuturistic and Afro-pessimist traditions, which are both extensions of the black radical imagination. L. H. Stallings (2013) engages Robin D. G. Kelley's notion of "surrealism" to draw attention to how creativity, dreams, ingenuity and so on have provided space for conceptualizing "liberation." #BlackGirlMagic provides a way for black women to reckon with centuries of emotional, physical, and verbal abuse from a society in which they have been rendered "socially dead" and seek "freedom" in the only context truly attainable within these frameworks—by accessing alternative temporal and/or geo-physical realms.

*Dead*

# 12

## "Dance to the Distortion"

The Queens of Pop vs. Donald Trump

**Jocelyn Kelvin**

"Are you ready to shake up the world?" Madonna called from the podium of the Women's March on Washington on January 21, 2017. "Yes!" the gathered protesters yelled back in unison. "Welcome to the revolution of love," she continued. "To the rebellion. To our refusal as women to accept this new age of tyranny." The audience cheered loudly, supporting her words. Madonna's voice rang in opposition to Donald Trump, a man whose misogynistic, racist, bigoted platform won him the presidency of the United States (though not the popular vote). Throughout history, many musicians have used their microphones to share political messages. At this unique moment in 2017, with Trump in office, nearly all the American women at the top of the pop machine—Madonna, Lady Gaga, Katy Perry, Beyoncé, and Taylor Swift, as defined by *Forbes*'s list of the highest paid women in music (Greenberg 2015, 2016)—chose to use their unusually wide-reaching female voices to represent an alternative to Trump's prejudice. These women used their live performances in the first six months after the election to depict a spectrum of civic engagement. On one end of that spectrum was Madonna, who, unsurprisingly, has been the most partisan in her political participation; on the other was Taylor Swift, whose silence created an opportunity for the alt-right to deify her as their icon. The other three performers—Beyoncé, Gaga, and Katy Perry, all of whom were vocally supportive of Hillary Clinton during her campaign—used their performances to make political statements with varying degrees of directness, contributing to the civic imagination of their (often young) fans.

In this discussion, I will not attempt to be comprehensive; many of these women crafted a political side of their persona long before the

2016 election, and a whole book (or many) could be written about each one. This chapter will focus on singular performance events that occurred in 2017 that exemplify how each of these pop stars has chosen to represent the female voice in an era in which the leader of the country openly and unapologetically practices and supports misogyny.

## Madonna's Revolution

Madonna strives to wake people up and is not afraid to make enemies in the process. Her persona is that of the rebel fighter, the controversy-stirring provocateur: she models a civic approach of direct attack, speaking her mind in rejection of tyranny, support of freedom of expression, and enjoyment of a distinctly female sexuality and power. Her response to Trump's election was no exception. At the podium on January 21, she wore a black version of the march's symbolic pussy power hat and a shirt defining feminism as "the radical notion that women are people." Solemnly, she called out, "Let's march together through this darkness and with each step know: That we are not afraid. That we are not alone. That we will not back down. That there is power in our unity and that no opposing force stands a chance in the face of true solidarity. And to our detractors that insist that this march will never add up to anything, fuck you. Fuck you. It is the beginning of much needed change" (Matthews 2017). Her curse was met with a swell of voices and the smile of those visible behind her on the stage. Madonna's contribution to the civic imagination of her liberal audience is to give voice to their anger in a way that allows for emotional release and incites fire and action. She directly engages the question of power and voices the deservingness of women and other minorities openly and forcefully.

But as a result, she has often played the role of the enemy for conservatives. Her curses led to mainstream media outlet CNN cutting their live coverage of her speech, and after the event, most media disparaged her anger, focusing on a single sentence in which Madonna admitted she had "thought a lot about blowing up the White House." They separated her words from their context, for she immediately followed her statement by calling to the crowd to instead "choose love." In response, President Trump himself called her "disgusting," saying she "was disgraceful to our country" (R. Reed 2017).

While Madonna is the second most successful female musical artist of the past century (Lynch 2017), she has not achieved this by generalizing her voice in an attempt to be palatable to all. Madonna uses her voice directly and forcefully to shock and therefore draw attention to her message. The self-proclaimed "Unapologetic Bitch" performed the same role in response to Trump's election as she has throughout her career—as a controversy-courting feminist provocateur—giving the left a voice for their anger and the right an enemy to smear. While Madonna's self-invention as both a musical artist and a political commentator paved the way for the younger artists chronicled in this chapter, she remains the most outspoken and divisive of them all.

## Queen Bey

With the release of her groundbreaking visual album *Lemonade*, Beyoncé has transformed into the most imaginatively political pop performer other than Madonna. If Madonna's Women's March archetype was that of a rebel fighter of the resistance, in Beyoncé's most visible performance of 2017, she gave her persona mythological proportions, utilizing the archetype of the goddess to lift her audience's sense of self and celebrate majestic womanhood, motherhood, and blackness. At the 2017 Grammys, where *Lemonade* was notably overlooked, winning only two of nine nominations and losing repeatedly to Adele's *25* in a questionably race-based way that made even Adele uncomfortable, Beyoncé performed as a serene golden goddess. She appeared first in a projection—her strikingly pregnant belly framed only by a golden chain bikini, a silk drape billowing behind her in a nod to African water spirit Mami Wata—and on stage, she wore a transparent, embroidered golden dress symbolizing Oshun, the Yoruba water goddess of female sensuality, love, and fertility. Her golden headdress, similar to medieval depictions of the black Madonna (Baila 2017), was echoed by her dancers' halos as they undulated around her, holding hands, weaving through, and supporting each other, at one point laying a golden drape over her crown, similar to depictions of Hindu goddess Kali, who is associated with sexuality, death, and motherly love (Mettler 2017). Beyoncé's celebration of female power and motherhood was clear through these visuals as well as her lyrics and spoken-word poetry, such as when her voice rang out,

"Your mother is a woman—and women like her cannot be contained." Notably, she used only female dancers—so for the nearly ten minutes of her performances, the conversation was for, by, and about women.

When she accepted the award for Best Urban Contemporary Album, Beyoncé didn't mention Trump by name but used her microphone to call for representation of black lives:

> We all experience pain and loss, and often we become inaudible. My intention for the film and album was to create a body of work that would give a voice to our pain, our struggles, our darkness and our history. To confront issues that make us uncomfortable. It's important to me to show images to my children that reflect their beauty, so they can grow up in a world where they look in the mirror, first through their own families—as well as the news, the Super Bowl, the Olympics, the White House and the Grammys—and see themselves, and have no doubt that they're beautiful, intelligent and capable. This is something I want for every child of every race. And I feel it's vital that we learn from the past and recognize our tendencies to repeat our mistakes. (Russonello 2017)

Beyoncé is explicitly asking for change: for complex, equal representation of people of every race. As race becomes the center of the national conflict, Beyoncé holds a unique position as the sole American woman of color at the top of the pop world, and therefore her engagement with the civic takes on different challenges and responsibilities. The Trump presidency has brought an increased risk for people of color, and in this climate, Beyoncé used her 2017 Grammys appearance to model for her fans a black woman honoring her own strength rather than lowering herself to the level of those who would silence her. Her performance showed the power of a woman, specifically a black woman, representing the uniquely female power of creation, rising above the moment, serene and impossible to dethrone.

## Could Gaga Be "The Cure"?

While Lady Gaga often seems to emulate Madonna, she does not match her spiritual predecessor's political provocativeness. Gaga's boundary pushing occurs in her visuals and her acceptance of the bizarre in herself and others, but she does her best not to make enemies. Where Madonna rallies the troops by admitting to her anger, Gaga soothes them, playing the role of "Mother Monster" to her "Little Monster" fans. Her Super Bowl LI halftime performance in February 2017 held to this nonabrasive methodology. Though Gaga made her stance on the election clear—for example, posting a photo of herself on the eve of Trump's win standing on a dump truck outside Trump Tower holding a "Love Trumps Hate" sign—when given a rare, national megaphone, rather than create a directly political dialogue, Gaga chose to keep her opinions on everything but self-acceptance somewhat under the radar.

Gaga began her halftime performance high above the crowd, singing parts of "God Bless America" and Woody Guthrie's "This Land Is Your Land" and reciting the "one nation under God" portion of the Pledge of Allegiance before descending to the stage and performing a campy, feel-good extravaganza of her hits from the last decade. She made no direct visual political jabs at Trump (the National Football League required her not to mention him by name), but as always, she trumpeted acceptance and inclusiveness through her existence as well as her multicultural backup dancers and staged audience. In a queer milestone, she was the first to use the words *lesbian*, *gay*, *bi*, and *transgender* during the Super Bowl, and though her song "Born This Way" was released six years ago, this celebration of sexual diversity proved particularly important in a moment where hatred of queer Americans is supported by Trump—and Vice President Pence, in attendance that afternoon (Lang 2017). Additionally, the use of Guthrie's protest song, written in the 1940s as a retort to "God Bless America," heartened members of the resistance, who noticed the subliminal messaging: when Gaga sang "This land is your land," red drones behind her lit up, and on "This land is my land," blue drones joined them (Stryker 2017).

Yet the political content of her performance was up for interpretation. Gaga called to the crowd, "We're here to make you feel good," and some liberals were frustrated by the "confrontationally apolitical" missed opportunity of that mission statement: "Worst of all," Sonia Saraiya wrote in *Variety* (2017), "[Gaga] appears to have willingly sanded down the politically charged subtext of her own art into a commodified piece of Americana that could be experienced without being truly understood." Meanwhile, many pro-Trump Americans took to Twitter to thank Gaga for "not making it political" (Enloe 2017). Rather than make a direct statement that engaged the bipartisan realities of 2017, Gaga and her team developed a purposefully uncontroversial performance that strove to draw Americans together with camp and heart at a moment when the country had never felt more divided. Gaga used her performance solely to model self-celebration for her diverse, nationwide audience.

## "Purposeful Pop": Katy Perry Gets Woke AF

For Katy Perry, whose pop has historically been characterized by oversized candy, whipped cream–shooting bras, and goofiness, 2016's election was a major turning point. Perry became one of Hillary Clinton's most ardent celebrity supporters, and her involvement in Clinton's campaign reshaped Perry's image, though this newfound persona is still in development. Perry's most powerful civic effect may be modeling for her teen fans as an avatar for their own experience of becoming civically engaged for the first time.

Her press for her 2017 album *Witness* prepared fans for a new era of, as Perry termed it, "political pop" (Bowles 2017). She changed her Twitter bio to "Artist. Activist. Conscious," and the music video for the first single, "Chained to the Rhythm," featured a 1950s-inspired futuristic amusement park with a dark underbelly of conformity and rides like the "American Dream Drop." At the Grammys, Perry performed in front of a white-picket-fenced clapboard house covered with projections of fire and other natural disasters before transforming into a backdrop upon which the Declaration of Independence was projected. She wore a white pantsuit, a symbol of Clinton's campaign and an ode to suffragettes, and an armband reading "Persist," a reference to Senator Elizabeth Warren's silencing by Mitch McConnell. Finally, she called out "No hate!" at the end of the number before the lights cut to black.

Of all the performers mentioned, Perry's outfit and imagery were the most directly related to the political moment, the most decidedly pro-Clinton and anti-Trump. But Perry is still maneuvering her way through her newfound message. In contrast to Madonna and Beyoncé, who model performances of self and femaleness that direct their audiences toward envisioning a better future, Perry's political imagery is deeply mired in the present. Perry's message to her fans is to "Resist!" She wants them to wake up from their complacency. But her imagery does not suggest what they should do once they've woken up; her representations are of the present or recent past—the white pantsuit of Clinton, the "persist" of Warren. Rather than offer a concept of a better future, Perry reflects to her audience their diseased present. While this may not precisely develop her fans' civic imagination, Perry aims to stoke their civic interest, and her unique strength is that her newness in this sphere can help her young fans confront their own fears about engaging in politics. And Perry's attempt to carry her young fans into a more aware, politically active space could have the potential for a real effect—especially given that she has about sixty-eight million more Twitter followers than the president does.

### Taylor Swift's "Reputation"

Unlike her peers, Taylor Swift has remained silent about politics. She has taken only two politically related actions: posting a photo of herself at a polling place on November 8, 2016, telling her followers to vote and tweeting after the Women's March demonstrations, saying, "I'm proud to be a woman today, and every day." Her silence has been greeted with widespread criticism, exemplified by *Noisey*'s Grace Medford (2017): "[For Taylor Swift] to stay silent is to be deafeningly noticeable. . . . To ignore is to not merely be 'unwoke' but to be embarrassingly out of touch with the public conversation. . . . To actively choose not to denounce a presidential candidate—now president—whose campaign promises set out to directly affect the women's rights you spoke so passionately about 12 months ago, is even more so."

A well-handled $1 lawsuit against a DJ who groped her at a photo op and then had the gall to sue her for damaging his reputation regained her some respect from liberal commentators. But the release of her first single from the *Reputation* album in August 2017 shattered some of this goodwill. The general consensus about its release in video form during the MTV Video Music Awards—which Swift did not attend—was well defined in *Elle*: "In a night dedicated to earnest pop culture displays of unity, the self-obsessed video for Taylor Swift's comeback single 'Look What You Made Me Do' stuck out like a can of Pepsi at a protest" (Snapes 2017; Wamsley 2017). But Swift's apolitical stance hasn't hurt her viewership—the video broke YouTube's record for the most watched video in a single day and the biggest debut, with 43.2 million views in its first twenty-four hours (McIntyre 2017).

However, Swift's silence has had negative repercussions: she has become an emblem of the civic imagination for the alt-right. In May 2016, *Broadly* (Vice Media's female-focused vertical) published an article titled "Shake It Off: How Taylor Swift became a Nazi Idol," in which Andre Anglin, founder of (now defunct) white supremacist blog the *Daily Stormer*, explained, "We are certain that as soon as Nazis saw her, they were magnetically drawn to her sculpted Aryan form and angelic demeanor. The entire alt-right patiently awaits the day when we can lay down our swords and kneel before her throne as she commands us to go forth and slaughter the subhuman enemies of the Aryan race" (Sunderland 2016). Other *Daily Stormer* headlines on Swift included "Taylor Swift, Avatar of European Imperialism" and "Aryan Goddess Taylor Swift: Nazi Avatar of the White European People." When we discuss the civic imagination, we have a tendency to focus on the liberal, inclusive imaginations that pop culture can create, but the fact that Swift's silence has enabled those who believe in hatred and violence to take her on as an emblem of their cause proves that like it or not, the women at the center of the pop-industrial complex have personas that define and shape many people's belief systems and understandings of culture. By nature of having such a visible place in our culture, each of these women contributes to the civic imagination of the American people—and if they don't define their belief systems, they cannot control the usage of their iconography.

While Trump may have the power of the government, among youths, he simply doesn't have the reach of these pop divas. For example, compare his 37.1 million Twitter followers to Katy Perry's 105 million, or his 7.4 million Instagram followers to Beyoncé's 106 million, and imagine how powerful a post urging followers to vote against him could have been from Taylor Swift (85.5 million Twitter followers and 102 million Instagram followers as of this writing). These five women have an extraordinary reach in shaping the perspective of younger generations. Calling for inclusion, love, and compassion, these women have cultural power to counter the narrative of racism, sexism, entitlement, and hatred.

# 13

## Changing the Future by Performing the Past

Budhan Theatre and Transformation of
Youth Identities

### Manisha Pathak-Shelat

> Theater gives you the power to speak out. . . . You are not just
> talking to yourself or your small community, you are talking to
> the larger society. . . . For me, the right to speak out is devel-
> opment; not buildings or some such things. . . . When you bring
> out your inner suffocation, the burden of years of stigma through
> theater, . . . that catharsis is your way to development.
> —Dakxin Chhara, founding member, Budhan Theatre Chhara

This is the story of Budhan Theatre in Ahmedabad, India, led by a community of marginalized youths. Through their story, I trace the process of
the transformation of their identities from that of outcasts, criminals, and
victims to agents of social change through critical creative engagement.

These youths belong to a denotified tribe known as "Chhara" and re-
side in a community called "Chharanagar" in the heart of the sprawl-
ing city of Ahmedabad in the state of Gujarat, India. The Chharas have
a unique burden to carry from their past. Their ancestors were recognized as skilled thieves and labeled as habitual offenders. The Chharas
are among the tribal groups that followed a nomadic lifestyle, much like
the Romas in Europe, and were classified as "dangerous" by the then
ruling British colonizers. In the nineteenth century, India had hundreds
of such nomadic tribes that survived by gathering forest products and
providing street entertainment through folk arts. Most of these tribes
were labeled as "criminals" in 1871, when an act was passed for the "no-
tification of criminal tribes." (Please see www.budhantheatre.org for a
detailed history of these tribes and the Chharas.)

As noted by Mukherjee (2016), these tribes were formally denotified in 1952 after India gained independence in 1947. The joy, however, was short-lived, and in 1959, they were classified again as "habitual offenders." As thievery was seen as their hereditary trait and carried a strong social stigma, there were minimal employment opportunities for these youths. They lived in segregated stigmatized communities such as the Chharanagar in Ahmedabad, where the Chharas have settled since the 1930s, and with no other options, they resorted to thievery and illicit liquor brewing as a means of survival. The stigma of being habitual offenders makes nomadic tribes especially liable to suspicion when crimes do occur. Even today, some sixty million people belong to such "denotified tribes" in India (www.budhantheatre.org).

What kinds of identities would such historical and political experiences shape for these generations of young people? And most importantly, how would they even see themselves as belonging to the larger community of their city or nation and capable of envisioning a future that is distinctly different from their present?

The literature on identity recognizes several different types of domains and categories of identity—for example, moral identity, ethnic identity, national identity, gender identity, and civic identity, among others. Hart, Richardson, and Wilkenfeld (2011) note that "civic identity lies at the heart of common notions of citizenship and civic participation" and explain it as "a set of beliefs and emotions about oneself as a participant in civic life" (773). The literature on identity, however, also draws our attention to the fact that an individual can be labeled as having a certain identity based on birth, physical features, or perceived religious membership even when the person himself or herself may or may not personally see that identity as the most important one. When applied to the youths from the Chhara community, it is evident that society labeled them primarily as criminals, thieves, and outcasts, and at best, they saw themselves as victims of historical and political injustice. In such circumstances, when young people look at their place in the world, it is difficult for them to imagine themselves as meaningful actors.

In our interview, Dakxin narrates to me the story of his young neighbor, Jeetu (name changed to maintain confidentiality), that shows how socially imposed identities and stigmatizing experiences actually create negative identities. Jeetu, naughty and yet brilliant in studies, wanted to be a policeman and was studying in a local school. Once, during a police raid in their community, his house was searched. (Police raids are common incidents in such communities, and suddenly one hundred to two hundred policemen will descend on their homes to look for evidence of criminal activities, including illicit liquor brewing, as alcohol consumption is banned in Gujarat.) Jeetu's mother was involved in liquor brewing and hastily hid a container of liquor in the boy's school bag. Unaware, Jeetu carried the bag to school the next day, and the liquor was found. Jeetu was severely reprimanded and expelled from school. He tried hard to convince the authorities of his innocence but failed. The Chhara community youth leaders, including Dakxin, tried to plead with the school authorities, explaining the boy's innocence. They saw a ray of hope when the principal started showing some signs of understanding. The parents of other children in the class, however, put up a strong collective opposition to having a "criminal" studying with their own children. Jeetu could never study further, as no other school would accept him. His frustration, anger, and helplessness finally made him turn to criminal activities for survival. "Jeetu wanted to create a new identity for himself, but the society didn't let that happen and in fact imposed the identity of a criminal on him," says Dakxin, recounting the incident that left a permanent mark on him.

To self-identify as a valuable member of the larger society, one needs to develop a strong and positive civic identity. A full civic identity has three constituent elements: membership, participation, and a concern for rights (Hart et al. 2011). One has to have a sense of belonging to a geographical or social community, opportunities to participate in the functioning and shaping of this larger community, and some rights by virtue of being a member. When young people are denied all of the above three elements, they most likely feel angry, alienated, and oppressed. At times, such groups turn to extremism and rebellion. The Chhara youths have faced years of exclusionary treatment from the larger society, and the community has witnessed too many young people falling victim to the combined pressure of social stigma, lack of survival options, persecution by the authorities, and lack of opportunities to envision a different future. How did Dakxin and some of his fellow Chhara youths turn to creative engagement and expression as a way to imagine a better future for themselves and a more just and humane social environment for everyone? How did an initiative that started with a small community library and a few young men putting on plays to tell their own stories blossom into a powerful movement with more than three hundred active "artivists" (artists who are also activists) and an impact on the lives of several hundred families? That is the story of Budhan Theatre.

The noted writer and social activist Mahashwetadevi and literary critic and linguist Professor Ganesh Devy visited Chharanagar in 1998. Starting with a small community library, they facilitated the collective path to catharsis, critical thinking, and social action for a handful of Chhara youths such as Dakxin who were already interested in literature, art, and cinema. The youths first turned to theater as a means of unburdening themselves of years of frustration born out of a lack of options and their anger toward their oppressors amid the authorities and the larger society. They reenacted scenes from their own lives and the lives of those around them, asking questions, challenging assumptions, and in the process staking a claim for their own voices and their right to be heard. From seeing themselves as criminals and those harmful to the larger society, they started recognizing how the social stigma and ostracization had harmed them. From seeing themselves as criminals, they started recognizing themselves as victims. Their identity transformation had begun but had not yet reached its full civic potential.

Dakxin sees theater and all other art forms as a way to positively channel energy. For marginalized communities that have little possibility of affecting positive change in real life, these forms offer a way to imagine a different future, a way to dream of a different society. Street theater or participatory theater, in that sense, is not a new medium for social change. There has been a long history of street theater and political performance in India. Theater is increasingly being used as a tool by activists and organizations for fostering justice, engagement, recognition, and reconciliation. Contemporary theorizations in Indian participatory theater developed a trajectory rooted in the ideas of countering hegemonic political and social structures. Badal Sircar's Third Theatre, the Indian People's Theatre Association (IPTA), Habib Tanvir's Naya Theatre, and Safdar Hashmi's Jana Natya Manch (JANAM) are some well-recognized examples of emancipatory or political theater in India. Da Costa (2010) underlines that this form of theater allows citizens and activists to see the world as a "malleable world of possibility" rather than an infallible system of constructed realities. Today, whether it is the Jana Sanskriti Center for the Theatre of the Oppressed in West Bengal; the Bangalore-based Centre for Community Dialogue and Change (CCDC); the Society for Rural, Urban and Tribal Initiative (SRUTI), which operates across thirteen Indian states; or several emerging street theater groups in colleges across India, theatrical activism is slowly but steadily gaining momentum to rework the perceptions of citizenship and reclaim dignity.

There is also growing evidence from all over the world hailing the transformative and liberating power of performance. For example, grassroots theater in Rwanda was introduced after the 1994 genocide in the country with an aim to cultivate a unified idea of nationality in the largely divided postwar nation. As Breed (2008) points out, the performances went beyond political reconciliation of conflicted tribes. These acts were performing the intimate actions of confession and forgiveness between the perpetrators and survivors, between the oppressors and the oppressed. Theater is a powerful medium that not only allows the development of consciousness toward injustice but also encourages collective reflection and action. Erel, Reynolds, and Kaptani (2017) acknowledge the transformative potential of participatory theater in their study on migrant mothers in London and how these participatory experiences prove emancipatory simply by giving these communities the capability of envisioning different reactions to challenge and ways to intervene in embodied situations. Thompson and Santiago-Jirau (2011) use theater as a motif to reiterate the same agency of transformation through their work with queer youths based in New York, wherein they propose how the "spect-actors"[1] often continue the portrayal of their roles even after they have stepped off the stage. These representations become necessary and successful in challenging the conventional understanding of identity and prevalent images of communities in the social tapestry.

An incident in February 1998 had a profound impact on the Chhara youths and led to the process of giving a formal name and shape to their theater group. Budhan Kheria of the Sabar community in West Bengal's Purulia district died in police custody, and the Chhara youths strongly empathized with Budhan's circumstances. They had witnessed police brutality, atrocities, and injustice in their daily lives. They had seen their fathers getting beaten up just as Budhan did. Their deep anguish and rising anger led them to write and stage the play *Budhan Bolta Hai*

(Budhan Speaks . . .). The play has been performed numerous times since then, and the theater group was formalized as Budhan Theatre, with the goal to "demonstrate that Chharas and other groups like them are not born criminals—they are humans with real emotions, capacities, and aspirations" (www.budhantheatre.org). The group has outlined their vision on the theater's website:

> We, at Budhan Theatre perform hard truths and real facts, no matter how disturbing, because it is in this way we connect with our history. It is in this way that we use theatre to show our people that we need to change our future. It is in this way the many people of India, from common people to mainstream society members, to policymakers, to educators/intellectuals, to government officials and beyond, may finally recognize the human needs of the Chhara community. It is in this way that we fight for dignity and social justice for all De-notified tribes of India.

Budhan Theatre's vision and mission are palpable in the themes and rhetorical techniques of the more than forty plays they have created and performed. Their style is starkly realistic, and the themes are drawn from their daily lives and also contemporary social and political issues. These include experiences of police brutality, deprivation, corruption, and exploitation of the marginalized by the society's power centers (e.g., *Budhan Speaks, Death of Pinya Hari Kale, Encounter*, and *Pata—the Tracks*) as well as issues of gender justice, forest rights, housing rights, and the right to clean drinking water (as reflected in plays such as *Ulgulan, Hamari Zindagi*, and *HallaBol*). Some other productions are based on works by the stalwarts of Indian literature, such as Mahashweta Devi (*Choli ke picche kya hai*, based on *Stan Dahini*, exposes the gender violence and struggles of lower-class women against exploitation by landlords) and Badal Sircar (*Bhoma* highlights the daily issues faced by common people on the Indian streets). Dakxin Chhara and Atish Indrekar, children's theater coordinator, actor, and theater coach at the Budhan, both have had formal training in theater and exposure to world theater. This has encouraged them to experiment with the adaptation of internationally acclaimed plays such as Jean Ganet's *La Balcon, Accidental Death of an Anarchist* by Dario Fo, and Maxim Gorky's *The Lower Depth*, molding them to reflect grim Indian realities.

The content is the key, and the actors remain authentic to the characters they are playing. It feels as if those on stage are actually living their lives in front of you. Atish notes that such content compels people to think, "as they get to know the reality they were never exposed to, the truth they never knew." There is no attempt to whitewash or sugarcoat or dilute anything. The emotions are raw, the dialogue hard hitting. There are minimal props, but the actors, all masters of their craft, use their bodies and voices to the optimum to convey the terror, brutality, and insensitivity of the oppressors on one side and the pain, anguish, and helplessness of the oppressed on the other. The chorus has a powerful role, with stirring songs and group movements accompanied by Indigenous instruments such as the dhol and everyday objects such as kitchen utensils and bottles. According to Dakxin, audiences never fail to respond when you emotionally connect with them: "They will watch if there is an emotional connection; they will think over what they have watched, discuss it with friends and family. . . . Therein lies the possibility of change." Atish recalls several incidents when members of the audience shared the deep impact the plays left on them. "Some of them admit to not being able to sleep for days after watching our plays," says Atish.

Their performances have given the members a new confidence in their own capacities for social action, and they are proud of their new identities as social action leaders. Their reach now extends much beyond their theater performances. Previous troupe members have gone on to become successful professionals in journalism and other creative industries. Short films and documentaries are their other chosen media. Some examples are Dakxin's short film *Birth*, which demands self-respect for Chhara youths, his first feature-length film, *Sameer* (2017), based on the 2008 serial bomb blasts in India, and Atish's short film *Who Am I*, which raises issues of identity and belonging. Both *Sameer* and *Who Am I* were shown at the 131st Leeds International Film Festival in the United Kingdom in November 2017. *Bulldozer* (directed by Dakxin Bajrange), a film revolving around housing rights of marginalized communities, was screened at the United Nations in 2007 and at many institutions in India.

Dakxin, Atish, and other Budhan members understand that theater can plant the seeds for change, but until the impact of the change manifests in the material lives of marginalized people, their struggle is not over. Budhan Theatre is also engaged in the rehabilitation and resettlement activities and housing rights of the Denotified Tribes and Nomadic Tribes of Ahmedabad. "Through our plays we have provided residences for two hundred marginalized families, and the soon-to-be-inaugurated complex is named 'Theatre Village'," says Dakxin with pride. The other priority for civic action for Budhan is the education of Chhara children. Budhan Theatre runs an informal community school in Chharanagar and has facilitated formal schooling for thirty-six children. They also equip Chhara girls with income-generating skills to provide better survival options and engage them in theater activities. Atish also shares their plans to expand these activities to seven other states in India.

"We have spent precious time of our lives just getting rid of the social stigma," says Dakxin. His eagerness to move to more constructive social action is palpable. The Budhan Theatre leaders will have to protect the new empowered identities of the Chhara youths against a social backlash and hierarchical power dynamics. They seem to be acutely aware of their continued struggle and are already training the second cadre of youth leaders. Today, however, they have much to celebrate and much to look forward to.

The journey of Budhan Theatre certainly shows the promise of autobiographical stories and the rewards of sharing them. Performing the stories of their history and lived realities has brought the Chharas closer as a community. The catharsis allowed by theater has shifted their self-identification from criminals to victims, and speaking out to the authorities and the larger society has further strengthened their identities as social change leaders. They have had a positive material impact on the lives of several hundred marginalized families and are now better equipped and more empowered to imagine a better world. Yet their struggle continues. The play goes on.

## Note

1 Augusto Boal coined the term *spect-actor* to symbolize the idea that everyone has the capacity to act in the "theater" of their own lives; everybody is at once an actor and a spectator and therefore "spect-actors." In the many theater forms under the Theatre of the Oppressed, the spectators have the possibility to intervene in the unfolding plot of the play and become actors to suggest a new possibility for action.

**14**

## Mirroring the Misogynistic Wor(l)d

Civic Imagination and Speech Mirroring Strategy
in Korea's Online Feminist Movement

**Donna Do-own Kim**

It's the honest thought of *foxes* to wish *her* future *husband* is
a virgin. . . . So *men*, modestly take care of your body as if it's a
precious jewel like a *gentleman* and give the precious, beautiful
gift called virginity to your future *wife*. [emphasis added]
—"The Honest Thought of Foxes," a mirroring response by a
Megalia user posted on DC Inside (Femiwiki 2017)

How do people imagine alternative social realities, and through what
process do they act upon such visions? This chapter examines the significance of "mirroring"—a parodic, gender-swapped mimicking of
misogynistic texts—in the development of Korea's feminist movement,
propelled by the online feminist community Megalia. Gender inequality
has been one of the most serious social problems in Korea; according to
the 2016 Global Gender Gap Report (World Economic Forum), it ranks
116th in gender inequality among 144 countries. Megalia, established in
August 2015, was understood as a response to misogyny both online and
offline. Its name originated from "MERS (Middle Eastern Respiratory
Syndrome) Gallery," a forum in the largely male user-based website DC
Inside (DC), where the movement was born, and Gerd Brantenberg's
novel *Egalia's Daughters: A Satire of the Sexes*, which depicts a world
where female is the normative gender. Megalia served as a key hub of
radical feminist activism, actively producing mirrorings of misogynistic
texts and leading social justice campaigns that combated issues such as
revenge pornography and hidden cameras, generating as many controversies as conversations until it finally dispersed into multiple splinter

groups at the end of 2015. However, despite its apparent dormancy, Megalia continues to symbolically prosper in discourses on equality, showcasing not only its impact but also its legacy.

While the history of Megalia is intertwined with the progression of the mirroring movement, mirroring, not Megalia, is the focus of this chapter. Megalia will be examined as the vehicle that facilitated the civic imagination (Jenkins et al. 2016) that led to remarkable solidarity and participation in Korea's feminist activism. However, because they are closely associated, Megalia's timeline provides the necessary contextual background to understand how mirroring helped foster both individual and collective empowerment. Therefore, it is from the birth of Megalia that I begin. In addition to examining digital records and existing literature, I conducted four 40- to 90-minute in-depth interviews with participants and observers of the movement.

## The Birth of Megalia

In the summer of 2015, amid the MERS outbreak, female users of the popular website DC began to collectively hold mirrors up to the country's deep-rooted misogyny. Some records claim that the mirroring movement was sparked by the flood of sexist hate speech that followed a false rumor that two Korean women suspected of MERS infection refused quarantine in Hong Kong (Singh 2016; Lee and Soep 2016), and others say it started due to speculations about male users' reactions to a scenario in which the first MERS patients were female instead of male ("Megalia" Femiwiki 2017). Both allude to two important social backdrops for the movement.

The first is the recognition of deepening misogyny within and beyond online spaces. Yoo (2015), drawing from Langton's (1993) speech act theory, explained how hate speech toward women had structurally silenced female speech in Korea. The proliferation of gender-specific slurs, such as "kimchi-girl/bitch" (*-nyeo/-nyeon*), in both traditional and new media illustrates his point. Although users claim the terms refer only to women who abuse gender roles to achieve materialistic goals, they have been used to censor the general female population. Accompanying contrasting ideals, such as "sushi-girl" (*sushinyeo*) and "right-minded-girl" (*gaenyeomnyeo*), highlight this. People used the term sushi-girl to

condemn kimchi-girls by contrasting them with the stereotypical subservient Japanese woman, with "sushi-" invoking the image of Japanese
culture. Its juxtaposition to "kimchi-" suggests that kimchi-girl/bitch
could easily be used as a negative stereotype of Korean women that all
must defend themselves against. To escape the label, women were forced
to successfully perform the idealized womanhood of the subservient yet
economically independent right-minded girl, devoid of everything its
binary pair kimchi-girl/bitch represented. In line with Yoo's analysis,
this misogynistic dichotomy rendered women silent by pressuring them
to continuously police and prove themselves against the arbitrary criteria of the kimchi-girl/bitch, becoming what Megalians called "corsets."

The second is pertinent to DC's characteristics and its relationship to
Korea's digital culture. The mirroring movement differed from previous attempts because it started "openly" across the publicly accessible
forums in the largely male user-based website DC (Jang 2016). Although
female online communities existed, most were closed, membership-only
web cafés hosted by the portal Daum. Conversely, male-based online
communities ranged from web cafés to stand-alone websites that seldom
necessitated membership and even promoted anonymity. Referring to
the participatory model of spreadable media (Jenkins, Ford, and Green
2013), Jang argued that DC's openness positively affected the spread and
impact of the mirroring movement through its accessibility and circulation. However, prior to it, the spreadable media environment had been
assisting the high visibility and active circulation of male-centric discourses, feeding into a vicious cycle of marginalization of female voices.
This spreadability meant that misogynistic culture was not bound to one
specific community. Although the notoriety of the website Ilbe[1] often
overshadows hate speech in other parts of the Korean web, even Ilbe
began as an archive of DC's popular posts (Kang 2013). Major websites'
paradoxical reactions to the growing mirroring movement called attention to how normalized misogyny had become. For instance, DC was
criticized for restricting mirrored posts and comments on the grounds
of profanity and obscenity while leaving their original versions viewable to the public. Jang (2016) explained that other platforms, such as
Facebook, reacted similarly, unearthing the discriminatory power structure in the digital sphere. It was out of such exclusion from established
platforms that the independently run web community Megalia was

**Figure 14.1.** Megalia.com's logo

born—funded, developed, moderated, and frequented by mostly female subjects who avowed to collectively fight against misogyny.

## Mirroring

Mirroring was Megalia's core strategy. With slogans like "Small penis, small mind" (*sochusoshim*) and a website logo that openly ridiculed undersized penises, Megalia promulgated its objective to tackle misogyny and its determination to do so in an aggressive manner. A post on Megalia titled "Megalia's Flaws in My Opinion" hints at the political purpose of their aggressiveness: "Megalia tries to slaughter K[Korea]-man-bugs (*hannamchoong*) with logic when K-men[2] never practiced misogyny with logic" (October 14, 2015). That is, their approach was not simply to mirror individual instances of vulgar source texts but to be a mirror of misogyny itself. Under this logic, those accusing Megalia of female chauvinism only further confirmed mirroring's potency in addressing male chauvinism: after all, a mirror only reflects the original.

The process by which mirroring instigated the civic imagination can be divided into five stages, which are not mutually exclusive:

1. The corset-identifying/countering stage, which involved individual or small-group engagement with mirrorings

2. The collective play stage, during which shared experiences and problems were identified through the generation, appropriation, and circulation of mirrorings

3. The collective action stage, in which participants moved beyond mirrorings to take organized action against the identified problems

4. The collaboratively achieved success stage, where participants' confidence and solidarity were reinforced

5. The expansion stage, where the scope of the civic imagination both broadened and segmented to encompass a wider range of issues and participants

## Corset-Identifying/Countering

The first two stages are closely tied with two key traits of mirrorings. The first key feature is playfulness. According to Douglas (1975), "All jokes have . . . [a] subversive effect on the dominant structure of ideas" (95). Mirroring evokes satirical humor; the more normalized and extreme the misogyny expressed in the original, the odder and funnier their mirrored parodies seem. Then, as in Megalia's logo, the embracement of vulgarity helps provide a sense of fun and lightness to a potentially emotionally burdensome project. Mirroring has an easy rule as well: simply swap males with females and vice versa. This makes engagement into a puzzle or game anyone could play, enhancing its spreadability. Hyunmo, a youth media creator affiliated with alternative media Misfits and ALT, said "[Mirroring was] not like 'let's thoroughly analyze and dissect the syntax' but changing the subject and the object in the stories they've heard, having great fun" (Hyunmo Koo, phone interview, July 29, 2017).

Second, mirrorings have the political purpose of fighting for gender equality. "Kimchi-man" (*kimchinam*), "right-minded man" (*gaenyeomnam*), "K-man-bug," and "god-Western-man" (godyangnam) are some examples of popular mirrored vocabulary. As the structural similarity suggests, they were coined to mirror disempowering terms such as kimchi-girl, right-minded girl, and sushi-girl. Whereas kimchi-man and right-minded man are literal mirrorings, K-man-bug is an interpretive one that mirrors how hate speech like kimchi-girl has reinforced the subordinate status of women by functioning as a policing label. On the other hand, god-Western-man, which stands as the antithesis of sushi-girl (Cheon 2015), is based on the interplay of several cultural meanings. Taken literally, the term may evoke the image of the "white savior," as "god" is internet slang commonly used to praise whatever it modifies—in this case, "Western-man." However, Megalia's glossary stresses the word's mirroring function. A sufficient mockery of kimchi-men precedes its definition, which they explain "refers not only to White males but also Black, Latino, and other males who have citizenship in the West and believe in gender equality" (Cheon). Ha (2017) suggested that the frequency of the phrase "penis size" among god-Western-man's related expressions indicates its mirroring intent to ridicule misogynistic Korean men, despite the unfortunate rhetorical reliance on the idealized imagery of the West. One can also argue that this shortcoming shows that fighting misogyny was not just *one* of the motivations behind the initial stages of the mirroring movement but *the* motivation; other social injustices were of lesser importance.

The two features combined buttress the first and second stages of the civic imagination: playfulness fueled interest, and the political undercurrent helped the generated interest keep its focus. Sejung, a feminist activist in her twenties and a member of the women's rights organization Flame Femi Action, mentioned that she thinks "'The Honest Mind of Foxes'[3] had been what really got the word out on Megalia" (Sejung Kim, phone interview, August 8, 2017). Chloe (pseudonym; phone interview, August 1, 2017), a female in her twenties who got involved in feminist activism (including a collaborative publication) through her Megalian experiences, recalled sharing funny screenshots with her friends and said that "many felt extremely gratified." Likewise, Sejung mentioned mirroring as "cider," an expression Koreans use to describe the delight of complete gratification by referring to the refreshing sensation of soda. As described, the satisfaction from blatant subversions of norms played a crucial role in the humor that drew people into mirroring. Locating the humor in mirroring involved identification of normative assumptions and connecting them to personal or projected experiences, thus having the potential to crack "corsets." This resonates with Ott and Aoki's (2001) concept of counterimagination, which refers to "endeavors to provide historically marginalized subjects with decoding strategies that recognize and empower their voices and identities, rather than excluding and diminishing them" (140) This is why I call the first stage "corset-identifying/countering," although for analysis I limit it only to relatively small-scale or sporadic forms of engagement to distinguish between larger-scale, more involved participation.

## Collective Play

The first stage morphs into the second as people begin to communicate not only about or within particular mirrorings but through and across them. By collectively playing with mirrorings as creators, distributors, and audiences, the identified "corsets" can transcend the boundary of the private and become shared experiences. According to the Korean research company Ars Praxia's research on Megalia's discourse map (Cheon 2015), fear of crime, marriage, and gaze were the penetrating emotions in mirrorings. Ars Praxia explained that when they compared this map to that of Namuwiki—Korea's most active wiki, which has repeatedly discredited mirroring (Yoon 2017)—they found the latter's dominant feelings were perplexity, contempt, and rage against the movement (Cheon 2016). This contrast shows not only the deep-rootedness misogyny the mirroring movement tried to expose and counter but the experiences and problems shared among mirroring's participants. If mirroring's playfulness and its political undercurrent helped break the prolonged silence in more private spheres, such as one's inner self or friend groups, then collective play wove together those formerly private voices into a publicly recognizable outcry, with shared experiences as the thread.

## Collective Action

Megalia and its extended members became a community, and their collective identity enabled them to pursue actions not only within but beyond the boundary of mirroring and online spaces: cleansing major news services' comment sections of misogynistic comments, archiving misogynistic posts, creating a glossary of misogynistic celebrities, organizing boycotts and protests against companies like Namyang (accused of discriminating against female employees) and Maxim (criticized for fetishizing crimes against women), crowdfunding feminist goods, and significantly contributing to the shutdown of Sora.net—Korea's largest adult website, with more than one million registered users, featuring hidden camera and up-skirt photos, revenge pornography, and under-age prostitution (Ha 2017; Jang 2016; K. Koo 2013; Singh 2016).

## Collaboratively Achieved Success

Collective action is linked to collaboratively achieved success. Here, success can also refer to more subjective achievements, like empowerment. Chloe said, "[Prior to Megalia] . . . there existed the hesitation of even talking like this and the feelings of looking weird or risking revenge. . . . [Now] there are far more rallies, which used to be rare, not just offline but even online." Likewise, Sejung said that the offline protests were "opportunities [so] that we who existed only invisibly could recognize one another and come together" and were therefore "very meaningful." These experiences of unity showed that their voices were significant and could be heard.

## Expansion

In December 2015, controversies around inclusivity toward Othered groups such as queer people and people with disabilities surged. The critical controversy that led to megalia.com's downfall was whether mirroring gay men was justifiable. Some argued that as biological males, they too have benefited from patriarchy and have exercised misogyny regardless of their sexuality. Some closeted gay men's unfaithfulness to their unknowing female partners and their use of sexually objectifying slang (e.g., "bulger" [bbollokee], which identified biological females through their protruding breasts) emerged as controversial issues. Others advocated for unity among minorities in tackling what they viewed as the source of misogyny: patriarchy. This group was critical of the former's mirroring methods, such as attempting to out unfaithful gay men and using terms such as "asshole-bugs" (ddongkkochoong). There was no simple answer to the issues raised; Gikko, one of the showrunners of Gaesung-sidae, a popular podcast dedicated to gay men, commented that while he found some of the mirrorings excessive, he thought misogyny was an urgent problem the Korean queer community needed to confront (phone interview, July 29, 2017). In the end, the adamant contenders fragmented into separate communities, such as Womad, which describes itself as existing "only for 'female human rights'" (Chanel 2017).

Although Megalia disintegrated, traces of the mirroring movement still exist in Korea's heightened interest in equality. On an interpersonal level, Chloe noted, "Now . . . people—even men—can say, 'No, you can't say that [misogynistic statement].'" In regard to policies, Sejung commented, "After women poured outside, all presidential candidates had women's issues in their ten main policies, . . . [which] had been only supplementary before." As for range, Gikko mentioned, "Currently [the] political correctness movement is extremely strong," a trend he believed surfaced in 2016. Likewise, Hyunmo attributed the rise of "pro-uncomfortablers" (*peurobulpyeolleo*; similar to social justice warriors) to the feminist wave. It could be said that mirroring's civic imagination did not disintegrate but expanded to reach a broader range of Others in Korean society.

## Conclusion: Mirroring from Then On

I have discussed how the civic imagination, inspired and buttressed by mirroring, progressed in Korea's feminist movement using the timeline of the online community Megalia as a guiding axis. In addition, I have identified five stages: (1) corset-identifying/countering, (2) collective play, (3) collective action, (4) collaboratively achieved success, and (5) expansion. The capacity to imagine alternatives both individually and collectively through this process was crucial in giving voice to the silenced and bringing forth change. Nevertheless, "alternative" and "good" are not necessarily interchangeable. People have tried to counter-mirror the mirrorings and have used "Megalia" as an insult similar to feminazi, believing it caused a gender war and male oppression. To this group, the mirroring movement's civic imagination was not so "civic," hence their appropriation of the mirroring tactic (i.e., countermirroring) to realize their version of the "civic" imagination. The varying visions of the future and related deployment of the same tactic show that the civic imagination is a process, and therefore it is by who, about what, and toward what that its ethics should be discussed. Nevertheless, the civic imagination can build a strong bridge to social change, one that inspires and empowers. As Chloe said, "Seeing the society change . . . people around me changing . . . experiencing such things with my body, I could feel there exists hope and change does occur, even if it's by small steps. . . . That lasts. . . . Wherever we scatter to live, the thought that there are people who think like this and had come together with this thought . . . [and] live somewhere, somehow more grown up [lasts]."

## Notes

1   Ilbe (*Ilganbeseutujeojangso*) is a far-right online community that has been criticized for its display and enactment of hate against social minorities (Yoon 2013).
2   "-Bugs" was often purposefully omitted to normalize the bug-like quality as a default characteristic of Korean men.
3   Opening excerpt.

## 15

## Reimagining the Arab Spring

From Limitation to Creativity

**Yomna Elsayed and Sulafa Zidani**

On June 29, 2016, a group of Egyptian high school seniors broke out in protest against the postponement of their final examinations due to an alleged exam leak. Their protest was met with violence and arrests despite the students' young ages. This was one of the very few protests that erupted in the years following the 2013 military take-over of Egypt and its violent crackdown on opposition. What stood out in this protest, however (from the sheer number of social media shares and likes), was a picture of a single high school student running away from tens of black-clad state security officers stretching out their arms to catch him. This picture was picked up by Egyptian Facebook pages (mostly those run by Egyptian young adults close in age to the young man in the picture) featuring sarcastic memes[1] and amateur remix videos. The picture soon became a rallying point; various memes were created around it, expressing the multitude of feelings it evoked in this generation of youths who came of age during the Arab Spring and its aftermath. The memes reimagined the boy in various popular culture contexts: running away from an army in *Game of Thrones* (with a caption reading "Winter Is Coming"); escaping on a hoverboard as a character in the video game *Subway Surfer,* with the police pictured as inspectors; or fleeing from officers reimagined as dancers underneath a disco ball. One meme, however, resonated most with Egyptian social media users, earning the greatest number of likes and shares among all other similarly themed memes: a picture of the boy running over (or away from) a background shot of a map of Egypt. This meme condensed in one expressive picture what many young Egyptians yearned for at the time: an escape to a better future (figure 15.1).

**Figure 15.1.** Asa7be "high school student" memes

While many see the return to authoritarianism in most of the post–
Arab Spring countries as a sign of regression, the Arab Spring uprisings
and, interestingly, the increased repression that followed have set forth
an unprecedented wave of creative requestionings and reimaginings facilitated by online technologies. Thousands of social media pages have
been created since 2011, paralleled by the rise of social media personas
and satirical vloggers. The content of these pages ranges from satires and
parodies incorporating politicians or celebrities to creative commentar-
ies on everyday life. Critiques in these spaces range from the social to
the political, sometimes within the same creative work. An edited image
on the Mawtoura (distressed) Facebook page shows the Hollywood sign
changed to read "meen mekhdé (who will you marry)?," advancing a
feminist critique of society's pressure on women to marry and its preoccupation with social status. Another image on the same page features
the *La La Land* movie poster edited to read "La, la, la, akid, akid, akid"
(No, no, no, sure, sure, sure; figure 15.2), building on the resemblance
of "La" to the word *No* in Arabic in order to mock Lebanese politician
Samir Geagea's tendency to repeat words.

To gain insight into the driving force behind these creative pages, we
interviewed fifteen of the most popular creative content producers (with
thirty thousand to fourteen million followers), page administrators, and

**Figure 15.2.** Hollywood sign and *La La Land* meme.
Mawtoura, Facebook.

their fans; we then combined these interviews with textual and visual analyses of their Facebook pages. The content of these pages included memes, GIFs, and videos covering topics ranging from sports and global and local popular culture to feminist and political commentary. While the pages differed in their levels of popularity and the type of content shared (memes, videos, or text posts), they all mixed comedy and popular culture with subversive political or social critique. The pages analyzed included Asa7be Sarcasm Society, Tamat Al-Targama (Translation Was Done), Dubsmash Egypt, Mohammed Khamis, Hesham Afifi, Seif Al-Mosalamy, Fatma Abd-ElSalam, Mawtoura, Gif7alak, and Kharabeesh. Most of the pages were Egyptian, while the last three were Lebanese, Palestinian, and Jordanian, respectively.

Notably (and unlike the pre-spring subversion, which was predominantly political), the post-spring subversion was multilayered, targeting the underlying social and economic aspects that solidify and perpetuate political oppression. Although ostensibly nonpolitical in content, these pages enacted subversive politics through creative practices such as remixing, meme creation, and Twitter hashtag campaigns. Rather than curtailing young adults' imaginative capacities, structural and semiotic limitations brought forth new and creative forms of the civic imagination, forcing young adults to reimagine the way they practiced politics.

### Limitations as Conditions for Imagination

Subversive critiques based in humor are not a new phenomenon; throughout history, they are often concomitant with religious and political oppression. François Rabelais, known for his comic masterpiece

*Gargantua and Pantagruel*, lived in sixteenth-century France, a time marked by religious and political persecution. Yet no spatial or temporal boundaries in the world could fetter or restrict Rabelais's imagination (Bakhtin 1981). Bakhtin (1981) argues that in Rabelais's world, "all limitations [were] bequeathed to the dying world, now in the process of being laughed out of existence." What were generally seen as insurmountable obstacles of power and tradition—representatives of the real world such as monks, feudal lords, judges, or kings—were treated as those who were truly limited, "absurd and doomed" (240), with a "potential . . . utterly exhausted by their pitiful reality." Gargantua and Pantagruel, on the other hand, were folkloric kings who succeeded in overcoming their limitations and were "models for unlimited human potential" (240–41).

As in the post–Arab Spring context, *Gargantua and Pantagruel* was also set up in a stifling authoritarian, religiopolitical environment, yet it managed to pass a "subversive critique" under the guise of laughter and absurdity. While state and societal repression can pose a severe threat to public expressions of dissent, this violence can push resistance to the realm of the imagination, resulting in not necessarily escapism (which is viewed as a dissipation of energy) but rather a reformulation of this energy into more creative forms that can effect change gradually. Emirbayer and Mische (1998) note, for example, that "actors who feel blocked in encountering problematic situations can actually be pioneers in exploring and reconstructing contexts of action" (1009). Rather than curtailing imagination, the existence of limitations, such as the "conflicts and challenges of social life," can be an impetus for the culturally embedded process of negotiating paths and forming projects (984). Through a "hypothesization of experience," actors can reconfigure their inherited schemas of the past by generating alternative responses to problematic situations (Emirbayer and Mische 1998).

Several of our participants credited their turn to comedy to the idea that when all else failed, they could laugh at the situation. Nadia, a young fan of sarcastic pages, attributed their popularity to the fact that "people [were] fed up . . . of talking about problems in the same old ways." Amin from Asa7be noted that the polarization/bias that overtook the scene in Egypt following the uprisings and especially in the post-Morsi era has driven them to look for other methods of delivery:

"When [Sisi] comes out saying something nonsensical, and I say this is ridiculous, people would say, 'You should not criticize him; he is the one who saved us.' But if I got something similar from Morsi and Mubarak and showed them next to it, the message will reach people better." Saleh from Kharabeesh said they resorted to humor during the sensitive time of the Arab uprisings as an effective way of bringing up politics and crossing an otherwise red line without offending anyone. Sometimes, however, humor was frustrating for fans when it bordered on sarcasm.[2] Mawtoura explained that many followers do not understand sarcasm and therefore take personal offense at sarcastic posts about their favorite politicians or celebrities. However, humor combined with visual depictions and popular art generally acted as a gateway to otherwise closed-off worlds. As prominent New York illustrator Robert Grossman (2012) proposed, "The ever abundant productions of imagination—art, poetry, music and the like—are our real means of experiencing those other possible or impossible worlds" (113).

## Breaking Sanctity through Imagination

In today's digital age, memes, as visual depictions, act as vehicles for jokes and tacit messages. As a blend of popular culture and politics (Shifman 2013), memes are "visual shortcuts" that can create "complex narratives about times past that bear upon the present" (Hristova 2013, 93). In the post–Arab Spring context, by utilizing memes, youths were able to criticize previously sanctified figures of social, political, or religious authority. Simply superimposing the image of Sisi over a character being ridiculed in a movie opened the door to the possibility of criticism (Elsayed 2016). For example, in 2017, following a sharp devaluation of the Egyptian pound, an Asa7be meme surfaced with Sisi's face placed over that of a beaten-up bridegroom alongside a sad, scruffy bride. Viewers were able to recognize Egypt as the scruffy bride, and the smile on Sisi's face despite his beaten-up state alluded to inside jokes about his mental state and general incompetency.

This soon spread into a technique and a common language whereby youths passed off their criticism as jokes without explicitly feeling that they were being political, all while experimenting with sanctity. This became evident in the comment sections, which constituted spaces for

**Figure 15.3.** Sisi as a beaten-up bridegroom: Asa7be meme

scaffolding and participation (Jenkins 2015), where fans responded with their own memes.

On the eve of two terrorist church bombings in Cairo, Marcus from Dubsmash Egypt edited a version of a popular, ominous video of Muslim clerk Sheikh Sha'rawy addressing Hosni Mubarak, saying, "If you were our destiny, may God guide you, and if we were your destiny, may God help you get through it." Marcus pasted a picture of Sisi over Mubarak and fan-subbed it: "If you were our destiny, then f\*\*k you, and if we were your destiny, then f\*\*k you too." By condemning the Sisi failed administration, with this brief post, the page turned from entertaining content to political satire that went beyond what was considered a "safe" condemnation of terrorism (Elsayed 2018). Users recognized that a line was crossed; despite agreeing with the political message, they disapproved of using the sheikh as a trope for passing insults. In response, Marcus commented, "We try to spread awareness that no one is God and no one is above sarcasm. The video was targeting Sisi in the first place, but Skeikh Sha'rawy is not God either. We get many angry comments. . . . I try to diffuse them with sarcasm." Subtle visual humor worked to open the possibility of criticism without openly criticizing sanctified figures; it also helped develop their young audience's critical thinking skills.

## Imagination as a Pathway to Critical Thinking

While memes served to deliver punchlines and immediate messages, remix videos worked to deliver more layered messaging that could tap into the past, present, and future of the topics discussed. Generally seen as a form of projection into the future, imagination also entails an iterational aspect situated in a process of reflectivity over past and present problems that cannot be resolved with habitual solutions but rather require a "free play of possibilities in a state of non-involvement with respect to the world of perception or of action" (Emirbayer and Mische 1998, 989). Reflectivity in creative youths' remix videos focused on analyzing past and present mainstream productions. It signified maturation on the one hand but also enabled participants to express their frustrations with a persisting system of semiotic and physical oppression through the critique of its cultural productions (Elsayed 2018; figure 15.4).

By cutting videos, mainly of mainstream popular culture, into frames and dissecting them, vloggers and remix artists embedded multiple layers of criticism into their remixes and/or video analyses. Khamis, known for his analyses of TV shows and music videos, suggested that the role of his videos was to help people develop "critical thinking skills, lower their tolerance for mediocrity, and teach them to look for substantial content, such that content producers would either adjust themselves or die out." Fatma, a female vlogger, also suggested that the role of creative content producers was to use their imaginations to "help people stop

**Figure 15.4.** Frame from the widely ridiculed (once admired) historical TV show *Qutuz*

**Figure 15.5.** Female vlogger Fatma's video about women-targeted ads

and see things they do not see." Referencing her video about women-targeted ads and how they conform to traditional gender roles (figure 15.5), she noted, "Everything in the approach of detergent ads dates back to the eighties: women are the ones targeted. It's offensive! While the outcome is good in terms of color and professionality, the content is dated; there's no innovation. NGOs working on women's rights are busy teaching women in villages, which is great, but nobody is helping the contemporary [Arab] woman. She's worn out and does not even notice it."

Interestingly, fans did not describe these creative works as intentionally critical but rather viewed their creativity as producers' means of "getting more laughs and followers." This demonstrates how humor worked as a shortcut through affective, not cognitive, channels. By viewing critical thinking as a practice rather than a message, affect can work as a means for capturing and maintaining attention whereby the video or song discussed is no longer an end in itself but rather a training ground for paying attention to details and layers of the message. It can be argued that such content falls within the realm of critical reflectivity, which plays a significant role in perspective transformation in critical thinking and adult learning (Garrison 1991; Mezirow 1981). Serious messages, however, were masked with a "just for fun" disclaimer.

## "Just for Fun"

In their "About" sections, Facebook pages are typically described along the lines of "Here, farce talks" or "Fun for everyone." Kareem affirmed the entertainment purpose of his page, suggesting that "everyone on social media comes to escape real-world problems to live in the virtual world. . . . Yes, they sometimes come for news, but mostly sarcasm wins." Mahmood from Gif7alak suggested that in the Arab World, "we have a lot of news, a lot of seriousness, we're always in drama, and we lack a space to breathe and laugh." Entertainment was not only an end but a tactic as well. Ashraf noted that they used "just for fun" as a response to angry commentators. Marcus emphasized that they aimed to raise awareness through sarcasm, yet in the same breath, he added, "We are very trivial."

Fatma noted that while social media can serve as an escape from the daily pressures, they nevertheless open people's minds to possibilities not readily visible in their everyday lives: "The daily routine makes people not want to overwork their brains or change their habits. So it's our job, people whose job is to imagine, to help them pause and see the things they do not see. So at least there's hope for change, that life can be easier." Most of our interviewees emphasized imagination (including the act of imagining) as a means of empowerment. According to many of them, imagination plays a powerful role in changing reality for the better. Saleh saw part of Kharabeesh's role as showing people a better world to aid their imagination: "Through seeing it in [creative] content, people become able to imagine a better situation. Once people can imagine it, they will try to reach it and implement it."

Memes and videos worked to carry a multitude of people's contributions and creativity over the same trend. Nadia noted that the most pleasurable thing about memes was when "everyone, fans and followers, started adding [to] them." Soon, she noted, she would be able to use memes in conversations with friends, making social media content a constituent part of their conversational cultures.

## Conclusion

While not explicitly painting alternatives, creating memes and GIFs and remixing videos were acts of learning by doing, thereby slowly working to deconstruct the sanctity of revered figures of authority and morality. The very act of reimagining one's own country and culture and receiving responses with similar memes made sarcasm a shared practice and taught fans how to think and express themselves in memes that were funny and redemptive not only in their sardonic humor but also in their clandestine shared language of cumulative jokes constituting their common history. The limitations imposed on their material acts of physical or semiotic protest pressed their imaginations into artistic channels of creative humor and digital participation. To many, these creators' lifestyles may be described as escapist, as they sleep during the day and spend most of their nights editing videos or images. Nevertheless, they wake up to thousands of shares, comments, and contributions that no longer fit that notion of escapism but rather point to something more far-reaching and collaborative: a shared diligent practice of reimaging a space for expression and freedom of thought wherein they can set the rules.

The "just for fun" disclaimers say more than they purport: they set limits that dissuade the older, more scornful generation repulsed by the waste of time and unrestrained sarcasm from participating and invite the younger generation to have fun and express itself. While the lack of emphasis on politics may be read as an inability to grapple with the oppressive political reality through direct conflict, it can also be read as a deeper understanding of the ramifications of direct conflict gained through the experience of the five years that followed the Arab Spring. As Khairy, a fan of these pages suggested, "Many people are playing the game of time. Egypt's demographics are in favor of the younger generation. There seems to be common agreement that radical change would do more harm than good and that it must be gradual. So many people are in survival mode right now." After realizing that their struggle for freedom and innovation would be more prolonged and run deeper than they first expected, Arab youths have resorted to the realm of imagination, wherein they can reflect on as well as project a different reality. In the words of Mawtoura, "If we don't imagine a better country, we would have left it a long time ago."

## Notes

1  We define a meme as a "fundamental cultural unit" passed from one individual to another, a carrier of information, or "a combination of a picture and a tacit concept linked to the picture" (Coscia 2013, 102).

2  We distinguish between humor and sarcasm, where we consider the latter to be a more ambiguous, less polite form of humor.

# 16

## DIY VR

Google Cardboard's Handmade Approach to
Imagining the Future of Immersive Technology

**Gabriel Peters-Lazaro**

### The Spherical Gaze

Gazing around the central courtyard of the school where I teach—
University of Southern California's School of Cinematic Arts—I notice
archways, palm trees, and a fountain. When I look more closely at the
architecture, I see surprising jagged breaks in what should be the perfectly circular edges of the fountain and the vertical lifts of the columns
supporting the arches. In fact, I find these misalignments and breakages
more engrossing than the intended symmetry and sheen of the place;
they seem to offer a point of entry for alternative visions that aren't quite
so neat and tidy. After I've had my fill of the view, I lower my hands
from my face, removing the rudimentary virtual reality (VR) headset
I've been holding to my eyes, and feel a bit of that same disconnect and
misalignment now in my real world, and I like it. I'm sitting in a swivel
chair in my office, just a few hundred yards from the courtyard where I
created this immersive digital image with the help of my iPhone and an
app, but there's a sense that I've just stepped out of one reality and into
another. I've never experienced anything quite like it. And it's all the
more remarkable because I had the experience using a $10 contraption
made of cardboard and rubber bands that I could have made myself.

The contraption is Google Cardboard, a VR platform introduced
in 2014 amid a cyclical revival and interest in all things VR. Unlike
other emerging VR platforms of its moment, Cardboard was meant to
be cheap, easy, and accessible; rather than building and selling the hard-
ware themselves, Google published a set of specifications that allowed

anyone with access to a few low-cost materials and a smartphone to create a VR viewer that facilitated head-tracking immersive media experiences such as the one described above. In this chapter, I suggest that Google Cardboard can be understood as a tangible aspect and tool of the civic imagination in the ways that it supports a sense of agency in and around the processes of technological innovation. This chapter is largely speculative because I have yet to see this particular tool applied to explicitly civic endeavors, but by looking closely at the materials, affordances, and distinguishing characteristics of the Cardboard platform, I aim to identify qualities that are important to supporting the civic imagination and to better understand how we might recognize, plan for, and facilitate such windows of opportunity in the future.

## Agency in Innovation

As a VR platform, Cardboard is enmeshed in a complex lineage of claims around empathy, immersion, and transcendence. Without attempting a comprehensive gloss of the field, it is helpful to render a few broad strokes about the history of VR and the moment at which Cardboard emerged. As technologies of representation and attendant modes of storytelling emerge and evolve within global media culture, they are bound to influence the ways in which we conceive of imagination and our potential to translate it into a shareable experience. Since its conception in the 1960s, VR technology has traversed several cycles of enthusiasm and disappointment and has tended to exist just beyond the horizon of mass attainability. Adi Robertson and Michael Zelenko's "Voices from a Virtual Past" (2014) compiled oral history provides a good sense of the historical efforts of the people and institutions that have worked to bring these tools into reality and helps counteract some of the contemporary amnesia and erasure that happens in the shadows cast by the high-power light of current marketing and buzz. And Oliver Grau (1999) does excellent work toward situating the experiences and affordances of VR tech within a historical context, arguing that the totalizing visual experience of virtual reality and its implications of otherworldly transcendence evolve from creative traditions stretching back into antiquity.

For the purposes of this piece, I am interested in Cardboard less for its strengths or weaknesses as a virtual reality tool and more for its accessible character and those qualities by which I believe it nurtures a sense of agency in its users and, in turn, how we might understand that agency as an important component of civic imagination and engagement. Ethan Zuckerman (2016) describes the potential for low-cost civic participation facilitated by digital media to increase voice and civic agency. He provides a framework for understanding how the practices of digital media, such as writing computer code, can contribute to shifting cultural and social norms. He gives the example of political theorist Anthea Watson Strong's work at Google and how she "focuses on reducing the cost of participation, ensuring that Google searches provide citizens with the information they need to find a polling place or a town meeting" (57). Google Cardboard may not intervene in civic participation so directly, yet it shares some of these qualities for enhanced participation and amplification of voice within the cycles of production of consumer-targeted media devices.

## The Cardboard Experience

Google invites users into the Cardboard experience with the following statement on their website: "Get it, fold it and look inside to enter the world of Cardboard. It's a VR experience starting with a simple viewer anyone can build or buy." Rudimentary and aspirational, Google Cardboard requires an investment of imagination to serve its full potential; it is a step on a path toward a future vision of immersive media experiences, not an end. Its qualities might not appear explicitly civic, yet much of the experience and action it facilitates closely parallels the types of engagements we see as key to the civic imagination; it creates a collective site of aspiration and asks participants to lend their energy and efforts toward the realization of an emergent goal. The promise and progress of virtual reality have much in common with archetypal movements of political progress that we understand as emblematic of the civic imagination; the path is long, spans multiple generations, and works toward the realization of a new and better world being born from this one. And just as the machinations and evolutions of politics can at times seem beyond the realm and reach of everyday citizens, so too can the developments of consumer technologies seem to place their users into semipassive positions, left to make do with whatever corporate offerings come their way.

The Cardboard platform has gone through two revisions, but the experience has stayed basically the same. Users can download and follow instructions to build their own viewers, or since these instructions are also available to and targeted at manufacturers, users can choose from a wide selection of low-cost prebuilt cardboard viewer kits from third-party suppliers. The simplest Cardboard systems are literally made of cardboard, along with a few other items, including Velcro and rubber bands; the most technically advanced aspects of a cardboard system are the two lenses needed for proper viewing and the user-supplied smart-phone. At the time of writing, one could order a basic viewer online from Knox Labs for $7. More expensive viewers are made from plastic and may have better-quality lenses and mechanisms for holding the smartphone in place, but they follow the same basic design. In all cases, a user installs special Cardboard-compatible apps on her smartphone device, launches a given app, inserts her device into the Cardboard viewer, and holds the viewer up to her face, blocking out ambient light and peripheral vision so that the magnified image of the phone's screen fills a large percentage of her field of view. The smartphone's built-in accelerometer tracks head movements, allowing users to look around at whatever content they are viewing. A simple button on the side of the viewer triggers limited interactions and navigation within the experience depending on the design of the application.

The material nature of the Cardboard platform provides tangible opportunities for agency, as it can be a tool for translating imagination into real-world shareable objects. Cardboard itself—the mundane papery material, not the platform—is a resilient and inviting medium for imagination. Many of us can reach back to memories of childhood and the forts, spaceships, and time machines we built and the sense of agency experienced through making a significant, observable, actionable change within our physical environments in a way that allowed space for others to join, play, and participate in imaginative experiences. This kind of tangible play shares similarities with observations and links Lissa Soep makes in her afterword to Jenkins, Shresthova et al. (2016) between the DIY nature of transmedia practices and civic agency: "Fundamental to the whole concept of participatory politics is a transfer of agency from formal institutions, recognized elites, and sanctioned protocols over to young people who can work in less hierarchical and more decentralized ways to gain attention and bring about change. This process of gaining attention and sparking change is a kind of making in itself, and often requires transmedia storytelling to accomplish" (420). The same spirit underlies the use of cardboard and fuels the potential of the Cardboard platform as a vehicle for the civic imagination.

Another example in which cardboard served as a material of imagination but has already demonstrated explicit positive social outcomes is the case of *Caine's Arcade*, a short documentary film about a boy's home-made arcade that led to a global movement. When he was nine years old, Caine Monroy built a wildly creative cardboard arcade that inspired the production of this short documentary film that was viewed all over the world and eventually led to the creation of the nonprofit organization Imagination.org. *Caine's Arcade* demonstrates the power of imagination as an organizational impetus. For the civic imagination to take place, you have to be able to see your own potential to make changes in the world. By providing an entry into VR through a material that feels supremely graspable and mutable, the Cardboard platform gives a sense of participation and agency to the development of future technology and potentially to new forms of visual and immersive language through which we will reimagine and reshape our visions of ourselves and our world.

I have brought Cardboard into my classes at the University of Southern California and into workshops I have conducted there for professional media makers visiting from international locations. The novelty of such an immersive media experience paired with the simplicity of the device consistently puts users into an open-minded state that allows for fun. This state of being is a useful starting place for the civic imagination, and the most readily accessible Cardboard apps harness this potential for new ways of seeing the world. I have found that the best introduction to the use of Cardboard is the free Google Street View app, which though mainly used for geography and mapping, has a built-in spherical image tool that uses a smartphone's built-in camera to stitch together multiple images into a fully immersive visual sphere. This is how I created the experience of the School of Cinematic Arts courtyard. When you view these spheres within the Cardboard viewer, your visual experience is as though you are standing at the point where the images were created, and you are able to look up and down and all around you. In concept, the process is simple enough, but it constitutes a new way of representing the world and one's place within it and a new way of sharing that experience with others. My photosphere of the courtyard has been viewed 151,250 times as of this writing. It has reached more people than anything else I have ever authored and shared online. In and of itself, such an experience may not change the world, but any new invitations to imagine, share, and shape worldviews can be seen as potential tools for the civic imagination.

One communal result of the kind of excitement engendered by the Google Cardboard experience can be seen online in the Reddit community r/GoogleCardboard. As of this writing, the r/GoogleCardboard subreddit has 29,322 subscribers. A sticky post (one that maintains its position at the top of the forum rather than being displaced by newer posts) from Reddit user faduci, one of the forum moderators, provides answers to "basic cardboard questions" such as "What is the cheapest (used from eBay) phone that works?" The answers support the notion that people drawn to the Cardboard experience are looking for low economic barriers to entry and that the community values and supports members who may not arrive already in possession of a powerful smartphone. Other posts in the forum cover some of the same ground in terms of recommended viewers, smartphones, and apps, though there are also posts from developers looking for feedback on their own experience designs and from teachers looking for advice about how to integrate Cardboard into classroom experiences.

Google's product called Expeditions is targeted directly at teachers and promises to give them the ability to lead virtual field trips to "virtually anywhere" (Google Expeditions 2017). The technology is packaged in kits that include a viewer and phone for each student and a tablet from which the teacher can guide the experience. Kits start at $4,000 for a ten-student package. Though the cost is high and I do not personally see this route as the most exciting aspect of the Cardboard ecology, it is worth imagining how such a group activity could serve the goals of an activist community harnessing the civic imagination for their world-changing work. Expeditions allows users to create and curate their own tours through real and imagined spaces. Although the primary intention is to create tours using documentary photospheres linked with real ge-ographies, nothing in the system stops people from creating imaginative photospheres that mash up real and fictional elements to create purely aspirational spaces and link them together in sequence with narratives that inspire change.

The more common types of content available and popular on the Cardboard platform tend to fall into the categories of games, preren-dered experiences, and 360-degree video. (I should note that one could argue that all of these types of experiences are not true virtual reality because they do not allow full interaction with their depicted worlds. However, popular usage has deemed the umbrella of the term *VR* large enough to encompass all such experiences.) Games are self-explanatory and a mainstay of VR technology. Cardboard offers only limited game-playing experiences because of its rudimentary input systems and head tracking. Prerendered experiences that harness computer graphic de-signs but are not wholly responsive to user movement and feedback can present immersive spectacle experiences but are labor intensive to create and appear in rather limited quantity. The 360-degree video and images offer some of the best opportunities for using a Cardboard headset to step into another place and experience the world from a new perspective. There are also many low-cost and easy-to-use tools for cre-ating such content, including the free apps described above as well as 360-degree-capable video and still cameras from established manufac-turers such as Ricoh and GoPro but also from new and emerging players such as Rylo and Insta360.

## VR Content

Within the world of VR, content creators are already focusing on creat-ing content, including 360-degree video, with explicit social and civic missions. Nonny de la Peña and Chris Milk, for example, have been innovative in the field and created early VR works that brought visceral attention to such issues as the Syrian refugee crisis and the fight against Ebola in Africa, respectively. Such examples represent the work of large teams of creative professionals with significant financial and techno-logical resources behind them. In some cases, the outcomes of their efforts can be experienced on a Cardboard headset, but other times they require (or simply perform better on) more high-powered and costly VR rigs. Still, Google Cardboard is not the only instance of a more grass-roots DIY approach to VR.

Collectives of artists and researchers are modeling more democratic approaches to the tools and practices of VR that hint at wider applications for the civic imagination. EleVR is a collective of researchers who embrace a noncommercial experimental approach and share their findings widely. Hyphen-Labs, an interaction studio, created a VR experience called "Neurospeculative AfroFeminism" that premiered at Sundance in 2017 and that used VR to create a speculative vision of an Afrofuturist feminist technology inspired by the work of Octavia Butler and others.

Part of what is exciting about efforts such as these is the way they activate new creative networks, bringing together artists, scientists, and technologists to actively imagine and create the future together. Such practices resonate with those of the civic imagination and demonstrate how emerging media technologies such as VR can serve a positive function not only as literal devices for creation and experience but as inspirations and jumping-off points for new perspectives and new expectations for what media can be and for who gets to participate and shape the new pathways of the culture.

The flipside concern is the prospect that after a brief period of openness and possibility, the existing industrial power structures of traditional and dominant media forms will simply co-opt, reassert, and reinscribe the values of the status quo within the field of VR. There is real potential for VR to be a powerful tool of the civic imagination; it represents an opportunity for a new generation of citizens to develop their voices and visions in new ways and to create fantastically immersive experiences that share their vision in whole new ways. It is just important that we do not delude ourselves about who is being reached, who is being creative, and who is profiting from the efforts. The Cardboard platform represents an excellent way to create an inviting sense of participation that adds to a sense of agency rather than detracting from it. For now, Google continues to support and promote the Cardboard platform and compatible app development, though that seems likely to change in the face of successive generations of VR tech. Cardboard is still an evocative and inviting example of technological imagination that can help us think about the kinds of values and opportunities we want to design, promote, and make space for and how such choices contribute to the development of civic identity and agency.

Any time we can connect our civic imaginations with real-world objects that we can hold and share and use as a conduit between each other and our ideas, we will be moving the process forward. Thinking about the hands-on, low-cost inviting nature of Cardboard can help us keep looking for more objects and sites of imagination that can influence and inflect the otherwise walled-off corporatized approaches that hew to narrower forms of action and participation. We should always keep questioning the tools and understand that this investigative critical work within the shifting fields of media technology is a skill set that well aligns with civic imagination. Challenging ourselves to learn new forms of expression and to contribute to their openness and accessibility strengthens our organizational potentials and may open up new vehicles for the stories, ideas, and movement building that can arise from the imaginations of civic actors.

## PART IV

# How Do We Forge Solidarity with Others with Different Experiences Than Our Own?

In the Freirean framework introduced in the previous section, dominant narratives deny the humanity of "the other," justifying oppression until revolution breaks the chains of the process. By contrast, forging alliances across difference is a necessary step for meaningful social change. While aspects of this process may resonate with radical politics and the kinds of work described by Max Haiven and Alex Khasnabish in *The Radical Imagination* (2014), we do not frame the civic imagination as necessarily radical. Our desire to create a shared space where different communities may communicate their hopes for the future requires us to be open to a broader range of ideological perspectives. We are seeking to find the shared ideals that may make it possible to work through differences and challenge historic privileges; we err on the side of inclusion, seeing the free play of the imagination as one way by which we may lower the stakes in current conflicts and work toward long-term solutions that everyone might be able to live with.

The chapters in this section represent a variety of approaches to the challenges of building solidarity. They demonstrate how the sensibilities and emotional affordances of popular culture can inform strategies of political activism and how even the apparently objective truth of scientific research is not necessarily enough to forge solidarity among groups that accept the same facts. The narratives from which understanding emerges and the narratives that are constructed and deployed for civic purposes all play an important part in the emergence of solidarity among individuals and groups who might otherwise remain disparate, unaware, or uncaring of each other's struggles.

In chapter 17, Stephen Duncombe describes his work with various activist groups and the lessons they have learned from popular cultural outings and analyses. Duncombe helps these groups understand the human needs being satisfied by popular culture experiences that might otherwise fall outside their own habitus or seem at odds with their agendas. He suggests that even if you find something problematic, you can still open yourself to why it is appealing and possibly find something good to incorporate into your civic practices. Duncombe draws on his firsthand observation that activists tend to self-impose barriers between what they see as their social change practices and the entertainments that they might otherwise enjoy in their personal lives.

In chapter 18, Sam Ford argues that another pop cultural practice, pro wrestling, provides unique opportunities for participation and solidarity among groups that might otherwise be left out of larger political debates. Ford traces historical examples where politics and the pageantry of wrestling interconnect as a way of understanding contemporary controversies surrounding Donald Trump's use of violent imagery to define his relationship with the press. Ford is especially interested in how wrestling narratives can and often do shift in response to audience feedback. The negotiations between the wrestling franchise and its fans offer a productive model for new kinds of solidarity and new forms of compromise.

The shifting meanings of fictional violence are also an important part of chapter 19, in which Rebecca Wanzo describes the comic book hero Ms. Marvel as a model for twenty-first-century values. Ms. Marvel is a complicated character, relaunched within the Marvel superhero universe in 2014 with a young Muslim American character, Kamala Khan, stepping into the role. Wanzo describes a historical relationship in which superheroes represent the values and interests of the state in their use of physical violence. Ms. Marvel's relationship to violence and to the state is more complicated. She is reluctant to fight but willing to do so when necessary for the defense of the vulnerable, even if that defense puts her at odds with the policies of the state. Ms. Marvel represents a stance from which values and actions are bigger than group identity and national alignment and a way to understand one's personal responsibility to the well-being of others.

In chapter 20, joan miller also examines narratives of violence and the ways they spill into the real world in her exploration of the #GamerGate phenomenon. She argues that in the face of some gains in equality for marginalized communities, those who see themselves as being displaced within video gaming communities have joined together in a concerted backlash steeped in violent rhetoric and action. She traces the narratives and ideologies of #GamerGate backward and forward in time, illustrating the potencies of problematic narratives and their persistent power to divide in the face of other examples of increasing solidarity.

Coming to the conversation from a different direction but also underlining the potential of narrative to overcome division, in chapter 21, Candis Callison looks at the challenges of crafting fact-based narratives around issues of climate change. In the face of an issue that threatens the well-being of groups all over the world, Callison details both the necessity and the difficulty of building bridges and forming solidarity. In her account, even when groups are united in their understanding of facts, the narratives through which they make sense of and interpret those facts can impede their potential to take action together. Moreover, she argues that scientists should be better at adapting their vernacular to the narrative sensibilities of potential allies.

Finally, in chapter 22, Rachel E. Moran and Thomas J Billard argue that brand identity can be a powerful tool for participation and solidarity through networked practices. They focus on the iconic nature of the National Park Service (NPS) brand and the particular resonance of the Smokey Bear character as resources for popular resistance in the early days of the Trump administration. In a literal sense, Smokey and the NPS brand are subordinate to the power of the executive branch and the president at its top. But the brand and its icon carried popular meanings that were not easily realigned to a new agenda, offering symbolic resources that could be used to identify and protest potential shifts in the agency's mission. Popular identification with Smokey Bear made him a powerful symbol in struggles over environmental policy.

The characters, images, stories, and tropes of popular culture offer us opportunities to humanize, contextualize, and understand people who we would otherwise never have a chance to know and care about. They offer us ways to see that the gains of others don't have to mean losses of our own. By connecting the narratives of the past with the complexities of the present and our aspirations for the future, popular culture can give us models that unite us and stories that invite greater participation and solidarity among those who may not realize the alignment of their causes and interests. The authors in the next section expand on these notions and show how recognition and the sense of solidarity that grows from it can support the development of larger communities of action that can organize and work for change at ever larger scales.

## 17

## Training Activists to Be Fans

## "The Moral Equivalent" of Pop Culture

### Stephen Duncombe

In 1906, the American pragmatist philosopher and early psychologist William James delivered a lecture to pacifist students at Stanford University in California. The purpose of his talk was as much political as it was academic, as James, a pacifist himself, was helping the student activists strategize how their antiwar message might resonate with more people. His advice was surprising. He explained that instead of just telling people how bad war is, pacifist activists needed to understand what is *good* about it.

Yes, war is bloody and brutal, he acknowledged, but "I will refuse to speak of the bestial side of the war-regime (already done justice to by many writers) and consider only the higher aspects of militaristic sentiment" (James 1910, 464). James pointed out that good people support bad wars for all sorts of understandable, and even noble, reasons: self-sacrifice, camaraderie, solidarity, honor, bravery, and patriotism. (Today we might add a job, technical training, and a way out of one's hometown.) Speaking of potential appeals to a war supporter, James went on to state, "Showing war's irrationality and horror is of no effect upon him. The horrors make the fascination. War is the *strong life*; it is life in *extremis*" (James 2008, n.p.).

James argued that if pacifists wanted their message to have a broader appeal, they had to move past simple condemnation and "enter more deeply into the aesthetical and ethical point of view of their opponents" (James 2008, n.p.). His plea was for pacifism through empathy with the other side. Too often, James warned, activists do not respect that their adversaries believe what they believe, and do what they do, for good reasons. The first step in converting warmongers into peace lovers was to understand—and respect—them. But James didn't stop with empathy. After we acknowledge the complicated and sometimes contradictory justifications and rationalizations of those we disagree with, the job of the activist, he argued, is to create a "moral equivalent of war": an activity or institution that fulfills the same needs for people that war does— the *strong life*, life in *extremis*—minus the killing. In brief, James argued that it is not enough to merely condemn; we need to understand popular needs and desires and then reroute them—to "move the point," as he put it (James 2008, n.p.).

So what might a "moral equivalent to war" look like? James's idea was to create an army—with discipline, fellowship, and a sense of purpose— but instead of being targeted toward killing, its objective would be the betterment of society. US governmental programs such as the Civilian Conservation Corps during the 1930s, the Peace Corps in the 1960s, and AmeriCorps today enacted this idea—alas, none at nearly the scale and funding of the US military. However, James's idea of a moral equivalent can be applied to more than just war. It is a political way to think about the psychological principle of sublimation, a rechanneling of popular desire from something harmful into something productive. Learning from James, we start with the assumption that people are getting something they need—something rewarding and meaningful—from the things in which they invest their time and money, things like popular culture.

Along with the activist artist Steve Lambert, I run the Center for Artistic Activism (C4AA), a research and training institute located in New York. For nearly a decade, we have helped activists create more like artists and artists strategize more like activists. At the core of the C4AA are our workshops: intensive multiday trainings where we work directly with activists and artists. We've worked with Muslim American activists in New York, Iraq War veterans in Chicago, undocumented youth immigration activists in San Antonio, mothers of incarcerated youths in Houston, transgender artists and activists across Eastern and Western Europe, sex workers in South Africa and Ireland, artists working on anticorruption campaigns in West Africa, public health organizers in Kenya, Macedonian Queer and Roma rights activists, dissident artists from Russia, Pakistan, and China, and more. To date, we have trained more than one thousand people across the United States, in fourteen countries, and on four continents.

In our trainings, we incorporate James's century-old wisdom into contemporary practice. As part of our workshops, we take everyone out one evening for a "cultural event." When we announce this, most people assume we will partake in some sort of culture that is explicitly political, something that activists are *supposed* to do with their free time, like going to a poetry reading in support of domestic workers or watching a hard-hitting documentary on strip-mining.

This is not what we do.

Instead, we find out what all the nonactivists and nonartists are doing on a Saturday night in the area and go do that. We go to malls, bowling alleys, wax museums, casinos, wrestling matches, high school football games, nail salons, megachurches, and fast food restaurants; we watch horror movies, read celebrity magazines, and play Monopoly. We engage in all sorts of "cultural experiences"—our only rule is that it has to be popular.

Many activists and artists have an adverse reaction to popular culture, at least in their official position *as* artists and activists. This is not to say that artists and activists are not also fans of pop culture—they frequently are—but too often they have learned to separate and segregate the things they enjoy in their leisure time from the "serious work" they do to change the world. Furthermore, since pop culture in a liberal capitalist society is often synonymous with commercial culture, it is frequently thought of as part of the problem: a distraction from "real" issues at best and ideological garbage celebrating the rich and the privileged, the sensational, and the violent at worst. And in all cases, it is considered a culture that exists primarily to generate profit. In authoritarian regimes, it is no better. Popular culture is often synonymous with officially sanctioned culture and is seen as instrumental in reinforcing the values and perspectives of the ruling order.

As an alternative to popular culture, and often in opposition, artists and activists proudly create their own cultures: countercultures, subcultures, alternative cultures. As cultural expression, this is to be celebrated; as a political strategy, it is problematic. A subculture, by definition, is marginal culture that appeals to a minority of the population. In order to bring about democratic social change, however, you need a majority on your side, and to reach this majority, you need to be able to understand their passions and speak their languages. Pop culture—as *popular* culture—can help activists and artists do this.

We ask the workshop participants to suspend whatever prejudices they may have against pop culture and enter these cultural spaces with curiosity, not judgment. We encourage them to open their eyes and minds and try to understand the needs and desires being met through this patently popular culture. We want them to become anthropologists for the night, studying "the natives" in their natural habitat—including the parts of themselves that are "native" fans as well. Then, the next morning, after a night of pop cultural study and guilt-free enjoyment, we reconvene and talk. First, we discuss what people saw and heard and felt, throwing out observations and writing them on a whiteboard or sheets of paper taped to the walls. After thirty or so minutes of this, we turn to applications, asking how we might use these insights in our own creative activist practices. What might a moral equivalent to this pop culture look like? How do we *move the point* toward social change?

A few years ago, we were working with Iraq Veterans Against the War (IVAW). Since this was an antiwar activist group made up of veterans who had served in the War in Iraq, it was as good a test case as any of James's theories of a moral equivalent to war. As part of our workshop in Chicago with the IVAW leadership, we took the activists out to see the Cubs play (and, unsurprisingly for that season, lose) at Wrigley Field. The next morning, we discussed what people had noticed. Folks first commented on how boring the baseball game was—yet also how much fun they had. They observed how people would show up with jerseys and hats to mark their allegiance to the team and signal their loyalty to other fans. They noticed how the game was broken up by predictable events: the call to the Pledge of Allegiance, the routine change of sides each inning, the intermittent "da-da-de-dum-de-dum Charge!" motif played on the organ, and the seventh inning stretch (made surreal in my hometown of New York by the Yankees' ritualistic playing of the Village People's gay hang-out anthem "YMCA"). Broadening our view a bit, we discussed the importance of rituals, uniforms, and allegiance to a group.

It was then time to *move the point* and discuss how we might apply these lessons to their activism. We began by talking about the importance of uniforms. It was a touchy topic for service people who had just spent years in uniform fighting in a war they abhorred, but they recognized how essential it was to be able to visually identify a friend or foe. We discussed how they might work this visual identity into the IVAW, not just with the usual T-shirts with political slogans (though these were suggested and approved), but as a recognizable visual style for activists, since their bodies were the first thing noticed and judged in any encounter with the public. This analysis of style soon went beyond clothing and addressed the demeanor of activists. If activists appear angry and stressed out or, conversely, joyful and friendly, what messages are conveyed to people about joining their cause? How did IVAW activists want to appear?

From here the conversation turned to what we might learn from the recognizable rituals that make up such a large part of baseball. We came to the conclusion that fans enjoy these rituals because they offer a known and predictable quality to a game that can be hard to follow and whose outcome is uncertain (after all, the Cubs, surprising everyone, went on to win the World Series in 2016). We then segued into a discussion of meetings and protests and how so much attention is given to the agenda items to be covered in the meeting and what tactics will be employed in the protest, but so little attention is given to simple things like rituals signaling the beginnings and endings of meetings and protests or to ways to mark various stages within these events. Indeed, many protests end when the opposing team—the police—decides they will end. The IVAW activists recognized the need to devise rituals of their own to mitigate the fear and uncertainty that marks much of activist life, thereby making the unfamiliar and uncertain a bit more knowable and predictable. Coming out of the service, where rituals are an important part of military life, these veterans intuitively understood their function, but it wasn't until they could see them in action, and at a distance in a baseball game, that they gave any thought to how they might use them in their activist practice.

Finally, we talked about how boring yet simultaneously enjoyable a baseball game is. For a few hours on a hot and lazy summer evening, we left all the stresses and strains of life behind. We concluded that one of the most attractive qualities of baseball—and indeed much of pop culture—is *escape*. We then wondered how we might "move the point" on escape and make political engagement something that veterans would want to escape *to* rather than *from*. We started brainstorming about the different forms of escape people enjoy: sports, movies, dancing, music, drinking, bars. Bars—that was it!

The Veterans of Foreign Wars (VFW) runs meeting halls—and bars—throughout the United States. In most places, veterans from the Vietnam and even Korean wars run the VFW. As these vets get older, the halls and bars are going dormant. This was the opening we were looking for. Why not have IVAW members join the VFW and resurrect these bars all across the United States? The IVAW could provide a service for vets—by providing a place to escape and unwind with people who have had similar experiences—but at the same time, the VFW halls could provide much-needed locations for the IVAW to meet about their larger objective: to end war. And there could be fruitful overlap. If vets want to come in and just have a few beers and relax, that's cool. But if they have a gripe about the treatment they received at a Veterans Administration Hospital or have questions about their legal rights as soldiers or veterans, then there would be bartenders who would not only listen to their problems but give them the resources, teach them the skills, and hook them up with an organization that might actually solve some of the problems they were trying to escape from. Eventually, these vets might even join the IVAW. It was a win-win.

We've had similarly productive pop culture outings over the years. With a group fighting for the rights of youth prisoners and their families in Houston, Texas, we went to a megabar that filled an entire city block. The next day, a bit tired and bleary from dance and drink, we explored the popular appeal of such places. We theorized that unlike bars that cater to one particular age, class, ethnic, sexual, musical, or subcultural scene, this bar—in order to maximize clientele and profit—made room for *everyone*. There was a country and western room *and* there was an electronic dance music room. We then applied that insight to our own groups, asking ourselves, What do we do to open our doors . . . and to close them? We then strategized how we might make activist spaces more open, inviting, and appealing for those who don't already share our culture.

We've also gone to an amusement park with program officers from the Open Society Foundations, a major multinational funding organization. Their job is to solicit proposals from and award grants to social change advocacy groups, and they were looking for ways to encourage creativity in their grantees. So we went to ride the Cyclone roller coaster on Coney Island. Constructed nearly a hundred years ago on a wooden frame, the Cyclone is terrifying. At any moment, you feel that the creaking, rattling structure is going to give way and you are going to hurtle down the track to certain death. But the Cyclone is also relatively safe. At least we all made it off alive that night, and the next morning we discussed the thrill that comes from feeling danger and the security in knowing you are safe, which, in turn, allows you to court danger. From this insight we brainstormed ways to include "risk" as a necessary component of all proposals, asking grantees how they would build danger into their plans, how they planned to ensure safety, and most important, how they proposed to ride the line between the two.

When we worked with the famed Actions Team of Greenpeace, we were in a rural retreat in West Virginia in the dead of winter. The closest (and only) pop culture around was a movie theater at the local mall. Here, we watched the latest installment of the Star Wars franchise: *Rogue One*. As with all the Star Wars movies, this one provided fertile cultural ground for activists. A popular story of a band of scrappy rebels fighting against an evil empire? What could be better! The next morning we had a productive discussion about how Greenpeace—now a massive, global, and bureaucratic organization—might capitalize on these popular myths by resurrecting their "rebel" image, updating (and regendering) their old iconography of the dude in the Zodiac inflatable boat, standing down a looming whaling ship with the Greenpeace flag whipping in the air behind him.

But there came a time in the discussion, as there frequently does when we do this sort of work, in which someone suggested that we adopt the symbology directly from whatever pop culture we've been working with. Dub Darth Vader's voice onto a video of the president of Exxon making a speech! Make Big Oil into the evil empire! Dress like Princess Leia (or, it being Greenpeace, Chewbacca)! There's nothing wrong with this use of pop culture, and plenty of artistic activists have dressed up as superheroes and cast their opponents as fictional villains to great effect. But this type of appropriation just adapts the symbols and signs and doesn't get at the deep dreams and nightmares that the Star Wars films evoke. The point is not to replicate popular culture but to *learn* from it and tap into the basic human needs and desires it speaks to.

"We pin our hopes to the sporting public," Bertolt Brecht wrote in 1926 in an essay directed to his fellow playwrights and directors who were bemoaning the fact that the masses seemed to prefer soccer to socially relevant avant-garde theater. The radical playwright asked his fellow artists to look at the problem from a different angle: instead of complaining about what the masses don't like, try to learn from what they do like. His suggestion? Make political theater more like a soccer match. Brecht didn't mean that actors should wear jerseys, keep score, and take up opposing sides on a pitch. Instead, artists needed to understand why people went to the soccer stands. The primary lesson Brecht came away with was that people participate in what they enjoy, and unless theater was made enjoyable, the people wouldn't come.

But there is a larger lesson that transcends the particulars of why people go to soccer matches. Brecht was insisting that if art was to be politically relevant, it needed to speak to people where they *are*, not where they were once in the purer days of yore or where they will be in the glorious future after the Great Leap Forward. Radical artists, regardless of the fact that they are working to change society, need to create for the society of *today*.

*[handwritten margin note: society of Today]*

Once the artist (or activist) understands where people are and meets them there, the artistic activist is under no obligation to stay in that place. Brecht was not suggesting a public-opinion-poll politics of giving the people whatever they want and then slavishly following in their wake. He took the position of a strategic weathervane, testing the popular wind and fashioning a political theater that sailed with it. Brecht understood that catching the wind did not dictate the direction that one traveled, because, in his words, "Once one has a wind one can naturally sail against it; the only impossibility is to sail with no wind at all or with tomorrow's wind" (Brecht 2002, 184). With the wind in our sails, we can tack right and jibe left, choose to sail with the wind or against it. The only certainty is that without the popular wind, we're stuck, becalmed, and going nowhere.

Culture is our medium at the Center for Artistic Activism, and understanding our medium means being attuned to the cultures that people (particularly nonartists and nonactivists) enjoy—not what we think they *should* enjoy but what they actually *do* enjoy in today's complicated and compromised world. It is only by understanding this culture and embracing the pop culture fan that lurks in all of us that we will begin to understand the needs and desires that motivate people and be able to speak the languages they can hear. Where we go with that understanding and what we decide to communicate once we know the cultural code are up to us. With cultural knowledge, we can move the point.

**18**

## Tonight, in This Very Ring . . .
## Trump vs. the Media

Pro Wrestling as Articulation of Civic Imagination

**Sam Ford**

It was the 2017 US Independence Day weekend when the sitting US president set off some metaphorical fireworks. Donald Trump used his communication platform of preference—Twitter—to publish the meme heard 'round the world. Using the hashtags #FraudNewsCNN and #FNN, he tweeted a short video of himself tackling another figure outside of a pro-wrestling ring with a clothesline—a staple pro-wrestling move—and then repeatedly punching the figure in the face. However, the logo of cable news network CNN was superimposed over his opponent's face.

President Trump had been in overt confrontations with news outlets throughout his campaign and the first months of his presidency. Engaging in call-and-response tactics with crowds at his political events, then candidate Trump had developed a rhetorical style focused on framing media outlets as the enemy of him and his devotees and uniting his supporters in a war not just against other candidates or the opposing political party but the machine he positioned as repeatedly holding blatant bias against a fair representation of him as a candidate and later as president.

The use of professional wrestling as a representation for this confrontation with CNN was made all the more powerful considering the aggressor perpetrating the attack in the video was the president himself. Years before he was candidate Trump, Donald brought his real estate business and reality television fame into the "sports entertainment" realm of pro wrestling, where he engaged in a feud with the owner of World Wrestling Entertainment (WWE, the largest professional

Donald J. Trump ✔
@realDonaldTrump

Follow ⌄

#FraudNewsCNN #FNN

**Figure 18.1.** Tweet by @realDonaldTrump

wrestling organization in the world), a purported "battle of the billion-aires." It was WWE owner Vince McMahon whose face was covered in the video in a showdown at WWE Wrestlemania in 2007. In fact, President Trump is the only one of the forty-five commanders in chief to date who is a member of the WWE Hall of Fame.

The ties between President Trump and WWE are long-standing. Trump Plaza had hosted Wrestlemania events in 1988 and 1989, and then businessman Trump had made numerous cameos, on camera and backstage, at wrestling events for years prior to his on-screen feud with McMahon in 2007. That and a subsequent storyline that brought Trump back to WWE were attempts by NBCUniversal to cross-promote Trump's reality series, *The Apprentice*, with WWE's lineup, which is a foundational part of the programming block for the conglomerate's USA Network cable channel. And the ties run even deeper, considering that President Trump named former WWE CEO Linda McMahon—Vince's wife—as a member of his cabinet, heading the Small Business Administration.

However, Trump is not the only presidential-level political figure with a WWE appearance under his belt. John McCain, Hillary Clinton, and Barack Obama all made appearances on WWE television during the 2008 campaign. McCain had asked wrestling fans—echoing iconic pro wrestler Hulk Hogan's signature line—"Whatcha gonna do when John McCain and all his 'McCainiacs' run wild on you?" Clinton had suggested "Hill-Rod" as a wrestling-style nickname. And eventual election winner Barack Obama echoed famous wrestler and Hollywood star Dwayne "The Rock" Johnson's tagline by asking fans, "Do you smell what Barack is cooking?" (Hunt 2010). Former candidate Mitt Romney made news in 2016 when he donned a luchador mask and entered the ring for a charity event organized by his son (Diaz 2016). Meanwhile, a few wrestlers have launched into political careers, most notably in the United States, with Jesse "The Body" Ventura becoming Minnesota governor in 1998 (see Jenkins 2005).

But this unprecedented example of a sitting president using a scene portraying him inflicting injury on someone else to address his conflict with the media generated particularly widespread discussion about the appropriateness of using popular culture like the world of pro wrestling—where every plot necessarily ends in a physical, violent confrontation between characters—as a means of framing civic discourse. The video, which had originated from a Reddit user, ignited a controversy that lasted throughout the holiday weekend. The discussion focused on the degree to which the video should be seen as a call to arms against journalists or a humorous attempt to use the excesses of pro wrestling to taunt and needle the media.

CNN's response to the president's tweet was swift: "It is a sad day when the President of the United States encouraged violence against reporters" (Acosta 2017). Meanwhile, *New York Times* executive editor Dean Baquet was quoted as saying, "I think it is unseemly that the president would attack journalists for doing their job, and encourage such anger at the media" (Grynbaum 2017). Perhaps the title of Will Gore's piece for the *Independent* in the UK best summarized this strain of response: "Don't Laugh at Donald Trump Sharing That CNN Wrestling Video: At Its Core, It Is Violent, Frightening and Wrong" (Gore 2017).

On the other hand, commentators like *Fortune* journalist Mathew Ingram questioned the tone of the outrage, considering pro wrestling's performative nature. Ingram tweeted, "As much as I dislike Trump, the clip is pretty clearly a parody using cartoon-style violence from a fake

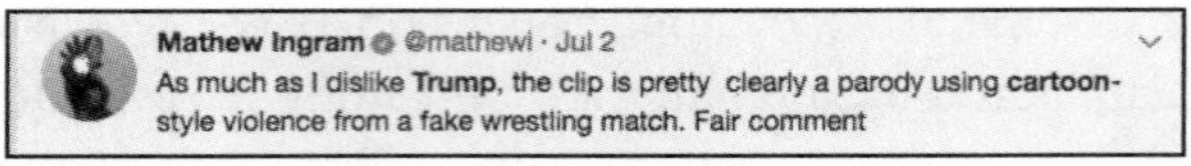

**Figure 18.2.** Tweet by @matthewi

wrestling match." And Jonathan Tobin (2017) wrote in the *National Review*, "Engaging in comic fantasies about body-slamming Trump's least favorite network is juvenile. But it's also important to point out that . . . the CNN gif was obviously a joke. One would think that it didn't need to be pointed out that WWE wrestling is fake, not real. . . . A pro-wrestling meme is silly entertainment, not scary video-game violence. It was an attempt to portray Trump as triumphing over the press, and while perhaps a trifle overoptimistic about the outcome, the ongoing dustup was clearly within the realm of fair comment and satire."

It should come as no surprise that pro-wrestling narratives prove useful as visual representations of social and cultural struggles both within the genre and in the wider culture. Wrestling villains have long represented cultural fears. Meanwhile, protagonists have sought to capture the populist mood of the moment: immigrant heroes such as Argentina Rocca, Bruno Sammartino, and Pedro Morales battling against all odds in markets like New York in the 1950s through the 1970s; the cartoonish superhero Hulk Hogan in the 1980s; the antiauthoritarian blue-collar worker "Stone Cold" Steve Austin in the 1990s; and the wise-cracking, resilient John Cena in the 2000s. Often, these exaggerated cultural figures have acted as points of reference beyond the pro-wrestling context. From the various ways that the image of the masked wrestling luchadors circulate throughout Mexican culture as a symbol of a battle against corruption and other evil forces (aided by some wrestling plots overtly focusing on the Mexican hero as social crusader; see Levi 2005) to the central use of wrestling character Andre the Giant in Shepard Fairey's "Obey" street art campaign, the verbal and visual excesses of wrestling characters often make for quick shorthand when referencing complicated ideals and cultural tensions.

Pro wrestling has a core narrative built on opposition and well over a century of providing a carnivalesque mirror on issues driving social angst. Thus the wrestling world's deep wells of call-and-response engagement, pithy catchphrases, and visual (and immediately intelligible) physical performance of anger and anguish are a frequent method for voicing cultural and political opposition. This is driven by what Roland Barthes (1957/1972) has called wrestling's nature as a "spectacle of excess" (15). Wrestling's narratives are frequently populist, antiauthoritarian, and critical of inept bureaucracy (embodied by the bumbling referee, who can't keep track of the action unfolding).

A battle for ideals inside the pro-wrestling ring can be one of optimism versus cynicism for what fans hold dear, such as a belief in the classic American dream myth versus a repudiation of it. It can pit free-speech advocates against hypocritical moral crusaders. Or the rich villain who has bought his way to the top of the ranks against the working-class underdog who fought his way up. The honored veteran against the arrogant young kid who says the other's time is past. The patriotic hero against the foreign menace. A non-gender-conforming heel against a defender of "traditional" gender norms. The proud representative of a racial minority population versus a bullying racist. The narrative may be progressive or reactionary, but it's almost always populist. And pro wrestling is rarely subtle about the ways in which the physical struggle between its characters becomes a stand-in for the battles society is having about itself. This framing is what Henry Jenkins (1997) has called "masculine melodrama," writing that "the populist imagery of melodramatic wrestling can be understood as one way of negotiating within these competing expectations . . . translating emotional expression into rage against political injustice" (75).

From a performance standpoint, a great pro-wrestling character focuses on pageantry and aura, an elaborate entrance, a brash style, creative insults, talking in soundbites that can be repeated in promo packages, and catchphrases that lend themselves to call-and-response. In that sense, pro wrestling is an ideal lens for simply and clearly contrasting opposing views in culture wars, for making sense of oppositional political discourse, and for understanding the nature of the discourse of both candidate and president Trump (*America with Jorge Ramos* 2015).

When considering the contrasting interpretations of the president's wrestling-themed tweet, it's worth noting that the parlance and language of the wrestling business and wrestling fandom focus overtly on the idea that the show is a con—selling to "marks" who are duped into believing the fiction of the athletic performance (S. Ford 2016). Not surprisingly, then, wrestling acts as a strong metaphor for seeing the world as "rigged." Considering how frequently and deeply coverage of Trump had been marketed by news programs, wrestling's narrative of everything being "fixed" and "part of the show" seemed an apt framing to many supporting the administration or, at least, critical of media response. From that angle, Trump's tweet was a wink and a nod that this "feud" was to some degree show business, while "the media" was seen as performing outrage for their own promotion and financial benefit, treating the audience as marks. Responses from major media outlets were contrasted with, for instance, the comment from CBS chairman Les Moonves's 2016 comment that Trump's candidacy "may not be good for America, but it's damn good for CBS" (Bond 2016), an oft-repeated quote that echoed criticism from left and right that the media's constant coverage of candidate and president Trump was driven by ratings—and that Trump was a master manipulator, using journalism's profit-driven performance against itself.

On the other hand, considering the long history of politicians and government leaders around the world perpetrating and calling for violence against journalists who speak against them, it should come as no surprise that many took Trump's tweet very seriously. However, one must understand the video in the context of President Trump's by-then extensive history of outlandish remarks against the media and his political opposition. And the president's tweet came only weeks after US congressional candidate (and eventual congressman) Greg Gianforte "body slammed" a reporter (as the act was most frequently called, itself a pro-wrestling move; Acuna 2017). Further, many of the journalists, activist communities, and others who saw the president's tweet viewed it without understanding the cultural context of the exaggerated performative nature of a pro-wrestling match. For that matter, many Trump supporters likely did as well. Thus those familiar with pro wrestling in general, or specifically with Trump's history in wrestling, were drawing on a much different set of cultural markers and references than the greater public who viewed the image and read the violence depicted in the brief clip much more literally. For those using pop culture as a catalyst for civic discussion, the wide range of familiarity with the source material, and orientation to that source material, can create drastically different readings. Of course, such differences in interpretation can also serve communicators well if, for instance, they are seeking to distinguish between those who "get it" and those who don't.

This debate between reading the president's depiction of violence as "real" or "fake" (the most frequent delineation discussed in relation to pro wrestling, by the way) also emphasizes the ongoing tension between understanding pro wrestling as a simplistic narrative using stereotypes to profit from culture wars or as an exaggerated parody of contemporary cultural tensions that allows society to look critically at those tensions. And it highlights consternation about where and how pop culture narratives of violent confrontation are used to illustrate opposition. After all, again, the endpoint of any pro-wrestling narrative is always the grudge match; bitter rivals only patch things up *after* the marquee violent confrontation has drawn significant money at the box office and on television.

A sitting US president tweeting a pro-wrestling meme depicting himself tackling the journalists who oppose him may be the ultimate case study for understanding the challenging ways that images of media violence are used to present and make sense of cultural tensions. It is an extraordinary circumstance but one that illustrates a long history of a wrestling match being used to demonstrate opposition in politics and culture wars. For instance, consider the ways in which pro-wrestling character creation engines in WWE videogames facilitate the presentation of political opposition.

**Figure 18.3.** Screenshot from Google+ user GrognougnouGaming

Or how wrestling narratives can portray fantasy "victory scenarios," such as a popular tweet that circulated on Election Day 2016 that portrayed defeated candidate Bernie Sanders "cashing in a money-in-the-bank contract" (a WWE storyline where a wrestler wins the contract to get a match for the title at any moment he chooses, often leading to a dramatic last-minute unexpected contest and a new champion in the narrative).

Or how the dramatic performance of confrontation in a wrestling ring can frame tensions in other realms, such as a popular 2017 video tweeted by Deadspin editor Timothy Burke (2017) depicting Senator

**glock** 🦋
@Glock__Lesnar                                    ( Follow )  ∨

## BAH GAWD!!! ITS BERNIE SANDERS!!!!! BERNIE SANDERS IS CASHING IN HIS MONEY IN THE BANK BRIEFCASE TO SAVE AMERICA!!!!!!!!

6:18 PM - 8 Nov 2016

**25,843** Retweets  **29,775** Likes

◯ 375    ⇄ 26K    ♡ 30K    ✉

**Figure 18.4.** Tweet by @Glock__Lesnar

Figure 18.5. Tweet by @bubbaprog

John McCain's dramatic defiance of Senate Republicans' push for an Affordable Care Act repeal with a pro-wrestling soundtrack, casting McCain as the antiauthoritarian wrestling hero "Stone Cold" Steve Austin. In this clip, McCain's dramatic "thumbs-down" vote in Majority Leader Mitch McConnell's face is accompanied by a soundtrack of Austin's entrance music as McCain walks into the Senate chamber and wrestling commentator Jim Ross pleads, "Don't do this, John!"

The ways in which wrestling narrative norms and storyline histories can comment on contemporary politics are perhaps best currently captured in the parody wrestling news website Kayfabe News, which occasionally includes parodies of political and social issues as part of their wrestling-focused satire.

**Figure 18.6a and b.** Screenshots from Kayfabe News

The persistent use of pro wrestling as a cultural reference point speaks to the power of its visual excesses to stoke civic imagination for a wide range of purposes. Within the pro-wrestling text, writers attempt to capture the mood of the culture by utilizing those tensions in their narratives. Meanwhile, those familiar with pro wrestling frequently use its characters and the visual opposition of a pro-wrestling contest to help make sense of the world outside wrestling's walls.

Most valuable to inspiring civic participation, though, is not the metaphor of the performers in the ring but rather the role modern pro-wrestling fandom plays in the text. In on the "con," wrestling fans present in the arena for a televised pro-wrestling text and those organizing online have the choice of whether to accept or reject the narrative on display in the ring and the ability through their live performance to directly challenge and potentially redirect the narrative. WWE fans have a history of working together to cheer on the character who is supposed to be the villain (as fan reactions once transformed Steve Austin from belligerent villain to embraced antihero), elevate performers who had been relegated to a sideshow (such as pressure in recent years for WWE to treat its female characters as seriously as male wrestlers and not primarily as sexualized "eye candy"), or reject the criteria by which promoters choose the top star (such as fans rebelling against the writers in order to move character Daniel Bryan to the top of the card despite his small size when the powers that be were routinely ignoring him in favor of much larger performers; Ford, forthcoming). Organizing together, fans have the ability to either bring a story to life through their support or subvert and directly challenge it through a resistant response. This ability is elevated by the role fans play as performers in televised shows in the arena as well as the fact that new live shows are produced weekly with no offseason, giving a new set of fans the chance to shape the text directly every week.

Wrestling fandom is a space where fans can playfully argue over their interpretations of the media text and, within the text itself, stage alternative readings that have the direct potential to shift the nature of the narrative. (Contrast that environment with a political rally, where acts of digression such as cheering the person depicted as the villain or speaking out against the purported protagonist might be met not with playful acts of opposition but—as seen in some political rallies and protests—with dangerous acts of violence.) The ability of wrestling fans to contest and resist the direction of the storyline has few parallels in the pop culture landscape. And contemporary wrestling fans debate when, where, and how to use this unique power (Ford, forthcoming). At a time when people across the US political spectrum sometimes feel that systems of democracy are not responsive to everyday citizens, that active political participation is futile, and that there aren't clear ways to have agency over the narrative, perhaps the unique power of pro-wrestling fans to collectively shape the direction of the narrative contains within it an ability to inspire an active civic imagination.

# 19

## Ms. Marvel Punches Back

Twenty-First-Century Superheroes and
Alienated Citizenship

**Rebecca Wanzo**

*Captain America*'s debut issue in 1941 depicted the titular hero punching Adolf Hitler in the face. "Punching Nazis" unexpectedly resurged as a conversational topic in 2017 after two key events. On January 17, President Donald Trump signed an executive order banning the entry of citizens from Iraq, Syria, Iran, Somalia, Sudan, and Libya (Sherlock 2017), sparking widespread protests and legal battles. In August, citizens aligned with various white nationalist groups and some of their supporters protested the removal of a Confederate soldier's statue as well as the presence of Jews and other racial and ethnic minorities in the United States. Many people chanted Nazi slogans and proudly sported symbols of the National Socialist German Workers' Party. One man rammed his car into counterprotestors, injuring many and killing a woman named Heather Heyer (Heim 2017). In the midst of these conflicts, a few people punched white nationalists, and a small debate ensued in the media: "Is it OK to punch a Nazi?" (Stack 2017).

T-shirts sporting slogans such as "Punch More Nazis" could be glimpsed in the streets, while many commentators argued that violence is never appropriate (Allen 2017). Legendary Marvel artist Jack Kirby's image of Captain America's muscular heroism occasionally circulated as a rhetorical rejoinder. Superheroes, whose modus operandi is the use of physical force, frequently punch Nazis and other state or planetary enemies. And outside the realm of the fantastic, colonial conquest, the American Revolutionary War, and World War II are moments of idealized violent conflict. Popular culture is filled with sanctioned violence: soldiers, cowboys, action heroes, vengeful vigilantes, and superheroes.

In the fantastic world of superhero comics, it is always appropriate to inflict violence upon Nazis and other adversaries of the nation or world peace. Superheroes have often embodied the state, either formally or as an extralegal form of a city's police force or military strength.

If the superhero represents the state or, more specifically, the state in its ideal form, superheroes of color have sometimes seemed to be dissonant figures. It is not surprising that the first two black superheroes with their own titles—*Luke Cage* (1972) and *Black Panther* (1973)—were alienated or not *of* the United States, respectively. Cage was unlawfully imprisoned and is a "hero for hire" who often resists altruism. The Black Panther is from the mythical nation of Wakanda, and while he has often worked with the Fantastic Four and has become more integrated with other heroes over the years, he was initially defined by his commitment to his isolationist state. Because black people have historically experienced much disenfranchisement, their happy work on behalf of state power might seem particularly jarring to readers, even in a fantasy world. Ms. Marvel, the first Muslim American superhero to have her own title, has also embodied such dissonance, as Muslim Americans were increasingly accused of being threats to the United States after 9/11. Ms. Marvel was created to illustrate the possibility of a member of a minority group being able to stand for the nation. But as rhetoric increased in the West that Muslims always already embody a threat, she came to stand both inside and outside of the comic as a protector of Muslim Americans *against* the state. The superhero's alignment with the state as an inherent good has been questioned many, many times, perhaps most notably by Captain America himself and in Alan Moore's groundbreaking comic *Watchmen* (1986–87), which queried who would hold morally questionable vigilante protectors accountable for their actions. But Kamala Khan as Ms. Marvel may have incorporated better than any other character before her a real multicultural citizenship model as opposed to the assimilationist model through which outsiders become state representatives. She represents not only difference but the *importance* of difference in illustrating values that might be imagined as central to the role of superheroes in the twenty-first-century imaginary.

Ms. Marvel was initially the identity of Carol Danvers, who became Captain Marvel as her character evolved over the decades. The title was relaunched in 2014 and the character reimagined as Pakistani American teenager Kamala Khan. The title received much attention. Marvel and the other major comics corporation—DC—had been under fire for a lack of diversity, and the new Ms. Marvel was part of a shift that saw black Latino Miles Morales take over as Spider-Man, African American Sam Wilson become Captain America, women take on the roles of Black Panther and Thor, and a number of other women receive their own titles. While the vice president of sales would later state that sales flagged "because people didn't want any more diversity" and that any character that "was diverse," "female," or "not a core Marvel character" did not sell, *Ms. Marvel* illustrated the questionable nature of the claim. It was clearly a success, with its trade paperbacks of collected issues landing on bestseller lists (Hoffman 2017).

Written by G. Willow Wilson, a white woman who converted to Islam, and edited by Muslim American Sana Amanat, the comic places a new twist on the urban allegiance of the superhero. Superman has Metropolis, Batman has Gotham, Spider-Man has New York, and Khan is very much a representative of Jersey City, New Jersey. Khan serving as representative and protector of her city updates a foundational comics allegory. Clark Kent offered an immigration metaphor of early twentieth-century Jews becoming ideal citizens, while Kamala Khan directly referenced a real immigration pattern of a second wave of South Asian immigration to the United States in the 1980s and 1990s (Fingeroth 2007). Khan's hometown has a large diasporic South Asian population, and in real life, this group has been the target of xenophobic violence. As Sunaina Marr Maira (2009) has argued, after 9/11, many Muslim youths had to negotiate their feelings of the United States as their home with the knowledge that many of their fellow citizens viewed them as enemies of the state (3–4). However, in the universe of *Ms. Marvel*, the signs of discrimination in the city are much less visible than the multicultural pleasures of her community. With her Italian Catholic love interest, her devout brother and head-covering best friend who challenge discourses of devout Muslim men and women, and a blonde cheerleader type who admits to her bigotry and later comes out as queer, Khan's Jersey City often models the best of what a multicultural city can be. Its ideality lies not in a utopia that ignores difference or in which conflict does not occur but in its citizens' recognition of the challenges in navigating cultural diversity and their willingness to confront their own prejudices and presumptions.

Early models of US citizenship idealized assimilation, or the "melting pot" ideal (Glazer and Moynihan 1963). But in the 1970s, various social movements placed pressure on the United States and other countries to adopt pluralistic models that embraced the idea of various identity groups maintaining their heritage (Kymlicka 1995, 14). Rogers Brubaker (2001) argues that the twenty-first century saw a return to an assimilation ideal in the West, albeit not in the chauvinist, Anglo-conformist form popular in the middle of the twentieth century that promoted sameness. For Brubaker, this newer mode of assimilation has transformed into something more heterogeneous, and it "has involved a shift from an overwhelming focus on persisting difference—and on mechanisms through which such cultural maintenance occurs—to a broader focus that encompasses emerging commonalities as well. Normatively, it has involved a shift from an automatic valorization of cultural differences to a renewed concern with civil integration" (542). In other words, policy makers are less interested in putting in place mechanisms for people to maintain their culture than in emphasizing national commonalities that people have in common as part of their commitment as citizens. At the same time, the rise in crimes against South Asians and Muslims after 9/11 and again after Donald Trump's presidential run suggests that Anglo-American sameness is still a desire of many citizens (Kishi 2016). *Ms. Marvel* is produced within this context, with Muslims profiled as people who have committed violence or wish to do so and with Muslim Americans emphasizing their right to maintain their culture while also equal status as Americans.

Khan emphasizes her unwillingness to injure others, and she is initially a reluctant practitioner of violence. Older superheroes such as the X-Men's Wolverine and Carol Danvers convince her of the necessity of force, but her reluctance affirms a reading of this Muslim American superhero as nonviolent. Thus she is in neither the physical nor affective tradition of most superheroes, who, as Jeffrey Brown (2009) argues, "are the quintessential expression of our cultural beliefs about what it means to be a man" (26). This representation of masculinity was also—not coincidentally—deeply linked to fascist representations of ideal male citizens in the early twentieth century (Brown 2009, 27). Friedrich

Nietzsche's *Ubermensch* (superman), a hard-bodied Aryan soldier, was often a point of reference for Nazi propaganda about the desired state. Kamala Khan is thus physically antithetical to the traditional ideal of the superhero, a point made explicitly when the "Terrigen Mist" that activates her Inhuman DNA initially transforms her into a superhero. Khan is a superhero fangirl who sees blonde and blue-eyed Carol Danvers as the ideal. Gifted with the ability to transform, she imagines herself as Danvers but decides that look is not appropriate for her. The flowing blonde wave of hair gets in her face, "the boots pinch," and the leotard gives her "an epic wedgie" (Wilson and Alphona 2015, issue #2). The humorous indictment of sexist superhero representations nonetheless gestures to the importance of her not being a mere replication of what canonical superheroes have been.

Ramzi Fawaz (2016) argues that in the decades after World War II, the superhero transformed from a "nationalist champion to a figure of radical difference mapping the limits of American liberalism and its promise of universal inclusion" (3). And indeed the roster of superheroes became more diverse over the course of the twentieth century, and creators negotiated issues of difference allegorically through characters like the X-Men and also addressed real political conflicts over identity. And yet the prototypical superhero continued to be white and male, and some fans have gone so far as to say that they *should* be white and male, because it makes it easier for people to identify with them (Ampi-kaipakan 2015). In this logic, white superheroes are universal, not threatening people of color with the specificity of political advocacy embodied by women and people of color. Of course, such a claim ignores the idea that the *white* hero embodied identity politics around class, gender, race, and nation. This perhaps became most apparent in a controversial *Captain America* story arc in 2017 that suggested that Steve Rogers (Captain America) had been working for Hydra—the Nazis—all along.

This was a controversial turn in the history of the character, and many fans argued that the move was a betrayal of the work of Jack Kirby and Joe Simon, the two Jewish creators of Captain America. However, Rogers's allegiance to Hydra turned out to be the result of a villain's trick and not a true rewriting of the character's entire history. Superhero comics often play with "what-if" versions of characters that create alternative worlds for longtime readers. At the same time, these "what-if" versions can be compelling reimaginings that push against the idea of the characters and who they represent. Mark Millar's *Superman: Red Son* (2003), for example, imagined that Kal-L had landed in the USSR instead of the United States but was just as noble and righteous in holding up the principles of communism as he was in representing the ideals of the United States. *Superman: Red Son* was, for Millar, very much a book about the United States after 9/11. It was "an Orwellian examination of what happens when the balance of power tilts in the world and one country finds itself the only world superpower" and about "the moral implications of one man or country policing the entire world" (Younis 2003). At their best, such revisions help people understand something different about the character. In the case of Captain America, the Hydra allegiance gestured to something that the character has struggled with throughout his history—namely, an awareness of how easily he could be used to support oppressive state power. Rogers has increasingly been a proponent of regulating state power over the decades for this very reason.

In contrast, as a brown-skinned Muslim girl, Kamala Khan is not transparently a sign of the United States to many people. But the promise of Ms. Marvel and many of these new superheroes who are people of color is that they should be. Most forecasts suggest that non-Hispanic whites will be less than 50 percent of the country's population by 2044 (Colby and Ortman 2015). This future is sometimes configured as posing a threat to the United States. Khan addresses this issue in her involvement in a Marvel crossover story event in which many of the characters are involved in the same storyline. In *Civil War II*, Khan's idol Carol Danvers discovers that one of the Inhumans—people with powers because of alien DNA—can predict that someone might commit a crime and enlists superheroes to stop crimes before they happen.

"Precrime" was the focus of Philip K. Dick's short story "The Minority Report" (1956), in which a police division arrests people before they have a chance to commit crimes. But with Khan at the center of the narrative, the story defamiliarizes the issues of profiling by having a Muslim character support it. Many citizens support profiling Muslims and people of color; the forty-fifth president's ban is rooted in the alleged potential of danger from these citizens. Khan's love for the beautiful, heroic Carol Danvers and what she represents made it difficult for her to push back against a policy that increasingly appeared unjust.

Khan's family history and community served to combat the pleasure of aligning herself with Danvers and thus the nation. The character's dialogue in the comic frequently gestures toward our real present rather than supernatural struggles. The opening of *Ms. Marvel #8* features Khan's great-grandparents fleeing to Pakistan after the Indian partition. Her pregnant great-grandmother reflects that her unborn child "doesn't yet realize that neighbors, friends can be turned against each other" (Wilson and Alphona 2016). In the storyline, Khan is concerned that they are profiling, but Danvers replies that profiling "was bad science" because it was based on "subjective data about a whole community." She believes her model is different because it targeted individuals. However, Khan's African American sister-in-law Ayesha presses her on how this law enforcement plan defines probable cause, arguing that "a whole generation" of black men "went to jail instead of college" because of "tough on crime" policies. When Khan suggests that the policy can save lives, Ayesha asks, "Whose lives? Did you ever think that the people committing the crimes need saving too?" After her love interest is hurt trying to rescue an incarcerated friend, Khan decides to shut the project down in her city, rejecting the idea that lives lost under the policy should be understood merely as "collateral damage." She tells Danvers, "If you lock somebody up before they've even committed a crime, you make them into a bad guy, even if they weren't before."

The story is an indictment of the policies that led to mass incarceration and that profile all Muslims as potential terrorists, fitting into a tradition of comics like *Watchmen* that sometimes question the efficacy of US policies that may create the conditions of crime or put people more at risk. Just as comics treat the superhero as representative of national ideals or as representatives who push the nation to represent its ideals, Khan is pushed to represent ideals articulated in her diverse, local community. Her moral authority comes from the community—her imam, her African American sister-in-law, her diverse group of friends, and her family history. This citizenship model imagines a nation grounded in a decentered moral authority.

In one variant of a *Civil War II* cover, artist Phil Noto depicts Ms. Marvel ripping a picture of beloved idol Carol Danvers in half. In January 2017, he circulated a revised version on social media, showing Khan tearing up a picture of President Donald Trump in the wake of his

Muslim ban announcement (Seifert 2017). One piece of fan art depicts Ms. Marvel punching Donald Trump in the face, the downed Trump wearing an armband with a *T* on it, drawing connections between this image and the Kirby *Captain America* cover. One fan modified an image from a *Ms. Marvel* issue in which the hero leads her community to the polls and fights back against attempts at voter suppression. In the modification, Khan yells, "Resist!" The other text, depicting her thoughts, remains unchanged: "Democracy. Sometimes a contact sport." Both the creators and some fans imagine a superhero who is sometimes in opposition to the state, but that conflict allows her to represent the people she has a responsibility to protect. Khan is thus well within the tradition of superheroes in her embrace of violence for protection and outside of it by being oppositional to the state when it threatens the vulnerable. By evoking such a foundational patriotic image in comics history and using her to talk about real conflicts, creators and fans ask people to reimagine what a representative American superhero looks like in the twenty-first century.

## 20

## For the Horde

Violent "Trolling" as a Preemptive Strike via
#GamerGate and the #AltRight

**joan miller**

In the United States on the morning of November 9, 2016, political
analysts and left-leaning citizens confronted the lingering and powerful prevalence of white, cisgendered, and heterosexual supremacist
ideology. While some avoided and denied the xenophobia at the heart
of the Republican campaign, others pointed to clear signs in social
data that were previously dismissed—among them, the #GamerGate
uproar. As the *Guardian* reported shortly after the US election, "The
culture war that began with games now has a senior representative in
the White House. . . . This hashtag was the canary in the coal mine, and
we missed it" (Lees 2016). The reporter traced direct connections
between #GamerGate and key players in the alt-right movement, such
as Steve Bannon and Milo Yiannopoulos. These links to the Trump
campaign will not be explicitly explored here, but I want such connections to linger over this examination of the underlying mechanics of
#GamerGate (#GG), a violent internet-based social movement, since the
signs of a fractured and violent public were there from the beginning.

Though #GG participants claimed noble purposes, their actions be-
trayed their intentions. As one writer (Elise 2014) commented, "Some
may be genuinely concerned with the ethics of video game journalists
and their relationships with developers, but the loudest supporters seem
to be those who are uneasy with the growing popularity of females on
the development side." Instead of critiquing journalists, #GamerGaters
primarily engaged in harassment campaigns against women in gaming.

The computer and video games industry, from its modest origins as
a pastime for people working in labs and tech companies, expanded

into arcades and later home entertainment system, and is today projected to earn more than ninety billion dollars of revenue worldwide per year as of 2020. For most of that history, the market for computer and video games skewed male. By the early 1990s, scholars were beginning to identify the emergence of a "girls' games" movement as companies such as Purple Moon and HerInteractive sought to broaden game content to attract more female players; feminist educators and activists saw playing games as a "head-start" program for boys at a time when women were grossly outnumbered in the technical fields (Cassell and Jenkins 1998). As of 2014, 48 percent of video game players in the United States were female, and they purchased 50 percent of computer games (ESA 2014), an increase of 36 percent in less than three decades (Donovan 2010). Female designers and entrepreneurs helped lead the charge, calling attention to workplace inequalities, advocating for broader representations and alternative play mechanics, pioneering more serious and artistic uses of the games medium (including, for example, games to teach or games for social change), and creating the infrastructure for indie games (Gray and Leonard 2018; Kafai et al. 2008, 2017). Women represented the core market for casual mobile games, for example, which is where some of the most dramatic growth in the market has occurred over the past decade. Online games critics questioned some of the tropes within existing games genres and the ways that they often degraded and devalued women and people of color.

Competing for market share, the major gaming companies sought to expand their outreach, partly through representation and customization. For example, the BioWare game *Dragon Age: Inquisition* (2015) allows customization of the gender, species, and skin color of the protagonist. The player can also choose to start a romance with male or female characters or both. Similarly, the latest edition of the Maxis series *The Sims 4* includes in its character creator a set of "custom gender settings":

Physical Frame: Masculine / Feminine
Clothing Preference: Masculine / Feminine
This Sim will be able to: Become pregnant / Get others pregnant / Neither
Can this Sim use the toilet standing? Yes / No. (*The Sims 4* 2014)

Such customization options represent one aspect of a shift toward greater inclusivity.

All of these efforts set the stage for #GamerGate, creating a context where some male gamers, threatened by their declining centrality within the games market, pushed back against women who they saw as embodying those changes. The "gamer" identity felt precarious, and some "hardcore gamers" struck out wildly. Something similar is occurring as demographic changes in America imperil white people's majority, which fuels the alt-right movement.

### #GamerGate: What Is It and Where Did It Come From?

#GamerGate is a hashtag used to aggregate discussion concerning "ethics in gaming journalism." More broadly, it is a violent, chauvinistic social movement. In 2013, Zoë Quinn released her independent game *Depression Quest*, an experiential treatise on the difficulties of the disease. It was not well received within certain factions of the gaming community:

> The hate mail began to arrive on "pretty much the same day." . . . Steam users argued that a game with such a gloomy subject had no place being distributed on the marketplace. Incredulous and angry user reviews filled [the] listing page. . . . Some of [Quinn's harassers] think that the darker themes are not suitable for video games, which they believe should be playful and primarily focused on entertaining. Others, especially those who have led the recent attacks, claim that the game has received an amount of coverage that is disproportionate to its quality. . . .
>
> The attacks on Quinn escalated when an ex-boyfriend posted a tirade . . . expos[ing] an alleged relationship . . . with a journalist who wrote about the game. The journalist in question pointed out that he had not reviewed the game, merely reported on its existence. Still, some justified their attacks on the "manipulative" Quinn in the name of ethics. (Parkin 2014)

Quinn was targeted by a faction of gamers who believed that she represented everything wrong with the gaming world, a world that rightfully belonged to them. They responded with attacks and harassment including doxxing (exposing private data to the public), verbal and sexual harassment, rape threats, and death threats. Many of the tactics employed by #GamerGaters were successful at their main objective: drawing a clear line between "us" and "them."

Thus #GamerGate can be described as an imagined public in revolt over the possession of the "gamer" identity. In analyzing the violence deployed by #GamerGate, I will demonstrate how their violent tactics of abjection create a "deadly certainty" (Appadurai 1998). #GamerGate represents a microcosm of a broader conflict in American culture; as increased equity among marginalized individuals creates a redistribution of privilege, displaced individuals respond with violent backlashes embodied by #GamerGate and the #AltRight. Attending to practices of identity and abjection within #GamerGate, we can scrutinize these imagined publics and their cleavages.

The chauvinist gaming public resists those voices that would change its shape. According to Dewey (1954), "To form itself, the public has to break existing political forms. . . . The public which generated political forms is passing away, but the power and lust of possession remains in the hands of the officers and agencies which the dying public instituted. This is why the change of the form of states is so often effected only by revolution" (31). He sees the public as the product of an internal struggle that resolves into a new social order. The difficulty lies in the resistance from those who benefit from the status quo. For #GamerGate, the threatened upheaval is a revolution of the ethos of gaming. A digitally connected network of individuals united by a demand for ethical treatment and representation constituted an existential threat for future #GGers. That threat is evidenced by their choice of targets. Anita Sarkeesian's *Tropes vs. Women in Video Games* (2013) series can be understood as a critical feminist historiography of games, while Quinn's *Depression Quest* is exemplary of the trend toward "serious games," including pieces like *That Dragon, Cancer* (2016); *Walden* (2017); and *Papers, Please* (2013). Another major target, Brianna Wu, was harassed, threatened and doxxed for no other reason than designing while trans. Backlash against the work of these three women shows us the barriers to political agency and participation for marginalized people in the face of supremacist ideals.

Supremacists who feel threatened "must abject that which is not [them] in order to form [their] identity" (Kristeva 1982, 185). #GamerGaters are protective of the identity because they expect games to be designed and produced for them, absent of "politicization." Difficult questions arise: What does it mean to be a gamer? Who's a gamer and who's not? How do we tell the difference? Gray areas present an unbearable anxiety. In response, #GGers employ radical measures. Affect studies scholar Arjun Appadurai (1998) argues, "Where one or more of these forms of social uncertainty come into play violence can create a macabre form of certainty and can become a brutal technique (or folk discovery-procedure) about 'them' and, therefore, about 'us'" (229). Violent separation turns gray areas into black-and-white answers. It reveals who is and is not on their side. Understanding this grasp toward certainty as a tool for control of a fractured public enables us to form an explanatory model for civic violence.

## "Ready? Fight!" Identity and Violence

The types of violence employed by #GamerGate illustrate the values and points of cleavage between the competing publics. Two dominant forms—threats and doxxing—constituted the majority of attacks. Though the violence is intangible, Appadurai (1998) affirms that "the body is the site of the worst possible infliction of pain, terror, indignity and suffering" (229). I include identity as part of the socioemotional body, the assemblage of one's emotional state, self-image, and perceived autonomy. Virtual terrorism and abuse represent extreme violence and a polity of hate.

Sexual and gendered threats indicate a preoccupation with identity and control. Rape threats especially indicate an objective: to dominate, to exercise power, to put "them" in their place. These abuses constitute a tactic of violent ejection, leaving the attacker in control of the disputed ground. This practice is highly effective: persistent abuse forced journalist Jenn Frank to permanently leave the gaming industry after her work became a "conflict of interest with [her] own terror" (C. Cox 2014). Frank's exile from the industry epitomizes the silencing of dissenting voices. In the #AltRight, we can see the same tactics when peaceful protestors are violently attacked and killed via shootings, vehicular manslaughter, and other crimes. This violent rejection produces a strong border between the threatener and the victim.

This possessiveness over the gamer identity forms an abhorrent object that must be destroyed. #GamerGaters, faced with ideals antithetical to their self-supremacy, resort to abjection. Their violent tactics cement their own identities at the expense of those who would displace them by claiming some control over the future of games. Dewey (1954) explains, "The line between private and public is to be drawn on the basis of the extent and scope of the consequences of acts which are so important as to need control, whether by inhibition or by promotion" (15). Acts that question the primacy of the normative subject are, for #GamerGaters, public, prescient, and vitally important.

We find exemplars in threats against the aforementioned Anita Sarkeesian, a strong and vocal critic of sexual objectification in games. Public support for her gamer ethos manifested in June 2012, when Sarkeesian crowdsourced more than 2,000 percent of her goal to produce the series *Tropes vs. Women in Video Games* (Sarkeesian 2013). In return, #GamerGate targeted her and her fans. In March 2014, an anonymous bomb threat was directed against her and thousands of supporters: "A bomb will be detonated at the Game Developer's Choice award ceremony tonight unless Anita Sarkeesian's Ambassador Award is revoked. . . . This is not a joke. You have been warned" (quoted in Totilo 2014). The goal is clear: prevent the spread of Sarkeesian's views. The award, bestowed by developers, represented an unconscionable betrayal to #GamerGaters. Sarkeesian was targeted again at Utah State University in October 2014:

> We live in a nation of *emasculated cowards* too afraid to challenge the *vile, misandrist harpies* who seek to destroy them. . . . Feminism has taken over every facet of our society, and women like Sarkeesian want to *punish us for even fantasizing about being men. This is why I've chosen to target her. Anita Sarkeesian is everything wrong with the feminist woman,* and she is going to die screaming like the craven little whore that she is if you let her come to USU [Utah State University]. I will write my manifesto in her spilled blood, and *you will all bear witness to what feminist lies and poison have done to the men of America.* (quoted in Alberty 2014, my emphasis)

Feminism is attacking this man; it has "taken over" society, and its proponents "want to punish" him. The threat represents a "violent and obscure revolt of the being against what is menacing it" (2010, 184). His tactic succeeded. Sarkeesian canceled her lecture, feeling that her safety and that of her audience were in jeopardy due to statewide open-carry laws and police indifference (Alberty 2014). Nonetheless, she persists; Sarkeesian continues to push the industry in a more feminist direction.

Doxxing represents another successful avenue of attack. A vengeful ex-boyfriend exposed Quinn's private life via a blog post, and Wu was forced out of her home after police established credible threats against her and her family (Elise 2014). Doxxing and other threats perform a violent abjection of marginalized others from the gaming public. Further, doxxing enacts social execution and dissection. Exposure of the subject's private life violently outs them and presents them for public judgment. Subjected to new and more dangerous forms of abuse, the victim cannot escape. They are left vulnerable and exposed, metaphorically stripped naked and paraded through the public square. #GamerGaters extract facets of the victim's personal history and serve them as evidence of otherness. Quinn's ex revealed her sex life to #GamerGaters as proof of her corruption and dishonesty. Her gender and sexuality became subjects of public dissection, ridicule, and punishment.

### "Continue?" Patience in Action

#GamerGate's violent tactics abject dissenting voices from gaming culture, using violence as "self-defense." Kristeva recognizes this paranoid hatred and proposes a remedy; she suggests a form of forgiveness that relies on the passage of time, a "patient dismantling" of the sources of the barrier between the subject and the dangerous other. "Through forgiveness, time for vengeance is suspended," and the fear and violence can be slowly disintegrated (Kristeva 2010). Rebuilding after violent conflict is a slow, difficult, and fragile process. Kristeva's patient dismantling strategy prioritizes long-term planning and the cumulative effects of small actions. Instead of seeking vengeance, we must doggedly continue our mission. We must make space for cultural critique in gaming; assert equality for nonnormative people; charge designers to explore the possibilities of gaming as a medium—including its potential for discomfort; and eliminate interpersonal violence within the gaming public.

To achieve these goals, we must change the conversation. Habermas's understanding of public discourse disregards identity as a component, but the omission is limiting. This model cannot explain the struggle over identity and intersectionality at the basis of not just #GamerGate but much of modern political conflict. Calhoun (1998) untangles the issue by attending to social movements: "[They] are occasions for the restructuring of not just issues but of identities. Throughout the modern era, social movements have been in part occasions for the legitimation of new voices . . . not just the inclusions of persons previously excluded, but also changes in identities from which included persons speak" (37). Here is the crux of #GamerGate: the argument over whose voices are legitimate and deserve to be included. #GamerGate's ideology inherently opposes the "inclusion of persons previously excluded." It is a countermovement against that inclusion, just as the #AltRight represents a countermovement against the political inclusion of perceived inferiors.

The resemblance between the #AltRight and #GamerGate is conspicuous; both groups cite the threat of displaced identity, and both use violence to control the boundaries of discourse. They demand the exclusion of others to support their own exclusivity and the freedom to assert dominance. Their freedom requires inequality, evidencing the major dilemma of our nation: how to reconcile the two. #GamerGate and the #AltRight embody the conflict and, not coincidentally, share much of the same membership. Wu argues that #GamerGate was crucial to the development of the #AltRight: "At the height of Gamergate . . . I had two calls with Obama's White House . . . and they told me they were going to get serious about prosecuting Gamergate. And they didn't. I personally blame Obama for Hillary losing. . . . I believe that if Obama had followed through on Gamergate and the prosecutions there . . . this playbook for the alt-right would not have poisoned the entire election" (quoted in Lagomarsino 2017). Such an intimate perspective is not to be taken lightly. Wu connects the two groups through their shared "playbook." Thus #GamerGaters' violent behavior should serve as a warning not to underestimate identity-based supremasists' capacity for violence.

As previously mentioned, Kristeva's approach requires patience. The sort required here is not the testy self-discipline we deploy under threat.

Instead, it is the patience that watches social movements rise and fall, causing the proverbial "wheel of progress" to turn. It turns only by the actions of those driving it. We might take an example of this philosophy in action from Wu, who recently announced her candidacy for a congressional seat in Boston's ninth district. Whether or not she wins the election, her deliberate action will serve as another push past supremacist ideology toward a truly inclusive and equal republic for all.

# 21

## Communal Matters and Scientific Facts

Making Sense of Climate Change

**Candis Callison**

In 2017, as Hurricane Irma bore down on the Caribbean Islands and southern Florida, the fierce power of environmental forces took center stage on every major news source. Hurricanes Jose and Katia remained offshore, and many were still cleaning up from Hurricane Harvey. The swirling, circular, animated cloud formations on satellite images only served to reinforce an ominous vision of multiple coincidental catastrophes far outside the bounds of human control. Veteran journalist Joseph B. Treaster, who has covered the last forty years of hurricanes, began his article following Hurricane Irma in the *New York Times* by stating, "Every hurricane tells a story." But what kind of story it tells largely depends on what kinds of data, experiences, and expertise matter—and who's speaking to whom.

Treaster describes shiny new towers and unchecked sprawls of coastal development that he's seen since Hurricane Andrew in 1992, and many scientists who study hurricanes have forcefully pointed out that this sprawl has been a bigger problem than the hurricanes themselves during the past two decades (Callison 2014; Mooney 2007). The images of the aftermath of a hurricane are profound and unforgettable precisely because of such coastal development. The smashed buildings, strewn with debris and inundated with storm surges and flooding, tell one kind of story: devastation. It's these images that leave an indelible impression of what catastrophe looks and feels like—and how much time, effort, and money are required to return to something like "normal." Even if it's the dominant one, the devastation of the aftermath is only one possible story to tell about hurricanes.

Following Hurricanes Katrina and Rita in 2005, many saw these storms as events that might engage American publics about climate

Climate Change

change. While the damage and loss were severe in these storms, those concerned about climate change pointed out that our whole concept of "normal" was going to change if people didn't do something to address it. What that actually meant during hurricane season was still a bit fuzzy, but with climate change as an ever-hovering specter, the story of storm-related devastation became a story of something much more pervasive and longer lasting. It became a story that spoke of prior civic imaginations and how our parameters for future imaginings would and could be shaped by current decisions and beliefs about what matters and what must change.

Fast-forward to the more recent 2017 hurricane season, and noted American climate scientist Michael Mann (2017) explained it this way in the *Guardian*: "While we cannot say climate change 'caused' Hurricane Harvey (that is an ill-posed question), we can say is that it exacerbated several characteristics of the storm in a way that greatly increased the risk of damage and loss of life. Climate change worsened the impact of Hurricane Harvey." This statement might still seem a bit convoluted for those who haven't been paying attention to climate change discourse and the evolution of explanations for and about its predictions, but the nuanced attribution and rejection of causality are clear. Mann both acknowledges the desire to blame it on climate change and recognizes the increased range of risks, impacts, and extremes due to the ongoing changes in underlying physical conditions (Benestad 2017). What this means in a future with climate change is not precise, but certainly, future hurricane stories will involve not less devastation but likely a lot more.

## Communal Lives and Facts

In the United States, as discussions about hurricanes aptly demonstrate, talking about climate change has been a particular and specific challenge and one that reflects both the diversity of experiences and civic imaginations in this country as well as attitudes toward science and scientists. Debates about whether climate change is "real," whether it is to blame, and its range of current and predicted future impacts reflect what scholars have been saying for some time—that scientific facts do not travel straightforward paths to garner either political action or public concern (see, e.g., Ellis et al. 2010; Jasanoff 2010). Certainly, the increasing separation between political parties regarding climate change demonstrates this in spades. In a poll during the 2016 presidential election, 56 percent of Hillary Clinton's supporters said they cared a great deal about climate change in contrast to 15 percent of Donald Trump's supporters (Kennedy 2016). In the same poll, this divide holds (51 percent to 17 percent, respectively) when people were asked whether climate scientists understand the causes of climate change.

Polls are quite good at illustrating differences in public sentiment, but engaging diverse US publics is not *only* a matter of belief or trust in scientific facts. Engaging the public is not the same as providing them with information, though that is part of it. Rather, engagement implies that diverse publics are paying attention to that information and want to know more about an issue or a problem so that there becomes a "right thing to do" and concern and/or action are a likely outcome (Callison 2014). Engagement might also be understood as that moment when a concern becomes part of a civic imagination that circumscribes how we want to live together and who should participate and take action (Baiocchi et al. 2014). Engagement is most often evident among social groups that already have a defined notion of their group's civic paths and imaginations, and I would argue that engagement at some point both requires and nourishes such collectivity and communality. Groups that have come together through politics, religion, work, or other identity-related affiliations around an issue like climate change provide some strong and diverse examples of this.

In the early 2000s, when concern about climate change had sunk to an all-time low in American public polling, I started talking with scientists, journalists, and groups as diverse as Inuit leaders across the circumpolar Arctic, US Evangelicals, and corporate social responsibility activists (Callison 2014).[1] What they held in common was an awareness of climate change and a commitment to informing or educating American publics, but how they talked about climate change, the stories they told about it, and why they thought it mattered sounded *very* different.

Inuit leaders like Sheila Watt-Cloutier who were at the forefront of global negotiations around climate change in the mid-2000s talked about it as a human rights issue. Arctic temperatures are already warming at a much higher rater than the rest of the world. Watt-Cloutier coined the phrase "the right to be cold" in order to account for the

The right to be warm

fundamental changes that had already begun to affect Inuit ways of life, cultural and social practices, and the location and resilience of their communities. Watt-Cloutier led a petition along with sixty-two other Inuit before the Inter-American Commission on Human Rights in 2006, effectively reframing climate change on Inuit terms and with Inuit knowledge of the environment. Her 2015 autobiography describes the petition as an effort to reach global populations who live in cities by pointing out the "profound interconnectedness" of the global environment. In her words, "As hard as it is for many people to understand, for us Inuit, ice matters. Ice is life" (2015, 221). These quite different terms for understanding climate change as happening on a global scale with distinct impacts in particular regions served to elevate notions of differentiated vulnerability as well as justice and the long history of colonialism in this region (Callison 2017; Whyte 2013). Arctic communities are disproportionate recipients of greenhouse gas emissions that emanate almost entirely from population centers in the South.

American Evangelicals working under a loosely organized submovement known as Creation Care in the 2000s took a markedly different tack. Organizers based some of their approaches on the positive response they had received from an earlier ad campaign aimed at fellow Evangelicals asking "What Would Jesus Drive?" in order to recast transportation as a "moral issue" (Callison 2014, 143). They organized the Evangelical Climate Initiative beginning in 2006, reflecting the wide range of support across the leadership of the estimated thirty million Americans who identify as Evangelical. It also garnered an opposing statement from other Evangelicals who denied or were skeptical of climate change, so it wasn't without internal resistance. Reverend Jim Ball of the Evangelical Environment Network said part of the work involved convincing evangelical leaders to "bless the facts" so that the issue would matter in Evangelical terms, and this required care and attention and because of the long history of distrust in science stretching back through a century's worth of American debates about evolution (2014, 137). In other words, *who* is saying climate change is a concern is as important as *what* they say. The messenger in this case is essential to and a constituent of the message.

Corporate social responsibility advocates working on behalf of the Boston-based organization Ceres started asking what was important to Wall

Street investors and corporate leaders. By asking this question, they learned how climate change fit into financial frameworks that require companies to account for risks that harm investments. Climate change concerns were rearticulated as "climate risks" in order to situate the issue within a management context and mobilize investors who were responsible for trillions of dollars to start asking questions about how companies were attending to this emergent risk (2014, 204). They also worked politically to mobilize investors to ask for policy changes that might support actions by businesses to address climate change, taking, as they put it "capital to the capitol" (226). Here too, then, who says what and how they say it connects climate change to existing concerns, the communal life of those concerns and facts, and a particular civic imagination.

In comparing these articulations to the work of scientists and science journalists to inform and educate diverse publics, what becomes apparent is that science is, in many ways, its own vernacular and mode of apprehending and relating to the natural world—and publics are likely to have their own histories with scientific facts, claims, and processes. Journalists and scientists who are committed to informing publics through various means must then not only translate science for wide public consumption but also negotiate with the ethical and moral implications of scientific findings and public attitudes toward science. In doing so, they grapple with their own professional norms and obligations around detachment and objectivity along a spectrum of what I term "near-advocacy" (2014, 167). Some scientists and journalists see part of their professional obligation as educating diverse publics so that publics see climate change as a pressing issue of concern, while others make a distinction between informing and educating and see their role as one of providing information only. The "So what?" and "Why should we care?" questions hang in the balance for some and require action for others.

For diverse publics to become engaged, we have to consider that social networks and affiliations matter and that scientific facts need to be invested with meaning, ethics, and/or morality in order to galvanize a response to consequences, predictions, and proposed solutions (Callison 2014). Questions related to climate change are about not only how it is defined but what it means both collectively and individually, how it is connected to other preexisting concerns and histories of concern, and who gets to speak for and about it. How individuals and groups respond to facts and predictions about climate change is deeply related to their civic imaginations, including a particular view of and agency in the past, present, and future.

## Double Binds and Credible Stories

I've come to think of climate change as posing a double bind. By this, I mean that in order to move publics to care, climate change must both maintain fidelity to scientific facts and at the same time become much more than that (Callison 2014).[2] The concept of a double bind reflects the contradictions we all live with on a daily basis. The double bind was first used in the 1950s to describe "no-win" situations where demands or messages are in conflict with one another and responding to one means failing at another (Bateson et al. 1962). Anthropologist Kim Fortun, in her work on the multisited advocacy work that followed the Bhopal gas disaster in the 1980s, adapted this concept to describe the way social groups negotiate related and equally valued contradictory obligations. Fortun (2001) defines it this way: "Double bind situations create a persistent mismatch between explanation and everyday life, forcing ethical agents to 'dream up' new ways of understanding and engaging the world. They provide a lens for observing experiences produced by established rules and systems, yet not adequately described in standard explanations of how these systems function and change" (13). Double binds are generative. They require explanations that relate to existing ways of approaching problems in the world and an articulation of newly configured problems and adaptations. Stories about double binds require a nonreductive approach to complexity that accounts for mismatched explanations and messages. This is a key challenge that resonates with what scientists and journalists like Mann and Treaster articulate when it comes to understanding hurricanes and climate change, and it's central to the work Inuit leaders, corporate social responsibility advocates, Evangelicals, and others do more broadly when it comes to telling stories of and about climate change on their own terms. Storytelling, then, is key to articulating a concern as part of a civic imagination and enrolling others to participate and collaborate in actualizing and/or evolving responses to that concern.

Stories and facts don't keep their distance, however. Rather, as historians and anthropologists of science are likely to point out, they inhabit the same terrain. Extending this notion in her recent work, feminist science studies scholar Donna Haraway (2015) elegantly expresses it this way: "We need stories (and theories) that are just big enough to gather up the complexities and keep the edges open and greedy for surprising new and old connections" (160). Telling a story doesn't involve a shift in the facts—though, unfortunately, it can. Corporate-funded political think tanks worked diligently from the 1980s onward to promote climate skepticism and denial by doing exactly this (see Oreskes and Conway 2010).

The work discussed in this chapter provides a stark contrast to those who use existing concerns to promote skepticism. For example, Watt-Cloutier explained how she worked with media, asking journalists to help her "tell the story" (Callison 2014, 72) That story drew not only on scientific facts from the Arctic Climate Impact Assessment but also on traditional Indigenous knowledge about the environment, Inuit lifeways, and long and diverse resistance to colonialism across the Arctic. Climate change is the latest crisis that layers new challenges and reorients existing ones (Callison 2017; Whyte 2013). It requires new ways of navigating and engaging the world for Arctic residents (Bodenhorn and Ulturgasheva 2017; Cochran et al. 2013).

Epistemology, or how we know what we know, is becoming increasingly open to consideration and investigation in our hybrid media and information sources (Chadwick 2013; Jenkins et al. 2013). Where we get our information, who we consider an expert, and how much our experience matters are not insignificant on any issue. Because of the debates about the veracity of climate change in the US context and the breadth of predictions and science related to it, credibility is perhaps a more embattled aspect than it is for many other issues. But questions about credibility and epistemology raise even more questions about how we envision a future together. If we can't agree on why something matters or can't handle the complexities of how it matters, can we still reach agreements on what we should do and how we should adapt?

The variation in ways of speaking about and for climate change raises broader questions that go beyond an uptake of scientific facts. If climate change is considered as only (or primarily) a science-based issue, then deeper discussions and questions about our relationships to the natural world and to each other get lost. The range of probable and possible outcomes and risks reminds us that we are part of deeply interconnected communities with historical *and* ongoing relationships with each other and the lands, waters, and nonhumans around us. Such efforts ask us to consider how climate change connects us, what the underlying structure of our relations are, and how and what we should consider in imagining our collective and interconnected future.

This work of understanding, negotiating, articulating, and rearticulating both for wider publics and for a specific group—this work of communal meaning making—is becoming that much more vital. President Trump has made clear his belief that climate change is a hoax and has begun dismantling federal-government-led efforts to address and provide information about climate change (Posner 2017). Negotiating plurality, inspiring action, and recognizing different ways of making sense of the world require more and different efforts than merely making the public aware of climate facts, and the stakes arguably have never been as high as they are now. This doesn't mean we all have to agree on a particular civic imagination or ethical rationales for action, but it does mean we have to find ways to work together among the communal lives of scientific facts like climate change.

## Notes

1   I discuss this in more detail in my 2014 book *How Climate Change Comes to Matter: The Communal Life of Facts*, but these brief summaries provide some idea of just how differently these groups approached science and translated it into their own *vernaculars*, a term I use in order to explain what I heard when I talked with those who are actively working to mobilize their concerns about climate change.

2   I consider climate change an emergent form of life in Wittgenstein's linguistic sense and in the expanded sense offered by anthropologist Mike Fischer. Fischer adapted Wittgenstein's concept to get at how emerging science and technology require new ways of thinking, teaching, and being in the world. What climate change means is not apparent only from its appearance as facts or a set of predictions—rather, its meaning must be negotiated—and rules, grammars, and associations for how to talk about climate change must be established.

# 22

## Imagining Resistance to Trump through the Networked Branding of the National Park Service

### Rachel E. Moran and Thomas J Billard

Hours after President Donald J. Trump's inauguration, the National Park Service (NPS) fell afoul of the new administration by retweeting a side-by-side photographic comparison of the crowd size in attendance that day compared to Barack Obama's first inauguration. After being forced to take down the tweet, the NPS was reportedly instructed not to use the social media platform at all (Potenza 2017). In response, members of the public took up the traditional branding of the NPS in order to create resistance, both online and offline, to the newly inaugurated president's strict control over the government's public communications. More specifically, the public used images and icons associated with the NPS as symbols of resistance to communicate messages critical of the new administration in direct response to both its actions against the NPS and its authoritarian politics in general.

For instance, individuals protesting Trump's political agenda redesigned classic advertisements featuring Smokey Bear to carry messages of general discontent with the new administration and to issue calls for civil resistance. The NPS logo—the agency's most identifiable brand resource—was redesigned into the shape of a fist, a symbol of the Black Power movement (see figure 22.1). Brand imagery was paired with riffs on Smokey Bear's slogans, such as "Only you can resist fascist liars" and "Smokey says resist" (e.g., figure 22.2), and "Wokey Bear," as he was redubbed, became a staple of protest signage at the multitude of anti-inauguration demonstrations. Beyond physical protests, these new branded images circulated online via the sharing of protest images on social media sites, the dissemination of new Smokey designs, and even the sale of merchandise featuring "Smokey the Resister" (e.g., Frazier 2017).

Yet the transformation of the NPS brand went far beyond the mere sharing of Wokey Bear imagery to include the creation of alternative NPS social media accounts dubbed "AltNPS" designed to mirror the brand strategy of governmental accounts in order to reclaim the agency's messaging in the face of censorship from the Trump administration. This use of the NPS's brand resources to protest governmental authority transformed the meaning of the NPS brand itself such that it now represents resistance to a government of which it is, in reality, a constituent part. Moreover, via this transformation, the NPS has become a site of civic imagination as citizens use the brand and iconography of the NPS to conceptualize what resistance to the Trump administration can mean and how it can be achieved.

The transformation of the NPS's brand identity, as well as its popular cultural meaning, illustrates the elasticity of branding in a networked communication environment. As brands—even governmental ones—attempt to cultivate social connections through and around their

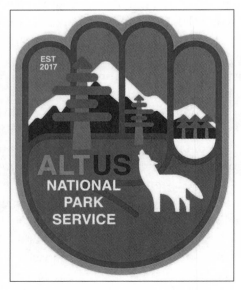

**Figure 22.1.** Redesigned National Park Service logo

**Figure 22.2.** National Park Service logo and "Wokey Bear" mascot

symbolic resources (Arvidsson 2005; Muniz and O'Guinn 2001), they open themselves up as spaces for the exchange of social and cultural meanings. Within these spaces, however, the networks of brand participants reify existing cultural meanings while also generating new ones that transform—and even contest—the identity of the branded entity (Billard 2016, 2019). This power over the structure and articulation of the NPS's brand meaning thus makes the NPS a focal point around which action and activism are organized and, consequently, alternative civic futures are imagined.

The cultural and iconographic significance of the NPS's brand resources and, in particular, the icon of Smokey Bear enabled this transformation. First released in 1942 during the Second World War (Rice

2001), Smokey was the central figure of public service campaigns raising awareness about wildfire prevention in the western United States. With so many able-bodied men away at war, the government could not spare the manpower to fight wildfires, so they needed to prevent them from beginning in the first place (Morrison 1995). In the intervening years, however, Smokey Bear has evolved beyond his role as a character in a public service announcement into a cultural icon (Helmers 2011). The subject of a 1952 song (which introduced the apocryphal name "Smokey *the* Bear"), radio plays, cartoons, children's books, comic strips, dolls, and toys, as well as the mascot of the Junior Forest Ranger Program, which inducted millions of American children (Morrison 1995; Wilson 2014), and of wildfire education programs at nearly every American school (Ballard, Evans, Sturtevant, and Jakes 2012), Smokey has a cultural resonance far beyond any other governmental marketing tool. Indeed, his cultural resonance is so great that in 1952, the US Congress passed the Smokey Bear Act, which removed Smokey from the public domain and placed his image under the control of the secretary of agriculture (Morrison 1995).

As Douglas Holt (2004) has written, "The crux of iconicity is that the person or the thing is widely regarded as the most compelling symbol of a set of ideas and values that a society deems important" (1), and Smokey stands in many ways as the most compelling symbol of the federal government's mandate to engage in public service. As is oft noted in scholarship and commentary on Smokey Bear, he is a warden figure (Morrison 1995), "a friendly and stalwart steward of nature" (Wilson 2014, 106), "a denizen of those woods you're visiting, and he cares about preserving them" (Earle 2000, 31). Whereas other symbols of governmental responsibility emphasize authority and dominion over the public, Smokey represents guardianship of the public's shared natural resources (DiSanza and Bullis 1999). As Marguerite Helmers (2011) notes, Smokey wears a hat that "aligns him with the authority of the Park Service rangers," but the rest of his apparel mirrors that of the Civilian Conservation Corps, "a group of workers who embodied the value of service and aligned it with patriotism and the parks" (48). Thus, as a branded image of the NPS, Smokey Bear communicates the government's obligation to nurture, rather than dominate, the public it serves, which made him—and the NPS he represents—the perfect brand image through which to criticize an administration that quickly revealed itself to hold alternative values of governance.

Individuals' resonance with Smokey Bear iconography and their reimagining of it in the service of political commentary reflect the ways in which communities are formed around brand imagery as well as how these communities become facilitators of political and civic imaginations. In their seminal work on "brand communities," Albert Muniz and Thomas O'Guinn (2001) argue that brands are social objects and are socially constructed (27). The communities that surround brands are united not simply by acts of consumption but by an affective bond with the brand itself as well as with others through connection to the brand. Muniz and O'Guinn further characterize this social connection as emblematic of wider trends in brand thinking that have moved beyond the traditional consumer-brand dyad to a consumer-brand-consumer triad. From this perspective, the NPS cultivates a triadic relationship wherein citizens facilitate social connection through their own connection with the NPS brand. This is particularly potent in the case of the NPS given its role in the personal history of millions of Americans who grew up going to—and continue to frequent—National Parks and for whom Smokey Bear is a resonant cultural icon.

The individual connection citizens feel with the public spaces guarded by Smokey and the NPS has been central to the NPS's branding efforts and can be seen clearly in their social media strategies. Rather than actively producing original brand content, the NPS relies on crowdsourced branding materials contributed by citizens through social media, which collectively builds a brand image reliant on their network of brand participants. The primary social media feeds used by the NPS—Twitter, Facebook, and Instagram—utilize the hashtag #findyourpark to source images from their wide network of visitors to populate their feeds. Currently, the Instagram version of the hashtag has been attached to more than one million images from users around the United States. Given the centrality of users to the maintenance of the NPS brand and the personal attachment individuals have to the public spaces being promoted, it is unsurprising that individuals feel an identity affiliation with the brand resources used by the NPS. Moreover, the move from "closed" to "open" brands seen in marketing in recent years (Pitt et al. 2006) affords brand communities a stake in the creative direction of the brand, thus opening space for brand imagery to be utilized in ways that may support or contest the brand's institutional image. Political activists' use of NPS brand imagery as resistance against the Trump administration is therefore a prime example of how civic engagement arises from brand communities.

Activists' use of NPS brand imagery is especially interesting given that they used it both to contest the burgeoning authoritarian tendencies of the incoming administration *and* to reify the traditional brand of the NPS as a public-serving entity. Rather than seeing this as an example of brand signifiers' vulnerability to hijacking for alternative causes, the NPS case illustrates the complexities of brand management in a networked era (Billard and Moran 2018). Despite the NPS being a governmental agency and thus subordinate to the executive administration, its reliance on the public for the development of its brand image distributes power over the brand's meaning across a network of individuals and institutions. Consequently, when institutional powers attempt to reclaim centralized control over the brand—for instance, the Trump administration's removal of information about climate change from the NPS's online presence—relations within the brand's network are disturbed. The locus of control over the brand's meaning no longer resides with the branded entity but rather is collectively held across the network of brand participants (albeit unevenly). This decentralization of power means that the government cannot prevent its own subordinate brand from becoming a site at which countergovernmental resistance can organize. Moreover, the "openness" of the NPS's brand imagery (including and especially Smokey Bear) offers a set of communicative resources through and with which the newly resistant brand network can express its collective political aims.

This alternative vision of the NPS—represented both by the resources reimagined by brand network participants and by the "AltNPS" social media accounts they created—launches from, yet moves beyond, the identity affiliations enabled by the brand's open nature and shifts into the collective imagining of alternative possibilities of governance and civic values. As Henry Jenkins, Gabriel Peters-Lazaro, and Sangita Shresthova discuss in their introduction to this volume, the civic imagination involves the ability to imagine positive alternatives to contemporary sociopolitical situations and to imagine oneself as empowered to bring about those changes, both of which are facilitated by a shared "cultural vocabulary" through which would-be activists communicate their imaginings. In the current case, the alternative future imagined through the NPS brand is one in which the federal government upholds its civic and moral obligation to preserve the environment for future generations and values democratic principles in its engagement with the public. The emergence of the AltNPS on social media is indicative of such imagining in practice. These social media feeds issue calls for action and #resistance from their followers in what we might consider a role-playing of the NPS in an imagined reality without the current political constraints. Further examples can be seen in how protesters employed Smokey Bear imagery in the March for Science in spring 2017 (see figure 22.3). Activists used NPS imagery on protest signs to contest the administration's downplaying of climate change, reaffirm the NPS's values as an environmental champion, and push for fulfillment of the government's role as a steward of the public. For those who employed the NPS brand in their protest activities, the NPS exists not only as a site of political contention, where conversations over policy priorities can take place, but also as a space within which civic futures can be imagined.

Individuals participating in the practices of networked branding were further emboldened as civic agents by repurposing the figure of Smokey Bear, an icon of collective civic responsibility, as an aspirational symbol of their own contributions. As a figure of both positive governmental authority and civic agency, Smokey Bear exists as a powerful cultural role model for individuals seeking ways to become involved in civic life in the wake of the Trump administration. Identification with this resonant cultural icon allowed individuals to put themselves in Smokey's boots and model their actions on those of the figure to whom they have looked since childhood as an ideal of collective responsibility. Reciprocally, in using the branded symbol of Smokey, they have attributed to him their own desires to become empowered civic actors and "resist fascist liars" (see figure 22.4).

By communicating their resistance through Smokey Bear and other NPS branding, in addition to attributing messages of resistance to his image, activists make salient how networked brands act as a cultural vocabulary allowing a multitude of political conversations. As such, the NPS's brand resources exist as pseudolinguistic resources that can be

**Figure 22.3.** Smokey Bear protest sign

used in *individual* acts of *collective* civic imagination. That is, the brand resources of the NPS can be—and indeed are—invoked in individuals' acts and articulations of dissent that contribute to the collective ethos of resistance. The polysemy of the NPS's brand resources further brokers political relationships through the unification of diverse political interest groups, each of which opposes different aspects of the Trump administration's agenda. For instance, activists used Smokey Bear imagery in both the Women's March and the March for Science as representative of both environmental and conservationist concerns as well as feminist critiques of the misogynistic policies of the incoming administration.

These uses and transformation of the NPS brand by individuals in service of political resistance are emblematic of what we have termed *networked branding* (Billard and Moran 2018). The networked nature of the NPS brand results from the confluence of several trends increasingly common in contemporary brand culture—namely, the participatory nature of branded entities' public communications, the cultivation of

**Figure 22.4.** Smokey Bear poster design

personal identity affiliations with brands, and the ease of digital manipulation of iconographic brand resources in an age of technologically empowered amateurs (Billard 2016, 2019). The very practice of networked
branding therefore enables the civic imagination to surface, as brands
have become collective resources with which, and transformative spaces
in which, civic associations can form and political consciousness can be
raised (Bennett and Lagos 2007).

The success of the NPS brand—both in its ability to take a central role
in the public's social relationships and in its open structure, which has
allowed it to be transformed in the service of the civic imagination—
stands as a testament to the revolutionary political potential of

contemporary brand culture. We view the practices discussed in this chapter as indicative of a brand culture—situated within a networked society (Castells 2010)—in which citizenship and consumer culture are not mutually exclusive categories and citizens are empowered to re-structure brand meanings for collective expression, even if that brand belongs to the government. Accordingly, we expect that the increasing prevalence of networked brands will facilitate an increase in popular political expression through the logics of consumer culture and, in par-ticular, contribute to the cultivation of the civic imagination.

## PART V

# How Do We Imagine Our Social Connections with a Larger Community?

Civic imagination helps communities build collective identities by allowing them to reflect on shared histories and envision alternative futures. Such community building operates on interconnected levels. Crucially, the civic imagination surfaces resonant tropes that identify affinities between community members. The civic imagination also helps people develop a narrative that frames their shared values. Finally, the civic imagination inspires civic action by defining collective goals. Storytelling plays a crucial role in each of these processes, helping us identify our collective identities, values, and goals and creating a strong sense that "we are all in this together."

Discussing storytelling in social movement contexts, Francesca Polletta (2009) notes, "Activists, like prophets, politicians, and advertising executives, have long recognized the power of a good story to move people to action" (33). Unlike an approach that emphasizes "framing" in terms of "clear, concise, and coherent" messaging, the power of these narratives lies in their "allusiveness, indeed, their ambiguity" (33), which encourages reflection and debate. We believe the invitation to participate in creating and exchanging such narratives is at the core of what we call "imagining communities," a reconceptualization of Benedict Anderson's (2006) "imagined communities."

Anderson (2006) accounted for the rise of nationalist movements in the late nineteenth and early twentieth centuries as the newspaper became the medium that brought together a diverse and dispersed population around more centrally composed messaging. Such communities were "*imagined* because the members of even the smallest nation will never know most of their fellow members, meet them, or hear of them, yet in the minds of each lives the image of their communion" (6). In Anderson's account, the imagination was a product, something produced by central authorities, rather than a process by which people seek to locate themselves in relation to others around them. Imagined communities are a byproduct of the homogenizing pressures of modernity (Gellner 1983) and the colonialist project. In speaking of imagining communities, we are interested in the processes by which people forge links with each other through their active participation in the production and circulation of media within an increasingly networked society.

Rather than collapsing differences, imagining communities value inclusion and diversity. Imagining communities maintain a dynamism and fluidity often lost in accounts of the imagined community. Building on Freire, imagining communities may be born through a process of decolonizing the mind, encouraging a questioning of inherited narratives in favor of the emergence of new structures of power and new forms of knowledge (above all, of self-knowledge). Postcolonial scholars (including Edward Said, Stuart Hall, and Partha Chatterjee) have challenged the linear trajectories implied in Anderson's formulation of the rise of nationalism as an outcome of the colonial experience. Chatterjee (1993) observes that Anderson assumes that "even our imaginations . . . must remain forever colonized" (5). Crucially, these critiques bring into sharp focus the uneven power relations of the colonial experience and the ways that these have impacted (and continue to impact) nation-building (and other community-building) efforts.

A struggle over national identity, here framed in terms of different forms of nostalgia, surfaces in chapter 24 in Henry Jenkins's account of the Broadway musical *Hamilton*, which he argues "embodied an America marked by multiculturalism, fluid boundaries, hybrid identities, and musical mash-ups." *Hamilton* offered an alternative framing of the founding of the American republic, one that Jenkins sees as an (almost) inevitable response from "diverse America" to the Tea Party movement, which sought to restore a lost nationhood (to "Make America great again").

In chapter 23, Sangita Shresthova discusses Bollywood dance as undergoing a moment defined by the ongoing struggle over competing narratives, especially as diasporic communities assert their own messages through its conventions. In this case, groups struggle to attach contested meanings to choreography inspired by Bollywood films to root their performances in local cultural and political realities. She describes critical discussions about who may perform Bollywood dance, what meanings are associated with it, and how it responds to current debates around the acceptance or rejection of cultural difference.

Through the cases included in this volume, we seek to update and nuance Anderson's term to stress contemporary modes of media production and circulation. Imagining communities "are not simply accepting an agenda constructed by mass media for their consumption, rather they are actively co-constructing the contents of the civic imagination through networked communications. They are building a group identity that might fuel their campaigns and, within those campaigns, they are developing ways of expressing their shared visions for what a better society might look like" (Jenkins et al. 2016).

Whereas Anderson's imagined communities depended on unified, shared narratives of national origins and Manifest Destiny, these imagining communities are defined through competing narratives as different participants propose alternative ways forward from historical divisions. These struggles are shaped by uneven access to communications tools and resources, cultural authority and political power, and systemic exclusions and inequalities, which result in an ongoing struggle between competing notions about the constitution of communities.

In chapter 25, Paromita Sengupta considers how the Humans of New York (HONY) initiative confronted such tensions as its core model was replicated in cities around the world and sought to move beyond collaborative storytelling toward other kinds of collective action. Sengupta describes how "members develop their own set of collaborative world-building practices, drawn from narrative empathy, and the creation of affective, parasocial relationships with the anonymous subjects of Stanton's photographs." The more strongly empowered participants felt, the more they bumped up against boundaries preset by the project's creator, who sought greater control over current and future HONY efforts.

Tracing the roots of the Black Lives matter to an older tradition of the black radical imagination as a powerful source of inspiration for black activists, artists, and leaders, in chapter 26, Chris Harris considers the theories of social change that informed the "Vision for Black Lives." This powerful manifesto envisions desired shifts in the relations between black citizens and public institutions, especially the police and the prisons, that directly impact their lives. Harris describes life-affirming rituals that allowed the black community to endure a long history of oppression and inequality and sustain a powerful emancipatory imaginary.

When read together, these case studies illustrate the *process* of imagining, the ongoing struggles that build and support communities, the unequal power dynamics that inform these struggles, and the ways the emerging imagery and narratives reinterrogate collective constructions of the past.

**23**

# Moving to a Bollywood Beat, "Born in the USA" Goes My Indian Heart?

Exploring Possibility and Imagination through Hindi Film Dance

**Sangita Shresthova**

Contestant Jennifer Davis's Bollywood dance performance caused controversy at the 2018 Miss America pageant because Davis could claim no connection to India or Indian heritage. Reacting to the flurry of posts triggered by her performance, Davis posted the following statement to her Facebook page in her defense: "'Why do you do Bollywood, are you even of the culture?' I get this question all of the time, and my response is because I LOVE it. The beauty of dance is that no matter where you come from we can have a common denominator, and that is a love of dance." The social media debate that unfolded focused largely on whether Davis should have chosen to perform a dance set to a Bollywood song as a non–Indian American. Commentor @MeganFaiFai applauded Davis for her "impressive" performance. Others, such as @AmyArgetsinger, were less charitable and compared her attempt to "playing Marimbas," a token gesture toward multiculturalism. Other commenters pushed further and questioned the ethics of Davis's decision, which they saw as problematic "#cultural appropriation" that undermined her stated commitment to diversity. They saw Bollywood dance as a specifically Indian dance style rooted in that country's national and cultural histories. The fact that Nina Davuluri, an Indian American contestant from Arkansas, had performed a Bollywood dance as a contestant in 2017 and had explicitly tied this performance to her cultural heritage strengthened this perceived connection. Davuluri had, in fact, won the Miss America title a few years earlier and appeared as a judge in the 2018 competition. Davuluri's poker-face reaction to Davis's performance inspired further remarks: "I am LIVING for @NinaDavu-luri's face after Bollywood debacle #sideeye."

The debate surrounding Davis's performance draws attention to the shifting meanings created by Bollywood dance performances in the United States. Specifically, it forces us to sharpen our understanding of how Bollywood dance emerged as a popular live dance form and why it has become a contested space in the current moment. We need to understand how live performances of Bollywood dance operate in the United States. How has its role evolved into a celebration of both diversity and Indianness? What sort of imagined communities do Bollywood dances inspire through this role? And are the meanings created contingent on a connection to Hindi films and Indian culture?

To understand how Bollywood dance has become a contested practice, we need to first explore it as a set of choreographic conventions that emerged out of India's Hindi-language cinema industries based in Mumbai, India. Colloquially, "Bollywood dance" describes both song-and-dance sequences in Hindi films and the live amateur and professional performances they inspire. India's Mumbai-based film industry dates back to the early 1900s, and choreographed movement sequences appear even in those early experiments. Indian filmmakers liberally borrowed from a myriad of theatrical and film traditions—including (most prominently) Parsi theater, religious drama, Weimar-era German films, and Hollywood—to inform the narrative conventions that later became the signature elements of Hindi films (Dudrah 2008; Gopalan 2002; Morcom 2007; Prasad 1998).

Over the decades, Hindi film dance directors (choreographers' official title in the industry) have borrowed from a variety of dance traditions to create dance sequences that would entice audiences and fulfill the dance's narrative functions. Commenting on this process ten years ago (in an era of DVD players), dance director Feroz Khan laughingly observed in an interview (in Shresthova 2011) that all dance directors return to India with suitcases full of dance DVDs every time they travel abroad. The demand for a mix of dance styles has also meant that dancers with training in various dance techniques, including India's classical dance traditions, have worked in the industry. As dance scholar Pallabi Chakravorty (2009) notes, "Many famous dancers and choreographers have appeared on the silver screen. They include GopiKishan, Waheeda

Rahman, Vaijantimala, Kamalahasan, Hemamalini and Madhri Dixit. Born out of Parsi theater (which blended the local idiom with received colonial aesthetic forms), Bombay cinema has been a fulcrum of creative hybridity" (218).

The contemporary global popularity of Bollywood dance was initially driven by enthusiasm expressed by Indian and other diasporic audiences for Hindi films in the 1990s. Enabled by technological innovations, reproductive possibilities, and digital spreadability, Indian diasporic communities initially turned to Hindi films as "temples of desire" (Mishra 2001) that nurture a sometimes nostalgic connection to an (often) imagined homeland. Translating song-and-dance sequences in Hindi films into live localized performances allowed audiences to literally experience Bollywood (and imagined versions of India) through their bodies, individually and collectively. The inherent mixing of styles and character-driven choreography that have inspired Hindi film dances since their inception imbued the process of creating localized Bollywood dances with a sense of permission (Prasad 1998, 88–115)—permission to mix film dance elements with local movements to create compositions that resonated with the audiences' desires and imagination.

The permission to appropriate Hindi film dance supported Bollywood dance as it grew into a participatory interpretive dance form. Soon dancers who were not connected to the industry felt that they could create, edit, and otherwise remix the dances to fit their local realities, needs, and preferences. Detailing the specifics of how Bollywood dance functions in South Asian diasporic communities, cultural studies scholar Anjali Gera Roy (2016) observes that the "syncretic song-and-dance sequences" in Hindi films "loosely draw on diverse performative traditions," which enables them to have a "wider South Asian appeal" (87).

Today, the college-level dance competition circuit is likely the most popular site for live Bollywood dance in the United States. The circuit involves thousands of young second- and third-generation Indian (and other South Asian) Americans. Many of these youths turn to Bollywood dance to explore their transnational and hyphenated identities in ways that break with the nostalgic return to an-imagined homeland that defined an earlier era of Bollywood dance in the country. To these young people, connections to a real or imagined India are only part of the draw of Bollywood dance. In fact, their relationships to India are often tenuous. Rather, the dancers lay claim to the permission to create and re-create dances that they see as central to Bollywood dance. As such, they increasingly use Bollywood dance to create dances that grapple with thorny issues and still-taboo social topics in South Asian communities. Before larger audiences in competition settings, these performances become important sites of imagination and negotiation and a coming of age for second- and third-generation Indian Americans who are breaking out of rather than reaffirming normative values and nostalgic longing.

A performance staged by Anubhav, a Hindi film dance competition team based at Northwestern University in 2014, defined a key moment for this trend in Bollywood dance. Anubhav's choreography grappled with issues of family, sexuality, and gender as told through the perspective of a young man coming of age in the United States. Through this performance, LGBTQ issues took center stage as Anubhav created a dance that told the story of a young Indian American man coming to terms with his homosexuality, a topic still taboo in many Indian communities, particularly as homosexual behavior is still a controversial issue in India.

In the opening moments of Anubhav's performance, the audience meets Neel, a young man who has grown up without his father and cares deeply about his mother. He has always tried to do "everything right" (we learn from the performance voiceover). He attended a good school and found a good job. Neel is engaged to Anjali, who was his "inspiration" and whom his mother also adored. But despite all this, Neel just couldn't "love her." Through the performance, set against the backdrop of wedding plans, the audience soon learns Neel's secret—that he is in love with another young man. As the performance progresses, Neel struggles to come to terms with his sexuality, but eventually, with Anjali's support, he decides to "be the person he was always meant to be."

Though it did initially raise some controversy among older judges, Anubhav's performance was enthusiastically received when the team performed their routine on the US college-level competition circuit that year. In fact, it was so well received that the team went on to win Bollywood America, which has established itself as the finalist "best of the best" annual event, where winners of all other regional competitions compete against each other.

Further evidence of the ways in which some dancers in the United States are moving beyond nostalgia in their approach to Bollywood dance is the fact that Anubhav's dance was co-choreographed by Yuri Doolan, a Korean American with no previous ties to the South Asian community. In fact, Doolan is the first to admit that he did not have any deep knowledge of Bollywood prior to his involvement with the team. The piece he choreographed for Anubhav was in part autobiographical and a big moment of truth for Doolan. When I interviewed him in 2015, he spoke about the community he found through Bollywood dance at college as a space that allowed him to connect with people and ultimately express his identity in ways that he was not able to in other spaces in his life. He explains, "The South Asian American [dance] community were very accepting and welcoming. I think that has to do with the fact that there's a lot of diversity in South Asian America. . . . A lot of times kids are coming from various different parts of India, speak different languages, are of a different religious background. With so much diversity, the fact that I was different wasn't a big deal. . . . I was never made to feel like an outsider." An article published on June 11, 2014, in *India Currents*, a popular Indian California community monthly magazine, put Doolan's observations and Anubhav's performance in a broader context when the author, Kamal Kamanth, argued, "This is what we need to do, as Indian Americans, to break the silence within our families and communities." For Kamanth, Bollywood, as a popular, recognizable, and participatory culture, can and should become an accessible "medium" that youths can use to "showcase [their] stand on this issue" so that the "message of both cultural and LGBTQ pride will be heard." For the youths, Anubhav's performance used Bollywood dance to explore the acceptance of multifaceted identities, which they felt were all part of what the Bollywood dance community could take on and embrace.

The Republican Hindu Coalition's (RHC) Hindus United Against Terror Charity Concert organized a Bollywood-dance-themed event on October 15, 2016, in Edison, New Jersey, that offered a very different—almost oppositional—interpretation of the meanings associated with Bollywood dance in the United States. The event sought to foster and support an explicitly Hindu Indian American community aligned with the antiterrorist and anti-Muslim rhetoric of Trump's presidential campaign. Attended by approximately two hundred people, the event featured performances by local Bollywood dancers and industry professionals flown in from the United Kingdom and India, recorded messages from American and Indian politicians, a live appearance by then presidential candidate Donald Trump, and Indian snacks.

A terrorism-themed Bollywood-like dance performed by amateur dancers was central to the event. In this sequence, four ethnically Indian dancers stepped out on the stage, a projection of the American flag looming large behind them. As waltz music began and they paired off and started to move, the background projection faded into a heart. Their Bollywood-like performance was soon rudely interrupted by a group of masked men who burst onto the stage bearing neon plastic automatic weapons. Amid screams and unintelligible shouting, the dancers were forced to kneel. Just as a violent ending seemed inevitable, another group of performers, dressed in army fatigues with the words "Navy Seal" sprawled across their backs, burst onto the stage. They overcame the masked men and joined the four dancers as the American national anthem began to play. More dancers came onto the stage to perform a synchronized flag-waving dance set to "Born in the USA." The projection of the American flag returned and faded to black as the dance concluded. In this instance, Bollywood-style dancing inspired an imaginary of fear and national sentiment. The dancers were not using dance to explore diversity; rather, they were using their performance to valorize the nation through the fear of terror.

Read through the lens of Anubhav's performance and many others like it, the dance staged at the RHC Hindus United Against Terror Charity Concert feels like an aberration, a departure from the largely progressive and expansive imaginary communities that Bollywood inspires among young Indian Americans who are using it to break out of existing limiting norms and expectations around Indian American identities. In contrast, the dance at the RHC event sets up an us-versus-them frame, one that reiterates Hinduism and American nationalism as a foundation for creating a shared imagination and, through it, a sense of shared community. This sense of aberration does, in fact, extend to the event itself, as the RHC likely represents only a relatively small percentage of Indian Americans. Statistics indicate that this population generally tends toward progressive politics (a 2012 Pew Research Center poll found that 65 percent of Indian Americans affiliate themselves with the Democratic Party).

Yet the RHC event performance can, and should, also be examined as reflective of nationalist narrative legacies in Bollywood films that are often, and perhaps too conveniently, overlooked by Indian American dancers committed to celebrating diversity and hybridity.[1] In particular, the narrative frame that pits "protagonist" (Hindu) Indians against dangerous outsiders (in particular, Pakistanis and Muslims) appears in Hindi films with distinct regularity. Examples of films such as *Veer Zara* (2004)—which involves a cross-border love story that bridges the Pakistan/India divide—notwithstanding, there is a strong tradition of conflict-centered Hindi films. For example, *Border* (1997), a film set in the Indo-American war of 1971, situates Indians (with recognizably Hindu names) as heroes. *Zameen* (Land 2003) opens with a (Pakistan-backed) terrorist attack on India's parliament building and follows the efforts of two (Hindu) protagonists as they struggle to stop future attacks. Set initially in Afghanistan, *Agent Vinod* (2012) portrays the Inter-Services International (ISI), Pakistan's secret service, as collaborating with the Taliban. The anti-Pakistani and anti-Muslim sentiments that surface in Bollywood films could, at first glance, even be seen as largely conciliatory. *Bajrangi Bhaijaan* (Brother Bajrangi 2015), for instance, tells the story of a devout (Hindu) Ram-devotee protagonist who rescues a mute Muslim girl and eventually returns her to her home in Pakistan. In the final guaranteed-tear-jerker moment of the film, as he crosses the militarized border to return to India, a young girl desperately waves to catch his attention. Against a background of awed copatriots on the Pakistani side, she shouts "Jai Shree Rama!" and thus effectively confirms the power of Hinduism and the protagonist's (superior) status as the man that broke her silence.

Themes contained in these films also tie into anti-Muslim, anti-Pakistan, pro-Hindu Indian rhetoric supported by India's prime minister, Narendra Modi; his Bharatiya Janata Party; and other affiliated parties and organizations, exemplified by increasing violence against Muslims in India and attempts to ban Pakistani artists (mostly actors) from working on Indian films following a terrorist attack in Jammu and Kashmir in September 2016. The RHC's support for Donald Trump's presidential campaign clearly articulate such pro-Indian nationalist and anti-Muslim sentiments. According to its website, the RHC specifically aims to support an "expansion of trade between India and United States to promote

'Made in America' opportunities and also encourage PM Modi's 'made in India' program." Through this statement, the RHC explicitly identifies itself as a connector between President Trump's agenda and the Modi administration in India. In fact, presidential candidate Trump was popular among India's Hindu nationalists, who saw him as a friend and ally who understood their worldview and anti-Muslim sentiments.

When read alongside this anti-Muslim and anti-Pakistani film tradition and the current political climate, the Bollywood dance staged at the RHC event appears to be very much an example of an exclusive and "othering" civic imagination inspired by Hindi films and expressed through Bollywood dance. Writing for *Quartz* (India), journalist Stanley Thangaraj (2016) makes this connection explicit when he states, "With a Hindu fundamentalist party in power in India, the wave of such conservatism and violence washes up easily onto the shores of the United States through transnational connections. The same fundamentalism shaping Indian politics finds a home with the Hindu Indian American community with their anti-Muslim rhetoric."

Thus read, the mechanisms celebrated by some dancers as tools that help support progressive and inclusive imaginary communities through Bollywood dance may also be used to advocate for causes that are antithetical to those progressive visions. The permissiveness and remixing of dance styles that some see as crucial to this movement style are at odds with the notion that Bollywood dance is a culturally rooted tradition. And the controversy that surrounded Jennifer Davis's performance at the 2018 Miss America competition confirms that Bollywood dance in the United States is indeed an intensely contested imaginary space. Through all this, Bollywood dance clearly has much to teach us about how popular culture can inspire contested imaginations.

## Note

1 See Rini Bhattacharya Mehta and Rajeshwari V. Pandharipande's *Bollywood and Globalization: Indian Popular Cinema, Nation and Diaspora* for a detailed examination of the nation, globalization, and Hindi cinema.

_Romantice_

**24**

## "Our" Hamilton

Reimagining the Founders for a "Diverse America"

### Henry Jenkins

America means certain things to people who come here. It
means the Declaration of Independence, it means Washington,
it means Lincoln. . . . Just as soon as the alien gets all that . . .
he is as much an American as the man who can boast of nine
generations of American forebears. He gets the tone of America,
and as soon as there is tone there is poetry.
—Robert Frost (1923)

American history can be told and retold, claimed and reclaimed,
even by people who don't look like George Washington and
Betsy Ross.
—Lin-Manuel Miranda (2016)

In mid-November 2016, not long after a traumatic presidential election,
future vice president Mike Pence took his daughter to see the Broadway musical *Hamilton*. *Hamilton* told the story of Alexander Hamilton,
the first US secretary of the Treasury, who is best known for his role
in creating the federal banking system and for his death in a duel
with Aaron Burr—unlikely material for a hip-hop musical. *Hamilton*
depicted America as a "young, scrappy and hungry" nation, embracing
an immigrant's ambitions as his guts and wits allow him to rise to the
highest circles of wealth and power. *Hamilton* did not pull punches in
representing the intense power struggles defining the infrastructure of
American democracy. But it became more than that—a key resource for
the contemporary civic imagination at a time of political struggles over
inclusion and representation. _yes_

As the Pences exited the theater, Brandon Victor Dixon (himself playing Vice President Aaron Burr), speaking on behalf of the cast, made some prepared remarks: "We, sir—we—are the diverse America who are alarmed and anxious that your new administration will not protect us, our planet, our children, our parents, or defend us and uphold our inalienable rights. But we truly hope that this show has inspired you to uphold our American values and to work on behalf of all of us. All of us. Again, we truly thank you for seeing this show, this wonderful American story told by a diverse group of men and women of different colors, creeds and orientations" (E. Nelson 2016). Pence took the incident in stride, evoking a conservative respect for American traditions: "I nudged my kids and reminded them that's what freedom sounds like" (E. Nelson 2016). But President Donald Trump was more reactionary, tweeting a hot-headed demand for an apology: "The theater must always be a safe and special place" (Healy 2016). The *Washington Post* noted that Trump had lost another chance to offer a divided nation "assurances that he would be a president for all Americans" (Rucker 2016). Peter Wehner, a former George W. Bush speechwriter, summed up the events as a "collision of two different Americas and two different visions and two different sets of experiences" (Rucker 2016).

*Hamilton* embodied an America of multiculturalism, fluid boundaries, hybrid identities, and musical mash-ups—what Dixon called "diverse America." Trump and Pence embraced an "America-first" vision of deportation police, walled borders, extreme vetting, and alternative facts. In many ways, this confrontation between competing civic imaginations was inevitable.

Since August 2015, *Hamilton* had been the hottest show on Broadway, winning multiple Tony Awards, reaching far more people with its top-selling soundtrack album than could see the sold-out performances, and spreading via social media in the form of YouTube clips and sound files. When the right created a hashtag campaign to #BoycottHamilton, many joked that it might increase their likelihood of getting tickets at a time when scalpers were charging upwards of $2,000 per seat. Ironically, *Hamilton* spoke for an America that by and large could not afford to attend its performances (despite various programs to discount tickets for inner-city youths).

What made *Hamilton* a symbol for a "diverse America" was not its story per se but how it was told—its mixture of different popular music traditions, its minority and mixed-race performers, the collective voice of its chorus, its alternative vision of "we the people" for an era of demographic flux, and the ways that the live event enabled more direct interplay between audience and performers. As Lin-Manuel Miranda, its Puerto Rico–born performer, playwright, and composer, noted, "Our cast looks like America looks now" (Major 2016). Renée Elise Goldsberry (who plays Angelica Schuyler) explained, "We have the opportunity to reclaim a history that some of us don't necessarily think is our own" (Perez et al. 2016).

Ron Chernow, the historian whose biography inspired the play, told *Newsweek*, "It was so daring and revolutionary to cast these parts with the very people who were excluded during this period from American history. . . . This came out at the point where more than 40% of the births in America were identified as an African-American, Asian American, Latino or biracial. We're seeing the same thing in American politics. You have one side of the aisle celebrating these changes and the other side of the aisle dismayed by all these changes" (Subin 2016). Amid these demographic shifts, there was an intensifying struggle over who belongs here, what an American looks like, and who "owns" the "founding fathers." By reimagining American history, Miranda encouraged audiences to reimagine America's future.

*Hamilton* represented a response from "diverse America" to the Tea Party movement. The Tea Party, which claimed to speak for "real Americans" who wanted to "take our country back," had embraced the Gadsen "Don't Tread on Me" flag as its symbol and the "Sons of Liberty" as its inspiration. The party consisted overwhelmingly of older white males with some college education who felt threatened by these demographic changes (Skocpol and Williamson 2012). One Tea Party supporter told political scientists Theda Skocpol and Vanessa Williamson (2012) that they felt they were "losing the nation they love[d], the country they planned to leave to their children and grandchildren" (7). This framing is a prime example of what Svetlana Boym (2001) calls "restorative nostalgia," a conservative desire to restore a lost homeland ("Make America great again") and a tendency to construct conspiracy theories to account for this fall from grace.

By contrast, *Hamilton* described America as an "unfinished symphony," suggesting that we still need to struggle if the nation is to live up to its founding ideals. Such comments represent what Boym (2001) calls "reflexive nostalgia," a form that "dwells on the ambivalences of human longing and belonging and does not shy away from the contradictions of modernity" (xviii). While restorative nostalgia starts from the assumption that it already knows all the answers, reflexive nostalgia represents an "ethical and creative challenge"—it asks questions, sparks debates, and encourages people to rethink their commitments to the past.

If *Hamilton* created a new countermyth about American history, it also embodied debates the country was already having in the wake of Obama's historic election and found itself briefly confronting the backlash against those changes that contributed to Trump's election success. The musical, allowed "diverse America" to fantasize about a country where "we"—"all of us"—had been there together, all along, even as it depended on audience recognition that many groups are still struggling for representation and inclusion. Accepting the Tony award a few days after a deadly shooting at an Orlando LGBTQ nightclub, Miranda (2016) broke down into tears as he proclaimed—in rhyming couplets, no less— "Love is love is love is love is love is love is love, cannot be killed or swept aside. Now fill the world with music, love, and pride." The conflict was less about "us and them" than about competing notions of what constituted the collective, possessive "we" that would define America's destiny. A democratic society lives and dies on the basis of whom it includes within its imagined community, and Miranda's arms stretched wide.

Responding to these same demographic shifts, political philosopher Danielle Allen (2014) wrote about "Our Declaration," recounting her experience as a mixed-race woman teaching one of America's founding documents in a night class of returning students, mostly people of color, at the University of Chicago. She described what it meant to these students to see these words as their birthright: "They found themselves suddenly as political beings, with a consciousness that had previously eluded them. They built a foundation from which to assess the state of their political world. . . . In reading the document with me, my students in fact re-gifted to me a text that should have been mine all along. They gave me again the Declaration's ideals—equality and freedom—and the power of its language" (31–35).

Far from Trump's apolitical conception of the Broadway musical as a "safe and special place," *Hamilton* had been strongly linked to the Obama administration, much as an earlier Broadway show, *Camelot*, came to embody the hopes and aspirations of John F. Kennedy's presidency. Miranda first tested material from his play as a surprise addition to a White House "evening of poetry, music and spoken word." Miranda was one of many who saw Obama as embodying the "hope" that there might be a way to achieve the promise of liberty and equality so long deferred and denied to American minorities: "This was a president that I had worked hard to help elect, and I wanted to show something about the American experience. . . . I don't know what his legacy will be. I do know that the thing that Hamilton and Obama have in common is that they're totally improbable stories—except they happened" (DiGiacomo 2015). The full cast returned for another performance at the White House after *Hamilton*'s Broadway success. Obama joked about Washington's partisan divide: "*Hamilton*, I'm pretty sure, is the only thing that Dick Cheney and I agree on" (Fabian 2016).

Courting millennial voters who had supported her primary opponent, Bernie Sanders, Hillary Clinton quoted the play in her speech accepting the Democratic nomination and told a young voter, "I've seen the show three times and I've cried every time—and danced hard in my seat" (Stoller 2017). Miranda was an outspoken Clinton supporter: "Are you going to vote for the guy who wants to build a wall, or for someone who's building bridges?" (Stoller 2017) Following Trump's win, the Broadway cast donated their salaries from one performance in support of the Women's March on Washington, while Miranda launched the Immigrants: We Get the Job Done Coalition, a collaboration between artists and immigrant rights nonprofits. (The organization's name echoes a line from the musical, celebrating the roles that Hamilton and Lafayette, both immigrants, played in the American Revolution—a line that consistently drew active audience response in the midst of a campaign season so heavily focused on issues of immigration reform.)

*Hamilton* fits into a long history of progressive works that explore contradictions that must be resolved if America is going to fulfill its promises. *Hamilton*'s performance at the Obama White House recalls a similar moment almost half a century before—the performance of Sherman Edwards and Peter Stone's *1776* at the Nixon White House, with the Broadway cast accompanied by the US Marine Band. The play had debuted in 1968, amid antiwar and civil rights protests, offering a story about the ways that John Adams and Thomas Jefferson had compromised on an antislavery clause, enabling delegates to the Continental Congress to approve the Declaration of Independence but setting the stage for conflicts that still divided America. This earlier musical's songs described the horrors of war ("Momma, Look Sharp"), implicated Northern merchants in the slave trade ("Molasses to Rum"); ridiculed a Congress that did nothing but "piddle, twiddle, and resolve"; and voiced Abigail Adams's demand that women be granted the franchise. Nixon's staff lobbied the producers to block "Cool, Cool, Considerate Men" from being performed before the president. In the midst of a song proclaiming "ever to the right, never to the left," John Dickinson, who opposed independence, cynically shares this political wisdom: "Don't forget that most men with nothing would rather protect the possibility of becoming rich than face the reality of being poor. And that is why they will follow us!" The cast refused to self-censor, though Nixon ally Jack Warner had the song removed from the film version (Lewis 2001). Howard Da Silva, the once-blacklisted actor, played Benjamin Franklin before Nixon, who had previously called Da Silva to testify before the House Un-American Activities Committee. The musical *1776* had offered a version of the nation's founding that was consistent with its era's skepticism. Written in a different time for a different audience, *Hamilton* pushed further to encourage a more utopian conception of what America might look like if it expanded its understanding of who its citizens were.

Myth-making about "founding fathers" dates back to the early years of the American republic. *Hamilton* made ironic comments about the growing cult surrounding George Washington ("There's nobody else in their country who looms quite as large"). Such myths persist because they articulate the things people value and want to carry with them into the future, because they embody the ways that Americans understand their place in the world. But such myths often involve simplifying complex and contradictory historical figures into something more iconic, turning flesh-and-blood humans into marble statues. Yale history professor Joanne B. Freeman (2015) tells us, "The real Hamilton was a mass of contradictions: an immigrant who sometimes distrusted immigrants, a revolutionary who placed a supreme value on law and order, a man who distrusted the rumblings of the masses yet preached his politics to them more frequently and passionately than many of his more democracy-friendly fellows."

Given the historical Hamilton's many rough edges, he remains a divisive figure. While the musical stresses his commitment to abolitionism, Hamilton bought and sold slaves on behalf of his in-laws, the Schuyler family, leading black critic and author Ishmael Reed (2015) to denounce the production: "If Hamilton had negotiated the sale of white people, do you think that an audience would be paying $400 per ticket to see a musical based upon his life?" Democratic Senator Elizabeth Warren bluntly described the historical Hamilton as a "plutocrat" (Stoller 2017). As the *Hamilton* chorus sings, "Who lives, Who dies, Who tells your story?" The irony was how many American youths in early 2016 were voting for Bernie Sanders yet singing songs about the founder of Wall Street.

Historian Andrew Burstein's book *Democracy's Muse* (2015) explores "how Thomas Jefferson became an FDR Liberal, a Reagan Republican, and a Tea Party fanatic, while being dead." *Hamilton* portrays Jefferson as a partisan politician who threatens to destroy those who disagree with him and who shows contempt for Hamilton's lowly birth. Aaron Burr had been a charming antihero at the center of Gore Vidal's 1973 novel *Burr*, published at the height of the Watergate era—a novel far less sympathetic to Hamilton, Washington, and Jefferson. In *Hamilton*, Burr becomes an opportunist with no fixed political beliefs (advising Hamilton to "speak less, smile more") even as he sings about being in "the room where it happens." As these stories are retold in different historical moments, different figures emerge as protagonists or antagonists, and different values are assigned to them.

Over the years, Alexander Hamilton has more often been seen as an icon of elite interests than as an embodiment of "diverse America." When conservative judges ground their rulings in "original intent," they often reference the Federalist Papers, which Hamilton wrote with James Madison and John Jay. Franklin Delano Roosevelt felt Hamilton embodied the values of the moneyed interests that aligned themselves against the New Deal (Stoller 2017). Popular Front dramatist Norman Corwin depicted Hamilton as a champion of the repressive Alien and Sedition Acts in *Together Tonight: Hamilton, Jefferson, Burr*. Several leading American conservatives, including David Brooks and William

*Reclaim Ham*

Kristol, recently started a movement to reclaim Hamilton, alongside Teddy Roosevelt and Henry Clay, as what they called "national greatness conservatives" (Stoller 2017). Progressive economist Robert Rubin started the Hamilton Project at the Brookings Institution, which laid the framework for the Obama administration's neoliberal financial policies (Stoller 2017). Each represents a different attempt to mobilize Hamilton and other iconic American leaders in the service of contemporary causes.

*Twisting History*

Writing for *Politico*, Republican Senator Mike Lee (2017a), who rose to power in Washington as part of the Tea Party movement, denounced what he called "the Hamilton Effect": "Twisting history to suit one's ends, willfully ignoring and ultimately erasing it when it stands in your way." He saw *Hamilton* as "propaganda" for a stronger federal government: "If we knew our history—the true and complete stories of how our nation came to be—we'd know how to fight back against the progressive agenda." Lee (2017b) published his own book, *Written Out of History: The Forgotten Founders Who Fought Big Government*, which reclaimed anti-Federalists such as Elbridge Gerry, George Mason, and Mercy Otis Warren as part of the conservative tradition. So once again, we see the ideological stakes as different groups lay claim to America's founding ideals as cultural capital in the service of their own causes. Once again, we see the Tea Party pitted against "diverse America," restorative nostalgia against reflexive nostalgia. As Boym (2001) writes, "Fantasies of the past determined by needs of the present have a direct impact on realities of the future" (xvi). How we think about where we have come from shapes how we imagine where we are going, and on that question, America remains deeply conflicted.

*Ideological stakes*

We might close with yet another story that illustrates this larger history of struggles over America's most iconic public figures. Following a decade-long campaign to feature a historic woman on American currency, the US Treasury announced plans to put Harriet Tubman, the abolitionist leader who organized the Underground Railroad, on the $10 bill, displacing Hamilton. However, the decision received an intense backlash, since the musical had inspired a new appreciation of Hamilton's contributions. So the Treasury Department announced Tubman would replace Andrew Jackson on the $20 bill, a decision candidate Trump denounced as "pure political correctness." Trump, who often compares himself to Jackson as a disruptive figure in American politics, argued that Jackson represented "somebody . . . very important to this country" and that he thought it might be "more appropriate" to place Tubman elsewhere (Wright 2016). It remains to be seen how big a priority putting Tubman on the currency will be under the Trump presidency. Ironically, in this case, *Hamilton*'s success may have delayed rather than enabled a more inclusive representation of American history by focusing attention on Hamilton as a historic individual rather than on the desire to represent those otherwise excluded or marginalized from our national symbols.

# 25

## Participatory Action in Humans of New York

### Paromita Sengupta

Street photographer Brandon Stanton started Humans of New York (HONY) in 2009 with the aim of gathering ten thousand photographs of New Yorkers framed against an interactive map of the city. To put his subjects at ease, Stanton frequently made conversation with them and turned these snippets of conversation into captions for his photographs. The microstorytelling format and the lack of closure were an invitation to Stanton's Facebook fan community to fill the gaps in the narratives and bring the stories to a satisfying conclusion. Between 2012 and 2017, HONY gradually transformed from a photography project to a pathway for civic intervention, taking its cue from the affective parasocial relationships cultivated by the fan community. In the wake of Hurricane Sandy, HONY and Tumblr teamed up to raise $100,000 in donations from the HONY fan community. Other, more personal civic intervention projects included the "Let's Bring Richard Home" campaign, in which the HONY community raised money to help the Watkins family pay the expenses to adopt a little boy from Ethiopia. The community has also come together to help subjects of Stanton's photographs locate missing pets, find employment, prevent a local bakery from going bankrupt, and get pro bono legal counsel for immigration. These calls to action are spontaneously driven by an impulse to improve the conclusions of those stories through participatory efforts.

Stanton is part of a growing network of celebrities who encourage their fan communities to use affective labor practices to enact social change. However, HONY is an interesting case study of a civic fan community that has gone beyond its founder's original political vision and created a version of the civic imagination that challenges, and even subverts, some of Stanton's own assumptions. My chapter contributes to what Jenkins et al. (2016) theorize as the civic imagination by exploring how the HONY community creates alternate modes of thinking about participatory action. In HONY's original iteration, this involved imagining better alternatives for the subjects of Stanton's photographs, but the emergence of HONY spinoff groups also inspired a collective vision of an alternate form of participatory action that moved away from large-scale global philanthropy and instead focused on local issues and grassroots action.

## The Civic Imagination and HONY

Jenkins (2016) defines the civic imagination as "the capacity to imagine alternatives to current social, political or economic institutions or problems," or the belief that one cannot change the world unless one can imagine what a better world might look like. Put into action, the civic imagination encompasses a set of collaborative practices that encourage problem-solving and building social consciousness through the simple act of imagining better alternatives to the world's contemporary social and political problems. The online HONY community often parallels the workings of the civic imagination—members develop their own set of collaborative world-building practices drawn from narrative empathy and the creation of affective, parasocial relationships with the anonymous subjects of Stanton's photographs. The desire to imagine better alternatives for the subjects of these stories provides the subsequent impetus for participatory civic action, such as fundraising or providing legal help. HONY uses communal storytelling and fan advocacy to create an alternate template of political activism that moves away from organized groups and political mobilization and instead advances a form of social reform based on collaborative problem-solving and networks of affect.

Stanton himself invoked the earliest iteration of the civic imagination. In August 2012, a representative of the fashion label DKNY approached Stanton about displaying his photographs in their showrooms. Stanton turned down their offer but later came to know that a DKNY store in Bangkok was using unlicensed HONY photos in their window display. Instead of filing a lawsuit, Stanton asked DKNY to donate $100,000 to help underprivileged children attend summer camp. DKNY issued a formal apology but negotiated the donation down to $25,000. Stanton turned to the HONY fan community and asked for help in raising the remaining money. Over the next four days, thousands of fans pitched in with donations, collectively raising $103,710. Following this incident, the HONY community successfully raised money for a plethora of charitable causes, gradually garnering more and more global attention for Stanton's reform photography. His fundraiser for the Mott Hall Bridges Academy raised $1.4 million to send three successive cohorts of sixth graders from local low-income families to a summer school program at Harvard University and even garnered a public platform from celebrity philanthropists like Ellen DeGeneres.

These examples shed some light on the way Stanton imagines civic action through HONY. Although he clearly understands the potential of participatory action and storytelling in enacting social change, the actual participation of the HONY community is limited to raising money, creating awareness, and above all, generating a spirit of goodwill and kinship in the community. This is not to imply that there is no value to this form of participatory action, but the HONY community has consistently shown signs of pushing back against these imposed boundaries and instead reimagining alternate forms of participation. The political ideology of HONY is framed around what Bennett and Segerberg (2012) call "connective action"—activist initiatives with low barriers of participation and deeply personalized narratives that gain mass popularity by traveling through digital networks. The Facebook comment threads that form around HONY photographs engage in various forms of microstorytelling through which the community forges affective social bonds with the subjects and other members of the community. Within these threads, the civic imagination takes on a more layered and nuanced form.

Stanton once posted a three-part photo series featuring a young woman who admitted to being in a submissive relationship with an older married man. Her self-expressed confusion about BDSM practices concluded with the confession, "I think I'm using this relationship to try to pull myself out of a dark, dark hole." The captions detailed how an adolescent interest in bondage had led the young woman's parents to put her on antidepressants to curb her "deviant" sexuality. The story coincided with the backlash against what was widely regarded as the romanticization of abuse in the name of BDSM in the novel *Fifty Shades of Gray* and the BDSM community's attempts to raise awareness about safe and ethical bondage practices. On the comment thread, the conversation moved from expressions of shock and sorrow at her description of parental abuse to an empathetic intervention from bondage practitioners, who explained that rather than being an assortment of sexually deviant individuals, those who practiced BDSM put a great deal of emphasis on the idea of community. The thread started out as a critical discussion of media representations of bondage, but it gradually became something of a support group for neophytes within the BDSM community to exchange their own stories and for more experienced members to share contact details of specialists who could help her understand her sexuality without feeling alienated and isolated. Unlike Stanton's visibly larger fundraising projects, the civic impact of this iteration of the civic imagination is nebulous and uncertain. It is impossible to determine whether the anonymous subject ever read the comments or whether the offers for help ever affected her relationship with BDSM. However, the thread is indicative of another form of the civic imagination in the HONY community—the use of personal narratives to develop empathy, the understanding that individuals coming together can be agents of change, and the collaborative imagination of a better alternative to a current predicament.

Stanton's philanthropic fundraising projects have led to his growing commercial success, with talk shows, book deals, and a web series on Facebook TV. In 2014, the UN recruited Stanton to go on a fifty-day global peace tour to war-ridden countries to publicize their Millennium Development Goals project (Stanton 2014). In press releases for the tour, Stanton stated that he wanted to visit Ecuador to "highlight the plight of the indigenous people" and Iraq because it was a misunderstood place that needed to be unveiled as more than a place of war, with "people trying to develop, people with hopes and dreams." This impulse to humanize misunderstood groups and redeem them in the eyes of the viewers is an integral part of Stanton's political vision. However, the rhetoric of humanization invoked a problematic white savior complex through its overtly sentimental impression of global fellowship. The HONY Facebook group underwent a strict filtration process, and comments that questioned Stanton's ethical practices or raised uncomfortable queries were deleted. The contrived culture of positivity and alignment with global power structures such as the UN cast Stanton in the light of an institutionally aligned philanthropic vehicle that perpetuates a viewpoint of privilege. Smyth (2015) echoes this sentiment in her critique of HONY's Millennium Development tour, in which she says that Stanton's constant reiteration of the universal humanity of people all over the world comes dangerously close to advocating a form of ethical neocolonialism meant to "convince the viewing public that liberal interventionist policies provide the solutions to the gulfs of privilege that prevent these people from obtaining these things." The UN tour, with its humanitarian interventionist connotations, was conducted by a lone American photojournalist who had very limited contact with the Indigenous peoples and cultures of the countries he visited and made virtually no attempt to synthesize his views with local cultural politics.

## HONY and Spreadability

Jenkins et al. (2013) define media spreadability as a participatory logic that leads audiences to "retrofit material to the contours of their particular community." Unlike media virality, spreadability depends on the degree to which the content stimulates audience engagement through participatory remixing. Shifman (2014) uses the notion of spreadability to comment on meme culture by outlining how memes do not propagate in a single mode; instead, individuals and movements adapted them to suit their own agendas. The spreadability of HONY as a meme, or a template for affective political engagement and connective action, led to a profusion of global "Humans of" microcommunities that could retrofit the civic potential of HONY to suit the needs of their particular communities and imbue it with their local political inflections through grassroots civic action and connective networks. Humans of New York has inspired the creation of a vast array of these subgroups, including Humans of Tel Aviv, Portraits of Boston, Souls of San Francisco, and Faces of Andover. These groups continue to utilize Facebook to share their content and use the familiar HONY format of a photograph followed by an anonymous, decontextualized quote. However, unlike Stanton's Anglocentric ideas about universal humanity, these groups try to create spaces that highlight their affective engagement with local issues and political conditions.

For instance, even though Facebook is banned in Iran, the Humans of Tehran Facebook page is an active community, with more than 160,000 followers who access the page through virtual private networks (VPNs) such as NordVPN and IPVanish, which allow Iranian users to encrypt their personal information and get around federal content blocking. Shirin Barghi, the founder of the page, describes their mission as the presentation of local narratives to build "a new visual vocabulary through which the world can communicate and connect with Iranians, who have been politically, and in many other ways, isolated in recent years." She invited Iranian photojournalists to change misperceptions of their culture as being repressive, antiquated, and in need of humanizing: "One thing that never sat well for me was that Western journalists and photographers frequently describe their work as 'giving voice to the voiceless.' . . . Our project decentralizes the 'voiceless' approach and we strive to take foreign intermediaries out of the creative process" (Aslan Media 2013). Barghi's comment is especially interesting in light of Stanton's own photographic tour of Iran in 2013, during which he said, "Americans are especially loved [in Iran]. . . . The vast majority of people will associate you with a culture they admire and respect." The privilege and cultural myopia of this remark elucidate Stanton's attempt to derive a culture of normalcy in terms of an uncritical expression of global fellowship and humanity without engaging with any nuances or local perspectives. In an article on Western photojournalism in Iran, Shams (2013) voices a similar perspective: "It seems that just about every other week another Western journalist 'discovers' Iran and its 'manically welcoming' people, explaining to the world for the fifty-millionth time that contrary to the audience's assumptions, Iran is a pretty nice place to visit." In contrast, Barghi's Humans of Tehran page retrofits HONY's template to reflect a more localized and contradictory perspective of Iran. One photograph depicting two Islamic clerics is wryly captioned, "Contrary to what many would think, not all clerics are into politics and power. There are some who steer clear of state affairs and are rather openminded on religious and theological questions." The comments, posted in both Farsi and English, incited a dynamic Facebook discussion thread about the roles religious figures play in Iran's political life. Another photograph features what looks like an ordinary newsstand, but the caption underneath says, "Newsstands in Tehran are absolutely awesome—you can find anything in them, lock, stock and barrel." This was a covert reference to the fact that newsstands in Iran run a flourishing trade in alcohol and marijuana even though alcohol presumption is prohibited by the government and drug dealing is punishable by death. The page also raises awareness about Iran's persecuted Afghan immigrant population by sharing photographs and captions describing the ethnic discrimination faced by this community in solidarity with the "We are all Afghans" advocacy campaign in Iran. The explicit evocation of Iranian political and cultural issues through a spreadable digital format allows the community of Humans of Tehran to envision alternatives to their current subjectification to rhetorics of Orientalism and demonization and map new pathways for youth networks to think about reform.

Other HONY spinoff groups engage in grassroots politics by documenting local political issues and activist movements, modulating their methods to fit the specific institutional and cultural contexts of each microcommunity. Humans of Berkeley covered the December 2014 Ferguson demonstrations through photos of armed policemen prowling around Berkeley's Telegraph Avenue, arresting and herding off student protestors. Humans of Vanuatu teamed up with the UNICEF Pacific communications team and extensively covered the aftermath of Cyclone Pam. They posted photographs of the extensive damage, updates about reconstruction initiatives, and calls for financial aid. The Pacific Institute of Public Policy later used their images to create a photo essay to raise public awareness about the cyclone. Humans of Kolkata is an archival source for grassroots activism in India that documents campus activism, the annual Rainbow Pride Walk, and social media campaigns organized by transgender advocacy groups in Kolkata.

The microstorytelling format employed by the captions uses a diverse array of rhetorical styles ranging from political criticism, to pathos, and even satire. Humans of Hindutva, which parodies the right-wing Hindutva ideologies of India's Bharatiya Janata Party (BJP), effectively employed the latter. Hindutva is a form of militant, neofascist nationalism in India premised on notions of the racial superiority of India's upper-caste Hindu population, and since 1989, it has been the official ideology of the BJP, the political party affiliated with Prime Minister Narendra Modi. The BJP's rhetoric of militaristic Jingoism has been used to incite racial riots against the Muslim and Dalit communities in India over issues such as the ban on selling and consuming beef through the analogy of the *gau mata*, or the cow as the holy mother. In 2015, Hindutva militants burned a teenage Muslim truck driver to death because they suspected him of transporting beef. A year later, a group of Dalit tanners were publicly stripped and beaten for their role in skinning dead cows for leather. Humans of Hindutva uses the spreadability of HONY to criticize this militant rhetoric through a series of mock interviews. For instance, a stock photo of a cow uses the HONY microstorytelling format to narrate the following:

> My mother was a single mother and worked in the agricultural industry. However, she always found the time to give us her milk or urine. She is at her happiest standing in a field or when she suddenly runs on the highway to gives heart-attacks to BMW drivers. As a kid when I asked her why the sky is blue she very cryptically said, "MOO." When I asked her for help with my homework she said, "MOO." When I told her that I am willing to kill people for her, she looked at me blankly and said "MOO."

The joke used reductio ad absurdum to take the maternal analogy to its most extreme limit, pointing to the absurdity of Hindutva nationalism, while the underlying critique of Hindutva's role in inciting instances of domestic terrorism against the beef-eating minorities in India provoked a lively discussion of racial politics in the unmoderated comment section.

## Conclusion

Stanton's original conception of Humans of New York was the impetus behind the creation of a novel form of the civic imagination centered on the practice of participatory storytelling and affective connections to imagine better conclusions to deliberately truncated narratives. The community originally came together through their shared appreciation of Stanton's photography, but it gradually morphed into a space for critical discussion and collaborative action to imagine better alternatives for the subjects of stories that aroused feelings of sympathy and kinship. However, as Stanton started getting global recognition as a celebrity philanthropist and collaborating with international organizations like the UN, the participatory potential of his fan community became limited to fundraising and following along with Stanton's social media activities. More problematically, people of color from within the HONY fandom found their cultures being homogenized in a misdirected attempt to "humanize" the unfamiliar for a white Western audience. However, the spreadability of HONY as a template for actionable photography makes it possible for spinoff groups to engage more directly with local politics and representations. "Humans of Tehran" and "Humans of Hindutva" display structural similarities to HONY that make them a part of the HONY spinoff tradition, but they deconstruct the model of universal humanity, push back against Western colonial understandings of the cultural Other, and encourage the community to regain control over their narratives. Their use of connective action offers ways of redefining activism as a decentralized, communal activity with low barriers of participation, participatory political strategies, and deeply personalized narratives that gain mass popularity by traveling over networked platforms. Together, these two fan spinoff pages confirm that fans can engage with the civic imagination in a myriad of different ways, some of which might even conflict with the ideologies of the original fan text. By reimagining the very nature of the civic imagination, these groups develop new ways of thinking about the infrastructures of collective action by remixing resources and practices and developing social links with a larger collective.

Although the "Humans of" spinoff groups lack Stanton's capacity for media outreach and fundraising, the sheer variety of these groups and the issues that they engage in are indicative of the spreadability of HONY as a template for civic action. Their use of connective action offers ways of redefining activism as a decentralized, communal activity with low barriers of participation, participatory political strategies, and deeply personalized narratives that gain mass popularity by traveling over networked platforms. By reimagining the very nature of the civic imagination, these groups collaboratively develop new ways of thinking about the infrastructures of collective action by remixing resources and practices and developing social links with a larger collective.

# 26

## A Vision for Black Lives in the Black Radical Tradition

### Christopher Harris

> Forced to cope with the nadir of political evil over centuries, Black people have responded consistently by forging advanced concepts of a deeply politicized love. Perhaps precisely because brutality and oppression can make people decidedly unlovable, African people in America have been adept at finding ways to perceive something left to love inside themselves and in others. That ability has enabled their survival, the preservation of their humanity, and their emergence as the nation's foremost champions of democracy and social justice.
>
> —George Lipsitz (2017)

In August 2016, the Movement for Black Lives, a united front composed of more than fifty organizations from across the United States, published a document advancing a visionary agenda committed to the goal of societal transformation and black liberation. The platform, entitled *A Vision for Black Lives: Policy Demands for Black Power, Freedom, and Justice* (*AVBL*), was created as a direct response "to the sustained and increasingly visible violence against Black communities" in the United States and abroad. This manifesto is the product of a collaborative project initiated during the final days of the Movement for Black Lives Convening held in Cleveland in the summer of 2015 (AV4BL 2016). Operating under a mandate to articulate and unite behind a collective vision and strategy for liberation, the yearlong process—which included multiple convenings and fervent dialogue, debate, and discussion—was led by veteran organizers representing groups such as Black Youth Project 100, the Center for Media Justice, and Dream Defenders. The resulting document issues six major

demands calling for an end to all violence against black people; a realloca-
tion of resources from prisons and the military to the health, education,
and safety of black people; and economic justice, community control, and
political power for black people within a genuine democracy.

These seasoned human rights activists and organizers authored *AVBL*
as a means to amplify the multitude of efforts championing the value of
black lives currently under way across the country. Seeking to supply
a generative resource for those engaged in long-term advocacy work,
*AVBL*'s contributors backed their demands with policy briefs outlining
tangible steps in the push toward liberation, extensive supporting data,
and legislative recommendations. The extended policy brief on the de-
militarization of law enforcement, which includes information on model
legislation as well as advice on how to use Obama-era executive orders
to pressure elected officials to reject military-grade equipment for local
police forces, illustrates the platform's practical value (McClain 2016).

However, the tool kit's most potent element may be its orienting vision. The declarations and demands set forth in *AVBL* are bold and
imaginative. Sincerely committed to the ideals of an inclusive democracy, the document insists on "elevating the experiences and leadership of the most marginalized Black people," including those who are
women, gender nonconforming, formerly/currently incarcerated, cash
poor / working class, and undocumented/immigrants (AV4BL 2016).
Although principally focused on black American concerns, the platform
proclaims solidarity with other oppressed peoples of the world, referring
to them as family and vowing to stand with them in the struggle for collective liberation. And in envisaging a world liberated from patriarchy,
exploitative capitalism, militarism, and white supremacy, valuing the
voices of the most vulnerable, and expressing solidarity with other oppressed groups, it exemplifies a use of imagination that moves beyond
merely envisioning the *as yet* and embraces an imagining guided by empathy. It recognizes that the world can and should be changed, but it also
grasps that the world to come must be cultivated through an inclusive
democratic process that privileges the concerns of those most harmed
by the world at present. In this regard, the orienting vision espoused by
*AVBL* stands as a brilliant example of radical imagination.

Radical imagination is, first of all, "the ability to imagine the world,
life and social institutions not as they are but as they otherwise might

be" (Haiven and Khasnabish 2014, 3). It is about innovation through empathy and begins with pushing ourselves to identify with "the beautiful which exists in thought, action, or person, not our own," allowing us to put ourselves "in the place of another and of many others" (Shelley 1904). However, emancipatory visions must also be underpinned by a deep awareness of historical contexts. Radical imagination "is not just about dreaming of different futures. It's about bringing those possible futures 'back' to work on the present, to inspire action and new forms of solidarity today. . . . [It] is about drawing on the past, telling different stories about how the world came to be the way it is, and remembering the power and importance of past struggles and the way their spirits live on in the present" (Haiven and Khasnabish 2014, 4). Historically, the radical imaginings of US black folks, like those articulated in *AVBL*, have been driven by empathy and rooted in the aforementioned interplay among past, present, and future. Whether expressed by musicians, poets, and playwrights or scholars, politicos, and pastors, black freedom dreams have always revolved around affirming the humanity and dignity of the vulnerable. These utterances and undertakings flow from and contribute to a robust radical tradition—a collective intelligence forged over centuries of struggle and colored by the blues sensibilities that underlie blacks' experience as a shunned people in a racist land.

From the moment the first African bondsmen disembarked in the American South, black people's relationship to and encounters within this nation have been haunted by the specter of racial oppression. Continued survival in the face of dehumanizing brutality—suffered through the long night of slavery, the plagues of convict leasing and Jim/Jane Crow, and more recently, racialized mass incarceration and police shootings—necessitated the development of effective coping strategies. As such, blacks created life-affirming rituals, customs, and worldviews through storytelling, music, and spiritual fellowship. They laughed, sang, danced, and prayed together, acknowledging each other's humanity and bolstering one another's self-worth in the midst of catastrophic circumstances. Pulsing through this equipment for living is an ethos called *the blues:* "an impulse to keep the painful details and episodes of a brutal experience alive in one's aching consciousness, to finger its jagged grain, and to transcend it" (Ellison 1972, 78–79). This blues impulse animates a sustained mutual struggle to derive meaning from degradation, informing traditions and outlooks that continue to empower blacks in America with the will to endure on the margins of a society that has proven steadfast in its efforts to denigrate and dehumanize them.

Blacks, however, have done more than just endure in America. They have emerged "as an aggrieved and insurgent polity. . . . [that,] insisting on their own humanity and the humanity of all people, even that of their oppressors," has consistently fought on the front lines of the battles for a more just world (Lipsitz 2017, 108–9). Consequent to these struggles, black peoples' oppositional undertakings have yielded an ever-evolving radical politics and culture—a blues-soaked tradition of striving stemming from "a collective consciousness informed by historical struggles for liberation and motivated by a shared sense of obligation to preserve the collective being" (Robinson 2000, 171). Awash in the blues ethos, the black radical tradition remains dedicated to upholding black personhood and dignity but pushes past strategies aimed simply at continued survival. Instead, it endorses the notion of intervention for the purpose of societal transformation and the engineering of a world in which blacks are able to exercise their full humanity.

According to its authors, AVBL "builds on the legacy of the Black radical tradition" (McClain 2016). It demands a more just world devoid of the obstacles that prevent the achievement of full humanity by all black people, particularly those who have been historically silenced within the black community, and provides "stepping stones and road maps on how to get there" (AV4BL 2016). It takes an explicitly Pan-Africanist tone in expressing a desire and commitment to work with other oppressed peoples of the world on the project of liberation. And it draws heavily on the spirit of previous policy efforts, such as the Black Radical Congress's *Freedom Agenda* and the Black Panther Party's *Ten-Point Program*, in its effort to identify and respond to the most pressing political exigencies impacting contemporary black Americans.

The language employed in AVBL reflects a keen awareness of the fact that black America is currently in an acute state of crisis. As blacks lead all groups in categories indicative of harm—including terminal disease rates, lack of access to health care, home foreclosures, missing persons, incarceration, and child poverty—the nature and consequences of this crisis are both economic and sociocultural (Glaude 2016). Responding to these dreadful conditions, contributors to the document forward a series of demands and suggestions that, taken together, aim to achieve black self-determination within a genuinely democratic society. Aspects of economic justice and community control are addressed at length—including calls for reparations for slavery, an end to the privatization of education, and improved protections for black workers. However, it is the rhetoric discussing black people's current relationship to law enforcement and the prison industrial complex that best captures the radical tone of *AVBL* and provides greater insight into the cultural context that influenced the platform's creation.

At present, the most high-profile dimension of the crisis afflicting black America is an escalating "epidemic of police harassment, brutality, corruption, and murder that threatens . . . the lives and personhood of . . . African Americans in every city and suburb" (Taylor 2016, 13). Blacks are currently twice as likely as other racial minorities, and three times as likely as whites, to be victims of lethal police violence. Statistics, however, only speak to part of the story. Take, for instance, the behavior of law enforcement after the murder of Michael Brown—the black teen whose death, at the hands of Ferguson, Missouri, police officer Darren Wilson, ignited a series of intense standoffs between protestors and local police that thrust the claim "Black lives matter" to the forefront of national consciousness. On the day Brown was killed, Ferguson police left his bullet-riddled body facedown in the middle of the street, in full view of his family members and neighbors (including young children) who had gathered at the scene. For more than four hours, they refused to allow his parents to identify him, and they brandished their weapons and used police dogs to threaten the crowd (Richardson 2015). Months later, on the day that Wilson's name was finally released to the public, Ferguson's police chief chose to also release blurry security camera footage that appeared to show Brown shoplifting at a local convenience store on the day he was killed. As Wilson was unaware that Brown was suspected of involvement in any crime, the motive for the release of the footage became maddeningly clear: by portraying him as a petty thief, police sought to alter public perception of Brown from victim to suspect. A final affront to Brown's humanity came when the prosecuting attorney overseeing the investigation of the shooting elected not to indict Wilson—essentially sanctioning the murder. Sadly, the egregiously dehumanizing practices undertaken by law enforcement officials in the wake of Brown's death are far from unique. During the highly publicized recent rash of police killings of black men, women, and children, victims' bodies, families, and reputations have been routinely disrespected and disparaged by police, prosecutors, and irresponsible reporters alike (Taylor 2016).

In response to this grievous trend, members of the Movement for Black Lives called for an end to the war on Black people—more specifically, an end to the criminalization and dehumanization of black youths; an end to the mass surveillance of black communities; an end to the militarization and privatization of the police; and immediate improvements to the conditions of all jails, prisons, and detentions centers. Though primarily concerned with the literal preservation of black life, these demands are about much more than making black people safer. While there is little doubt that the deprivatization of police forces coupled with an end to the mass surveillance of black communities would increase police accountability to the public and drastically reduce black people's vulnerability to overzealous policing, the most radical elements of these demands flow from a focus on the way that blacks are viewed by law enforcement.

Legislation enacted in the aftermath of the 9/11 terror attacks ushered in changes to training, tactics, and weapons that have police forces across the United States equipped and behaving like occupying armies—approaching law enforcement as war and excessively deploying militarized methods against those they deem as enemies (Balko 2014). Owing to the continued conflation of blackness and criminality in the American psyche—a bias established through the nineteenth-century practice of convict leasing and expanded on by the dog-whistling discourse of the unending war on drugs—black people, and particularly black youths, are disproportionately forced into this adversarial role (Coates 2015). Blacks' proscribed status as *enemies* of the law due to the presumption of their inherent criminality is time and again used to justify the violent tactics too often used against them by police officers. Ending the criminalization of black youths across all areas of society and demilitarizing the police would remove any rationale for the police to continue seeing blacks as *enemies*. The framers of *AVBL* hope that the curtailing of racist assumptions of black criminality and the elimination of police officers' current need for readily identifiable antagonists will help end police violence against blacks.

Although exceptionally comprehensive, the call to end the war on black people advanced in *AVBL* is just one of many recent black responses to the menace of racialized police violence. Over the last few years, a burgeoning black radical consciousness has fueled an upsurge in the intensity and frequency of performances and direct actions intent on championing the value of black lives. These interventions have come from black artists, activists, and athletes, as well as collectives of ordinary folks and draw from "deep wells of exhaustion among African-Americans who have grown weary of the endless eulogizing of Black people . . . killed by police" (Taylor 2016, 14). They have sought to disrupt mainstream acceptance and perpetuation of America's value gap by boldly challenging white supremacy—the "set of practices informed by the fundamental belief that white people are valued more than others" (Glaude 2016, 30). Voiced via a variety of platforms—ranging from social media, movies, and music to mass and symbolic protests—the recent salvos of black radical expression all emphasize the unequivocal assertion that *black lives matter*.

The year 2016 was a watershed for such statements. As black America celebrated the fiftieth anniversary of both the coining of the term *Black Power* and the founding of the Black Panther Party for Self-Defense, grassroots activists ratcheted up organizing efforts and demonstrations under the banner of #BlackLivesMatter, and black celebrities began to make greater use of their platforms to express pro-black sentiments. The year began with protestors blockading the San Francisco Bay Bridge on Martin Luther King Jr.'s birthday in an attempt to reclaim his radical legacy and pop icon Beyoncé's Super Bowl half-time performance in which she and her dancers donned black leather attire inspired by the uniforms of the Black Panther Party (Wong 2016). The year was also marked by actor Jesse Williams's strongly worded rebuke of American law enforcement's racist practices during the Black Entertainment Television Awards show; quarterback Colin Kaepernick's (and other NFL players') decision to silently protest during the playing of the national anthem before football games to raise public awareness of racist police practices; and a proliferation of music, memes, and hashtags celebrating blackness, critiquing police brutality, and encouraging audiences to *stay woke*.

The pro-black actions and utterances of the current moment are powerful manifestations of the black radical tradition and offer imaginative defenses of black life that are empathetic, historically informed, and attuned to the events, trends, and technologies of the times. For example, writers for the heralded Netflix series *Luke Cage* elected to have the bulletproof black superhero protect Harlem (the longtime cultural capital of black America) from crime and corrupt cops while wearing a hooded sweatshirt in an overt tribute to Trayvon Martin—the black teenager whose murder rose to national prominence when George Zimmerman, the unremorseful vigilante who killed him, was found not guilty by a Florida jury. It was Martin's murder and Zimmerman's subsequent acquittal that inspired Patrisse Cullors, Alicia Garza, and Opal Tometi to found the now global social media movement known as #BlackLivesMatter. Cage's hooded sweatshirt honors as heroes both Martin and those who were inspired to build and participate in a social movement in response to his tragic death.

At their best, such utterances are generative as well, seeking to encourage honest and decent dialogue around social problems, compel critical self-reflection, and inspire audiences to endeavor to bring about a better world. The recent national anthem protests by professional athletes are readily observable instances of such expressions. As mentioned above, NFL players began silently protesting during the pregame playing of the national anthem early in the 2016 season. Their stated goal was to bring attention to the reality that the rights and freedoms America claims to stand for are not conferred equally to all Americans and force a public conversation about the police's mistreatment of black people. As an overwhelming majority of players in the NFL—the most popular and influential American professional sports league—are black, while most fans are white, the players' actions immediately sparked controversy and generated intense debate in both the sports and news media around race, patriotism, and policing. Kaepernick's and others' initial acts of defiance inspired a wave of players to follow suit and prompted NFL executives and owners to come out publicly in support of criminal justice reform. Athletes in other sports at all levels (professional, college, and high school) have begun to engage in similar protests, increasing social pressure on politicians and law enforcement agencies to take steps to curb police violence.

*AVBL* is a superbly imaginative intervention that draws from the torrent of expression radiating out of present rearticulations of black radicalism. It is a magnificently worded and thoroughly researched manifesto forged from genuinely inclusive democratic praxis by thinkers who view the achievement of black freedom dreams as both ends and means in the global push for collective liberation. *AVBL* is "more than a platform. It is a remarkable blueprint for social transformation . . . a plan for ending structural racism, saving the planet, and transforming the entire nation" (Kelley 2016). In calling for an end to the war on black people and demanding reparations for the harms inflicted by colonialism and slavery, it highlights the links between the termination of racist policies and practices and the creation of new democratic institutions. In calling for economic justice, community control, and political power for blacks, it stresses the centrality of the role that black self-determination must play in ensuring that these new institutions uphold black personhood and dignity. And in lambasting US foreign policy and calling for drastic reductions in military spending, divestment from apartheid regimes abroad, and an end to the industrial use of fossil fuels, it declares solidarity with the world's oppressed. Empathetic, visionary, and pragmatic, *AVBL* fulfills the charge given to its collaborating authors and carries forward the legacy of black radical struggle, conceptualizes the contours of a more just society and world, and seeks to empower those who will dare to build such a world.

## PART VI

# How Do We Bring an Imaginative Dimension to Our Real-World Spaces and Places?

In this volume, we have made a case for why imagining alternative universes may serve useful political purposes—allowing us to step outside of the constraints of current reality and explore other possibilities. But politics also often begins at home, localized in particular spaces. These spaces become places when we collectively and individually feel a sense of possession over them. Places anchor memories. Places serve as points of departure for many aspirations. Places also are where the civic imagination often is staged for others. Though clearly significant and colloquially prevalent, place and space are quite difficult to define. David Harvey (1993) notes,

> There are all sorts of words such as milieu, locality, location, locale, neighborhood, region, territory and the like, which refer to the generic qualities of place. There are other terms such as city, village, town, megalopolis and state, which designate particular kinds of places. There are still others, such as home, hearth, "turf," community, nation and landscape, which have such strong connotations of place that it should be hard to talk about one which out the other. "Place" also has an extraordinary range of metaphorical meanings. We talk about the place of art in social life, the place of women in society, our place in the cosmos, and internalize such notions psychologically in terms of knowing our place, or feeling we have a place in the affections or esteem of others. (3)

The multilayered meanings of place summon up Henri Lefebvre's (1991) theorization of place, which articulated three intertwined but distinct fields: "The fields we are concerned with are, first, the *physical*—nature, the Cosmos; secondly, the *mental*, including logical and formal abstractions; and thirdly, the *social*. In other words, we are concerned with logico-epistemological space, the space of social practice, the space occupied by sensory phenomena, including products of the imagination such as projects and projections, symbols and utopias" (14). Read through this theoretical frame, the civic imagination helps us overcome the possible disjunctions/breaks/schisms (Lefebvre) between the "real" and imagined dimensions of place.

The City Formerly Known as Cambridge project invited participants to proposed new names for physical locations in the city to better reflect their own experiences and aspirations, recognizing that naming is an assertion of the community's identity and priorities. This exercise sought to map the interplay between real and imagined spaces. Catherine D'Ignazio (2016, 26) encouraged participants to think past the local politics and history that led to current street names, to refuse the idea that this inherited set of spatial practices was inevitable, and to assert their rights as the current occupants to remap these spaces to reflect their own cultural identities. The project's focus on "what if" rather than "what is" allowed participants to look at the city around them with fresh eyes.

The cases in this section all engage with the interplay between imagination and place in similar ways. Detailed by Ethan Zuckerman in chapter 27, the construction projects in Haiti conducted by the Fondation Connaissance et Liberté (FOKAL)—including a sculpture park in one of Port-au-Prince's most violent neighborhoods—also actively engage the local as the starting point for the civic imagination. FOKAL understands that "beautiful public spaces" are crucial to the country's future as they "dare to imagine what Haiti could be. And then they go ahead and build it." The result is an inhabitable future, one rendered tangible through the act of rebuilding. The ability to imagine alternatives to physical places is thus integral to Haiti's understanding of its past, present, and future.

Like Zuckerman's study of FOKAL, this section's other case studies engage place through their discussion of the ways in which the civic imagination is layered onto physical geography. This layering of meaning is captured in chapter 28, Clint Schnekloth's case study of the politics of Southern identity. Schnekloth, a Lutheran pastor from the Midwest who moved to Fayetteville, Arkansas, observes that "Many progressive Southerners feel as if they are engaged in the Sisyphean task of repeatedly disambiguating their regional identity from the stereotypes of Southerners." He describes a South that is being redefined through changing dynamics, as the so-called Bible Belt recognizes the emergence of a progressive Christian identity that embraces place-based struggles for social justice as central to its mission.

The experience of place-based imagination does not always have to be connected to an actual mappable location to be spatially significant. In Robin D. G. Kelley's (2002) discussion of the shifting imaginaries that have fueled black civil rights movements in the United States, ancient Africa, an imagined historical location, fueled the black imagination by opening a "window into our dreams of a New Land" (29). In chapter 30, Rogelio Lopez's discussion of "Aztlán," the "mythical homeland of the once nomadic Aztec people," evokes a similarly elusive place that allows Chicanx (people of Mexican origin residing in the United States) to access their cultural heritage and actively participate in "co-creating a new world" that situates their social and civic struggles within a longer place-based history. In Lopez's account, "Aztlán" facilitates a remapping of belonging and home for people who otherwise feel they are "ni de aquí, ni de allá" (neither from here nor from there).

The layered meanings created through remembered and imagined dimensions of place are also at the center of *Tzina: Symphony of Longing*, an immersive virtual reality project. *Tzina*, as described by Ioana Mischie in chapter 29, sought to archive both the geography and the local resident narratives of Dizengoff Square, an elevated square in Tel Aviv, Israel, that was demolished in 2016. The project also worked to capture the physical experience of being in the space by using immersive technologies. Organized around times of day (from sunrise to sunset) that coincide with particular sensibilities (Awakeness, Home, Emptiness, Disappointments, and Loneliness), the project invited "visitors" to engage with the atmosphere of the square and to "talk" with its visitors by hearing their first-person accounts of their lives—their aspirations, their regrets, their accomplishments. As Mischie notes, *Tzina* invited audiences to engage with an imagined, no-longer-existing place as an entry into an imagined past and future.

Read together, the case studies included in this section describe how the physical and mythical experience of place becomes a powerful tool for the civic imagination. Put differently, the civic imagination draws our attention to what Harvey (1993) would identify as the "dialectical interplay between experience, perception and imagination in place construction" (17).

## 27

## "Without My City, Where Is My Past?"

## Ethan Zuckerman

Haitian architect Farah Hyppolite asks this question as she leads visitors to Port-au-Prince, Haiti, on the tour of a worksite where Belgian and Haitian experts work to rebuild an ornate, wood-framed "gingerbread house." These richly ornamented houses, striking hybrids of tropical and European architecture, were built at the turn of the twentieth century for the city's wealthy merchants and can be found throughout older parts of the city, often in advanced states of decay.

The builders work from photographs of a building damaged by neglect and crippled by Haiti's 2010 earthquake and the hurricanes and tropical storms that preceded and followed it. The building Hyppolite is overseeing will be a reconstruction, as similar to the original building as possible for a successor that contains none of the original timber and is rebuilt on a dirt lot using locally harvested lumber and hand tools. All old buildings are ships of Theseus, their elements replaced one after the next until only the original shape remains. But the house Hyppolite is reconstructing was imagined into being as part of a plan to re-create a neighborhood of gingerbread houses within Port-au-Prince's crowded downtown, a tourist attraction, and most importantly, a reminder of the city and its past.

Hyppolite's question comes in response to a query often asked of the foundation she works for: "Given all of Haiti's problems and suffering, why is historical preservation a priority?" Haiti is not short on suffering. Europeans first encountered Haiti when Christopher Columbus's ship crashed on the northern coast of Hispaniola. With no immunity to European diseases, a huge percentage of the Indigenous population died, and the remainder were enslaved by Columbus's crew and forced to collect gold for Spanish treasuries. Since then, Haiti has survived colonial rule by France and Spain, occupations by Germany and the United

States, three decades of kleptocratic dictatorships, foreign-backed coups, AIDS and cholera epidemics, and an extensive catalog of natural disasters.

As the poorest nation in the Western Hemisphere, Haiti has practically become shorthand for poverty, hardship, and dysfunction (World Bank in Haiti 2019). Well before the earthquake, Haiti's economy was in shambles, the result of both domestic mismanagement and countless international interventions and depredations. In 1970, 70 percent of the government's revenues came from international aid, a number that's subsequently risen. Despite massive unemployment (as high as 75 percent in the 1990s) and enormous aid dependency, per-capita aid to Haiti in 2008 was only $92.30 per person, the vast majority of whom lived in abject poverty (Ramachandran and Walz 2015). Wealthy nations are resilient and can cope with calamity; fragile nations cannot. In 2002, the national budget for Haiti, a country of ten million people, was equivalent to the national budget for the city of Cambridge, Massachusetts, a city of one hundred thousand people (Ramachandran and Walz 2012).

In one sense, Hyppolite's employer, Fondation Connaissance et Liberté (FOKAL), is part of the international complex that's been both aiding and plaguing Haiti for years. But FOKAL is distinctively Haitian. FOKAL is the Kreyol acronym for Fondation Connaissance et Liberté, a Haitian foundation that is part of the George Soros–funded Open Society Foundations but whose founders, board, and management are Haitian. In most countries where Open Society Foundations works, local foundations support work on human rights, access to justice, fiscal transparency, and strengthening the free press. Rarely do Open Society Foundations projects focus on aid and reconstruction, and almost never do they focus on new construction or historical reconstructions.[1]

FOKAL is different because of Michèle Pierre-Louis, its founder, who served as Haiti's first prime minister during President René Préval's term. An activist and leader in Haiti through the purges and terror of the Duvalier years (during which François Duvalier and his son Jean-Claude ran a dictatorship that killed over thirty thousand Haitians, led many educated Haitians to flee the island, and then subsequently destroyed Haiti's population and economy),[2] Pierre-Louis's ambition has been not to bandage the nation's wounds but to give the nation permission to imagine better.

Under Pierre-Louis's leadership, FOKAL has built public spaces that would be considered ambitious in other contexts and that strain credulity against the backdrop of contemporary Port-au-Prince. An elegant waterfall runs down a hill to a library named for American choreographer Katherine Dunham, who spent her career exploring Haitian voudou and bringing it into her dance. Filled with French, Kreyol, and English books—and dozens of schoolchildren enjoying them in groups—it is one of several public spaces FOKAL has brought to the city. FOKAL's downtown headquarters opens directly to the street—an unusual feature in a city where many buildings are protected behind courtyard walls—and features another library, a theater and screening room, and spaces for talks and performances.

The new buildings FOKAL constructs are architecturally inventive, with unexpected angles, bold colors, and creative juxtapositions. While FOKAL also works on combating cholera, rebuilding the legal system, strengthening agriculture, and protecting human rights, they do also something most aid groups do not: they build and restore beautiful public spaces, creating sources of neighborhood and national pride. While many international organizations are focused on helping Haitians access the bare minimum of health care and education, FOKAL dares to imagine what Haiti could be—and then they go ahead and build it.

All nations are the product of the civic imagination, the dream of a people to be united by history, purpose, or place. Haiti's civic imagination has been especially ambitious. Inspired in part by the American and French Revolutions, the hundreds of thousands of African slaves imported by the French to cultivate sugar cane rose up against their masters and chased the "planters" from the island. (To quote Lin-Manuel Miranda in *Hamilton*, "We know who was doing the planting.") Revolutionary France responded by both seeking to control the island and also banning slavery throughout French colonies, led by Robespierre and the Jacobins at the National Convention. The leader of the slave revolt, Touissant Louverture, proceeded to liberate neighboring Spanish Santo Domingo (the contemporary Dominican Republic) from slavery. Haiti was not only the only nation formed from a successful slave revolt but also the first successful decolonizer of the Western Hemisphere, chasing off French, Spanish, and English occupiers.

Haitians paid dearly for the audacity of imagining a free, black, post-colonial nation. When Charles X sought to restore the French monarchy, he threatened Haiti with a naval blockade until Haitian leaders agreed to compensate France tens of millions of francs for their loss of territory. The payments crippled Haiti's economy for generations to come. The United States, still ostensibly a revolutionary nation, failed to recognize Haiti until the abolition of slavery after the Civil War. From 1915 to 1935, US marines occupied Haiti after seizing the treasury of Haiti's national bank over fears that the nation would not repay the millions it owed to France, Germany, and the United States. As with so many "underdeveloped" nations, Haiti's contemporary situation is not just a product of corruption, mismanagement, and bad luck; it's the predictable, deliberate outcome of centuries of racial discrimination manifested through economic and military revenge.

Benedict Anderson (2006) tells us that nations imagine themselves into being through shared symbols and practices: flags, maps, museums, a daily newspaper we imagine to be on the breakfast table of every other citizen in the nation. In Port-au-Prince at least, Haiti's national imagination is embedded in the city's buildings—or was before the earthquake. The downtown of Port-au-Prince is constructed around broad avenues that celebrate Haiti's postcolonial leaders, landmarked by government and commercial buildings. Hyppolite can no longer navigate downtown after the earthquake: her landmarks have been destroyed.

The 2010 earthquake killed an estimated sixty thousand to eighty thousand Haitians and left at least one million homeless (Kolbe et al. 2010). A year after the devastation, one major Port-au-Prince landmark had been reconstructed: the Marché en Fer, or the Iron Market. Originally built with Moroccan architectural flourishes, the market was intended to be a Cairo railway terminal but ended up anchoring Port-au-Prince's Avenue Dessalines since 1891. The market, burned in 2008 during food riots and leveled by the earthquake, was back to life a year later, the beneficiary of the ambitious campaign of Irish billionaire investor Denis O'Brien, who invested $12 million of his own money in the reconstruction effort.

O'Brien's billions come in part from his ownership of Digicel, Haiti's dominant cell phone carrier, and in the restoration, he became the majority owner of a joint stock company that will oversee the market for the next fifty years, so his motives may have been commercial as well as civic. But the choice of Marché en Fer was one with deep symbolic meaning for residents of the city. Port-au-Prince mayor Jean-Yves Jason told the *New York Times*, "Anyone born in Port-au-Prince, who has shopped in Port-au-Prince, they all have a story, a memory, from the market" (Bhatia 2011). Demonstrating that the building could be rebuilt within a year was a reflection of UN Special Envoy for Haiti Bill Clinton's hopes that Haiti would "build back better."

Reconstructed much like the gingerbread houses Hyppolite re-creates, Marché en Fer maintains the shape of the remembered market, and some of the bricks and iron columns are salvaged from the previous market's ruins. Other parts of the market were rebuilt in France, where the market was originally assembled; its clock faces were painted to resemble the originals. In a part of Port-au-Prince where buildings routinely lack exterior walls or have trees growing out of their ruined roofs, Marché en Fer is neatly painted, carefully signed, and gleaming. Much like its audacious timeline for reconstruction—documented in the BBC film *From Haiti's Ashes*—the market is as much symbol as place, the dream of Haiti's rebirth rendered in iron columns.

But just as the reconstructed gingerbread houses have a different meaning as historical landmarks than as residences celebrating the city's prosperity, the new Marché en Fer means something new in a city radically reshaped by calamity. While the market has been rebuilt, it is no longer the city's commercial center. Pétion-Ville, a wealthy neighborhood once considered a separate city from Port-au-Prince, attracted many of the merchants whose stores near the Iron Market were leveled in the earthquake. Pétion-Ville was less damaged by the quake and was popular with the influx of aid workers who came to help the city, so this once-distant part of town is now central to both the retail and tourist economies. In the 1960s, cruise ships docked near the downtown so tourists could roam the Iron Market, buying paintings and mahogany carvings. When I visited in 2017, shootings near the market happened routinely, and my friends would let me visit only for a few moments, worried that my presence could lead to a kidnapping attempt.

Central to the "build back better" vision was an influx of aid, gifts from the wealthy countries to one of the world's poorest. Of the $500 billion in aid initially promised, roughly $6 billion had actually materialized a year after the earthquake (Vulliamy 2011), and only $15 billion appeared five years later (Connor, Rappleye, and Angulo 2015). Despite the gap between promises and realities, huge sums have been deployed in Haiti, often with little to show for the funds spent.

Jonathan Katz, author of *The Big Truck That Went By: How the World Came to Save Haiti and Left behind a Disaster* (2014), argues that the money deployed to Haiti was not misspent in the sense that it was stolen but that it was spent in a shortsighted way, providing immediate relief with little consideration of what Haiti needed in the longer term. Vijaya Ramachandran and Julie Walz, reporting for the Center for International Development in 2012, observed that less than 1 percent of humanitarian relief money and only 15 to 21 percent of longer-term aid went to the Haitian government (2011). The majority went to international aid agencies and contractors, who often misunderstood local needs and built projects that were inappropriate, unsustainable, or unsuccessful.

One possible explanation for Haiti's stalled recovery is the country's low level of underlying infrastructure, making it difficult to support new projects. Attempts to build hospitals flounder because the electric grid cannot support the power needs of construction equipment or the donated medical equipment; attempts at rural agricultural development collapse when unusable roads make it impossible to bring food to urban markets or to ports for export. Another possibility is that endemic corruption, the concentration of power in the hands of a few families, dooms projects to failure. In addition, the violence that's erupted in neighborhoods filled with unemployed young men makes movement through the city dangerous, dooming efforts to assist those marginalized communities.

FOKAL offers another explanation, one so unexpected that it seems almost fanciful. Maybe the failure of Haiti is a failure of the civic imagination. Like many developing nations, Haiti is a young country, and the vast majority of Haitians cannot remember the 1960s, when Haiti's educational institutions were strong enough that the nation sent doctors and professors to the newly independent Democratic Republic of Congo, which was rumored to have only thirty university graduates at the end of Belgian colonialism. (Many of those professionals were fleeing Papa Doc's Tontons Macoutes, progovernment thugs who targeted Haitian elites, among others. But that doesn't minimize the pride many Haitians took in their ability to aid a new postcolonial nation.)

For most Haitians, their nation has been in crisis their entire lives, the victim of internal, external, and natural forces beyond their control. FOKAL invites Haitians to imagine a different nation, one that deserves not just shelter and food but libraries and theaters. When Pierre-Louis and her team build parks and public spaces and restore its historic buildings, they are inviting Haitians to imagine a Haiti that debates its future and celebrates its past. Against a backdrop of violence, unemployment, and poverty, their ambitions can feel unfamiliar or even inappropriate. But perhaps their ability to imagine a better Haiti—and to invite a generation to imagine with them—is one of the forces that will transform the nation again.

Like the gingerbread houses and the Marché en Fer, a new Haiti is emerging, bearing the shape of the past and the materials of modernity. Whether that nation is built better than before depends in large part on what Haitians are able to imagine for themselves.

## Notes

1   The author serves as an advisor to the president of the Open Society Foundations.
2   Haiti was the epicenter of the AIDS epidemic in the Western Hemisphere, and the close association between Haiti and AIDS destroyed the country's briefly burgeoning tourist industry.

# 28

# Reimagining and Mediating a Progressive Christian South

## Clint Schnekloth

From our forms of speech, to our religious commitments, to our sense of communal identity, we are a nation of diverse regional cultures. And part of regional imagination is recognizing differences among those regions. As a Christian pastor, I have recently experienced how the interplay of regionalism and new media informs our civic and religious imagination. That's the story I wish to tell here. As a Gen Xer raised on a farm in rural Iowa, my move to Fayetteville, Arkansas, constituted a transition from one significant regional culture to another.

To use Colin Woodard's (2012) memorable remapping of the American "nations," I actually moved not from the North to the South but from the *Midlands*, where people designate their ethnicity by their European or other ancestry (German, Norwegian, Polish, Vietnamese, Pakistani), to *Greater Appalachia*, "rendered perfectly in the Census Bureau's map of the largest reported ancestry group by county: its inhabitants virtually the only counties in the country where a majority answered 'American.'" As the Midlands and the South have become more diverse, shaped by global immigration and internal migration, their religious landscape has also changed: increasing numbers in both places self-identify as secular or nonreligious. There is a new mind of the South, captured succinctly by Southerner Tracy Thompson (2014), who writes, "[There is a] mismatch of history and identity that so many Southerners up through my generation have had, this vague sense of cognitive dissonance that comes with growing up in a world where nothing you see around you quite fits with the picture of history made available to you." Lyndon B. Johnson famously remarked as he signed the Civil Rights Act of 1964 that "we have lost the South for a generation" (Obama 2014). His prediction was premature, but by the time I arrived in Arkansas, it had become a reality. Mark Pryor's (Democratic) Senate seat had flipped to (Republican) Tom Cotton, and in 2017, "in a region stretching from the high plains of Texas to the Atlantic coast of the Carolinas, Republicans controlled not only every Senate seat, but every governor's mansion and every state legislative body" (Cohn 2014). Regional imagination is finally catching up with shifting political reality, but it surprised many in a state that proudly birthed Bill Clinton.

Many also believe that the United States is quickly losing religiosity, with significant percentages of the emerging generations identifying with no specific religious tradition (Pew Forum 2015). For those who remain committed to the Christian faith but whose civic imagination aligns with the progressives (a larger percentage of whom are "nones"; D. Williams 2017), some basic and essential questions arise. *Does it matter whether Christianity offers anything other than secular humanism?* Charles Taylor (2007) maps out the new conditions of secularity: "The change I want to define and trace is one which takes us from a society in which it was virtually impossible not to believe in God, to one in which faith, even for the staunchest believer, is one human possibility among others" (3). Taylor is describing a world that is increasingly secular not in the nonreligious sense of that term but in the sense that many forms of religiosity can live side by side and even mutually support one another. Recall the classic dictum of Christian humanist Nikolai Grundtvig, who frequently stated, "Human first, then Christian." The world increasingly recognizes shared interests across multiple religious and secular perspectives.

Yet for Grundtvig, there was still "then Christian." What is this "then Christian"? The answer hovers around issues of resistance and sanctuary, both resources in Christianity not as clearly present in or adjacent to various kinds of humanism. Dominant forms of Christianity in the United States allow a co-optation by "moral majorities" who believe the perpetuation of racism, sexism, and homophobia are part and parcel of the maintenance of Christianity as the dominant religion. In my (progressive) way of imagining, Christianity contains unique resources for repentance and resistance, for giving preference to the poor and migrants, and for radical neighbor love that overturns the morality of capitalist self-interest.

Many progressive Southerners feel as if they are engaged in the Sisyphean task of repeatedly disambiguating their regional identity from the stereotypes of Southerners. According to Brooks Blevins (2009), "Arkansas has for one reason or another undergone more caricaturing and stereotyping in the American imagination than has just about any other state" (4). The main negative stereotype that makes an average Arkansan self-conscious is that they are low class, uneducated, and poor. Arkansans have learned that such stereotypes are dealt with most effectively through humor. Blevins ends the introduction to his book with the following rejoinder: "Even if we don't get to the very bottom of this, perhaps we'll be better able to laugh at ourselves. . . . At the very least, you found a friend to read this book to you, and I found a friend to write it. Yee-haw, indeed" (10).

Such representational hyperawareness has significant political ramifications. For example, at a recent rally in Fort Smith, Arkansas, Senator Cotton said,

> Go home tonight and turn on one of the nighttime comedy shows. Tomorrow morning, turn on one of the cable morning-news shows. This Saturday, watch "Saturday Night Live." . . . All the high wardens of popular culture in this country, they love to make fun of Donald Trump, to mock him, to ridicule him. They make fun of his hair, they make fun of the color of his skin, they make fun of the way he talks—he's from Queens, not from Manhattan. They make fun of that long tie he wears, they make fun of his taste for McDonald's. . . . What I don't think they realize is that out here in Arkansas and the heartland and the places that made a difference in that election, like Michigan and Wisconsin, when we hear that kind of ridicule, we hear them making fun of the way *we* look, and the way *we* talk, and the way *we* think. (quoted in Toobin 2017)

Although this is a breathtaking leap, Cotton is right about one thing: inasmuch as Southerners perceive themselves to be subject to ridicule by the "high wardens of popular culture," they then are tempted to imagine a kind of solidarity between Trump and Southerners, even if on every other level—his wealth, his (im)morality—he diverges from a Southern Christian imaginary. Their solidarity under ridicule unites them, and this interplay of the regional social imaginary with mass media content informs their voting habits and political preferences even more than their religious commitments.

During the February 2017 congressional recess, Republican Cotton hosted a town hall meeting in Springdale, Arkansas. Springdale is part of the "new" or emerging South: population seventy thousand, 40 percent Latino, 8 percent Pacific Islander. It would certainly fit in Tracy Thompson's chapter "Salsa with Your Grits" in her *The New Mind of the South*. Cotton was taking a lot of heat, along with many other elected officials, for his support of a repeal of the Affordable Care Act and the proposal of the RAISE Act that would dramatically curtail immigration and refugee resettlement.

Although historically the landing place for migrants from all over the world, especially Europe, America did not begin to resettle significant numbers of refugees until it was forced to by the Holocaust and the great need to provide a safe place for Jews to flee during World War II. Since World War II, the United States has slowly and steadily increased its commitment to offering refuge to those fleeing various dangers around the world. Partnering with the Office of the United Nations High Commissioner for Refugees, over the last decade, the United States has resettled on average around seventy-five thousand refugees. These refugees come to America because each year the executive designates admissions levels. One of nine primarily faith-based refugee resettlement agencies, one of the largest of which is the Lutheran Immigration and Refugee Service (LIRS), oversees the actual resettlement.

In 2015, when the Syrian refugee crisis entered the global conversation, a large group of us in Northwest Arkansas began looking into establishing a refugee resettlement center. In just a year, we built a nonprofit, and in 2016, we began welcoming refugees. Then Donald Trump was elected president, and his first action in January 2017 was to announce a Muslim ban, which also paused the entire refugee resettlement program. Suddenly, we dropped from 110,000 refugees arriving in the last year of the Obama administration to fewer than 45,000 refugees in the first year of the Trump administration.

Because we had recently begun resettling these refugees to Northwest Arkansas and because our congregation participates in a lot of social justice ministry in alignment with immigrants and refugees, my presence at the 2017 Springdale town hall was essential. I got there early and stood in line with the thousands of other (mostly anti-Cotton) attendees. It was exhilarating and frightening: a media frenzy. All the national networks were there. To my surprise, I had the opportunity to ask a question at the town hall, advocating for expanded refugee resettlement not only in our state but in our nation, and I did so out of the biblical imagination that recommends providing hospitality for the stranger, for "you were once strangers in the land of Egypt" (Deuteronomy 10:19).

Imagine thousands of attendees in a high school auditorium in Springdale, Arkansas (which incidentally has more Marshallese and Latino students than Anglo), chanting support for refugees and immigrants. I responded to Cotton's characterization of Muslims as a threat with "We love Muslims!" The noise at that point was deafening. Surprised by the breadth and depth of the progressive (Christian) support for immigrants and refugees in our state (remember those media elites and their perceptions of us), the media followed up with several days of televised interviews. Standing in front of an MSNBC camera, I again became mindful of this deep truth: when Southerners speak on the national stage, we are always concerned for our image. There is this representational hyperawareness. I wanted to make the South, or at least Arkansas, look good. I wanted to do them proud. We don't want to feed into the stereotypes. I'm not sure all regional peoples feel this way when they emerge on the national stage, but I know Arkansans do. "Arkansas people remain first and foremost cognizant of the state's place in the American consciousness" (Blevins 2009, 186), and many progressive Christians are equally cognizant of national perceptions of Christianity.

The Southern imagination functions in a circular fashion, with the South mirroring to the world and then sometimes undermining and sometimes reinforcing the world's imagination of the South. So Arkansans were aware of not only how they looked to the world (including the frustration by some that someone with Cotton's views represents us in the Senate) but also the outside perspective on us, their fascination with the town hall's size and tenor, and Rachel Maddow's surprise that an Arkansas pastor would make a comparison between the town hall and Prime Minister's Question Time in the House of Lords. Similarly, the progressive Christian community frequently encounters surprise when articulating their faith: "You're a Christian and you believe that?"

The media layers and recenters regional and religious imaginations, with institution building, television and newspaper presence, and new social media platforms all interlocking in a seamless fashion to energize a religiously informed civic imagination. So, for example, the development of our refugee resettlement agency, Canopy NWA, only happened because we began local conversations after a Twitter post from the governor of the state opposing refugee resettlement; our efforts were strengthened and streamlined as we organized like-minded people of faith to form the nonprofit and solicit resources. Our presence on television and radio and in the newspaper (Jordan 2017) has meant that our model is inspiring others to replicate the development in other locations, while widespread media coverage affects our own and external stereotypes of our region. Transform how the wider world perceives the Southern Christian imagination and you might expand the civic imagination on both sides of the Mason-Dixon Line. John Edge (2017) describes such a transition in his recent book on the changes in Southern food culture:

> The South was once a place that did not brook intrusion. Now it's the region with the highest immigration rates. When I was a boy in 1970s Georgia, a barbecue sandwich and a Brunswick stew with soda crackers was my go-to meal. Jess (my son) prefers tacos al pastor, hold the cilantro, and cheese dip with fryer-hot tortilla chips. In his South, Punjabi truck stop owners in Arkansas fry okra for turban-wearing reefer jockeys. And Korean bakers in Alabama turn out sweet potato-gorged breakfast pastries. His South is changing. For the better, mostly. In fits and starts, yes. New peoples and new foods and new stories are making their marks on the region. In those exchanges, much is gained. What was once a region of black and white, locked in a struggle for power, has become a society of many hues and many hometowns. His generation now weaves new narratives about what it means to be Southern, about what it takes to claim this place as their own. Given time to reconcile the mistakes my generation made with the beauty we forged amid adversity, his generation might challenge the region of our birth to own up to its promise. (350)

Consider the growth of Indivisible, an activist group started after the presidential election of 2016, which is locally focused and has implemented a defensive congressional advocacy strategy to protect their values. A founding member, Billy Fleming, is actually from Arkansas, and their model for developing the Indivisible movement was to publish reproducible resources (an "indivisible guide") that could fuel a progressive grassroots network of local groups to resist the Trump agenda (www.indivisibleguide.com). Although the guide was published online and designed for the entire social media network, by offering a replicable model that local groups could put in place in each district, Indivisible had become—within months—a national movement with chapters (sometimes multiple chapters) in each US congressional district. In Northwest Arkansas, the chapter meets regularly at our church building. We find creative ways weekly and monthly to fuse the church's mission with Indivisible's advocacy activities. Clearly, going mass media actually facilitates going local if those using new social media forms are savvy. Indivisible goes big by going small with national issues energized at the local level.

In my work, I have learned one mantra from the Arkansas United Community Coalition, an immigrant rights advocacy group. They frequently say, "Nothing about us without us," a slogan first popularized in the disability rights movement (Charlton 2000, 3). As a white pastor in a predominantly white church who spends significant time in refugee and immigrant spaces, I have learned how to listen, support, walk alongside, amplify. It's a slogan I wish other prominent leaders might heed: whether it's the Evangelicals publishing their Nashville Statement or multiple attorney generals and President Trump threatening to end the Deferred Action for Childhood Arrivals Act, they should live by the slogan "Nothing about us without us" coupled with Grundtvig's slogan "Human first." Christians hoping their message might be life-giving and attractive can learn much from both slogans, not the smallest of those lessons being that the first shall be last and the last shall be first (Mark 10:31). It's awfully hard to build a progressive *Christian* movement when the largest and loudest Christian voices encourage strategies quite opposite those of progressives—and Jesus. Nevertheless, it has probably always been so. Effective progressive movements find ways to keep their imagination indigenous to the region (the actual region rather than the stereotype), open to the resonances of the wider movements with which they partner, amplified by new media in order to be even more effectively local, cognizant of the traditions of all, and respectful of the humanity in each.

We might remember that "there has been consensus for several decades among political historians of the early modern period that

European theories of resistance found their first articulation in the Lutheran tradition" (DeJonge 2019, 198). One significant moment in the Reformation was the emperor's push early on to suppress reform. When Martin Luther died in 1546, Charles V published the Augsburg Interim, which put all German lands back under Roman Catholic rule. All the cities and towns acquiesced with the exception of one—Magdeburg. The pastors of Magdeburg published a confessional document explaining why their magistrates were right to resist. Not as well known as some other confessional documents of the early modern period, the Magdeburg Confession functioned as a first example of regional resistance to empire and became a source for other articulations of resistance, such as the Declaration of Independence. It informed the thought of such a significant resister as Dietrich Bonhoeffer (quoted in DeJonge 2019), who wrote,

> There are thus three possibilities for action that the church can take vis-à-vis the state: first, questioning the state as to the legitimate state character of its actions, that is, making the state responsible for what it does. Second is service to the victims of the state's actions. The church has an unconditional obligation toward the victims of any societal order, even if they do not belong to the Christian community. "Let us work for the good of all." These are both ways in which the church, in its freedom, conducts itself in the interest of a free state. In times when the laws are changing, the church may under no circumstances neglect either of these duties. The third possibility is not just to bind up the wounds of the victims beneath the wheel but to seize the wheel itself. Such an action would be direct political action on the part of the church. (210)

To claim that all forms of resistance have Christian origins is a stretch, but Christianity provided a very significant resource for resistance in the West. Consider sanctuary. Of the many German cities, only one resisted the Augsburg Interim. During the Holocaust, a small remnant (the Confessing Church) resisted the Nazis. So also with sanctuary: a small percentage of the whole of American congregations offer sanctuary. But repentance is in the Christian tradition. The first call of Luther's Ninety-Five Theses, in fact, states that the whole life of the Christian is to be one of repentance. So when Christians heed their own tradition, they can confess their failure to live into their own best practices and recenter themselves on the social imaginary that defines them.

Sanctuary may become even more important in this next era, as immigrants and others seeking refuge approach the church in their time of need. The original Sanctuary Movement was "a religious and political campaign to provide safe-haven for Central American refugees fleeing civil conflict in their homelands during the 1980s" (De La Torre 2017, 130) Reverend John Fife, one of the architects of the Sanctuary Movement, still works along the border, leading efforts to protect the undocumented in their perilous travels. Fife, a strategic troublemaker, adopts a peculiar way of practicing "then Christian." In a nation that has for decades understood Christianity to be the dominant cultural form of religiosity, it may be surprising to lift up *disruption* of the status quo as an especially Christian practice, but nevertheless, there it is—part of being Christian is being "a royal pain in the ass . . . shout[ing] from the mountain top what is supposed to be kept silent . . . audaciously refusing to stay in [the] assigned place [and] . . . upsetting the prevailing Panopticon social order designed to maintain the law and order of the privileged" (De La Torre 2017, 210). In this instance, practicing sanctuary, providing actual physical sanctuary to undocumented immigrants or refugees, is both human and Christian at the same time: human because it is simply doing the right thing and Christian because it uses the religious space itself (sanctuary) precisely in the way it is named—as sanctuary. When sanctuary breaks the law, precisely there it is sanctuary. A community wrestling with how to do it and how much to sacrifice doing it will expand the progressive Christian social imaginary in ways we have yet to imagine. And if you make fun of us for our disruptive activity, we will join you and exercise self-mockery, which we will then use strategically to our advantage.

## 29

## *Tzina:* Symphony of Longing

Using Volumetric VR to Archive the Nostalgic
Imaginaries of the Marginal

**Ioana Mischie**

If "nostalgia is rebellion against the modern idea of time" (Boym 2001),
can we consider it a form of civic imagination? Does the civic imagination activate our past as well as our future?

Even though it has seen several major controversial redesigns,
Dizengoff Square is still considered one of the most iconic highlights
of Tel Aviv.[1] Before its recent demolition in 2016, the elevated square
and its marginalized residents were captured in a pioneering volumetric
virtual reality (VR) experience directed by Shirin Anlen called *Tzina:
Symphony of Longing*. If, as André Bazin (1976) claimed, "photography embalms time" and cinema "is mummified," volumetric (three-
dimensional) VR has the potential to revitalize subjective glimpses of
reality. In this chapter, I focus on the relation between the Dizengoff
Square space and its VR archive, created through interviews, personal
experimentation, and external sources.

As she traces competing histories in relation to the reconfiguration of
public spaces in the Middle East, Susan Slyomovics (1998) observes, "In
both Palestinian Arab and Jewish culture, active remembrance is seen
as a guarantee of cultural survival; each has developed narrative codes,
remarkably similar, to transform individual memory into public history."
In this context, can a volumetric VR archive depicting the longing of
marginalized people become a meaningful facet of a public space?

## Dizengoff Square: The Chronology of a Remixed Public Space

The original design of the square was inaugurated in 1938 as the "Étoile of Tel Aviv" (figure 29.1a). The square was nicknamed Zina (Tzina) as an homage to the wife of Meir Dizengoff, the first mayor of Tel Aviv. The first major redesign of the space was proposed in 1978. The architectural plan, signed by Tsvi Lissar, proposed to elevate the square and add bridges and ramps (Kamisher 2017) to ease congestion of the urban space and support traffic flow. Although it faced criticism, the planned redesign took place in 1983. In 1986, a fountain designed by Yaacov Agam, "Fire and Water" became central to the square (figure 29.1b). The sculpture is now revered for its kinetic qualities.

In the 1990s, the elevated square became the birthplace of punk in Israel, which brought a community of rebels and homeless to the area. Over time, the majority of the residents grew to despise it due to "poor maintenance of the square and homeless people living underneath the elevated pedestrian walkway" (Kamisher 2017). Acknowledging these realities, Shirin Anlen became "fascinated by the space" (Anlen, personal interview, 2017) and decided to conserve the stories of the square's marginalized residents in a volumetric VR experience.

In 2016, the authorities decided to demolish the elevated square and bring it back to street level (figure 29.1d). The new plan included bike lanes, an underground infrastructure, and reconstructed streets (figure

**Figure 29.1.** Evolution of Dizengoff Square: (a) original ground of Dizengoff Square; (b) elevated Dizengoff Square; (c) still from *Tzina*, an interactive experience; (d) predemolition view; (e) demolition (photo by Omer Shalev); and (f) future projection of Dizengoff Square (remixing the past ground level and the current kinetic sculpture)

29.1f). The full reconfiguration process was scheduled to finish in early 2018 and cost sixty million Israeli new shekels (NIS) (Kamisher 2017). Although most Tel Aviv residents approved of these plans, those personally invested in the space held a different, loss-filled, view. Anlen expressed this sentiment when she recalled, "The day they demolished it I cried. It was like they took something that was a part of me" (Anlen, personal interview, 2017).

## A Battle of "Splendors": Investigating the Modus Operandi of Multiple Imaginaries

> Catastrophe is the past coming apart. Anastrophe is the future coming together.
> —Sandie Plant and Nick Land (1994)

Tsvi Lissar, the architect of the elevated square, argued that the decision to bring it back to ground level was a mistake: "Restoring the square to its original splendor—as ruining its current form is often referred to— would actually mean going back to a traffic island" (Kamisher 2017). His observation touches on a battle of "splendors." Whose view holds more weight? Who determines how meaning is created? In this political and cultural context, what feels celebratory to some is a disillusion to others. As a result, the quality and meaning of imaginaries in the public space[2] become hard to determine.

What do we lose through the act of redesigning a space? What do we gain? And once a public space is in a transition process, "how much of the past will be allowed to survive" and "how can we manage this mediated survival with its inequalities, inequities?" (Bliss Cua Lim 2017). Though there are no absolute answers to these questions, nostalgia, as experienced through personal memories and imagination, can give us a sense of the indecipherable flux that surrounds such change. Boym (2001) distinguishes between two categories of nostalgia: restorative ("total reconstructions of monuments of the past," a view that may be associated with the position of the authorities in relation to restoring Dizengoff Square to its original form) and reflective nostalgia (one that "thrives in algia," "lingers on ruins, the patina of time and history, in the dreams of another place and another time," which is more suggestive of the views held by the square's residents).

## *Tzina: Symphony of Longing*: A Groundbreaking Volumetric VR Experience

*Tzina: Symphony of Longing*[3] is an Israeli room-scale volumetric VR experience and an interactive web-based documentary in which residents of Dizengoff Square "muse on their lives, loves, longing and loneliness" (IDFA DocLab 2016). The walkable VR experience is central to the story universe, while the web interactive version facilitates greater worldwide accessibility to the narrative.

Created by Anlen and her team in 2016, the project became a pioneering work. It was one of the first walkable VR experiences selected by the International Documentary Film Festival Amsterdam (IDFA), the first VR/web student thesis project, and the first interactive VR experience selected for Israeli documentary festivals. The project reunites ten interviewed characters recorded with Depthkit volumetric shooting technology through forty-five minutes of footage and eighteen minutes of volumetric VR (Anlen, personal interview, 2017).

### Facets of Personal History: A Museum of Vulnerabilities

> I long therefore I am.
> —Svetlana Boym (2001)

Shirin Anlen had a personal connection to Dizengoff Square—she saw it as a symbol of *home*. As a child, her grandmother had an apartment with a view of the square. When developing the project, Anlen returned to the same apartment after enduring a painful divorce. To her, the public space of the square became "a kind of personal space" (Anlen, personal interview, 2017). Perhaps this is why the subjectified VR square resembles "a shelter for the broken ones" (Anlen interviewed by Holmes 2017). Dizengoff Square for Anlen, like Kaliningrad-Konigsberg for Boym, "resembles a theme park of lost illusions" (Boym 2001). In 1945, the former German city of Königsberg, known as the hometown of Immanuel Kant, was annexed by the Soviet Union, renamed Kalinin-grad, and gradually populated by new citizens. This major shift, with its numerous cultural, social, and political implications, is a clear example of how the too-quickly changed identity of a space impacts the identity, memory, and nostalgia of its residents and vice versa.

The merit of *Tzina* lies in the archiving of the public square and in the process that led to the project's creation. While conducting research in the square, Anlen noticed a steadfast routine: people would return to the space at precise times. Though they generally did not interact, their isolation was characterized by a profound sense of solidarity.

While many audiovisual projects carefully curate their characters in advance, *Tzina* embraces a more genuine approach to archiving. For sixteen days, the team arrived at Dizengoff Square fully equipped with 3-D spatial capture technology and waited for the passersby to settle. They then approached them and requested to record them: "Sometimes we waited for a whole day, sometimes two. Sometimes a character just wasn't in the mood to be filmed, another was sick and one got cold feet and disappeared for a while, so we just packed and came back the next day" (Anlen 2017). Most of the characters were chosen solely because they were present in the square.

Anlen and her team learned that the square would be demolished while the project was under way. The news shifted the focus of the VR piece: "When we found out that [it was] going to be destroyed, we started to work differently on the project. Before that, I thought mostly about the characters, and then the place became a character that was much more significant" (Anlen, personal interview, 2017). The project shifted from primarily an emotional experience to a virtual archive of the elevated Dizengoff Square.

The team focused on conserving the space accurately in VR. Every-thing was scanned—the kinetic fountain, the one-hundred-year-old trees,[4] the textures of the square, the imperfections of the benches, the graffiti marks—and recomposed according to the architectural plan. As Anlen explains, "*Tzina* offers you a visit [to] a place that no longer exists" (Anlen interviewed by Holmes 2017).

## The User Experience: Decoding Imaginaries

I first experienced the VR version of *Tzina* in May 2017, displayed on an HTC Vive VR headset in the NEXT Pavilion at Cannes Marché du Film. As soon as I put on the headset, I was isolated and placed in another dimension that I can most accurately characterize as a guided meditation. The director's poetic voice invited me to explore and get deliberately lost in the virtual square. I soon started to connect with the solitary characters.

Once immersed in the room-scale experience, I explored the personal stories of those present in Dizengoff Square. The square became a place that healed lost love, expressed longing, and invited solitude through a layering of experiences, regrets, and mistakes that normally remain hidden. This was a fertile urban space for observation, remembrance, and imagination. As I encountered the characters in the walkable virtual square, I engaged with their vulnerabilities and, to some extent, was encouraged to feel comfortable with my own.

The *Tzina* VR experience is nonlinear and conceived in five episodes: Awakeness, Home, Emptiness, Disappointments, and Loneliness. Each episode connects to a time of day, ranging from sunrise to sunset. While the webVR version of the project allows the users to wander endlessly, in the volumetric VR experience, the player can switch from one chapter to another any time by looking at the sun. Reflecting on the collected narratives, Anlen observed, "The morning characters are more positive than the night characters" (Anlen, personal interview, 2017). There was a metaphysical change in their narratives in relation to the time of the day; therefore, temporality became vital to the piece.

## The Meaningful Nobodies: Redefining *Dramatis Personae*

The volumetric characters who frequent the square are ordinary people, "nobodies" (Anlen, personal interview, 2017). Most are old men and women who have experienced emotional loss. They are widowed, unmarried, or divorced. They recall their past loves, their challenges, their mistakes, their moments of joy. They imagine how different choices would have impacted their lives. Anlen does not reveal their financial, health, or social dramas; rather she focuses on their emotions (Anlen, personal interview, 2017).

The names of the characters are not revealed and do not even seem relevant. We remember them. We do not remember their names. We remember their feelings. Their uncertainties ("Sometimes I do not know what I want . . ."), decisions ("In order to survive, I have to forget . . ."), accomplishments ("He was the love of my life . . ."), and regrets ("Most of my friends are married, everyone is married, everyone is with children . . . I ran around all over the place . . .") are the expressions of their identities. All together, they are facets of the ordinary, facets of modern nostalgia, facets of retroactive imagination.

The absence of a protagonist allows the user to oscillate between the characters, to decide for how long he or she wants to listen to each story. The VR experience democratizes the story structure and blurs power inequalities between characters and users: "I wanted to affect the viewers' physical body and to encourage them to go down on their knees when they interacted with the characters. To be equal, as humans," explained Anlen (Holmes 2017). The space created through *Tzina* becomes a playground for connecting otherwise distinct civic imaginations.

## Volumetric VR: An Innovative Catalyst for Shared Humanity

The project presents us with a paradox in which "technology is in a stage of reminding us what it means to be human" (Anlen 2017). If VR was so far associated with empathy (Milk 2015), intensity (Rosenthal 2017), and embodiment (Slater 2016), volumetric VR is increasingly associated with an unprecedented sense of presence. Creators like Aaron Koblin (2015) attribute an additional dimension—"it's almost like people across the planet are dreaming together." The novelty of the volumetric technology and the documentary's theme of longing creates an interesting contrast for analyzing distinct imaginaries.

The characters are strangers sitting alone in the square. Their imperfect volumetric figures, at times distorted by technical glitches, remind us of our own ordinariness: we all are works in progress spiritually, mentally, physically. The technical imperfections reinforce the imperfections of humanity. The project deliberately uses volumetry as a parallel discourse on ephemerality: "One of the project's cornerstones was our approach to work within technological constraints. We did not act to hide the limitations we worked within, but rather adopted them as an ideology" (Anlen 2017).

The virtual experience prioritizes physical actions such as exploring, looking, sitting, wondering: "I insisted not to have controllers and not to have clicks. You feel [as if you are] inside a world, not inside an interface" (Anlen, personal interview, 2017). The exploration is conceived almost as choreography: "In spatial VR humans have more opportunities to expose themselves and to be vulnerable" (Anlen 2017). In the web interactive version of the project, users can decode additional layers of meaning. Created as a multiuser experience, all users exploring the project are displayed as pigeons navigating the square and are thus indirectly in dialogue with each other. This particular element makes loneliness and togetherness inseparable feelings. The creator herself emphasized the notion of "us together as a power" (Anlen, personal interview, 2017), and the "comfort in shared loneliness" (Anlen 2017) thus became a vital layer of the experience.

## A Feedback Loop: Shifting Perceptions

The *Tzina* VR experience was included in fifteen festivals worldwide and received an array of reactions. In particular, the 2017 premiere in Tel Aviv was important for the creators and for the residents. Anlen said, "I felt I really need to bring it back to TLV [Tel Aviv]" (Anlen, personal interview, 2017). In Tel Aviv, "everyone stayed up until the last second in the VR version of 18 minutes" because "they knew the place, they recognized themselves" (Anlen, personal interview, 2017). For Yaacov Agam, the ninety-year-old sculptor of the kinetic fountain, who was also a character in the documentary, the VR experience offered a unique opportunity to archive his work (Anlen, personal interview, 2017). For others, the volumetric VR experience shifted their perceptions of the square: "A lot of people that hated the space told me that after they saw *Tzina*, they went to the square and looked at it differently, understood it differently, and that was really powerful" (Anlen, personal interview, 2017). These experiences raise important questions. What is the relationship between the archive and the original? How does it change over time? Is one becoming more persistent than another?

## Nostalgic Imaginaries, Imaginative Nostalgias

> One is always nearer by not keeping still.
> —Thom Gunn, "The Sense of Movement" (2015)

According to a Russian proverb, "The past has become much more unpredictable than the future" (Boym 2001). We need to explore how the plurality of civic imaginations operated in the past in order to anticipate how these imaginations may work in the future. As Boym (2001) underlines, "Nostalgia itself has a utopian dimension, only it is no longer directed toward the future. Sometimes nostalgia is not directed toward the past either, but rather sideways."

According to Peter Frase (2016), "It's up to us to build the collective power to fight for the futures we want." Similarly, I believe we need to fight for the pasts and presents that represent us. *Tzina* is only one example that points to a much bigger movement: a movement that strives to understand marginalized ordinariness as a form of enrichment rather than treat it with derision. Volumetric technology allows us to archive, express, and expand humanity. The result is a movement that aims to create a compelling "memorializing consciousness" of the residents (Slyomovics 1998)—a movement that strives to reconcile nostalgia and imagination.

### Notes

1　My connection with Tel Aviv began in 2015, when I visited the square for the first time. As a tourist, I could not decode its local urban poetry in depth. However, when I experienced *Tzina: A Symphony of Longing*, I felt as if I knew it extensively. The stories of the square residents in the context of the square's demolition activated the deepest feelings of longing for a no-longer-existent urban cocoon.

2　According to Stuart Hall, "The meaning of a cultural form and its place or position in the cultural field is not inscribed inside its form. Nor is its position fixed once and forever. This year's radical symbol or slogan will be neutralized into next year's fashion; the year after, it will be the object of a profound cultural nostalgia" (quoted in Storey 2013, xvi)

3　See http://tzina.space/.

4　All the trees were later cut down during the demolition process.

## 30

## What's Civic about Aztlán?

Reflections on the Chican@ Promised Land

**Rogelio Alejandro Lopez**

### Remnants of an Imagined Homeland

Olvera Street, Plaza Mexico, and Boyle Heights's "El Mercadito" are Mexican American cultural centers in Los Angeles whose cultural products often reflect a playful hybridity that gives the city its distinct character. From T-shirts depicting Star Wars's Chewbacca as musta-chioed Mexican revolutionary "El Chuy" to smartphone cases featuring Day of the Dead–inspired "calavera" Pokémon, the centers' artifacts fuse traditional Mexican culture with American (and international) popu-lar culture. One artifact in particular stood out on a recent visit to *La Placita Olvera*—a gray Dodgers T-shirt with the word *Aztlán* spelled using the baseball team's logo standing in for the letters *L* and *A*. As a Chicano Angeleno, I am familiar with both the "Aztlán Dodgers" and the "Aztlán Raiders," the fandoms of Chicana/o[1] sports fans in Los Angeles. While the term *Aztlán* continues to be used to describe communities of Chican@s, people of Mexican descent living in the United States, it has come a long way since the Chicano movement popularized it in the late 1960s to describe both a nation and a homeland for Chican@ people.

This chapter examines the rise of the concept of Aztlán as an example of "civic imagination," the idea that collectively reimagining the world is the first step toward social change, with an emphasis on the role of cultural production. Looking specifically at the earliest years of the Chicano movement, three central questions guide and frame this work: (1) Why is Aztlán relevant to the civic imagination? (2) What was the role of cultural production in creating and cultivating the shared con-cept of Aztlán? (3) What can the potentials and limitations of Aztlán teach us about utopias and dystopias? Although the concept of Aztlán has been the subject of various academic works (Chávez 1994; Gaspar de Alba 2004; Hidalgo 2016; Miner 2014; Pérez 2011; Pérez-Torres 2016), it's worth considering in the context of civic imagination for several reasons: Aztlán is a notable concept that can inform how people of color and social movements harness the imagination for social change; as a cautionary tale, the story of Aztlán shows both the potentials and pitfalls of imaginaries—the thin line between utopia and dystopia; and despite its deserved criticism for perpetuating regressive politics (mainly patriarchy and toxic masculinity), Aztlán as a concept continues to endure, for better or for worse.

## The People of the Sun: The Citizens of Aztlán

Not Mexican Enough or American Enough

Aztlán has been an important, although contested, "place" linked to Chican@ imaginaries in the United States (Hidalgo 2016; Miner 2014), representing physical space, an aspirational utopia, and an Indigenous worldview. But what exactly is Aztlán?

Chican@s, people of Mexican descent in the United States, have long voiced their sense of displacement from both the United States and Mexico alike, feeling they are "ni de aquí, ni de allá" (neither from here nor from there) amid discriminatory race politics at home and nostalgia for a "homeland" they knew only through a vibrant culture (LaWare 1998). This deep sense of homelessness, of not belonging, led many Chicana/o youths in the late 1960s to rediscover Mesoamerican culture and reimagine their place in US society through the Chicano movement, which began in the 1960s as a social movement for the liberation and empowerment of Chican@s in the United States.

While its timeline and histories remain contested (Watts 2004), a central narrative of the Chicano movement concerns Aztlán, the mythical homeland of the once nomadic Aztec people. Myths aside, many Chican@s considered Aztlán to be a physical place in the southwestern United States (Hidalgo 2016). According to Indigenous-Mexican codices, a prophecy led the Aztec people away from Aztlán and south through the deserts of Northern Mexico for years in search of a promised land. The location of this promised land would be revealed by a divine apparition—an eagle, perched upon a cactus, devouring a snake (a symbol now included on Mexico's national flag). This historical connection between Indigenous Mexicans and the present-day United States inspired Chican@ activists to use the concept of Aztlán to lay claim to the Southwest as their long-lost homeland (Hidalgo 2016; Miner 2014). Reestablishing historical ties to the United States through land claims became particularly important for Chican@s who were regularly othered by xenophobia and nativism, and Aztlán reinforced Indigenous migration patterns that opposed divisive national borders.

## Making the Homeland: Imaginaries and Cultural Production

Aztlán, Aztlán
a call for justice
Aztlán, Aztlán
a call for freedom
Aztlán, Aztlán
a call for nationhood
dedicated to the humanization
of man and woman
dedicated to the preservation
of earth and sun
rooted in brotherhood and sisterhood
rooted in collective labor and self-sacrifice.
—Alurista, "The History of Aztlán" (Miner 2014, 66)

While Aztlán has been historically used by Chican@ activists as a concept linked to geographic space, it has also informed Chican@ imaginaries as a means to reclaim indigeneity, affirm collective identity, and imagine a new homeland—especially through cultural production.

Since the 1960s, Chican@ activist groups, organizations, artists, public intellectuals, and poets have conjured the idea of Aztlán to imagine a place of belonging amid a hostile and discriminatory world. The rise of the Chicano movement coincided with a widespread rediscovery of Mesoamerican, pre-Columbian culture and philosophy (Gómez-Quiñones and Vásquez 2014), which inspired poets like Alurista to link the struggles of US-based Chican@ people to the historic Indigenous struggles across the American continents (Gómez 2016). In "The History of

Aztlán," Alurista moves beyond Aztlán as a physical place and outlines how the concept can forge community and identity through shared commitments and priorities, such as justice, freedom, humanization, and a relationship to the earth (Miner 2014).

The concepts of nationhood and nationalism have also been linked to Aztlán (Chávez 1994; Hidalgo 2016; Miner 2014). Some scholars (Miner 2014) consider Aztlán to follow an Indigenous rather than a Western concept of nationhood, emphasizing the affirmation of identity and culture in the tribal sense. Others note a type of nationalism that often accompanied Aztlán called "chicanismo," which focused on a reclamation of Indigenous places, cultures, and identities and served as the basis for community building, empowerment, and political consciousness (Chávez 1994). In either sense, Aztlán named and identified a "Chicano Nation," one composed of people of color at a time when Mexican Americans were legally considered Anglo despite their racial othering and status as second-class citizens. Rodolfo "Corky" Gonzales's influential poem "I Am Joaquin" is often cited as laying the foundations for both Aztlán and a wider Chicano community. The Chicano movement's founding manifesto, *El Plan Espiritual de Aztlán* (The Spiritual Plan of Aztlán), written in 1969, notably asserts Aztlán as a new nation and homeland and Chicanos as its people (Chávez 1994). This manifesto was widely read by Chican@s across the United States, forging an imagined community based on citizenship in the aspirational homeland of Aztlán (C. Anderson 2016).

The Chicano art movement, composed of activist-artists inspired to create art based on the ideals of the Chicano movement (Gaspar de Alba 1998), became particularly important for translating Aztlán from the realm of the imagination into physical space. Miner (2014) discusses how Chican@ art came to reflect not only Aztlán but its priorities and values, especially through Mesoamerican iconography. Murals depicting Mesoamerican architecture, Indigenous faces and patterns, Aztec deities, Nahuatl script, and the cultivation of maize became the visual vernacular of Chican@ barrios from Los Angeles to Chicago (Gaspar de Alba 2004; Miner 2014). Aztlán used elements of the past to reimagine both the present and the future. LaWare's (1998) study of the community art center "Casa Aztlán" in Chicago documents how Chican@ murals often depicted Aztlán as a place of hybridity, a homeland that mirrored Chican@s' sense of "mestizaje," or racial and cultural blending, by mixing Indigenous, Spanish, Mexican, and American elements visually. The murals of Chicano Park in San Diego, California, similarly emphasize hybridity by depicting Quetzalcoatl, the Aztec deity of knowledge and creation, alongside Frida Kahlo, Ernesto "Che" Guevara, and Cesar Chavez. In this sense, Aztlán was less about depicting a specific "place" and more about reclaiming history to create an aspirational vision for the present and future when juxtaposed with contemporary barrio life.

## From Outcasts to Cocreators of the World

Aztlán stands as a notable example of how social movements harness the imagination to reenvision the world and inform action. However, as far as the civic imagination is concerned, a key question remains: *What's civic about Aztlán?* The following section attempts to uncover the "civic" dimensions of Aztlán, mainly (1) its use to reconceptualize belonging, (2) its cultivation of identity as empowerment, and (3) its potential to facilitate various types of civic processes.

First, vital to healthy civics is a strong sense of community and belonging and a shared commitment to a common good—whether through formal or alternative channels (Boyte 2011; Putnam 2003). Historically, formal politics prevented many Chican@s from reaching this civic potential. Prior to the Chicano movement, people of Mexican descent in the United States were relegated to second-class citizenship: exploited for cheap labor (Ganz 2010), segregated to subpar neighborhoods and schools (Gonzalez 2013), and politically disenfranchised (Chávez 1994). As a geographically and sociopolitically displaced people, Chicanos turned to activism to become empowered and to Aztlán to imagine a place to belong—often through art.

Public-oriented art, from murals to street art, played a key role in reclaiming space and spreading the priorities of *El Movimiento* in an accessible visual format (LaWare 1998). Many Chican@ murals reflected what Aztlán could be: a place for hybridity and cultural blending; a fluid mashup of past, present, and future; and a space to represent people of color in dignified and empowered ways (LaWare 1998; Miner 2014). Through this type of "people's art," the symbolism of Aztlán countered exclusion and displacement by publicly embracing and celebrating difference, giving Chican@s a sense of both home and pride. Boyle Heights's low-income housing project "Estrada Heights" became such a place to reimagine belonging with murals, with one in particular depicting Che Guevara in an Uncle Sam pose accompanied by the phrase "We are NOT a minority!" Because mainstream US (and Mexican) society had discarded them for being Chican@, these murals became the signposts for a new nation where they could belong. In short, the concept of Aztlán—especially the conjuring of its symbolism through art—allows us to consider the importance of place and belonging to civics and the civic imagination.

Second, identity and a sense of self are also important to the civic imagination. The ability to see oneself as an "agent of change," with a sense of civic efficacy to enact influence and social change, often accompanies the exercise of reenvisioning the world (Jenkins et al. 2016). This idea echoes Paulo Freire's (2018) notion of "conscientization," the idea that a combination of reflection and action, or "praxis," can lead marginalized groups to critically understand the social order and see their capacity to meaningfully intervene in the creation of the world. While Aztlán cannot take full credit for this transformation of self, its emergence is linked to the development of an empowered "Chicano consciousness" (Gómez-Quiñones and Vásquez 2014). The Brown Berets, a Chicano group modeled after the Black Panther Party, used symbolic occupations of space as a means to raise and develop political consciousness with the March through Aztlán in 1971 (Gómez-Quiñones and Vásquez 2014). Media texts from the movement also reflected elements of Aztlán while raising consciousness, such as the struggle to reconcile cultural and racial hybridity in Gonzales's "I Am Joaquin." If Aztlán was the answer to "Where are you from?," then Chican@ became the answer to "Who are you?" Much like place and belonging, this affirmation of an empowered identity encouraged countless Chican@s to see themselves as agents of change. In this sense, Chican@s developed their own sense of citizenship wherein their duties and sense of belonging were tied to the empowerment of Chican@s and to Aztlán.

Third, many of Aztlán's associated ideas and priorities seemed to facilitate civic processes, such as activism, shared knowledge production, and community work. I define civic processes as various actions and activities that promote, cultivate, or sustain civic engagement, such as democratic decision-making, the managing of pooled resources, community building, and a commitment to a common good. Not only were

Chican@s urged to define their homeland and themselves, but Aztlán also called for an active part in cocreating a new world. In particular, key movement texts like *El Plan de Santa Bárbara* moved Aztlán into the realm of knowledge, learning, and education. Much like the Chicano movement manifesto before it (*El Plan Espiritual de Aztlán*), *El Plan de Santa Bárbara* addressed the displacement of Chican@s in educational institutions and academia (González 2002). Through scholarship, ethnic studies departments, and the student group MEChA in particular, the discourse of Aztlán became key to interpreting belonging, hybrid culture, and identity (Gómez-Quiñones and Vásquez 2014).

MEChA, an acronym for Chicano Student Movement of Aztlán, was one of the outcomes of the Santa Barbara plan, and its purpose was to empower young Chicanos through education and activism (Gómez-Quiñones and Vásquez 2014). To this day, the symbols of Aztlán can be found on many MEChA emblems, such as the black eagle holding an Aztec *macuahuitl* on the UCLA group's banner. For decades, MEChA cultivated consciousness in countless students through cultural awareness, community mentorship and volunteering, and educational attainment (Gómez-Quiñones and Vásquez 2014; Valle 1996). In essence, Aztlán became a kind of rallying cry used to bring Chican@s together and enact change through action, bridging elements of the imagination with grassroots social change.

## The Dark Side of Aztlán: From Chicano Utopia to Chicanx Dystopia?

While Aztlán offered a radical vision for society centered on the inclusion and empowerment of a racial and ethnic group, some early versions prioritized racial politics over gender and sexuality, alienating women and queer Chicanxs along the way. In this sense, Aztlán became dystopian for some by perpetuating hostile and exclusionary gender and heteronormative politics (Gaspar de Alba 2004; Pérez 2011). The civic imagination potential of these early versions of Aztlán may have been held back by regressive and arguably "anticivic" elements—namely, a gendered and heteronormative vision of the world.

Although Aztlán offered an alternative vision for what the world could be, this vision was predominantly created by men of the movement—and its priorities were often male- and hetero-centric (Gaspar de Alba 2004).

From the very beginning, the Chicano movement's manifesto, *El Plan Espiritual de Aztlán*, framed the liberation of men through a gendered use of language: the male variation of "Chicano," an emphasis on Indigenous "forefathers," and even the designation "People of the Sun"—in reference to the male Aztec sun god of war (Gaspar de Alba 2004). Furthermore, pockets of the Chicano art movement often depicted Aztlán as a utopia for men, where they could express their masculinity as conquering Aztec warriors worthy of both land and women as trophies. The Aztec "sleeping woman" myth of the princess Ixtaccíhuatl and the warrior Popocatepetl has become a ubiquitous visual story in Chican@ communities. According to Garber (1995), "This image epitomizes woman as sex object, woman as tied to man, and because Popocatepetl is usually depicted as holding the dead Ixtaccihuatl in a Pieta arrangement, the passive woman protected by active man" (221). Across barrios in the United States, the visual depiction of Aztlán coincided with a nostalgia for male Aztec warrior culture (Gaspar de Alba 2004). This vision was translated from texts and art into the political formations of the movement, as men regularly held visible leadership roles, taking credit for its accomplishments, while women were relegated to the heavy lifting in the shadows (Blackwell 2011). Women who spoke out against patriarchy and sexism in the movement were often considered traitors to the cause.

Aztlán continues to be a compelling and powerful concept for many young Chicanxs developing their political consciousness. While this chapter tracks the "rise and fall" of an early "version" of Aztlán tied to the rise of the Chicano movement, there are many versions that have come since. Notably, Gloria Anzaldúa's groundbreaking Chicanx feminist text *Borderlands/La Frontera: The New Mestiza* offered displaced Chicanas and Chicanx people a new metaphor for home and belonging in the *borderlands*—which some scholars (Watts 2004) consider as a reclamation and expansion of Aztlán into a more inclusive transnational feminist project.

## Note

1   As a Spanish word, the use of the letter *o* to end a pronoun designates a male/masculine role. As a more inclusive signifier, activists prefer the use of the term with gender-inclusive variations, such as those ending in *a/o*, *@*, *e*, or *x*.

# References

Abad Faciolince, Hector. 2017. "Contra Las Buenas Noticias." *El Espectador*, June 17.

Acosta, Jim (@Acosta). 2017. "CNN response: 'It is a sad day when the President of the United States encourages violence against reporters . . .'" Twitter, July 2, 2017, 8:28 a.m. https://twitter.com/acosta/status/881534997894770688?lang=en.

Acuna, Alicia. 2017. "Greg Gianforte: Fox News Team Witnesses GOP House Candidate 'Body Slam' Reporter." *Fox News*, May 24. www.foxnews.com/politics/2017/05/24/greg-gianforte-fox-news-team-witnesses-gop-house-candidate-body-slam-reporter.html.

Adewunmi, Bim. 2014. "Kimberle Crenshaw on Intersectionality." *New Statesman*, April 12. https://www.newstatesman.com/lifestyle/2014/04/kimberl-crenshaw-intersectionality-i-wanted-come-everyday-metaphor-anyone-could.

Akomfrah, J., dir. (1996). *The Last Angel of History*. United States: Black Audio Film Collective.

Alberty, E. 2014. "Anita Sarkeesian Explains Why She Canceled USU Lecture." *Salt Lake Tribune*, 16 October/12 December.

Alexander, Michelle. 2012. *The New Jim Crow: Mass Incarceration in the Age of Colorblindness*. New York: New Press.

Ali, Mahershala. 2017. "Mahershala Ali Acceptance Speech | 23rd SAG Awards." YouTube video, 2:33. Posted by "SAG Awards," January 29. https://www.youtube.com/watch?v=e59q6jsWS6Q.

Allen, Danielle. 2012. "Toward Participatory Democracy." *Boston Review*, April 16.

———. 2014. *Our Declaration: A Reading of the Declaration of Independence in Defense of Equality*. New York: W. W. Norton.

———. 2017. "No, Don't Punch More Nazis." *Washington Post*, August 24.

Amaya, Hector. 2013. *Citizenship Excess: Latinos/as, Media, and the Nation*. New York: New York University Press.

America with Jorge Ramos. 2015. "Why the WWE Is to Blame for Donald Trump's Political Rise." *Fusion*, November 12. http://fusion.net/video/231139/donald-trump-wwe-political-rise/.

Ampikaipakan, Umapagan. 2015. "The Oxymoron, the Asian Comic Superhero." *New York Times*, December 25. https://www.nytimes.com/2015/12/26/opinion/that-oxymoron-the-asian-comic-superhero.html?mcubz=3.

Anderson, Benedict. 2006. *Imagined Communities: Reflections on the Origin and Spread of Nationalism*. London: Verso.

———. 2016. *Imagined Communities: Reflections on the Origin and Spread of National-ism*. Rev. ed. London New York: Verso.

Anderson, Carol. 2016. *White Rage: The Unspoken Truth of Our Racial Divide*. New York: Bloomsbury.

Anderson, Tre'vell. 2017. "New CAA Study Says Diverse Casting Increases Box Of-fice Potential across All Budgets." *Los Angeles Times*, June 21. www.latimes.com/entertainment/movies/la-et-mn-caa-diversity-study-exclusive-20170622-story.html.

Angry Asian Girls United. 2013. "The Other Asia and Cho Chang." *Angry Asian Girls United* (blog), April 16. http://angryasiangirlsunited.tumblr.com/post/48171033352/the-other-asia-and-cho-chang.

Anlen, Shirin. 2017. "Symphony of Conclusions." *Medium*, January 30. https://medium.com/volumetric-filmmaking/symphony-of-conclusions-56b907bb6fd5.

Appadurai, A. 1998. "Dead Certainty: Ethnic Violence in the Era of Globalization." *Public Culture* 10 (2): 225–47.

Arendt, Hannah. 1966. *The Origins of Totalitarianism*. New York: Harcourt, Brace & World.

Arvidsson, Adam. 2005. "Brands: A Critical Perspective." *Journal of Consumer Culture* 5 (2): 235–58.

Aslan Media, 2013. "Kodachrome Tehran." www.aslanmedia.com/arts-culture/mideast-art/21517-kodachrome-tehran.

Baila, Morgan. 2017. "This Is Where You've Seen Beyoncé's Divine Grammys Perfor-mance Before." Refinery29.com, February 13. https://www.refinery29.com/en-us/2017/02/140654/beyonce-grammys-inspiration-religious-symbols-meaning.

Bailey, Alyssa. 2016. "Katy Perry on What She'll Be in Donald Trump's America." Elle.com, December 1. https://www.elle.com/culture/celebrities/news/a41137/katy-perry-post-election-feelings-instagram/.

Bailey, M. 2010. "They Aren't Talking about Me." Crunk Feminist Collective. Accessed August 6, 2018. www.crunkfeministcollective.com/2010/03/14/they-arent-talking-about-me/.

Baiocchi, Gianpaolo, Elizabeth A. Bennett, Alissa Cordner, Peter Taylor Klein, and Stephanie Savell. 2014. *The Civic Imagination: Making a Difference in American Political Life*. Boulder: Paradigm.

Bakhtin, M. M. 1981. *The Dialogic Imagination: Four Essays*. Austin: University of Texas Press.

Balko, Radley. 2014. *Rise of the Warrior Cop: The Militarization of America's Police Forces* New York: Public Affairs, 2014.

Ballard, Heidi L., Emily Evans, Victoria E. Sturtevant, and Pamela Jakes. 2012. "The Evolution of Smokey Bear: Environmental Education about Wildfire for Youth." *Journal of Environmental Education* 43 (4): 227–40.

Banet-Weiser, Sarah. 2007. *Kids Rule! Nickelodeon and Consumer Citizenship*. Durham: Duke University Press.

———. 2012. *Authentic™: The Politics of Ambivalence in a Brand Culture*. New York: New York University Press.

———. 2015. "'Confidence You Can Carry!': Girls in Crisis and the Market for Girls' Empowerment Organizations." *Continuum: Journal of Media and Cultural Studies*, https://doi.org/10.1080/10304312.2015.1022938.

———. 2018. *Empowered: Popular Feminism and Popular Misogyny*. Durham: Duke University Press.

Baquero, Luis Enrique Rodríguez. 2006. *Historia de Colombia: Todo lo que hay que saber*. Ontario: Taurus.

Barthes, Roland. (1957) 1972. "The World of Wrestling." In *Mythologies*, translated by Annette Lavers, 15–25. New York: Hill and Wang.

Bates, Daniel. 2014. "Ferguson Protestors Scrawl Hunger Games Slogan on Landmark as Tense Town Waits for Grand Jury Decision on Indicting Officer Darren Wilson over Killing of Michael Brown." *Daily Mail*, November 24.

Bateson, Gregory, Don D. Jackson, Jay Haley, and John H. Weakland. 1963. "A Note on the Double Bind—1962." *Family Process* 2 (1): 154–61.

Battle, N. T. 2016. "From Slavery to Jane Crow to Say Her Name: An Intersectional Examination of Black Women and Punishment." *Meridians: Feminism, Race, Transnationalism* 15 (1): 109–36.

Bazin, André. 1976. *Qu'est-ce que le cinéma?* Paris: Cerf.

Benestad, Rasmus. 2017. "Why Extremes Are Expected to Change with a Global Warming." *Real Climate*, September 5. www.realclimate.org/index.php/archives/2017/09/why-extremes-are-expected-to-change-with-a-global-warming/#more-20607.

Bennett, W. Lance, and Taso Lagos. 2007. "Logo Logic: The Ups and Downs of Branded Political Communication." *Annals of the American Academy of Political and Social Science* 611:193–206.

Bennett, W., and A. Segerberg. 2012. "The Logic of Connective Action." *Information, Communication and Society* 15 (5): 1–30.

BestBuy. 2017. "Google Expeditions I Best Buy Education." Accessed September 1. https://www.bestbuy.com/site/bestbuy-education/googleexpeditions/pcmcat748302046351.c?id=pcmcat748302046351&utm_source=ExpWeb&utm_medium=web.

Bhatia, N. 2016. "Bollywood and South Asian Diaspora." *Topia 26*, April 10.

Bhatia, Pooja. 2011. "A Symbol of Hope for Haiti, a Landmark Again Stands Tall." *New York Times*, January 10. https://www.nytimes.com/2011/01/11/world/americas/11haiti.html.

Billard, Thomas J. 2016. "Fonts of Potential: Areas for Typographic Research in Political Communication." *International Journal of Communication* 10:4570–92.

———. 2019. "Citizen Typography and Political Brands in the 2016 US Presidential Election Campaign." *Marketing Theory*, 18 (3): 421–31. https://doi.org/10.1177/1470593118763982.

Billard, Thomas J, and Rachel E. Moran. 2018. "Toward 'Networked Branding': Rethinking Brand Logic in a Networked Communication Environment." Unpublished manuscript.

Blackwell, Maylei. 2011. *Chicana Power! Contested Histories of Feminism in the Chicano Movement*. 1st ed. Austin: University of Texas Press.

Bleecker, Julian. 2009. "Design Fiction: A Short Essay on Design, Science, Fact and Fiction." *Near Future Laboratory*, March 17. http://drbfw5wfjlxon.cloudfront.net/writing/DesignFiction_WebEdition.pdf.

Blevins, Brooks. 2009. *Arkansas/Arkansaw: How Bear Hunters, Hillbillies, and Good Ol'Boys Defined a State*. Fayetteville: University of Arkansas Press.

Bliss Cua Lim. 2017, 20 October. Keynote Address. Contagion Conference, University of Southern California, Los Angeles, California, SCA 112.

Bodenhorn, Barbara, and Olga Ulturgasheva. 2017. "Climate Strategies: Thinking through Arctic Examples." *Philosophical Transactions of the Royal Society A* 375 (2095): 20160363.

Bogle, D. 2001. *Toms, Coons, Mulattoes, Mammies, and Bucks: An Interpretive History of Blacks in American Films*. New York: Bloomsbury Academic.

Bond, Paul. 2017. "Leslie Moonves on Donald Trump: 'It May Not Be Good for America, but It's Damn Good for CBS.'" *Hollywood Reporter*, February 29.

Booker, M. Keith. 2013. "On Contemporary Speculative Fiction." In *Critical Insights: Contemporary Speculative Fiction*, edited by M. Keith Booker, xiv–xxvii. Ipswich: Salem Press.

Bosman, Julie. 2012. "Amazon Crowns 'Hunger Games' as Its Top Seller, Surpassing Harry Potter Series." *New York Times*, August 17.

Bowles, Hamish. 2017. "Katy Perry Is Leaving Her Cutesy Style behind and Going Androgynous, Architectural, and Political." Vogue.com, April 13.

Boym, Svetlana. 2001. *The Future of Nostalgia*. New York: Basic Books.

———. 2002. *The Future of Nostalgia*. New York: Basic Books.

Boyte, Harry C. 2011. "Constructive Politics as Public Work: Organizing the Literature." *Political Theory* 39 (5): 630–60.

Brecht, Bertolt. 2002. "Emphasis on Sport." In *Cultural Resistance Reader*, edited by Stephen Duncombe, 183–85. New York: Verso.

Breed, Ananda. 2008. "Performing the Nation: Theatre in Post-Genocide Rwanda." *TDR/The Drama Review* 52 (1): 32–50.

Brough, Melissa M., and Sangita Shresthova. 2012. "Fandom Meets Activism: Rethinking Civic and Political Participation." In *Transformative Works and Cultures*, no. 10. http://dx.doi.org/10.3983/twc.2012.030.

Brown, Adrienne Maree, and Walidah Imarisha, eds. 2015. *Octavia's Brood: Science Fiction Stories from Social Justice Movements*. Oakland: AK Press.

Brown, David G. 2015a. "Why Star Wars the Force Awakens Is a Social Justice Propaganda Film." Return of Kings, December 20.

———. 2015b. "Star Wars Lost 4.2 Million Because of Our Reporting That Identified It as SJW Propaganda." Return of Kings, December 20.

Brown, Jeffrey A. 1999 "Comic Book Masculinity and the New Black Superhero." *African American Review* 33:25–42.

Brown, N., and L. Young. 2015. "Ratchet Politics: Moving beyond Black Women's Bodies to Indict Institutions and Structures." *National Political Science Review* 17:45–56.

Brubaker, Rogers. 2001. "The Return of Assimilation? Changing Perspectives on Immigration and Its Sequels in France, Germany, and the United States." *Ethnic and Racial Studies* 24:531–48.

Burstein, Andrew 2015. *Democracy's Muse: How Thomas Jefferson Became an FDR Liberal, a Reagan Republican, and a Tea Party Fanatic, All the While Being Dead.* Charlottesville: University of Virginia Press.

Butler, Judith. 1990. *Gender Trouble: Feminism and the Subversion of Identity.* Oxfordshire: Routledge.

———. 1997. *Excitable Speech: A Politics of the Performative.* Oxfordshire: Psychology Press.

Button Poetry. 2013. "Rachel Rostad—'To JK Rowling, from Cho Chang' (CUPSI 2013 Finals)." YouTube video, 3:52. Posted by "Button Poetry." April 13, 2013. https://www.youtube.com/watch?v=iFPWwx96Kew.

Cabosky, Joseph. 2015. "'For Your Consideration': A Critical Analysis of LGBT-Themes Film Award Campaign Advertisements: 1990–2005." *Journalism History* 41 (2): 73–84.

Calhoun, C. 1998. "The Public Good as a Social and Cultural Project." In *Private Action and the Public Good*, edited by W. Powell and E. Clemens, 20–35. New Haven: Yale University Press.

Callison, Candis. 2014. *How Climate Change Comes to Matter: The Communal Life of Facts.* Durham, NC: Duke University Press.

———. 2017. "Climate Change Communication and Indigenous Publics." *Oxford Encyclopedia of Climate Change Communication*, September 27.

"Campaña Soy Capaz: Reporte final." 2014. Bogotá, Colombia.

Carey, Aaron. 2015. "Why You Should Not Go See Mad Max: Feminist Road." Return of Kings, May 11.

Cassell, Justine, and Henry Jenkins, eds. 1998. *From Barbie to Mortal Kombat: Gender and Computer Games.* Cambridge: MIT Press.

Castells, Manuel. 2010. *The Rise of the Network Society.* 2nd ed. Oxford: Wiley-Blackwell.

Chadwick, Andrew. 2013. *The Hybrid Media System: Politics and Power.* Oxford: Oxford University Press.

Chakravorty, P. 2009. "Moved to Dance: Remix, Rasa, and a New India." *Visual Anthropology* 22 (2–3): 211–28. https://doi.org/10.1080/08949460902748113.

Chaletain, M., and K. Asoka. 2015. "Women and Black Lives Matter." *Visual Anthropology* 63 (3): 54–61.

Chanel. 2017. "Banghwanghaneun yuibeul wihan WOMAD annaeseo" [WOMAD Guide for Wandering Visitors]. WOMAD, February 7. https://womad.me/4445.

Charles Taylor. 2007. *A Secular Age.* Cambridge: Belknap Press.

Charlton, James I. 1998. *Nothing about Us without Us: Disability Oppression and Empowerment*. Berkeley: University of California Press.

Chase, M. 2015. "#Digitalborderlands: Shaping Social Justice Discourse in Digital Spaces." Scholarworks @ CSU San Marcos. https://csusm-dspace.calstate.edu/bitstream/handle/10211.3/139182/ChaseMatthew_Spring2015.pdf?sequence=1.

Chatterjee, Partha. 1983. *The Nation and Its Fragments: Colonial and Postcolonial Histories*. Princeton: Princeton University Press.

Chavers, L. 2016. "Here's My Problem with #BlackGirlMagic." *Elle Magazine*, January 13.

Chávez, Ernesto. 1994. "Creating Aztlán: The Chicano Movement in Los Angeles, 1966–1978." PhD diss., University of California, Los Angeles.

Cheon, Gwanyul. 2015. "'Megalian' . . . Yeoseonghyeomoe dallyeondoen 'museoun eonnideul'" ["Megalian" . . . "Scary Sisters" Who Are Misogyny-Trained]. *SisaIN*, September 14.

———. 2016. "Jeonguiui pasukkundeul?" [The Guardians of Justice?]. *SisaIN*, August 22.

Cheon, Jung Hwan. 2016. "Gangnamyeok sarinsageonbuteo 'Megallia' nonjaengkkaji" [From Gangnam Station Murder Case to the "Megalia" Controversy]. *Critical Review of History*, August, 353–81.

Coates, Ta-Nehisi. 2015. "The Black Family in the Age of Mass Incarceration." *Atlantic*, October.

Cochran, Patricia, Orville H. Huntington, Caleb Pungowiyi, Stanley Tom, F. Stuart Chapin, Henry P. Huntington, Nancy G. Maynard, and Sarah F. Trainor. 2013. "Indigenous Frameworks for Observing and Responding to Climate Change in Alaska." *Climatic Change* 120 (3): 557–67.

Cohn, Nate. 2014. "Demise of the Southern Democrat Is Now Nearly Complete." *New York Times*, December 4. https://www.nytimes.com/2014/12/05/upshot/demise-of-the-southern-democrat-is-now-nearly-compete.html.

Colby, Sandra L., and Jennifer L. Ortman. 2014. "Projections of the Size and Composition of the U.S. Population: 2014–2060." *Current Population Reports*.

Collins, Patricia Hill. 1998. *Fighting Words: Black Women and the Search for Justice*. Minneapolis: University of Minnesota.

———. 2000. *Black Feminist Thought: Knowledge, Consciousness, and the Politics of Empowerment*. New York: Routledge.

———. 2008. *The Hunger Games*. New York: Scholastic Press.

———. 2009. *Catching Fire*. New York: Scholastic Press.

———. 2010. *Mockingjay*. New York: Scholastic Press.

Confino, Alon. 2014. *A World without Jews: The Nazi Imagination from Persecution to Genocide*. New Haven: Yale University Press.

Connor, Tracy, Hannah Rappleye, and Angulo, Erika. 2015. "What Does Haiti Have to Show for $13 Billion in Earthquake Aid?" *NBC News*, January 11.

Coontz, Stephanie. 1992. *The Way We Never Were: American Families and the Nostalgia Trap*. New York: Basic.

Cooper, A. J. 1988. *A Voice from the South by a Black Woman of the South*. New York: Oxford University Press.

Cooper, B. 2016. "Intersectionality." In *The Oxford Handbook of Feminist Theory*, edited by L. Disch and M. Hawkesworth, 385–406. New York: Oxford University Press.

Cornell, Drucilla, and Stephen D. Seely. 2017. "What Happened to the Public Imagination, and Why?" *global-e*, March 21.

Coscia, M. 2013. "Competition and Success in the Meme Pool: A Case Study on Quickmeme.Com." In Proceedings of the *International Conference on Weblogs and Social Media*, 2013. https://arxiv.org/abs/1304.1712.

Cox, C. 2014. "Female Game Journalists Quit over Harassment, #GamerGate Harms Women." Mary Sue, December 12.

Cox, Susan. 2015. "Star Wars the Force Awakens Provides the Kick-Ass Female Lead We've Been Waiting For." *Feminist Current*, December 27.

Crenshaw, K. 1989. "Demarginalizing the Intersection of Race and Sex: A Black Feminist Critique of Antidiscrimination Doctrine, Feminist Theory, and Antiracist Politics." *University of Chicago Legal Forum* (1): 139–67.

———. 2012. "From Private Violence to Mass Incarceration: Thinking Intersectionally about Women, Race, and Social Control." *UCLA Law Review* 59:1419–72.

Crenshaw, K., P. Ocen, and J. Nanda. N.d. *Black Girls Matter: Pushed Out, Overpoliced, and Underprotected*. Center for Intersectionality and Social Policy Studies. https://static1.squarespace.com/static/53f20d90e4b0b80451158d8c/t/54d2d37ce4b024b41443b0ba/1423102844010/BlackGirlsMatter_Report.pdf.

Crenshaw, K., A. J. Ritchie, R. Anspach, R. Gilmer, and L. Harris. 2015. *Say Her Name: Resisting Police Brutality against Black Women*. New York: African American Policy Forum, Center for Intersectionality and Social Policy Studies.

Crenshaw, Kimberle. 1991. "Mapping the Margins: Intersectionality, Identity Politics, and Violence against Women of Color." *Stanford Law Review* 43 (6): 1241–99.

Cullors, Patrisse Marie. 2017. "It Is Our Duty to Dismantle White Supremacy." Broadly, August 23. www.broadly.vice.com/en_us/article/ywwn9k/blm-co-founder-it-is-our-duty-to-dismantle-white-supremacy.

Cunningham, Joel. 2016. "Rewriting H.P. Lovecraft, Reclaiming the Mythos: A Writers' Roundtable." *B and N Sci-Fi and Fantasy Blog*, August 16.

Da Costa, Dia. 2010. "Subjects of Struggle: Theatre as Space of Political Economy." *Third World Quarterly* 31 (4): 617–35. https://doi.org/10.1080/01436591003701133.

Dahlgren, Peter. 2003. "Reconfiguring Civic Culture in the New Media Milieu." In *Media and Restyling of Politics: Consumerism, Celebrity and Cynicism*, edited by John Corner, 151–70. Thousand Oaks: Sage.

———. 2009. *Media and Political Engagement: Citizens, Communication, and Democracy*. Cambridge: Cambridge University Press.

Davis, Viola. 2017a. "Viola Davis Acceptance Speech | 23rd SAG Awards." YouTube video. Posted by "SAG Awards," January 29. https://www.youtube.com/watch?v=akMEM4gDtMw.

———. 2017b. "Viola Davis Wins Best Supporting Actress." YouTube video. Posted by "Oscars," April 3. https://www.youtube.com/watch?v=xbo9GVmv87Y.

———. 2017c. "Viola Davis Wins Best Supporting Actress at the 2017 Golden Globes." YouTube video. Posted by NBC, January 8. https://www.youtube.com/watch?v= maxrpiA2dnM.

de Camp, L. Sprague. 1975. *H. P. Lovecraft: A Biography*. New York: Doubleday.

De La Torre, Miguel A. 2017. *Embracing Hopelessness*. Minneapolis: Fortress Press.

DeJonge, Michael P. 2017. *Bonhoeffer's Reception of Luther*. Oxford: Oxford University Press.

Denning, Michael. 2011. *The Cultural Front: The Laboring of American Culture in the 20th Century*. New York: Verso.

Denskus, Tobias. 2010. "Peacebuilding Does Not Build Peace." In *Deconstructing Development Discourse: Buzzwords and Fuzzwords*, edited by Andrea Cornwall and Deborah Eade, 235–44. Rugby, Warwickshire: Oxfam Practical Action.

Dery, Mark. 1993. *Culture Jamming: Hacking, Slashing, and Sniping in the Empire of Signs*. Vol. 25. Westfield, NJ: Open Media.

———. 2002. *Black to the Future: Afro-Futurism 1.0*. www.detritus.net/contact/rumori/ 200211/0319.html.

Dewey, J. 1954. "Search for the Public." In *The Public and Its Problems*, 3–36. New York: Swallow Press.

Diaz, Hector. 2016. "Mitt Romney Donned Wrestling Tights, a Cape and a Luchador Mask for Charity." *SBNation*, June 12.

Dickey, Josh. 2015. "Don't Give into Your Anger: That #BoycottStarWarsVII Hashtag Was the Work of Trolls." Mashable, October 20. http://mashable.com/2015/10/20/ boycott-star-wars-hashtag-trolling/#Noq_CcGx.Gqi.

DiGiacomo, Frank. 2015. "*Hamilton*'s Lin-Manuel Miranda on Finding Original-ity, Racial Politics (and Why Trump Should See His Show)." *Hollywood Reporter*, August 12.

D'Ignazio, Catherine. 2017. "Civic Imagination and a Useless Map." In *DIY Utopia: Cultural Imagination and Remaking of the Possible*, edited by Amber Day, 21–46. London: Lexington Books.

DiSanza, James R., and Connie Bullis. 1999. "'Everybody Identifies with Smokey the Bear': Employee Responses to Newsletter Identification Inducements at the U.S. Forest Service." *Management Communication Quarterly* 12 (3): 347–99.

Douglas, Mary. 1975. "Jokes." In *Implicit Meanings: Essays in Anthropology*, edited by Mary Douglas, 90–115. London: Routledge.

Dourish, Paul, and Bell, Genevieve. 2011. *Divining a Digital Future: Mess and Mythol-ogy in Ubiquitous Computing*. Cambridge: MIT Press.

Dudrah, R., and J. Desai. 2006. *The Bollywood Reader*. London: Open University Press.

Duncombe, Stephen. 2004. "Ethical Spectacle." Beautiful Trouble. http://beautifultrouble .org/theory/ethical-spectacle/.

———. 2012a. "Imagining No-Place." *Transformative Works and Cultures* 10. https://doi .org/10.3983/twc.2012.0350.

———. 2012b. "Introduction: Open Utopia." Open Utopia. http://theopenutopia.org/full
-text/introduction-open-utopia/.

———. 2012c. "Utopia Is No Place." *Walker Primer*, August 27. https://walkerart.org/
magazine/stephen-duncombe-utopia-open-field.

———. 2017. "Opening Up Utopia." In *DIY Utopia: Cultural Imagination and the Remaking of the Possible*, edited by Amber Day, 3–20. Lanham: Lexington.

Dunne, Anthony, and Fiona, Raby. 2013. *Speculative Everything: Design, Fiction, and
Social Dreaming*. Cambridge: MIT Press.

Dyer, Richard. 1985. "Entertainment and Utopia." In *Movies and Methods II*, edited by
Bill Nichols, 175–89. Berkeley: University of California Press.

Earle, Richard. 2000. *The Art of Cause Marketing*. New York: McGraw-Hill.

Edge, John T. 2018. *The Potlikker Papers: A Food History of the Modern South*. New
York: Penguin.

Egan, Danielle. 2013. *Becoming Sexual: A Critical Appraisal of Girls and Sexualization*.
Oxford: Polity Press.

Elise, A. 2014. "What Is the GamerGate Scandal? Female Game Developer Flees Home
amid Online Threats." *International Business Times*, September 24.

Ellis, Rebecca, Claire Waterton, and Brian Wynne. 2010. "Taxonomy, Biodiversity and
Their Publics in Twenty-First-Century DNA Barcoding." *Public Understanding of
Science* 19 (4): 497–512.

Ellison, Ralph. 1972. *Shadow and Act*. New York: Vintage.

El Pais.com. 2016. "'El Proceso de Paz No Tiene Vuelta Atrás': Raúl Castro." June 23, 2016.

Elsayed, Y. 2016. "Laughing through Change: Subversive Humor in Online Videos of
Arab Youth." *International Journal of Communication* 10 (20): 5102–22.

———. 2018. "Modes of Cultural Resistance in Post-Arab Spring Egypt." Unpublished
diss. University of Southern California.

Emirbayer, M., and Mische, A. 1998. "What Is Agency?" *American Journal of Sociology*
1034:962–1023.

Emrys, Ruthanna. 2017. *Winter Tides*. New York: Tor.com.

Enloe, Chris. 2017. "The Difference between Lady Gaga's Super Bowl Halftime Show
and Beyoncé's Couldn't Be More Apparent." TheBlaze.com, February 6. www
.theblaze.com/news/2017/02/06/the-differences-between-lady-gagas-super-bowl
-halftime-show-and-beyonces-couldnt-be-more-apparent.

Erel, Umut, Tracey Reynolds, and Erene Kaptani. 2017. "Participatory Theatre for
Transformative Social Research." *Qualitative Research* 17 (3): 302–12. https://doi.org/
10.1177/1468794117696029.

Eshun, Kodwo. 1998. *More Brilliant than the Sun: Adventures in Sonic Fiction*. London:
Quartet Books.

———. 2003. "Further Considerations of Afro-Futurism." *CR: The New Centennial
Review* 3 (2): 287–302.

Evans, Christina. 2015. "The Nuts and Bolts of Digital Civic Imagination." DML
Central, March 26. https://dmlcentral.net/the-nuts-and-bolts-of-digital-civic
-imagination/.

Fabian, Jordan. 2016. "Obama: '*Hamilton* Is the Only Thing Dick Cheney and I Agree On.'" *The Hill*, March 14.

faduci. 2017. "7,000 Subscribers Extra: Basic Cardboard Questions and Answers • r/GoogleCardboard." Reddit. Accessed September 1. https://www.reddit.com/r/GoogleCardboard/comments/39t5tl/7000_subscribers_extra_basic_cardboard_questions/.

Faiola, Anthony. 2017. "Colombia's FARC Rebels Launch a Political Party, Trading Bullets for Blazers." *Washington Post*, September 2.

Fawaz, Ramzi. 2016. *The New Mutants: Superheroes and the Radical Imagination of American Comics*. New York: New York University Press.

Femiwiki. 2017. "Megalia." https://femiwiki.com/w/%EB%A9%94%EA%B0%88%EB%A6%AC%EC%95%84.

Fienberg, Daniel. 2017. "Critic's Notebook: Lady Gaga's Super Bowl LI Halftime Performance Is Confrontationally Apolitical." HollywoodReporter.com, February 5.

Fingeroth, Danny. 2017. *Disguised as Clark Kent*. New York: Continuum.

Fischer, Michael M. J. 2003. *Emergent Forms of Life and the Anthropological Voice*. Durham, NC: Duke University Press.

Fiske, John. 1996. *Media Matters: Race and Gender in US Politics*. Minneapolis: University of Minnesota Press.

Flood, Alison. 2014. "World Fantasy Awards Pressed to Drop Lovecraft in Racism Row." *Guardian*, September 17.

Fora TV. 2015. "Brandon Stanton: The Scourge of Internet Anonymity." YouTube video, 4:31. Posted by "Fora.tv," May 26. https://www.youtube.com/watch?v=g4nAWqKYBdk.

Ford, A. 2016. "There Is Nothing Wrong with Black Girl Magic." *Elle*, January 13. www.elle.com/life-love/a33251/there-is-nothing-wrong-with-black-girl-magic/.

Ford, Sam. 2016. "'I Was Stabbed 21 Times by Crazy Fans': Pro Wrestling and Popular Concerns with Immersive Story Worlds." In *Seeing Fans: Representations of Fandom in Media and Popular Culture*, edited by Paul Booth and Lucy Bennett, 33–43. New York: Bloomsbury.

Ford, Sam. Forthcoming. "The Marks Have Gone Off Script: Rogue Actors in the WWE's Stands." In *#WWE: Professional Wrestling in the Digital Age*, edited by Dru Jeffries. Bloomington: Indiana University Press.

Fortun, Kim. 2001. *Advocacy after Bhopal*. Chicago: University of Chicago Press.

Foucault, Michel. 1967. "Of Other Spaces: Utopias and Heterotopias." *Diacritics* 16 (1): 22–27.

Frase, Peter. 2016. *Four Futures—Life after Capitalism*. New York: Verso.

Frazier, Reid. 2017. "Pittsburgh Company Gets 'Cease-and-Desist' Letter over Anti-Trump T-Shirt." *Allegheny Front*, March 10.

Freeman, Joanne B. 2015. "How Hamilton Uses History." *Slate*, November. www.slate.com/articles/arts/culturebox/2015/11/how_lin_manuel_miranda_used_real_history_in_writing_hamilton.html.

Freire, Paulo. 2000. *Pedagogy of the Oppressed*. 30th-anniversary ed. New York: Continuum.

Gaiman, Neil. 2013. "Why Our Future Depends on Libraries, Reading and Daydreaming: The Reading Agency Lecture 2013." *The View from the Cheap Seats: Selected Nonfiction*, 5–25. New York: Harper Collins.

Galuppo, Mia. 2016. "Disney's Bob Iger on Rogue One: There Are No Political Statements in It." *Hollywood Reporter*, December 12.

Ganz, Marshall. 2010. *Why David Sometimes Wins: Leadership, Organization, and Strategy in the California Farm Worker Movement*. New York: Oxford University Press.

Garber, Elizabeth. 1995. "Teaching Art in the Context of Culture: A Study in the Borderlands." *Studies in Art Education* 36 (4): 218. https://doi.org/10.2307/1320936.

Garrison, D. R. 1991. "Critical Thinking and Adult Education: A Conceptual Model for Developing Critical Thinking in Adult Learners." *International Journal of Lifelong Education* 10 (4): 287–303.

Gaspar de Alba, Alicia. 1998. *Chicano Art Inside/Outside the Master's House: Cultural Politics and the CARA Exhibition*. 1st ed. Austin: University of Texas Press.

———, Alicia. 2004. "There's No Place like Aztlan: Embodied Aesthetics in Chicana Art." *CR: The New Centennial Review* 4 (2): 103–40. https://doi.org/10.1353/ncr.2005.0007.

Gates, Kelly A. 2011. *Our Biometric Future: Facial Recognition Technology and the Culture of Surveillance*. New York: New York University Press.

Gehlawat, A. 2014. "Shuddh Desi Romance: Impurely Bollywood." *Cineaction: Performing Arts Periodicals Database*.

Gellner, Ernest. 1983. *Nations and Nationalism*. Ithaca: Cornell University Press.

Gera Roy, A. 2016. "Meanings of Bhangra and Bollywood Dancing in India and the Diaspora." *Topia* 26.

Gerbaudo, P., and E. Trere. 2015. "In Search of the 'We' of Social Media Activism: Introduction to the Special Issue on Social Media and Protest Identities." *Information, Communication and Society* 18 (8): 865–71. www.tandfonline.com/doi/full/10.1080/1369118X.2015.1043319.

Giddings, Paula. 1984. *Where and When I Enter: The Impact of Black Women on Race and Sex in America*. New York: Harper Collins.

Ginwright, Shawn. 2016. *Hope and Healing in Urban Education: How Urban Activists and Teachers Are Reclaiming Matters of the Heart*. New York: Routledge.

Girl Scouts Organization website. Accessed January 2018. www.girlscouts.org.

Glaude, Eddie S., Jr. 2016. *Democracy in Black: How Race Still Enslaves the American Soul*. New York: Crown.

Glazer, Nathan, and Daniel P. Moynihan. 1963. *Beyond the Melting Pot: The Negroes, Puerto Ricans, Jews, Italians, and Irish of New York City*. Cambridge: MIT Press.

Gómez, Alan Eladio. 2016. *The Revolutionary Imaginations of Greater Mexico: Chicana/o Radicalism, Solidarity Politics, and Latin American Social Movements*. 1st ed. Austin: University of Texas Press.

Gómez-Quiñones, Juan, and Vásquez, Irene. 2014. *Making Aztlán: Ideology and Culture of the Chicana and Chicano Movement, 1966–1977*. Albuquerque: University of New Mexico Press.

Gómez-Suárez, Andrei. 2016. *El Triunfo Del No: La Paradoja Emocional Detrás Del Plebiscito*. Bogotá, Colombia: ICONO.

Gonzalez, Gilbert G. 2013. *Chicano Education in the Era of Segregation*. Denton, TX: UNT Press.

González, Kenneth P. 2002. "Campus Culture and the Experiences of Chicano Students in a Predominantly White University." *Urban Education* 37 (2): 193–218. https://doi .org/10.1177/0042085902372003.

Google Cardboard. 2017. "Google Cardboard—Google VR." Accessed September 1. https://vr.google.com/cardboard/.

Google for Education. 2017. "Google Expeditions." Accessed September 1. https://edu .google.com/expeditions/#about.

Google Play Music. N.d. "Lyrics for Lady Gaga's 'The Cure.'" https://play.google.com/ music/preview/Twwtqepyegk5n2cbtahhsmayzym?lyrics=1&utm_source=google& utm_medium=search&utm_campaign=lyrics&pcampaignid=kp-lyrics&u=0#.

Google VR. 2015. "Google Cardboard for Manufacturers Specifications and Tolerance Guides." September. https://static.googleusercontent.com/media/vr.google.com/en/ /cardboard/downloads/manufacturing-guidelines.pdf.

Gopalan, L. 2002. *Cinema of Interruptions: Action Genres in Contemporary Indian Cinema*. London: BFI.

Gordon, Eric, and Stephen Walter. 2016. "Meaningful Inefficiencies: Resisting the Logic of Technological Efficiency in the Design of Civic Systems." In *Civic Media: Technology, Design, Practice*, edited by Eric Gordon and Paul Mihailidis, 243–66. Cambridge: MIT Press.

Gore, Will. 2017. "Don't Laugh at Donald Trump Sharing that CNN Wrestling Video: At Its Core, It Is Violent, Frightening and Wrong." *Independent*, July 3.

Grau, Oliver. 1999. "Into the Belly of the Image: Historical Aspects of Virtual Reality." *Leonardo* 32 (5): 365–71.

Gray, Jonathan, Cornel Sandvoss, and Lee C. Harrington. 2017. *Fandom: Identities and Communities in a Mediated World*, 2nd ed. New York: New York University Press.

Gray, Kishonna L., and David J. Leonard, eds. 2018. *Woke Gaming: Digital Challenges to Oppression and Social Justice*. Seattle: University of Washington Press.

Greenberg, Zack O'Malley. 2015. "The World's Highest-Paid Women in Music 2015." Forbes.com, November 4. https://www.forbes.com/sites/zackomalleygreenburg/ 2015/11/04/the-worlds-highest-paid-women-in-music-2015/#60175ca53db3.

———. 2016. "The World's Highest-Paid Women in Music 2016." Forbes.com, November 2. https://www.forbes.com/pictures/eeel45fhgfm/highest-paid-women-in-mu/ #68f510f4267f.

Greene, Maxine. 1995. *Releasing the Imagination*. San Francisco: Jossey Bass.

Grossman, R. 2012. "Occupy This: Humor versus Reality." *Social Research* 79 (1): 113–16.

Grynbaum, Michael M. 2017. "Trump Tweets a Video of Him Wrestling 'CNN' to the Ground." *New York Times*, July 2.

Ha, Soojung. 2017. "Megallia nonjaenge gwanhan dansangdeul" [Thoughts on the Megalia controversy]. *Left Daegu* 12 (January): 70–82.

Haimerl, A. 2015. "The Fastest-Growing Group of Entrepreneurs in America." *Fortune*, June 29.

Haiven, Max, and Alex Khasnabish. 2014. *The Radical Imagination: Social Movement Research in the Age of Austerity*. London: Zed Books.

Hall, Gina. 2014. "'Hunger Games: Mockingjay—Part 1' Set for World Premiere in London." The Wrap, October 14. www.thewrap.com/hunger-games-mockingjay-part-1 -set-for-world-premiere-in-london/.

Hall, Stuart. 1981. "Notes on Deconstructing 'The Popular.'" In *People's History and Socialist Theory*, 227–40. London: Routledge and Kegan Paul. Reprinted in John Storey, ed., *Cultural Theory: A Reader*, 508–18. Harlow: Pearson Longman.

——. 1992. "What Is This 'Black' in Black Popular Culture?" In *Black Popular Culture*, edited by Gina Dent, 465–75. Seattle: Bay Press. Reprinted in John Storey, ed. *Cultural Theory: A Reader*, 374–82. Harlow: Pearson Longman.

Hammond, Pete. 2014. "'12 Years a Slave' Telling Voters 'It's Time'—but How Will It Resonate?" *Deadline Hollywood*, February 19. http://deadline.com/2014/02/oscars -12-years-a-slave-telling-voters-its-time-but-how-will-it-resonate-685914/.

Han, Woori. 2017. "SlutWalk Korea: Translation, Cultural Production, and the Politics of Possibility." *Communication, Culture and Critique* 10 (2): 221–40. https://doi.org/ 10.1111/cccr.12161.

Haraway, Donna. 2015. "Anthropocene, Capitalocene, Plantationocene, Chthulucene: Making Kin." *Environmental Humanities* 6:159–65.

Harrari, Yuval Noah. 2015. *Homo Deus: A Brief History of Tomorrow*. London: Harvill Secker.

Harris, Aisha. 2014. "The Publicity Team behind *12 Years a Slave* Think 'It's Time' You See Their Movie." *Slate*, January 31. http://deadline.com/2014/02/oscars-12-years-a -slave-telling-voters-its-time-but-how-will-it-resonate-685914/.

Harris, Mark. 2010. "The Red Carpet Campaign: Inside the Singular Hysteria of the Academy Awards Race." *New York Magazine*, February 7.

Hart, Daniel, Cameron Richardson, and Britt Wilkenfeld. 2011. "Civic Identity." In *Handbook of Identity Theory and Research*, edited by Seth J. Schwartz, Koen Luyckx, and Vivian L. Vignoles, 2:771–87. Berlin: Springer-Verlag New York.

Harvey, David. 1993. "From Space to Place and Back Again: Reflections on the Condition of Postmodernity." In *Mapping the Futures: Local Cultures, Global Change*, edited by John Bird, Barry Curtis, Tim Putnam, George Robertson, and Lisa Tickner, 3–29. New York: Routledge.

Havel, Václav. 1991. "Stories and Totalitarianism." In *Open Letters: Selected Writings (1965–1990)*, translated by Paul Wilson. New York: Alfred A. Knopf.

Healy, Patrick. 2016. "*Hamilton* Cast's Appeal to Peace Ignites Showdown with Trump." *New York Times*, November 19.

Heikkilä, Niko. 2017. "Online Antagonism of the Alt-Right in the 2016 Election." *European Journal of American Studies* 12 (2). https://journals.openedition.org/ejas/12140.

Heim, Joe. 2017. "Recounting a Day of Rage, Hate, Violence, and Death." *Washington Post*, August 14.

Helmers, Marguerite. 2011. "Hybridity, Ethos, and Visual Representations of Smokey Bear." *JAC* 31 (1/2): 45–69.

Henson, Taraji P. 2017. "Hidden Figures Acceptance Speech | 23rd SAG Awards." You-Tube video. Posted by "SAG Awards," January 29. https://www.youtube.com/watch?v=87-FkkZYDuM.

Herrera, Linda. 2012. "Youth and Citizenship in the Digital Age: A View from Egypt." *Harvard Educational Review* 82 (3): 333–52.

Hidalgo, Jacqueline M. 2016. *Revelation in Aztlán: Scriptures, Utopias, and the Chicano Movement.* New York: Palgrave Macmillan.

Hoffman, Charles Paul. 2017. "No, Diversity Didn't Kill Marvel's Sales." CBR.com, April 3. www.cbr.com/no-diversity-didnt-kill-marvels-comic-sales/.

Holmes, Kevin. 2017. "Experience a Ghostly 'Symphony of Longing' in This Interactive Vr Doc." Vice.com, March 21.

Holt, Douglas B. 2004. *How Brands Become Icons: The Principles of Cultural Branding.* Boston: Harvard Business Press.

hooks, bell. 1990. "Postmodern Blackness." *Postmodern Culture* 1 (1).

———. 1991. "Theory as Liberatory Practice." *Yale Journal of Law and Feminism* 4 (1): 1–12.

———. 1992. *Black Looks: Race and Representation.* Boston: South End Press.

———. 2003. *Teaching Community: A Pedagogy of Hope.* New York: Routledge.

———. 2014a. "Representations of Whiteness in the Black Imagination." In *Black Looks: Race and Representation*, chap. 11. New York: Routledge.

———. 2014b. *Teaching to Transgress.* New York: Routledge.

Hristova, S. 2013. "Occupy Wall Street Meets Occupy Iraq on Remembering and Forgetting in a Digital Age." *Radical History Review*, no. 117: 83–97.

Hume, T. 2016. "Army Reserve Officer Deshuana Barner Crowned Miss USA 2016." *CNN*, June 6.

Hunt, Kasie. 2010. "WWE: Obama, Clinton, McCain Appeared." Politico, October 15. www.politico.com/story/2010/10/wwe-obama-clinton-mccain-appeared-043657.

IDFA DocLab. 2016. "Tzina: Symphony of Longing." IDFA DocLab. https://www.doclab.org/2016/tzina-symphony-of-longing/.

Im, Jeeyoung. 2015. "'Megalliaui ttaldeul' yeoseong hyeomoreul malhada" ["Daughters of Megalia" speaks of misogyny]. SisaIN, July 28. www.sisain.co.kr/?mod=news&act=articleView&idxno=23931.

"Informe ¡Basta Ya! Colombia: Memorias de guerra y dignidad: Estadísticas del conflicto armado en Colombia." n.d. Centro Nacional de Memoria Histórica.

Institute for the Future. 2013. "Framework: Public Imagination." *ReConstitutional Convention.*

Internet archive. "Megalian.com." 2017. Internet Archive Wayback Machine, September 13. https://web.archive.org/web/*/megalian.com.

Ip, C. 2014. "How Do We Know What We Know about #Gamergate?" *Columbia Journalism Review*, December 12.

Iton, Richard. 2008. *In Search of the Black Fantastic: Politics and Popular Culture in the Post-Civil Rights Era*. Oxford: Oxford University Press.

Itzkoff, Dave. 2014. "Those Were the Days, Not Simple or All Sweet." *New York Times*, October 5. https://www.nytimes.com/2014/10/06/arts/norman-lears-memoir-even-this-i-get-to-experience.html.

James, William. 1910. "The Moral Equivalent of War." Edited print version of 1906 speech. *McClure's Magazine*, August, 463–68.

———. 2008. "Proposing the Moral Equivalent of War." Transcript of speech delivered at Stanford University 1906. *Lapham's Quarterly* 1 (1). https://www.laphamsquarterly.org/states-war/proposing-moral-equivalent-war.

Jang, Min-Gi. 2016. "Dijiteol neitibeu yeo/seongjuche (Digital Native Fe/Male Subject) ui undong jeollyak" [Social movement strategy of digital native fe/male subject: Focused on "Megalia"]. *Media, Gender and Culture* 31 (3): 219–55.

Jasanoff, Sheila. 2010. "A New Climate for Society." *Theory, Culture and Society* 27 (2–3): 233–53.

Jenkins, Barry. 2017. "'Moonlight' Wins Best Picture." YouTube video. Posted by "Oscars," April 3. https://www.youtube.com/watch?v=GCQn_FkFElI.

Jenkins, Barry, and Tarell Alvin McCraney. 2013. "'Moonlight' Wins Best Adapted Screenplay." YouTube video. Posted by "Oscars," April 3. https://www.youtube.com/watch?v=kTEi8Cfo4FY.

———. 2017. "Moonlight Wins Best Screenplay at the 2017 Film Independent Spirit Awards." YouTube video, 3:19. Posted by "Film Independent," February 25. https://www.youtube.com/watch?v=qc6RflX3YTY.

Jenkins, Henry. 1997. "'Never Trust a Snake': WWF Wrestling as Masculine Melodrama." In *Out of Bounds: Sports, Media, and the Politics of Identity*, edited by Aaron Baker and Todd Boyd, 48–78. Bloomington: Indiana University Press.

———. 2004. "Chasing Bees without the Hive Mind." *MIT Technology Review*, December 3. www.technologyreview.com/s/403444/chasing-bees-without-the-hive-mind.

———. 2005. "Afterword, Part I: Wrestling with Theory, Grappling with Politics." In *Steel Chair to the Head: The Pleasure and Pain of Professional Wrestling*, edited by Nicholas Sammond, 295–316. Durham, NC: Duke University Press.

———. 2011. "From New Media Literacies to New Media Expertise: 'Confronting the Challenges of a Participatory Culture' Revisited." *A Manifesto for Media Education* (blog), January 2011. www.manifestoformediaeducation.co.uk/2011/01/henryjenkins.

———. 2017. "Imaging the Future at Sankofa City." *Confessions of an ACA Fan* (blog), June 23. http://henryjenkins.org/blog/2017/6/15/imagining-the-future-at-sankofa-city.

———. Forthcoming. "'What Else Can We Do with Them?': Superheroes and the Civic Imagination."

Jenkins, Henry, Thomas J Billard, Samantha Close, Yomna Elsayed, Michelle C. Forelle, Rogelio Lopez, and Emilia Yang. 2018. "Participatory Politics." In *Keywords in Remix Studies*, edited by Eduardo Navas, Owen Gallagher, and xtine burrough. New York: Routledge.

Jenkins, Henry, Sam Ford, and Joshua Green, eds. 2013. *Spreadable Media: Creating Value and Meaning in a Networked Culture*. New York: NYU Press.

Jenkins, Henry, and M. Ito. 2015. *Participatory Culture in a Networked Era: A Conversation on Youth, Learning, Commerce, and Politics*. Hoboken: John Wiley and Sons.

Jenkins, Henry, R. Purushotma, M. Weigel, K. Clinton, and A. Robison. 2009. *Confronting the Challenges of Participatory Culture: Media Education for the 21st Century*. Cambridge, MA: MIT Press.

Jenkins, Henry, Sangita Shresthova, Liana Gamber-Thompson, and Neta Kligler-Vilenchik. 2016. "Superpowers to the People! How Young Activists Are Tapping the Civic Imagination." In *Civic Media: Technology, Design, Practice*, edited by Eric Gordon and Paul Mihailidis, 295–320. Cambridge: MIT Press.

Jenkins, Henry, Sangita Shresthova, Liana Gamber-Thompson, Neta Kligler-Vilenchik, and Arely M. Zimmerman. 2016. *By Any Media Necessary: The New Youth Activism*. New York: New York University Press.

Johnson, Brian David. 2011. "Science Fiction Prototyping Designing the Future with Science Fiction." *Synthesis Lectures on Computer Science* 3 (1): 1–190.

Johnson, Kij. 2016. *The Dream-Quest of Vellitt Boe*. New York: Tor.com.

Jones, Jimbo. 2017. "How Toxic Femininity Turned Men into Tranny Chasers." Return of Kings, August 1. www.returnofkings.com/126811/how-toxic-femininity-turned -men-into-tranny-chasers.

Jordan, Miriam. 2017. "A Refugee Family Arrives in Arkansas, before Door Shuts." *New York Times*, June 13. https://www.nytimes.com/2017/07/13/us/trump-refugee-ban .html.

Joshi, S. T. 1990. *H.P. Lovecraft: The Decline of the West*. Rockville: Wildside Press.

———. 1996. *H.P. Lovecraft: A Life*. West Warwick: Necronomicon Press.

Jung, In-Gyung. 2015. "Tajahwareul neomeo, seoro dareun du jucheui sotongeul jeonmanghanda: yeoseong Hyeomoreul Hyeomohanda" [Beyond otherization to prospecting the communication between two different subjects: Hating hatred of females]. *Journal of Asian Women* 54 (2): 219–27.

Kafai, Yasmin B., Carrie Heeter, Jill Dinner, and Jennifer Y. Sun, eds. 2008. *Beyond Barbie and Mortal Kombat: New Perspectives on Gender and Gaming*. Cambridge: MIT Press.

Kafai, Yasmin B., Gabriela T. Richard, and Brendesha M. Tynes, eds. 2017. *Diversifying Barbie and Mortal Kombat: Intersectional Perspectives and Inclusive Designs in Gaming*. Cambridge: MIT Press.

Kamisher, Eliahu. 2017. "Dizengoff Square Demolition: Residents Applaud, Architects Call It a Mistake." Jpost.com, January 9. www.jpost.com/Israel-News/Dizengoff -Square-demolition-Residents-applaud-architect-calls-it-a-mistake-477907.

Kang, Jung-suk. 2013. "Ilganbeseuteujeojangso, Ilbeui busang" [Daily best archive, the rise of Ilbe]. *Cultural Science* 75 (September): 273–302.

Karvelas, Patricia, 2015. "Star Wars Is a Game-Changer, Awakening the Feminist Force in Little Girls Everywhere." *Guardian*, December 30.

Katz, Jonathan. 2014. *The Big Truck That Went By: How the World Came to Save Haiti and Left behind a Disaster*. New York: St. Martin's Griffin.

Kelley, Robin D. G. 2002. *Freedom Dreams: The Black Radical Imagination*. Boston: Beacon Press.

———. 2016. "What Does Black Lives Matter Want?" *Boston Review*, August 17.

Kennedy, Brian. 2016. "Clinton, Trump Supporters Worlds Apart on Views of Climate Change and Its Scientists." Pew Research Center, October 10. www.pewresearch .org/fact-tank/2016/10/10/clinton-trump-supporters-worlds-apart-on-views-of -climate-change-and-its-scientists/.

Khan, Jessica. 2016. "William Daniels and Lin-Manuel Miranda Riff on *1776* and *Hamilton*." *Broadway World*, March 16. www.broadwayworld.com/article/William -Daniels-and-Lin-Manuel-Miranda-Riff-on-1776-and-HAMILTON-20160316.

Kim, Jinsook. 2017. "#iamafeminist as the 'Mother Tag': Feminist Identification and Activism against Misogyny on Twitter in South Korea." *Feminist Media Studies* 17 (5): 1–17. https://doi.org/10.1080/14680777.2017.1283343.

Kishi, Katayoun. 2016. "Anti-Muslim Assaults Reach 9/11 Era Levels, Data Shows." *Fact Tank: News in the Numbers*. Pew Research, November 21.

Klein, Naomi. 2017. "Daring to Dream in the Age of Trump." *Nation*, July 3–10. https:// www.thenation.com/article/daring-to-dream-in-the-age-of-trump/.

Kligler-Vilenchik, Neta. 2016. "'Decreasing World Suck': Harnessing Popular Culture for Fan Activism." In *By Any Media Necessary: The New Youth Activism*, by Henry Jenkins, Sangita Shresthova, Liana Gamber Thompson, Neta Kligler Vilenchik, and Arely Zimmerman, 102–48. New York: New York University Press.

Kline, D. 2017. "The Pragmatics of Resistance: Framing Anti-Blackness and the Limits of Political Ontology." *Critical Philosophy of Race* 5 (1): 51–69.

Kniesler, Sarah Margaret. 2013. "'We Both Know They Have to Have a Victor': The Battle between Nature and Culture in the *Hunger Games* Trilogy." In *Critical Insights: Contemporary Speculative Fiction*, edited by M. Keith Booker, 17–30. Ipswich: Salem Press.

Knowlton, Linda Goldstein, dir. 2015. *The Radical Brownies: A Documentary*. http:// radicalbrowniesmovie.com.

Knoxlabs. 2017. "Knox V2." Accessed September 1. https://www.knoxlabs.com/ products/knox-v2.

Koblin, Aaron. 2014. *Clouds Trailer*. https://www.cloudsdocumentary.com/#trailer.

Kolbe, Athena R., et al. 2010. "Mortality, Crime and Access to Basic Needs before and after the Haiti Earthquake: A Random Survey of Port-au-Prince Households." *Journal of Medicine, Conflict and Survival* 26 (4): 281–97. https://doi.org/10.1080/ 13623699.2010.535279.

Koo, Ken. 2013. "Korean Dairy Giant Namyang Apologizes as Scandal Widens."
KoreaBang, May 15. https://www.koreabang.com/2013/stories/korean-dairy-giant
-namyang-apologises-as-scandal-widens.html.

Kraidy, Marwan M. 2016. *The Naked Blogger of Cairo: Creative Insurgency in the Arab
World*. Cambridge: Harvard University Press.

Kristeva, J. 1982. *Powers of Horror: An Essay on Abjection*. Translated by Leon S. Roud-
iez. New York: Columbia University Press.

———. 2010. *Hatred and Forgiveness*. Translated by Jeanine Herman. New York: Columbia University Press.

Kymlicka, Will. 1995. *Multicultural Citizenship: A Liberal Theory of Minority Rights*.
Oxford: Oxford University Press.

Lachenal, Jessica. 2015. "#BoycottStarWarsVII: People Boycott *The Force Awakens*
Because It Promotes 'White Genocide.'" Mary Sue, October 19. https://www
.themarysue.com/boycott-star-wars-vii-because-why-again/.

Lagomarsino, J. 2017. "Brianna Wu Says the Gamergate Playbook Poisoned the Election." *The Outline*, February 1. https://theoutline.com/post/983/brianna-wu-says
-the-gamergate-playbook-poisoned-the-election?zd=1&zi=d6waxznw.

Lang, Nico. 2017. "The Super Bowl's Big Queer Milestone: Lady Gaga Was the First
Singer to Reference LGBT People during a Halftime Show." *Salon.com*, February 6.

Langton, Rae. 1993. "Speech Acts and Unspeakable Acts." *Philosophy and Public Affairs*
22 (4): 293–330. https://doi.org/10.2307/2265469.

LaValle, Victor. 2016. *The Ballad of Black Tom*. New York: Tor.com.

Lawrence, Francis, dir. 2013. *The Hunger Games: Catching Fire*. Santa Monica:
Lionsgate.

———. 2014. *The Hunger Games: Mockingjay—Part 1*. Santa Monica: Lionsgate.

———. 2015. *The Hunger Games: Mockingjay—Part 2*. Santa Monica: Lionsgate.

Lederach, John Paul. 2005. *The Moral Imagination: The Art and Soul of Building Peace*.
Oxford: Oxford University Press.

Lee, Clifford, and Elisabeth Soep. 2016. "None but Ourselves Can Free Our Minds:
Critical Computational Literacy as a Pedagogy of Resistance." *Equity and Excellence
in Education* 49 (4): 480–92.

Lee, Mike. 2017a. "How the *Hamilton* Effect Distorts the Founders." Politico, June 30.
www.politico.com/magazine/story/2017/05/30/senator-mike-lee-forgotten
-founders-hamilton-effect-215194.

———. 2017b. *Written Out of History: The Forgotten Founders Who Fought Big Government*. New York: Sentinel.

Lee, Yeji. 2016. "Megalia: South Korea's Radical Feminist Community." 10 Magazine
Korea, August 2. https://www.10mag.com/megalia-south-koreas-radical-feminism
-community/.

Lees, Matt. 2016. "What Gamergate Should Have Taught Us about the 'Alt-Right.'"
*Guardian*, December 1. https://www.theguardian.com/technology/2016/dec/01/
gamergate-alt-right-hate-trump.

Lefebvre, Henri. 1991. *The Production of Space*. Cambridge, MA: Blackwell.

Lempert, William. 2015. "Navajos on Mars: Native Sci-Fi Film Futures." Medium, September 21. https://medium.com/space-anthropology/navajos-on-mars -4c336175d945.

Letofsky, Irv. 1990. "Roseanne Is Sorry—but Not That Sorry." *Los Angeles Times*, July 28. http://articles.latimes.com/1990-07-28/local/me-537_1_roseanne-barr.

Lewis, Ferdinand. 2001. "Heated Debate about 'Cool' Cut." *Los Angeles Times*, September 7. http://articles.latimes.com/2001/sep/07/entertainment/ca-42982.

Lindsay, Kitty. 2015. "Radical Monarchs: A Social Justice Twist on the Girl Scouts." *Ms. Magazine*, May 29.

Lipsitz, George. 2006. *The Possessive Investment in Whiteness: How White People Profit from Identity Politics*. Philadelphia: Temple University Press.

———. 2007. *Footsteps in the Dark: The Hidden Histories of Popular Music*. Minneapolis: University of Minnesota Press.

———. 2017. "What Is This Black in the Black Radical Tradition?" In *Futures of Black Radicalism*, edited by Gaye Theresa Johnson and Alex Lubin. London: Verso.

Littler, Jo. 2017. *Against Meritocracy: Culture, Power and the Myth of Meritocracy*. London: Routledge.

Lombana Bermudez, Andres. 2016. "Mobilizing the Civic Imagination: New Media in the Context of Colombia's Peace Agreement and Referendum." *vVvAlog* (blog), September 19, 2016. http://andreslombana.net/blog/2016/09/19/mobilizing-the-civic -imagination-in-colombia/.

Lorre, Chuck. 2012. "Interview for the Archive of American Television by Nancy Harrington." Television Academy Foundation. February 25. http://emmytvlegends.org/ interviews/people/chuck-lorre.

Lovecraft, H. P. 2005. *Tales*. New York: Library of America.

———. 2010. *A Means to Freedom: The Letters of H.P. Lovecraft and Robert E. Howard*. Edited by S. T. Joshi, David E. Schultz, and Rusty Burke. New York: Hippocampus Press.

———. 2011. *Letters to James F. Morton*. Edited by David E. Schultz and S. T. Joshi. New York: Hippocampus Press.

———. 2016. *Letters to C. L. Moore and Others*. Edited by David E. Schultz and S.T. Joshi. New York: Hippocampus Press.

———. 2017. *Dawnward Spire, Lonely Hill: The Letters of H.P. Lovecraft and Clark Ashton Smith*. Edited by David E. Schultz and S.T. Joshi. New York: Hippocampus Press.

Lucas D'Oyley, D. 2016. "Elle, You Just Don't Understand #BlackGirlMagic." The Root, January 14. www.theroot.com/elle-you-just-don-t-understand-blackgirlmagic -1790853913.

Lynch, John. 2017. "The 50 Best-Selling Music Artists of All Time." BusinessInsider .com, September 13.

Lyons, Matthew N. 2017. "Ctrl-Alt-Delete: The Origins and Ideology of the Alternative Right." *Political Research Associates*, January 20. www.politicalresearch.org/2017/01/ 20/ctrl-alt-delete-report-on-the-alternative-right/#sthash.Q7TY2bhT.dpbs.

Maira, Sunaina Marr. 2009. *Missing: Youth, Citizenship, and Empire after 9/11*. Durham: Duke University Press.

Major, Melissa. 2016. "7 Ways *Hamilton* Has Impacted America." *Great Performances*, September 7. www.pbs.org/wnet/gperf/hamilton-american-musical-changed -musical-theater/52.

Mann, Michael E. 2017. "It's a Fact: Climate Change Made Hurricane Harvey More Deadly." *Guardian*, August 28.

Marc, David. 1989. *Comic Visions: Television Comedy and American Culture*. Malden, MA: Blackwell.

Marez, Curtis. 2016. *Farm Worker Futurism: Speculative Technologies of Resistance*. Minneapolis: University of Minnesota Press.

Martin, Adam, Brooke Thompson, and Tom Chatfield. 2006. "Alternate Reality Games White Paper." *International Game Developers Association (IGDA)*. http://igda.org/ arg/resources/IGDA-AlternateRealityGames-Whitepaper-2006.pdf.

Martin, Courtney. E. 2012. "From Young Adult Book Fans to Wizards of Change." *New York Times*, March 21.

Martinez, Alejandra. 2017. "From Quinceañera to Protest: Tejana Teens Fight SB 4 Immigration Law." Latino USA, July 17. https://www.latinousa.org/2017/07/17/ quinceanera-protest-tejana-teens-fight-sb-4-immigration-law/.

Massanari, Adrienne. 2015. "#Gamergate and the Happening: How Reddit's Algorithm, Governance, and Culture Support Toxic Technocultures." *New Media and Society*, 19 (3): 329–46. https://doi.org/10.1177/1461444815608807.

Mather, Kate. 2016. "Richard Che Risher, 18." *Homicide Report, Los Angeles Times*, August 29. www.homicide.latimes.com/post/richard-che-risher/.

Matthews, Lyndsey. 2017. "Here's the Full Transcript of Madonna's Speech at the Women's March." Elle.com, January 21. www.elle.com/culture/career-politics/news/ a42336/madonnas-womens-march-speech-transcript/.

Mayer, R. 2000. "Africa as an Alien Future: The Middle Passage, Afro-Futurism and Postcolonial Waterworlds." *Amerikastudien/American Studies* 45 (4): 555–66.

Mazza, Ed. 2017. "NPR Tweeted Declaration of Independence, and Trump Supporters Flipped Out." *Huffington Post*, July 5. www.huffingtonpost.com/entry/npr -declaration-of-independence_us_595c6525e4b0da2c7325bd50.

McClain, Dani. 2016. "What Does Black Lives Matter Want? Now It's Demands Are Clearer Than Ever." *Nation*, August 1.

McCormick, R. 2014. "Stephen Colbert Takes on Gamergate with Anita Sarkeesian." *The Verge*, December 12.

McDowell, Alex. 2015. "Prejudicial Narratives: Building Tomorrow's World Today." *Architectural Design* 85 (4): 26–33.

McIntyre, Hugh. 2017. "Taylor Swift's 'Look What You Made Me Do' Video Has Shattered YouTube Records." Forbes.com, August 29.

McMillan Cottom, T. 2016. "Black Cyberfeminism: Ways Forward for Intersectionality and Digital Sociology." In *Digital Sociologies*, edited by J. Daniels, K. Gregory, and T. McMillan Cottom, 528. Bristol: Policy Press.

McMurtry-Chubb, T. 2015. "#SayHerName #BlackWomensLivesMatter: State Violence in Policing the Black Female Body." *Mercer Law Review* 67 (3): 3–38. https://libraries.mercer.edu/ursa/handle/10898/9637.

McPherson, Tara. 2003. *Reconstructing Dixie: Race, Gender and Nostalgia in the Imagined South.* Durham: Duke University Press.

Medford, Grace. 2017. "Why Not Even Taylor Swift Can Exist in a Political Vacuum." Noisey.Vice.com, January 31. https://noisey.vice.com/en_us/article/ypnwdb/taylor-swift-trump-inauguration-muslim-ban-self-promotion.

Mehta, Rini Bhattacharya, and Rajeshwari V. Pandharipande. 2010. *Bollywood and Globalization: Indian Popular Cinema, Nation, an Diaspora.* New York: Anthem Press.

Mettler, Katie. 2017. "The African, Hindu and Roman Goddesses Who Inspired Beyoncé's Stunning Grammy Performance." WashingtonPost.com, February 13.

Mezirow, J. 1981. "A Critical Theory of Adult Learning and Education." *Adult Education* 32 (1): 3–24.

Mickenberg, Julia L. 2005. *Learning from the Left: Children's Literature, the Cold War, and Radical Politics in the United States.* Oxford: Oxford University Press.

Milk, Chris. 2015. *How Virtual Reality Can Create the Ultimate Empathy Machine.* TED Talk. https://www.ted.com/talks/chris_milk_how_virtual_reality_can_create_the_ultimate_empathy_machine.

Miller, Taylor Cole. 2011. "Too Short to be Quarterback, Too Plain to Be Queen." *gnovis* 11 (2). http://www.gnovisjournal.org/2011/04/04/too-short-to-be-quarterback-too-plain-to-be-queen/.

———. 2017. "Syndicating Queerness: Television Talk Shows, Rerun Syndication, and the Serials of Norman Lear." PhD diss., University of Wisconsin–Madison.

Miner, Dylan. 2014. *Creating Aztlán: Chicano Art, Indigenous Sovereignty, and Lowriding across Turtle Island.* Tucson: University of Arizona Press.

Miranda, Boris. 2016. "Las Razones Por Las Que el 'No' se Impuso En El Plebiscito En Colombia." *BBC Mundo*, October 3.

Miranda, Lin-Manuel. 2016. "Tony Acceptance Speech." YouTube video. https://www.youtube.com/watch?v=UPSyx7nu6Fs.

Mischie, Ioana. 2017. "Berlinale 2017—the VR Focus: Empathy, Embodiment, Experience, Part I." *Storyscapes* (blog), February 26. https://storyscapes.wordpress.com/2017/02/26/berlinale-2017-the-vr-focus-empathy-embodiment-experience-part-i/.

Mishra, V. 2001. *Bollywood Cinema: Temples of Desire.* New York: Routledge.

Mooney, Chris. 2007. *Storm World: Hurricanes, Politics, and the Battle over Global Warming.* Orlando: Harcourt.

Morcom, A. 2007. *Hindi Film Songs and the Cinema.* Hampshire: Ashgate.

———. 2015. "Terrains of Bollywood Dance: (Neoliberal) Capitalism and the Transformation of Cultural Economies." *Ethnomusicology* 59 (2): 288–314.

Morrell, E. 2008. *Critical Literacy and Urban Youth Pedagogies of Access, Dissent, and Liberation.* New York: Routledge.

Morrison, Ellen Earnhardt. 1995. *Guardian of the Forest: A History of Smokey Bear and the Cooperative Forest Fire Prevention Program.* Alexandria, VA: Morielle Press.

Moten, F. 2003. *In the Break: The Aesthetics of the Black Radical Tradition*. Minneapolis: University of Minnesota Press.

Movement for Black Lives. N.d. "A Vision for Black Lives." https://policy.m4bl.org/.

Mukherjee, Tutun. 2016. "Transformative Energy of Performance: 'Budhan Theatre' as Case Study." In *Cultural Studies in India*, edited by Rana Nayar, 222–36. Oxon, New York: Routledge.

Muniz, Albert M., and Thomas C. O'Guinn. 2001. "Brand Community." *Journal of Consumer Research* 27 (4): 412–32.

Muñoz, Juan Sebastián, and Juan David Herreño. 2016. "Pais(es) Divergente(s): Radiografia Del Plebiscito." *El Espectador*, October 13. https://www.elespectador.com/colombia2020/pais/paises-divergentes-radiografia-del-plebiscito-articulo-854881.

Murch, Donna. 2003. "The Prison of Popular Culture: Rethinking the Seventy-Fourth Annual Academy Awards." *Black Scholar* 33 (1): 25–32.

Mydans, Seth. 2014. "Thai Protestors Are Detained after Using 'Hunger Games' Salute." *New York Times*, November, 20.

National Center for Education Statistics. 2010. "Status and Trends in the Education of Racial and Ethnic Groups 2018." NCES 2019-038, Degrees Awarded.

———. N.d. "Degrees Conferred by Race and Sex." https://nces.ed.gov/fastfacts/display.asp?id=72.

Nelson, Alondra. 2002. "Introduction: Future Texts." *Social Text* 20 (2): 1–15.

Nelson, Eliot. 2016. "Mike Pence's *Hamilton* Recollection Conflicts with Donald Trump's Take." *Huffington Post*, November 21. www.huffingtonpost.com.au/entry/mike-pence-donald-trump-hamilton_us_5831bbf8e4b058ce7aab9dd7.

Newcomb, Horace, and Paul M. Hirsch. 1983. "Television as a Cultural Forum." *Quarterly Review of Film Studies* 8 (3).

Noble, S. 2016. "A Future for Intersectional Black Feminist Technology Studies." *Scholar and Feminist Online* 13 (3)–14 (1). Retrieved from http://sfonline.barnard.edu/traversing-technologies/safiya-umoja-noble-a-future-for-intersectional-black-feminist-technology-studies/0/.

NPR. 2016. "'Black-ish' Creator Kenya Barris Says Show Will Take New Direction Post-election." November 13. https://www.npr.org/2016/11/13/501904251/black-ish-creator-kenya-barris-says-show-will-take-new-direction-post-election.

Obama, Barack. 2014. "Remarks by the President at LBJ Presidential Library Civil Rights Summit." White House Office of the Press Secretary, April 10. https://obamawhitehouse.archives.gov/the-press-office/2014/04/10/remarks-president-lbj-presidential-library-civil-rights-summit.

Okorafor, Nnedi. 2011. "Lovecraft's Racism and the World Fantasy Award Statuette, with Comments from China Miéville." *Nnedi's Wahala Zone Blog*, December 14. http://nnedi.blogspot.com/2011/12/lovecrafts-racism-world-fantasy-award.html.

Oliver, Myrna. 2002. "Whitney Blake, 76; Star of 1960s' 'Hazel' Helped Create 'One Day at a Time,'" October 2. http://articles.latimes.com/2002/oct/02/local/me-blake2.

Olson, G. A., and Worsham, L. 2015. *The Politics of Possibility: Encountering the Radical Imagination*. London: Routledge.

O'Neill, Brian. 2015. "Presidents Fade, but 'The Simpsons' Endure." *Pittsburgh Post-Gazette*, September 24. http://www.post-gazette.com/opinion/brian-oneill/2015/09/24/Brian-O-Neill-Presidents-fade-but-The-Simpsons-endure/stories/201509230178.

Oreskes, Naomi, and Eric Conway. 2010. *Merchants of Doubt: How a Handful of Scientists Obscured the Truth on Issues from Tobacco Smoke to Global Warming*. New York: Bloomsbury.

Ott, Brian L., and Eric Aoki. 2001. "Popular Imagination and Identity Politics: Reading the Future in Star Trek: The Next Generation." *Western Journal of Communication* 65 (4): 392–415. https://doi.org/10.1080/10570310109374718.

Oyelowo, David. 2015. "*Selma* Star David Oyelowo: Academy Favors 'Subservient' Black Roles." YouTube video. Posted by "Scott," February 2. https://www.youtube.com/watch?v=jlUL6oyDnWc.

Parker, A. 2011. "Twitter's Secret Handshake." *New York Times*, June 10.

Parkin, S. 2014. "Zoe Quinn's Depression Quest." *New Yorker*, December 12.

Patterson, O. 1982. *Slavery and Social Death*. Cambridge, MA: Harvard University Press.

Pendleton-Jullian, Ann, and John Seely Brown. 2016. *Pragmatic Imagination: Prequel to Design Unbound*. San Francisco: Blurb.

Perez, Adam, Ashley Ross, and Salima Koroma. 2016. "Why History Has His Eyes on *Hamilton*'s Diversity." Time.com, December 15. http://time.com/4149415/hamilton-broadway-diversity/.

Pérez, Annemarie. 2011. "Splitting Aztlán: American Resistance and Chicana Visions of a Radical Utopia." PhD diss., University of Southern California, Los Angeles.

Pérez-Torres, Rafael. 2016. "Refiguring Aztlán." In *The Chicano Studies Reader: An Anthology of Aztlán, 1970–2015* (3rd ed.), edited by C. A. Noriega. Los Angeles: UCLA Chicano Studies Research Center Press.

Perry, Katy (@katyperry). 2017. "NOT TOO LATE TO PICK UP THE PHONE." Twitter, February 6, 2017, 2:18 p.m. https://twitter.com/katyperry/status/828729592974237696.

Pew Forum. 2015. "U.S. Public Becoming Less Religious." Pew Research Center, November 3. www.pewforum.org/2015/11/03/u-s-public-becoming-less-religious/.

Phillips, Whitney. 2015. *This Is Why We Can't Have Nice Things: Mapping the Relationship between Online Trolling and Mainstream Culture*. Cambridge: MIT Press.

Phillips, Whitney, and Ryan M. Milner. 2017. *The Ambivalent Internet: Mischief, Oddity and Antagonism Online*. Cambridge: Polity.

Pitt, Leyland F., Richard T. Watson, Pierre Berthon, Donald Wynn, and George Zinkhan. 2006. "The Penguin's Window: Corporate Brands from an Open-Source Perspective." *Journal of the Academy of Marketing Science* 34 (2): 115–27.

Plant, Sandie, and Nick Land. 1994. *Cyberpositive*. In *Unnatural: Techno-Theory for a Contaminated Culture*, edited by Matthew Fuller. www.sterneck.net/cyber/plant-land-cyber/index.php.

Polletta, Francesca. 2006. *It Was like a Fever: Storytelling in Protest and Politics*. Chicago: University of Chicago Press.

Popescu, Delia. 2012. *Political Action in Václav Havel's Thought*. Plymouth, UK: Lexington Books.

Posner, Sarah. 2017. "Can Irma Finally Blow through the GOP's Climate Change Denial?" *Washington Post*, September 11. https://www.washingtonpost.com/blogs/plum-line/wp/2017/09/11/can-irma-finally-blow-through-the-gops-climate-change-denial/.

Potenza, Alesandra. 2017. "The National Park Service Is Slyly Taunting President Trump on Twitter." The Verge, January 20. www.theverge.com/2017/1/20/14341882/national-park-service-twitter-account-anti-trump-messages-inauguration.

Press, A. 2016. "Colombian President Says Nobel Peace Prize Win Helped End Civil War." *Guardian*, December 10.

Proctor, William. 2018. "'I've Seen a Lot of Talk about the #BlackStormtrooper Outrage, but Not a Single Example of Anyone Complaining': *The Force Awakens*, Canonical Fidelity and Non-toxic Fan Practices." *Participations: Journal of Audience and Reception Studies* 15 (1): 160–79.

Proctor, William, and Bridget Kies. 2018. "Toxic Fan Practices and the New Culture Wars." *Participations: Journal of Audience and Reception Studies* 15 (1): 127–42.

Punathambekar, A. 2013. *From Bombay to Bollywood: The Making of a Global Media Industry*. New York: NYU Press.

Putnam, Robert. 2003. "Community-Based Social Capital and Educational Performance." In *Making Good Citizens: Education and Civil Society*, edited by Diane Ravitch and Joseph P. Viteritti, 58–95. New Haven, CT: Yale University Press.

Quayle, James Danforth, III. 1992. "Reflections on Urban America." Speech given to the Commonwealth Club of San Francisco, May 19. http://voicesofdemocracy.umd.edu/quayle-murphy-brown-speech-text/.

Quinlan, Casey. 2016. "How Racial Bias Affects the Quality of Black Students' Education." Think Progress, July 18. www.thinkprogress.org/how-racial-bias-affects-the-quality-of-black-students-education-642f4721fc84/.

Quinn, Z., et al. 2013. "Depression Quest." DepressionQuest.com. December 12, 2014.

Radical Monarchs website. Accessed January 2018. www.radicalmonarchs.org.

Ramachandran, Vijaya, and Julie Walz. 2012. *Haiti: Where Has All the Money Gone?* CGD Policy Paper 004. Center for Global Development. www.cgdev.org/content/publications/detail/1426185.

———. 2015. "Haiti: Where Has All the Money Gone?" *Journal of Haitian Studies* 21 (1): 26–65.

Reddit. "Google Cardboard VR." 2017. Accessed September 1. https://www.reddit.com/r/GoogleCardboard/.

Reed, Ishmael. 2015. "*Hamilton*: The Musical: Black Actors Dress Up like Slave Traders . . . and It's Not Halloween." *Counterpunch*, August 21. https://www.counterpunch.org/2015/08/21/hamilton-the-musical-black-actors-dress-up-like-slave-tradersand-its-not-halloween/.

Reed, Ryan. 2017. "Donald Trump on Madonna: 'She's Disgusting.'" Rollingstone.com, January 27.

Renegar, Valerie R., and Stacey K. Sowards. 2009. "Contradiction as Agency: Self-Determination, Transcendence, and Counter-Imagination in Third Wave Feminism." *Hypatia* 24 (2): 1–20. https://doi.org/10.1111/j.1527-2001.2009.01029.x.

Rice, Ronald E. 2001. "Smokey Bear." In *Public Communication Campaigns*, edited by Ronald E. Rice and Charles K. Atkin, 276–79. 3rd ed. Thousand Oaks, CA: Sage.

Richard, Stuart. 2016. "Overcoming the Stigma: The Queer Denial of Indiewood." *Journal of Film and Video* 68 (1): 19–30.

Richardson, John H. 2015. "Michael Brown Sr. and the Agony of the Black Father in America." *Esquire*, January 5.

Robertson, Adi, and Michael Zelenko. 2014. "Voices from a Virtual Past." The Verge. https://www.theverge.com/a/virtual-reality/oral_history.

Robinson, Cedric. 2000. *Black Marxism: The Making of the Black Radical Tradition.* Chapel Hill: University of North Carolina Press.

Rolsky, L. Benjamin. 2019. "The Return of Archie Bunker." CNN.com, April 26. https://www.cnn.com/2019/04/25/opinions/all-in-the-family-archie-bunker-returns-in-trump-era-rolsky.

Romano, A. 2014. "The Sexist Crusade to Destroy Game Developer Zoe Quinn." *Daily Dot*, 12 December.

Ross, Gary, dir. 2012. *The Hunger Games.* USA: Lionsgate.

Rostad, Rachel. 2013. "Response to Critiques of 'To JK Rowling, from Cho Chang.'" YouTube video, 5:12. Posted by Rachel Rostad, April 15. https://www.youtube.com/watch?v=04qQ1eNGJwM.

Rowling, J. K. 2008. "Text of J.K. Rowling's Commencement Speech." *Harvard Gazette*, June 5. https://news.harvard.edu/gazette/story/2008/06/text-of-j-k-rowling-speech/.

Rozsa, M. 2014. "The Racist #BlackStormtrooper Backlash Shows the Dark Side of Geek Culture." *Daily Dot*, December 2. https://www.dailydot.com/via/racist-black-stormtrooper-backlash-star-wars/.

Rucker, Philip. 2016. "Trump and Pence vs. Hamilton Cast: A Collison of Two Americas." *Washington Post*, November 19.

Russ, Joanna. 1976. "My Boat." *Magazine of Fantasy and Science Fiction*, January.

Russonello, Giovanni. 2017. "Beyoncé's and Adele's Grammy Speeches: Transcripts." NYTimes.com, February 12.

Saler, Michael. 2012. *As If: Modern Enchantment and the Literary Prehistory of Virtual Reality.* New York: Oxford University Press.

Samper Ospina, Daniel. 2014. "Soy Capaz de Apoyar 'Soy Capaz.'" Soy Capaz de Apoyar Soy Capaz, Por Daniel Samper Ospina. September 20.

Saraiya, Sonia. 2017. "Super Bowl Halftime Review: Lady Gaga Takes Safe Route with Hits and Spectacle." Variety.com, February 5.

Sarkeesian, A. 2013. "Tropes vs. Women in Video Games." Kickstarter. 12 December 2013.

Saxon, Levana. 2017. "Theater of the Oppressed." *Beautiful Trouble—a Toolbox for Revolution.* Accessed November 28. www.beautifultrouble.org.

Schechter, Patricia. 2015. "The Anti-Lynching Pamphlets of Ida B. Wells, 1892–1920." *During the Gilded Age.* http://gildedage.lib.niu.edu/wellspamphlets.

Schneider, M. 2011. "New to Your TV Screen: Twitter Hashtags." *TV Guide*, April 21. www.tvguide.com/news/new-tv-screen-1032111/.

Schuschke, J., and B. Tynes. 2016. "Online Community Empowerment, Emotional Connection, and Armed Love in the Black Lives Matter Movement." In *Emotions, Technology and Social Media*, edited by Sharon Y. Tettengah, 188. London: Academic Press.

Scott, K. 2015. "The Pragmatics of Hashtags: Inference and Conversational Style on Twitter." *Journal of Pragmatics* 81:8–20.

Sebastian, Michael. 2016. "Why Are So Many Women Sluts?" Return of Kings, September 29. www.returnofkings.com/97269/why-are-so-many-women-sluts.

Seifert, Mark. 2017. "Phil Noto Revises His #0 Civil War II Kamala Khan Ms. Marvel Cover Art in Reaction to Trump's Immigration Ban." Bleeding Cool, January 18. https://www.bleedingcool.com/2017/01/28/phil-noto-revises-civil-war-ii-0-kamala -khan-ms-marvel-cover-art-reaction-trumps-immigration-ban/.

Sexton, Jared. 2009. "The Ruse of Engagement: Black Masculinity and the Cinema of Policing." *American Quarterly* 61 (1): 39–63.

Sharpe, Donavan. 2017. "Seven Ways Women Are Just like Abandoned Dogs." Return of Kings, September 18. www.returnofkings.com/130126/7-ways-women-are-just -like-abandoned-dogs.

Shelley, Percey Bysshe. 1904. *A Defence of Poetry.* Indianapolis: Bobbs-Merrill.

Sherlock, Ruth. 2017. "Donald Trump's Chaotic Muslim-Majority Immigration Ban: The Full Story." *Telegraph*, January 30.

Shifman, Limor. 2013. *Memes in Digital Culture.* Cambridge: MIT Press.

———. 2014. *Memes in Digital Culture.* Cambridge: MIT Press.

Shresthova, S. 2011. *Is It All about Hips? Around the World with Bollywood Dance.* Delhi: Sage.

———. 2016. "Dance It! Film It! Share It! Exploring Participatory Dances and Civic Potential." In *Artistic Citizenship: Artistry, Social Responsibility, and Ethical Praxis*, edited by David J. Elliott, Marisa Silverman, and Wayne D. Bowman, 146–62. London: Oxford University Press.

Siegel, Tatiana 2016. "'Star Wars' Writers Get Political: Will Anti-Trump Tweets Hurt Rogue One?" *Hollywood Reporter*, November 21.

Sim, David. 2014. "Hong Kong: Defiant Protestors Give Hunger Games Three-Fingered Salute as Police Clear Camp." *International Business Times*, December 11.

Singh, Emily. 2016. "Megalia: South Korean Feminism Takes Powerful Twist." *Korea Exposé.* July 29. https://koreaexpose.com/megalia-south-korean-feminism -marshals-the-power-of-the-internet/.

Skocpol, Theda, and Vanessa Williamson. 2012. *The Tea Party and the Remaking of Republican Conservatism.* Oxford: Oxford University Press.

Slack, Andrew. 2015. "Op-Ed: Ad Campaign (Lip) Glosses over 'Hunger Games' Message." *Los Angeles Times*, November 25.

Slater, Mel. 2016. "Virtual Reality: Virtual Embodiment." YouTube video, 4:02. Posted by "Digital Catapult," November 7. https://www.youtube.com/watch?v= 0XsOJFPgJqA.

Slyomovics, Susan. 1998. *The Object of Memory—Arab and Jew Narrate the Palestinian Village*. Philadelphia: University of Pennsylvania Press.

Smith, Maya Enista. 2017. "Born This Way Foundation Hits the Road." Born This Way Foundation, July 28. https://bornthisway.foundation/born-way-foundation-hits-road/.

Smyth, Melissa. 2015. "On Sentimentality: A Critique of Humans of New York." Warscapes, January 16. www.warscapes.com/opinion/sentimentality-critique -humans-new-york.

Snapes, Laura. 2017. "Actually, the Old Taylor Swift Is Alive and Well." Elle.com, August 28.

Spam, Kwame. 2017. "Lady Gaga Opened Her Super Bowl Performance with a Protest Anthem." TheVerge.com, February 5.

Sperling, Nicole. 2017. "*Moonlight* Director Barry Jenkins Reflects on the Oscars the Morning after Its Big Win." *Entertainment Weekly*, February 28.

Spigel, Lynn. 1991. "From Domestic Space to Outer Space: The 1960s Fantastic Sitcom." In *Close Encounters: Film, Feminism, and Science Fiction*, edited by Constance Penley. Minneapolis: University of Minnesota Press.

Squires, C. R. 2002. "Rethinking the Black Public Sphere: An Alternative Vocabulary for Multiple Public Spheres." *Communication Theory* 12 (4): 446–68.

Stack, Liam. 2017. "Attack on Alt-Right Leader Has Internet Asking: Is It OK to Punch a Nazi?" *New York Times*, January 21.

Stallings, L. H. (2013). "Hip Hop and the Black Ratchet Imagination." *Palimpsest* 2 (2): 135–39.

Stanley, A. 2014. "Wrought in Rhimes's Image." *New York Times*, September 18.

Stanton, Brandon. 2013. "On Travel to Iran." Humans of New York. www .humansofnewyork.com/post/38682208638/on-travel-to-iran-the-us-government -has-a.

———. 2014. "The 8 Millennium Development Goals" Humans of New York. https:// www.humansofnewyork.com/post/94003381026/beginning-tomorrow-ill-be-taking -a-50-day-trip.

Stoller, Matt. 2017. "The *Hamilton* Hustle." The Baffler. https://thebaffler.com/salvos/ hamilton-hustle-stoller#.

Storey John, ed. 2013. *Cultural Theory and Popular Culture—a Reader*. New York: Routledge.

Streitfeld, David. 2017. "Writing Nameless Things: An Interview with Ursula K. Le Guin." *Los Angeles Review of Books*, November 17.

Strobele, Ursula, and Lawrence Weschier. 2015. *The Sense of Movement—When Artists Travel*. Ostfildern, Germany: Hatje Cantz Verlag.

Stryker, Sam. 2017. "If You Look Closely, Lady Gaga's Halftime Show Seemed Very, Very Political." Buzzfeed.com, February 6. https://www.buzzfeed.com/samstryker/ lady-gaga-halftime-show-politics?utm_term=.xvoM4d7oy#.crQN1qBop.

Subin, Nina. 2016. "Meet Ron Chernow, the Biographer Who Inspired the Broadway Hit, Hamilton." *Newsweek*, November 26. www.newsweek.com/hamilton -biographer-ron-chernow-502295.

Sunderland, Mitchell. 2016. "Can't Shake It Off: How Taylor Swift Became a Nazi Idol." *Vice*, May 23. https://www.vice.com/en_us/article/ae5x8a/cant-shake-it-off-how -taylor-swift-became-a-nazi-idol.

Sutherland, John. 2005. "George Lucas Could Be Messing with Your Head." *Guardian*, May 23. https://www.theguardian.com/film/2005/may/23/cannes2005 .cannesfilmfestival.

Taylor, Keeanga-Yahmatta. 2016. *From #Black Lives Matter to Black Liberation*. Chicago: Haymarket.

Terdiman, Daniel. 2015. "Why Volumetric VR Is The Real Future Of Virtual Reality." *Fast Company*, September 12.

Terrell, M. C. 1940. *A Colored Woman in a White World*. Amherst, MA: Prometheus.

Thomas, D. 2015. "Why Everyone's Saying 'Black Girls Are Magic.'" *Los Angeles Times*, September 9.

Thompson, Anne. 2014. *The $11 Billion Year*. New York: HarperCollins.

Thompson, Liana, and Arely Zimmerman. 2016. "DREAMing Citizenship: Undocumented Youth, Coming Out, and Pathways to Participation." In *By Any Media Necessary: The New Youth Activism*, edited by Henry Jenkins, Sangita Shresthova, Liana Gamber-Thompson, Neta Kligler-Vilenchik and Arely Zimmerman. New York: NYU Press. http://opensquare.nyupress.org/books/9781479899982/read/.

Thompson, S. Leigh, and Alexander Santiago-Jirau. 2011. "Chapter Eight: Performing Truth: Queer Youth and the Transformative Power of Theatre of the Oppressed." *Counterpoints* 416: 97–108. www.jstor.org/stable/42981331.

Thompson, Tracy. 2014. *The New Mind of the South*. New York: Simon and Schuster, 2014.

Thorpe, Patrick, ed. 2011. *The Legend of Zelda Hyrule Historia*. Trans. Michael Gombos, Takahiro Moriki, Heidi Plechl, Kumar Sivasubramanian, Aria Tanner, and John Thomas. Milwaukee, OR: Dark Horse Books.

Tiempo, Casa Editorial El. N.d. "¡Acuerdo Ya!, La Consigna de Las Movilizaciones En El País." *El Tiempo*.

Timetree. 2017. "Haengdonghaneun Megallia" [Acting Megalia]. Accessed August 22. http://timetree.zum.com/123516.

Tobin, Jonathan S. 2017. "Are We Connecting Dots Again on Speech and Violence?" *National Review*, July 5.

Toobin, Jeffrey. 2017. "Is Tom Cotton the Future of Trumpism?" *New Yorker*, November 13. https://www.newyorker.com/magazine/2017/11/13/is-tom-cotton-the-future -of-trumpism.

Totilo, S. 2014. "Bomb Threat Targeted Anita Sarkeesian, Gaming Awards Last March." *Kotaku*. 17 December. https://kotaku.com/bomb-threat-targeted-anita-sarkeesian -gaming-awards-la-1636032301.

*Tracking Ida*. N.d. "Tracking Ida Press Kit." http://trackingida.com/presskit.html.

Treaster, Joseph B. 2017. "After a Dozen Hurricanes and 40 Years, Familiar Dangers with Higher Stakes." *New York Times*, September 12. https://www.nytimes.com/2017/09/12/us/hurricana-irma-katrina-.html.

*Tzina: Symphony of Longing.* 2016. http://tzina.space/.

Valle, Maria Eva. 1996. "MEChA and the Transformation of Chicano Student Activism: Generational Change, Conflict, and Continuity." PhD diss., University of California, San Diego.

Vanity Fair. 2016. "Interview with *Transparent*'s Jill Soloway + Interactive Pfefferman Family Tree." September 23. https://www.vanityfair.com/hollywood/2016/09/interview-with-transparents-jill-soloway-interactive-pffeferman-family-tree.

Van Slyke, Tracy. 2014. *Spoiler Alert: How Progressives Will Break through with Popular Culture.* Citizen Engagement Lab. http://spoileralert.report/sites/sar/files/SpoilerAlert.pdf.

Van Wart, Sarah, K. Joyce Tsai, and Tapan Parikh. 2010. "Local Ground: A Paper-Based Toolkit for Documenting Local Geo-Spatial Knowledge." Proceedings of the First ACM Symposium on Computing for Development.

Vidal, Gore. 1973. *Burr: A Novel.* New York: Random House.

Villareal, Yvonne. 2017. "Lena Waithe of 'Master of None' Discusses Emmy Nomination." *Los Angeles Times*, August 5. http://www.latimes.com/entertainment/la-et-entertainment-news-updates-august-lena-waithe-glaad-1501966059-htmlstory.html.

Vulliamy, Ed. 2011. "How an Irish Telecoms Tycoon Became Haiti's Only Hope of Salvation." *Guardian*, January 8.

Wamsley, Laurel. 2017. "After Uproar, Pepsi Halts Rollout of Controversial Protest-Themed Ad." National Public Radio, April 5. https://www.npr.org/sections/thetwo-way/2017/04/05/522750764/after-uproar-pepsi-halts-rollout-of-controversial-protest-themed-ad.

Wang, Amy B. 2016. "Pence Says He 'Wasn't Offended 'by Hamilton as Trump Continues to Demand an Apology." *Washington Post*, November 20.

Warnock, Mary. 1978. *Imagination.* Berkeley: University of California Press.

Watson, Jeff. 2010. "ARG 2.0." *Confessions of an ACA Fan* (blog). July 7. Accessed December 12, 2017. http://henryjenkins.org/blog/2010/07/arg_20_1.html.

Watt-Cloutier, Sheila. 2015. *The Right to Be Cold: One Woman's Story of Protecting Her Culture, the Arctic and the Whole Planet.* Toronto: Penguin Canada.

Watts, Brenda. 2004. "Aztlán as a Palimpsest: From Chicano Nationalism toward Transnational Feminism in Anzaldúa's *Borderlands*." *Latino Studies* 2 (3): 304–21. https://doi.org/10.1057/palgrave.lst.8600104.

Wells, Ida B. 2013. *Crusade for Justice: The Autobiography of Ida B. Wells.* Chicago: University of Chicago Press.

———. 2014. *Southern Horrors: Lynch Law in All Its Phases.* Auckland: Floating Press.

West, Shearer. 2000. *The Visual Arts in Germany 1890–1937: Utopia and Despair.* Manchester: Manchester University Press.

Whyte, Kyle Powys. 2013. "Justice Forward: Tribes, Climate Adaptation and Responsibility." *Climatic Change* 120 (3): 517–30.

Wiedeman, Reeves. 2014. "Activism." *New Yorker*, December 22 and 29.

Wikstrom, P. 2014. "#srynotfunny: Communicative Functions of Hashtags on Twitter." *SKY Journal of Linguistics* 27: 127–52.

Williams, Daniel K. 2017. "The Democrats' Religion Problem." *New York Times*, June 23. https://www.nytimes.com/2017/06/23/opinion/democrats-religion-jon-ossoff.html.

Williams, Raymond. (1958) 1989. *Culture Is Ordinary*. In *Raymond Williams on Culture and Society: Essential Writings*, edited by Jim McGuigan, 1–29. New York: Sage.

Williams, S. 2016. "#SayHerName: Using Digital Activism to Document Violence against Black Women." *Feminist Media Studies* 16 (5): 922–25.

Wilson, G. Willow, and Adrian Alphona. 2015. *Ms. Marvel: No Normal*. New York: Marvel Worldwide.

———. 2016. *Ms. Marvel: Civil War II*. New York: Marvel Worldwide.

Wilson, Randall K. 2014. *America's Public Lands: From Yellowstone to Smokey Bear and Beyond*. Lanham, MD: Rowman and Littlefield.

Wittgenstein, Ludwig. 1953. 2001. *Philosophical Investigations*. Malden, MA: Blackwell.

Wong, Julia. 2016. "Black Lives Matter Protestors Block San Francisco Bay Bridge." *Guardian*, January 18.

Woodard, Colin. 2011. *American Nations: A History of the Eleven Rival Regional Cultures of North America*. London: Penguin.

Woolf, Nicky. 2016. "Breitbart Declares War on Kellogg's after Cereal Brand Pulls Advertising from Site." *Guardian*, November 30.

World Bank in Haiti. 2019. "Overview." World Bank. April 5. https://www.worldbank.org/en/country/haiti/overview.

World Economic Forum. 2016. "The Global Gender Gap Report 2016." https://reports.weforum.org/global-gender-gap-report-2016/.

Wright, David. 2016. "Trump: Tubman on the $20 Is 'Pure Political Correctness.'" CNN.com, April 21.

Yoo, Minseok. 2015. "Hyeomobareone gisaenghagi: Megalliaui ballanjeogin balhwa" [Being parasitic on hate speech: Megalia's oppositional speech]. *Journal of Feminist Theories and Practices*, no. 33 (December).

Yoon, Bora. 2013. "Ilbewa yeoseong hyeomo" [Ilbe and misogyny]. *Progressive Review* 57 (September): 33–56.

———. 2017. "Megalliaui 'geoul'i bichuneun myeot gaji jilmundeul" [A few questions Megalia's "mirror" reflect]. In *Geureomedo, peminijeum* [Yet still, feminism], by Bora Yoon, Seoyeon Cho, Bohwa Kim, Miri Kimhong, Eunhee Kim, Eunhasun, Na young, et al., 236. Seoul: Eunhaeng Namu.

Youis, Steven. 2003. "Exclusive Mark Millar Interview." Superman Homepage, March 10. https://www.supermanhomepage.com/comics/interviews/interviews-intro.php?topic=c-interview_millar3.

Zuckerman, Ethan. 2016. "Effective Civics." In *Civic Media: Technology, Design, Practice*, edited by Eric Gordon and Paul Mihailidis. Cambridge, MA: MIT Press.

# Index

# About the Contributors

Andrea Alarcón is a PhD student in communication at the University of Southern California. She studies imaginaries of technology in developing countries, particularly social media platforms as gateways to the web and transnational, online labor cultures. She received her MSc degree from the Oxford Internet Institute and her BSc in online journalism from the University of Florida.

Sarah Banet-Weiser is professor of media and communications and head of the Department of Media and Communications at London School of Economics. Her research interests include gender in the media; identity, citizenship, and cultural politics; consumer culture and popular media; race and the media; and intersectional feminism.

Thomas J Billard is a PhD candidate in the University of Southern California's Annenberg School for Communication and Journalism. He is a political communication scholar whose research focuses on transgender politics and graphic design.

Candis Callison is an associate professor at the Graduate School of Journalism at the University of British Columbia. She is Tahltan, an Indigenous people located in northern British Columbia, and the author of *How Climate Change Comes to Matter: The Communal Life of Facts* (2014).

Stephen Duncombe is professor of media and culture at New York University and is author and editor of six books on the intersection of culture and politics. Duncombe, a lifelong political activist, is also cofounder and codirector of the Center for Artistic Activism, a research and training organization that helps activists create more like artists and artists strategize more like activists.

Yomna Elsayed holds a PhD in communication from the University of Southern California. She studies how popular culture mechanisms, such as humor, music, and creative digital arts, can be utilized to sustain social movements all while facilitating dialogue at times of ideological polarization and state repression in authoritarian nationalist contexts.

Sam Ford is director of cultural intelligence at Simon & Schuster. He is also an affiliate of MIT Comparative Media Studies/Writing and Western Kentucky University's Popular Culture Studies Program and a Knight News Innovation Fellow for Columbia University's Tow Center for Digital Journalism.

Brooklyne Gipson is a third-year PhD student at the University of Southern California's Annenberg School for Communication and Journalism. Her research centers on the intersections of race and digital technology. She analyzes the ways in which traditionally marginalized groups utilize social media platforms and other digital tools to engage in political discourse.

Jonathan Gray, professor of Media and Cultural Studies, University of Wisconsin–Madison, is author of *Watching with* The Simpsons: *Television, Parody, and Intertextuality, Television Entertainment* (2011), *Show Sold Separately: Promos, Spoilers, and Other Media Paratexts* (2009), and *Television Studies* (with Amanda Lotz, 2019) and coeditor of numerous books, including *Keywords for Media Studies* (2017).

Christopher S. Harris is an associate professor of communication in the School of Liberal Arts and Sciences at Nevada State College. His research interests include fin-de-siècle rap music and neosoul, critical pedagogy, media portrayals of ethnicity/race, and the relationship/interplay between power and discourse in contemporary society.

Henry Jenkins is the Provost's Professor of Communication, Journalism, Cinematic Arts, and Education at the University of Southern California. His previous books include *Convergence Culture: Where Old and New Media Collide* (2006) and *Spreadable Media: Creating Meaning and Value in a Networked Society* (with Sam Ford and Joshua Green, 2013).

Jocelyn Areté Kelvin is an immersive avant-pop artist and assistant to Henry Jenkins. She is currently composing an intermedia concept album and producing immersive events as *Areté*. Her past work includes her first feature as director and producer, *Your Friends Close*, which premiered at the United Film Festival and is currently streaming on Amazon, Vimeo, and YouTube. In Chicago, she collaborated with dance companies Lucky Plush and the Moving Architects to direct site-specific dance films and performed in theaters including Victory Gardens, Lookingglass, Strawdog, and Red Orchid. www.arete.space.

Do-own (Donna) Kim is a communication PhD student at the University of Southern California and a Korea Foundation for Advanced Studies fellow. She is interested in mediated communication, culture, and technology, particularly in the impact and implications of new media technologies in user engagement and cultural practices.

Clifford H. Lee is an associate professor in the School of Education at Mills College. His research, teaching, writing, and social justice advocacy attempt to disrupt dominant ideologies and institutional practices. He also cohosts an online channel about cooking, gardening, and more with his son.

Diana Lee, PhD, is a content strategist, writer, and qualitative researcher passionate about storytelling for social change. For fifteen years, she has transformed complex ideas about education, culture, and society into engaging and accessible forms for diverse audiences, and she solemnly swears that she's been managing mischief for much, much longer.

Lauren Levitt is a PhD candidate at the University of Southern California, where she studies sex workers' support networks. She has published essays on RuPaul's *Drag Race* and *Paris Is Burning* and the TV show *Batman*, and she serves as services director for the Sex Workers' Outreach Project Los Angeles.

Rogelio Alejandro Lopez is a fifth-year doctoral candidate of communication at University of Southern California Annenberg, where he studies social movements, civic media, and youth culture. His dissertation explores how social movements tap into the civic imagination when developing and deploying media strategies to achieve their goals and reimagine the world through action.

joan miller is a fourth-year doctoral student at University of Southern California Annenberg. She studies media fandom and ecological inter-species communication. Yep, she talks to animals. Her favorite episode of *Star Trek: The Next Generation* is "Darmok and Jalad" because it con-denses all her research interests into one awesome episode.

Taylor Cole Miller, assistant professor of entertainment and media stud-ies at the University of Georgia, is academic director of the Peabody Media Center. He teaches media and cultural studies courses as well as courses in digital production and is currently collaborating with Nor-man Lear on a cultural history of his groundbreaking shows.

Ioana Mischie is a Romanian-born cinematic storyteller awarded for filmmaking and innovative concepts, Fulbright Alumna of University of Southern California School of Cinematic Arts and UNATC, currently completing her doctoral study on transmedia/holistic storytelling, and cofounder of Storyscapes, a transmedia-oriented NGO. Her cinematic works have been selected for more than fifty film festivals worldwide.

Rachel E. Moran is a doctoral candidate and endowed fellow at the Annen-berg School for Communication and Journalism at the University of Southern California. Her dissertation work seeks to understand how online news media producers cultivate relationships of trust with their audiences and how trust can be understood through the objects of journalism.

Tapan Parikh is an associate professor of information science at Cornell Tech in New York City. His research interests include human-computer interaction and the design and use of information technologies for sup-porting youth and community development. He currently teaches the Remaking the City course at Cornell Tech. He has received the NSF CAREER award, a Sloan Fellowship, and a UW Diamond Early Career Award and was named *Technology Review* magazine's Humanitarian of the Year in 2007.

Manisha Pathak-Shelat is professor of communication and chair, Center for Development Management and Communication, at MICA, India. She has taught and worked as a media consultant/training facilitator and researcher in India, Thailand, and the United States. Her special interests are new media; civic engagement; transcultural citizenship; young people's media cultures; the intersection of civic, popular, and consumer cultures; media literacy; and gender.

Gabriel Peters-Lazaro, MFA, PhD, is assistant professor of cinematic arts at the University of Southern California. In addition to the civic imagination, he works on theories and practices of hypercinemas. He grew up on a walnut farm in Northern California, where he was mostly homeschooled. He is an avid surfer.

William Proctor is senior lecturer in transmedia, culture, and communication at Bournemouth University, UK. He is coeditor of *Disney's Star Wars: Forces of Production, Promotion, and Reception* (2018) and author of the forthcoming monograph *Reboot Culture: Comics, Film, Transmedia*.

Michael Saler is professor of history at the University of California, Davis, where he teaches modern European intellectual history. He is the author of *As If: Modern Enchantment and the Literary Prehistory of Virtual Reality* (2012) and *The Avant-Garde in Interwar England* (1999); editor of *The Fin-de-siècle World* (2014); and coeditor, with Joshua Landy, of *The Re-enchantment of the World* (2009).

Raffi Sarkissian is a lecturer in media studies at Christopher Newport University. His scholarship covers LGBTQ representation in popular culture, participatory practices in digital video activism, and the politics of award shows—a favorite pastime ever since he began watching the Oscars at ten years old.

Clint Schnekloth is the author of *Mediating Faith: Faith Formation in a Transmedia Era* (2014). He serves as pastor of Good Shepherd Lutheran Church, Fayetteville, Arkansas; appears regularly on the local NPR; and blogs at Patheos. He has written for the *Christian Century* and other religious journals.

Paromita Sengupta is a doctoral student at the University of Southern California. Her research is situated at the intersection between politics, social media, and humor, and she is especially interested in networked laughter as an alternate way of engaging with political issues.

Sangita Shresthova is the director of research of the Civic Imagination Project@Civic Paths project based at University of Southern California. She is also the author of *Is It All about Hips? Around the World with Bollywood Dance* (2011) and continues to find time to teach and learn dance whenever she can.

Elisabeth Soep, PhD, is executive editor (Features and Special Projects) and senior scholar at YR Media (formerly Youth Radio), where she cofounded the Innovation Lab with MIT in 2013. YR Media's Peabody Award–winning newsroom serves as NPR's youth desk. Soep's books include *Participatory Politics* (2014), *Drop That Knowledge* (with Vivian Chávez, 2010), and *Youthscapes* (with Sunaina Maira, 2005).

Sarah Van Wart is an assistant professor of instruction at Northwestern University in the Department of Electrical Engineering and Computer Science. Her research examines approaches to teaching introductory data and computer science for high school and community college students, including designing computing technologies, activities, and learning environments.

Rebecca Wanzo is associate professor of women, gender, and sexuality studies at Washington University in St. Louis and author of *The Suffering Will Not Be Televised: African American Women and Sentimental Political Storytelling* (2009). She is also the author of *The Content of Our Caricature: African American Comic Art and Political Belonging* (NYU Press, 2020).

Emilia Yang is an activist, artist, and militant researcher. Her research interests and art practice span the role of memory in the political imagination and forms of political action and participation. Yang is currently pursuing a PhD in media arts and practice at the School of Cinematic Arts at the University of Southern California. For more information, see www.emiliayang.org.

Sulafa Zidani is a doctoral student at University of Southern California Annenberg. She researches new media, participatory culture, and digital language and power dynamics, with a special interest in China and the Arab World.

Ethan Zuckerman directs the Center for Civic Media at the MIT Media Lab. He studies the use of technology for social change and works with NGOs and foundations around the world to build diverse and inclusive civil society.